The
Kennedy–Khrushchev
Letters

Volumes in the Top Secret Series Published by New Century Books:

World War Two:
   U.S. Military Plans for the Invasion
   of Japan

FBI Files on Elvis Presley

The Vietnam War:
   Confidential Files on the Siege and
   Loss of Khe Sanh

FBI Files on the Lindbergh Baby Kidnapping

CIA Files on the U2 Plane Program, 1954–1974

The Kennedy–Khrushchev Letters

TOP SECRET:

The Kennedy–Khrushchev Letters

Thomas Fensch, Editor

New Century Books

Contents

List of Abbreviations

ACDA, Arms Control and Disarmament Agency

EUR, Bureau of European Affairs, Department of State

FRG, Federal Republic of Germany

G/B, Germany/Berlin

GDR, German Democratic Republic

ICC, International Control Commission

NATO, North Atlantic Treaty Organization

Niact, night action: communications indicator requiring attention by the recipient at any hour of the day or night

P, Bureau of Public Affairs, Department of State

SOV, Office of Soviet Union Affairs, Bureau of European Affairs, Department of State

S/AE, Special Assistant to the Secretary of State for Disarmament and Atomic Energy

S/S, Executive Secretariat, Department of State

S/S-RO, Reports and Operations Staff, Executive Secretariat, Department of State

TASS, Telegrafnoye Agentsvo Sovetskogo Soiuza (Telegraph Agency of the Soviet Union)

UN, United Nations

USA, United States of America

USRO, United States Mission to the North Atlantic Treaty Organization and European Regional Organizations

USSR, Union of Soviet Socialist Republics

USUN, United States Mission to the United Nations

List of Names

Adenauer, Conrad, Chancellor of the Federal Republic of Germany until October 1963

Adzhubei, Aleksei I., Editor in Chief of Izvestia and Khrushchev's son-in-law

Anderson, Harry L., Bureau of European Affairs, Department of State

Ball, George W., Under Secretary of State for Economic Affairs until December 1961; thereafter Under Secretary of State

Beam, Jacob D., Assistant Director for International Relations, Arms Control and Disarmament Agency, from March 1962

Bohlen, Charles E., Special Assistant to the Secretary of State until September 1962; thereafter Ambassador to France

Bolshakov, Georgi N., Editor in Chief of USSR magazine; Counselor at the Soviet Embassy in the United States from October 1962

Brezhnev, Leonid I., Chairman of the Presidium of the Supreme Soviet of the Union of Soviet Socialist Republics

Bundy, McGeorge, Special Assistant to the President for National Security Affairs

Castro, Fidel, President of Cuba

Chiang Kai-shek, Generalissimo, President of the Republic of China

Davis, Richard H., Deputy Assistant Secretary of State for European Affairs

de Gaulle, Charles, President of France

Dobrynin, Anatoly F., Chief of the American Countries Division, Soviet Foreign Ministry until March 1962; thereafter Ambassador to the

United States

Eisenhower, Dwight D., President of the United States until January 20, 1961

Farley, Philip J., Special Assistant to the Secretary of State for Atomic Energy and Outer Space from August 1961 until March 1962

Foster, William C., Director of the Arms Control and Disarmament Agency

Gromyko, Andrei A., Soviet Foreign Minister

Harriman, W. Averell, Ambassador at Large February-December 1961; Assistant Secretary of State for Far Eastern Affairs until April 1963; thereafter Under Secretary of State for Political Affairs

Harrison, James B., Executive Secretariat Staff, Department of State

Hartley, Charles R., Reports and Operations Staff, Executive Secretariat, Department of State

Henry, David H., Deputy Director of the Office of Soviet Union Affairs, Department of State, from July 1961

Home, Alexander Frederick Douglas (Lord), British Secretary of State for Foreign Affairs until October 1963; Prime Minister thereafter

Johnson, Lyndon B., Vice President of the United States until November 22, 1963; thereafter President

Johnson, U. Alexis, Deputy Under Secretary of State for Political Affairs

Kennedy, John F., President of the United States until November 22, 1963

Kennedy, Robert F., Attorney General of the United States

Khrushchev, Nikita S., Chairman of the

Council of Ministers of the Soviet Union

Kohler, Foy D., Assistant Secretary of State for European Affairs until August 1962; thereafter Ambassador to the Soviet Union

Kretzmann, Edwin M. J., Deputy Assistant Secretary of State, Bureau of Public Affairs, until March 1961

Kriebel, P. Wesley, Executive Secretariat Staff, Department of State

Kuznetsov, Vasily V., Soviet First Deputy Foreign Minister

Macmillan, Harold, Prime Minister of the United Kingdom until October 1963

McCloskey, Robert J., Public Information Specialist, Office of News, Bureau of Public Affairs, Department of State

McCloy, John J., Presidential adviser and coordinator for U.S.-Soviet negotiations over Cuba at the United Nations

McCone, John A., Director for Central Intelligence from November 1961

McNamara, Robert S., Secretary of Defense

McSweeney, John M., Director of the Office of Soviet Union Affairs, Bureau of European Affairs, Department of State, until October 1961; thereafter Minister-Counselor at Moscow

Mikoyan, Anastas I., First Deputy Chairman of the Soviet Council of Ministers

Ngo Dinh Diem, President of the Republic of Vietnam until November 1963

Nobbe, Richard, Executive Secretariat Staff, Department of State

Owen, Robert I., Officer in Charge of Bilateral Political Relations, Office of Soviet Union Affairs,

Bureau of European Affairs, Department of State

Ramsey, James A., Office of Soviet Union Affairs, Bureau of European Affairs, Department of State

Rusk, Dean, Secretary of State

Salinger, Pierre, President's Press Secretary

Sihanouk, Prince Norodom, Cambodian Chief of State

Smith, Bromley, Acting Executive Secretary of the National Security Council until August 1961; thereafter Executive Secretary

Souphanouvong, Prince, leader of the Pathet Lao; after June 1962, Vice Premier and Minister of Economy and Planning

Souvanna Phouma, Prince, leader of the neutralist political forces in Laos; after June 1962, Prime Minister of Laos and Minister of Defense, Veteran Affairs, and Social Action

Stevenson, Adlai E., III, Permanent Representative to the United Nations

Thompson, Llewellyn E., Jr., Ambassador to the Soviet Union until July 1962; Ambassador at Large from October 1962

Tully, Francis W., Policy Plans and Guidance Staff, Bureau of Public Affairs, Department of State

Tyler, William R., Deputy Assistant Secretary of State for European Affairs until August 1962; thereafter Assistant Secretary

Udall, Stewart, Secretary of the Interior

Valdes, Philip H., Office of Soviet Union Affairs, Bureau of European Affairs, Department of State

Veliotes, Nicholas A., Reports and Operations

Staff, Executive Secretariat, Department of State
 Weiner, Benjamin, Executive Secretariat Staff,
Department of State
 Zorin, Valerian A., Deputy Soviet Foreign
Minister and Permanent Representative to the
United Nations

Introduction

New Century Books is pleased to publish *The Kennedy–Khrushchev Letters,* the sixth volume in our Top Secret Series of formerly-classified documents.

We believe this may be the largest record extant of the relationship between President John F. Kennedy and Soviet premier Nikita Khrushchev, during the three-year period of November 1960 until the assassination of John Kennedy in November, 1963. These letters — totaling 120, including cables between diplomatic agencies on behalf of Kennedy and Khrushchev — should be an invaluable aid to understanding the years of the Kennedy administration and the Khrushchev regime.

In these letters we read the leaders congratulating each others on space achievements of the two countries and attempting to come to grips with events in Laos, Vietnam, the idea of Berlin as a free city, and most particularly, the Cuban Missile crisis and the Nuclear Test Ban Treaty.

We read them as individuals; Khrushchev mentioning taking a working vacation to the Black Sea and John Kennedy replying with remembrances of vacations to Hyannis Port. They share mentions of families and Nikita Khrushchev sends his condolences on the death of a newborn infant of John and Jackie Kennedy.

In one letter, cited as number 22, dated October 16, 1961, John Kennedy writes:

For my part the contents and even the existence of our letters will be known only to the Secretary of State and a few others of my closest associates in the government.(pp. 70)

We can only speculate if John Kennedy ever thought the correspondence would be revealed, or eventually published. He also writes:

I think it is very important that these letters provide us with an opportunity for a personal, informal but meaningful exchange of views. (pp. 70)

In those letters we can see John Kennedy and Nikita Khrushchev enjoying the exchange of views; some are in fact "pen-pal"-type letters. We read Khrushchev offering Russian folk tales as analogies (the Russian who vows to bring back a giant bear to his village; pp. 85) to international political events and leaders; we read Kennedy and Khrushchev becoming serious and argumentative, stating positions, challenging and refuting the position of the other. At times the exchange is as warm as two friends; on other occasions, the tones of the letters are official, bureaucratic and combative. A few of the letters were made public and the occasions of their public release are noted.

They are also fascinating, instructive, and offer extremely valuable insights of these two superpower leaders during the years in question. They show not only the personalities of Kennedy and Khrushchev, but their leadership styles, the cultures in which they lived and the cultural and international differences which they attempted to bridge.

These letters were collected by members of the Kennedy administration and the federal government, particularly the Foreign Service. The source of each letter appears in the footnote after the date of the letter. The mode of transmission of the message is also noted. Questions of translation from the Russian of Khrushchev's letters are also indicated. Questions of translation were coordinated and answered with the co-operation of Soviet governmental agencies.

We believe this is the first commercial publication of the Kennedy–Khrushchev correspondence.

Those interested in the John Kennedy administration, or in the Nikita Khrushchev regime, those interested in international diplomacy and modern global politics may make their own determination of the thrust and importance of this correspondence.

The volume ends not with a letter from John Kennedy to Khrushchev or a letter from Nikita Khrushchev to John Kennedy, but with a poignant — even heart-breaking — letter from Jacqueline Kennedy, thanking Russian leaders for their concerns and sympathies after the assassination of John Kennedy. While reading and becoming engrossed with this correspondence, it may almost come as a surprise to remember that John Kennedy was assassinated in Dallas in 1963. We almost hope that the correspondence would have continued — somehow — past that letter from an obviously shattered Jackie Kennedy.

TOP SECRET

New Century Books has made no changes to this correspondence, save moving the origin of each letter to a footnote, following the date of the letter (footnote number one in each case). We have also added a quotation in italic type at the top of each letter, solely as a key to an important topic in that letter. Otherwise, the text of each letter remains as it appears in the original archive. We have treated each letter as a separate chapter in this on-going correspondence and cited it separately. All letters appear in chronological order, as they were written.

These letters were placed on a CD-Rom for storage, then reprinted from the CD-Rom, then recoded for computerized "print-on-demand" technology. Every effort has been made to retain the accuracy of the Kennedy–Khrushchev correspondence, however, New Century Books does not guarantee the accuracy of the text, after the declassification, transfer to CD-Rom then the second-stage recoding for eventually publication in book form. (Nor can we determine if there have been other letters from John Kennedy or Nikita Khrushchev which do not appear in this volume. Original documents make no references to letters withheld from this archive during the years in question, but that still may be the case.)

We are extremely pleased to make this volume of the Kennedy–Khrushchev correspondence available to the public.

—*Thomas Fensch, Publisher*
New Century Books

The
Kennedy–Khrushchev
Letters

The
Kennedy–Khrushchev
Letters

"Allow me to congratulate you . . ."

1. Message From Chairman Khrushchev to President-elect Kennedy

Moscow, November 9, 1960./1/

ESTEEMED MR. KENNEDY, Allow me to congratulate you on the occasion of your election to the high post of the President of the United States.

We hope that while you are at this post the relations between our countries would again follow the line along which they were developing in Franklin Roosevelt's time, which would meet the basic interests not only of the peoples of the U.S.S.R. and the United States but all mankind which is longing for deliverance from the threat of a new war.

I think you will agree that the eyes of many people are fixed on the United States and the Soviet Union because the destinies of world peace depend largely on the state of Soviet-American relations.

We have declared and declare our respect for the peaceable and gifted people of the United States and we are ready to develop the most friendly relations between the Soviet and the American peoples, between the Governments of the U.S.S.R. and the United States.

We are convinced that there are no insurmountable obstacles to the preservation and consolidation of peace.

For the sake of this goal we are ready, for our

part, to continue efforts to solve such a pressing problem as disarmament, to settle the German issue through the earliest conclusion of a peace treaty and to reach agreement on other questions, the solution of which could bring about an easing and improvement of the entire international situation.

Any steps in this direction will always meet with the full understanding and support of the Soviet Government.

I wish you fruitful activity in the responsible capacity of United States President and prosperity to the American people./2/

/1/Source: *American Foreign Policy: Current Documents, 1960*, p. 476. No classification marking.
/2/Printed from an unsigned copy.

" . . . a just and lasting peace will remain a fundamental goal of this nation . . ."

2. Message From President-elect Kennedy to Chairman Khrushchev

November 10, 1960./1/

I am most appreciative of your courtesy in sending me a message of congratulations./2/ The achievement of a just and lasting peace will remain a fundamental goal of this nation and a major task of its President. I am most pleased to have your good wishes at this time./3/

3

TOP SECRET

/1/Source: *American Foreign Policy: Current Documents,
1960*, p. 476. No classification marking.
/2/Document 1.
/3/Printed from an unsigned copy.

*". . . the Soviet Government
is always ready to support
any good undertakings . . ."*

3. Message From Chairmen Khrushchev and Brezhnev to President Kennedy

Moscow, January 20, 1961./1/

DEAR MR. PRESIDENT: We congratulate you on the occasion of your inauguration. Availing ourselves of this opportunity we wish to express the hope that by our joint efforts we shall succeed in achieving a fundamental improvement in relations between our countries and a normalization of the whole international situation. We are convinced that, step by step, it will be possible to remove existing suspicion and distrust and cultivate seeds of friendship and practical cooperation between our peoples. On its side the Soviet Government is always ready to support any good undertakings in this direction and do everything in its power in order that durable peace may be established in the world, so that all nations may live in friendship and without enmity.

N. Khrushchev
Chairman of the Council of Ministers of the USSR

L. Brezhnev
Chairman of the Presidium of the Supreme
Soviet of the USSR

/1/Source: Department of State, Presidential
Correspondence: Lot 66 D 204. No classification marking.
The source text is a Department of State translation of a
commercial telegram from Moscow. Another copy of this
message is in the Kennedy Library, National Security Files,
Countries Series, USSR, Khrushchev Correspondence. This
message is also printed in *Public Papers of the Presidents
of the United States: John F. Kennedy, 1961*, p. 3, and
American Foreign Policy: Current Documents, 1961, p. 559.

"I welcome your expression of hope . . ."

4. Telegram From the Department of State to the Embassy in the Soviet Union

Washington, January 21, 1961, 6:34 p.m./1/

1174. For Ambassador. Please pass following
Presidential message to Khrushchev and
Brezhnev.

"N. Khrushchev, Chairman of the Council of
Ministers of the USSR

L. Brezhnev, Chairman of the Presidium of the
Supreme Soviet of the USSR, The Kremlin,
Moscow.

Please accept this expression of my appreciation for your kind message of congratulations/2/

on the occasion of my inauguration as President of the United States of America. I welcome your expression of hope for a fundamental improvement in relations between our two countries and in the world situation as a whole; it is a hope which we share. We are ready and anxious to cooperate with all who are prepared to join in genuine dedication to the assurance of a peaceful and a more fruitful life for all mankind. Speaking on behalf of the Government and people of the United States of America, as well as on my own behalf, I can assure you that the efforts of the United States Government will be directed toward this imperative goal.

/1/Source: Department of State, Central Files, 711.11-KE/1-2161. Unclassified; Niact. Drafted by McSweeney and Veliotes (SOV) and cleared by Goodpaster, Kretzmann, and Rusk. Another copy of this message is in the Kennedy Library, National Security Files, Countries Series, USSR, Khrushchev Correspondence. Also printed in *Public Papers of the Presidents of the United States: John F. Kennedy, 1961*, p. 3, and *American Foreign Policy: Current Documents, 1961*, p. 560.
/2/Document 3.

Sincerely, John F. Kennedy."

Message being released to press approximately 7:00 pm Washington time, January 21, 1961.

Rusk

"We shall watch its progress with interest and wish you success in another chapter of man's exploration of the universe."

5. Telegram From President Kennedy to Chairman Khrushchev

Washington, February 13, 1961./1/

I wish to extend my congratulations and those of the American people for the impressive scientific achievement represented by the launching of your space vehicle to Venus. We shall watch its progress with interest and wish you success in another chapter of man's exploration of the universe.

⁕ John F. Kennedy

/1/Source: Department of State, Central Files, 761.13/2-1361. Unclassified. Drafted by Rusk. A typed note on the source text indicates it was sent by commercial telegram. A copy of this message is also in the Kennedy Library, National Security Files, Countries Series, USSR, Khrushchev Correspondence, and Department of State, Presidential Correspondence: Lot 66 D 204.

"All agree to the fact that the solution of the problem of disarmament depends to a great extent on agreement between the Soviet Union and the United States of America."

6. Message From Chairman Khrushchev to President Kennedy

Moscow, February 15, 1961./1/

Received your telegram of congratulations on the occasion of the launching of the Soviet cosmic spaceship to the planet Venus./2/ I express gratitude to you for this telegram giving high appraisal to this outstanding achievement of peaceful science and for wishes for success in the new stage of the exploration of the cosmos. In your speech of inauguration to the office of President, and likewise in the message to Congress of January 30 you, Mr. President, said that you would like for the Soviet Union and the United States of America to unite their efforts in such areas as the struggle against disease, mastering the cosmos, development of culture and trade. Such an approach to these problems impresses us and we welcome these utterances of yours.

We consider that favorable conditions for the most speedy solution of these noble tasks facing humanity would be created through the settlement of the problem of disarmament. And we would like every country to make every effort for the solution of this problem with the establishment of such a strict international control under which no one could arm secretly and commit aggression.

All agree to the fact that the solution of the problem of disarmament depends to a great extent on agreement between the Soviet Union and the United States of America. If we reached such an agreement, it would be a great joy for all people on Earth and a great blessing for all mankind.

N. Khrushchev/3/

/1/Source: Department of State, Presidential Correspondence: Lot 66 D 204. No classification marking. The source text is a Department of State translation of a commercial telegram from Moscow. Other copies of this message are in the Kennedy Library, National Security Files, Countries Series, USSR, Khrushchev Correspondence, and Department of State, Central Files, 761.13/2-1561. The transliterated Russian text is ibid.
/2/Document 5.
/3/Printed from a copy that bears this typed signature.

"I hope it will be possible, before too long, for us to meet personally . . ."

7. Letter From President Kennedy to Chairman Khrushchev

Washington, February 22, 1961./1/

DEAR MR. CHAIRMAN: I have had an opportunity, due to the return of Ambassador

Thompson, to have an extensive review of all aspects of our relations with the Secretary of State and with him. In these consultations, we have been able to explore, in general, not only those subjects which are of direct bilateral concern to the United States and the Soviet Union, but also the chief outstanding international problems which affect our relations.

I have not been able, in so brief a time, to reach definite conclusions as to our position on all of these matters. Many of them are affected by developments in the international scene and are of concern to many other governments. I would, however, like to set before you certain general considerations which I believe might be of help in introducing a greater element of clarity in the relations between our two countries. I say this because I am sure that you are conscious as I am of the heavy responsibility which rests upon our two Governments in world affairs. I agree with your thought that if we could find a measure of cooperation on some of these current issues this, in itself, would be a significant contribution to the problem of insuring a peaceful and orderly world.

I think we should recognize, in honesty to each other, that there are problems on which we may not be able to agree. However, I believe that while recognizing that we do not and, in all probability will not, share a common view on all of these problems, I do believe that the manner in which we approach them and, in particular, the manner in which our disagreements are handled, can be of great importance.

In addition, I believe we should make more use of diplomatic channels for quite informal discussion of these questions, not in the sense of negotiations (since I am sure that we both recognize the interests of other countries are deeply involved in these issues), but rather as a mechanism of communication which should, insofar as is possible, help to eliminate misunderstanding and unnecessary divergencies, however great the basic differences may be.

I hope it will be possible, before too long, for us to meet personally for an informal exchange of views in regard to some of these matters. Of course, a meeting of this nature will depend upon the general international situation at the time, as well as on our mutual schedules of engagements.

I have asked Ambassador Thompson to discuss the question of our meeting. Ambassador Thompson, who enjoys my full confidence, is also in a position to inform you of my thinking on a number of the international issues which we have discussed. I shall welcome any expression of your views. I hope such exchange might assist us in working out a responsible approach to our differences with the view to their ultimate resolution for the benefit of peace and security throughout the world. You may be sure, Mr. Chairman, that I intend to do everything I can toward developing a more harmonious relationship between our two countries.

Sincerely, John F. Kennedy/2/

/1/Source: Department of State, Presidential Correspondence: Lot 66 D 204. No classification marking. At the top of the source text is written "2/22/62?". The final drafting of this message was done at a meeting at the White House on February 21 attended by the President, Rusk, Thompson, Harriman, Bohlen, Kohler, and Bundy. No record of this meeting has been found, but it is noted in Rusk's Appointment Book (Johnson Library) and the President's Appointment Book (Kennedy Library), and is also mentioned in the first sentence of a February 26 memorandum from Rusk to Kennedy scheduled for publication in volume V. At noon on February 22 Rusk, Kohler, and Harriman briefed French Ambassador Alphand and British Ambassador Caccia on the content of this message stating that it was general in nature and informing them that specific questions would be addressed in further messages after consultations with their governments. (Memorandum of conversation; Department of State, Central Files, 611.61/2-2261) Regarding delivery of this letter to Khrushchev, see vol. V, Document 28. Printed in part in Claflin, *The President Wants To Know*, pp. 50-51.
/2/Printed from a copy that bears this typed signature.

". . . for the safe flight of the astronaut in man's first venture into space."

8. Telegram From the Department of State to the Embassy in the Soviet Union

Washington, April 12, 1961, 1:24 p.m./1/

1724. Deliver following message to Khrushchev from the President. Message being released 2:00 p.m. April 12 Washington time.

"The people of the United States share with the people of the Soviet Union their satisfaction for the safe flight of the astronaut in man's first venture into space. We congratulate you and the Soviet scientists and engineers who made this feat possible. It is my sincere desire that in the continuing quest for knowledge of outer space our nations can work together to obtain the greatest benefit to mankind.

John F. Kennedy"

Rusk

/1/Source: Department of State, Central Files, 711.11-KE/2-1261. Official Use Only; Niact. Drafted at the White House. Also printed in *Public Papers of the Presidents of the United States: John F. Kennedy, 1961*, p. 257.

"I send you this message in an hour of alarm, fraught with danger for the peace of the whole world."

9. Telegram From the Embassy in the Soviet Union to the Department of State

Moscow, April 18, 1961, 2 p.m./1/

2550. Following letter to President Kennedy from Khrushchev handed me by Acting Foreign Minister Semenov at 12:15 today. *Begin text:*

Mr. President, I send you this message in an hour of alarm, fraught with danger for the peace of the whole world. Armed aggression has begun against Cuba. It is a secret to no one that the armed bands invading this country were trained, equipped and armed in the United States of America. The planes which are bombing Cuban cities belong to the United States of America, the bombs they are dropping are being supplied by the American Government.

All of this evokes here in the Soviet Union an understandable feeling of indignation on the part of the Soviet Government and the Soviet people.

Only recently, in exchanging opinions through our respective representatives, we talked with you about the mutual desire of both sides to put forward joint efforts directed toward improving relations between our countries and eliminating the danger of war. Your statement a few days ago that the USA would not participate in military activities against Cuba created the impression that the top leaders of the United States were taking into account the consequences for general peace and for the USA itself which aggression against Cuba could have. How can what is being done by the United States in reality be understood, when an attack on Cuba has now become a fact?

It is still not late to avoid the irreparable. The Government of the USA still has the possibility of not allowing the flame of war ignited by interventions in Cuba to grow into an incomparable conflagration. I approach you, Mr. President, with an urgent call to put an end to aggression against the Republic of Cuba. Military armament and the world political situation are such at this time that any so-called "little war" can touch off a chain reaction in all parts of the globe.

As far as the Soviet Union is concerned, there should be no mistake about our position: We will render the Cuban people and their government all necessary help to repel armed attack on Cuba. We are sincerely interested in a relaxation of international tension, but if others proceed toward sharpening, we will answer them in full measure. And in general it is hardly possible so to conduct matters that the situation is settled in one area and conflagration extinguished, while a new conflagration is ignited in another area.

I hope that the Government of the USA will consider our views as dictated by the sole concern not to allow steps which could lead the world to military catastrophe. End text.

Freers

/1/Source: Department of State, Presidential Correspondence: Lot 66 D 204. Secret; Niact; Limit Distribution. Another copy of this message is in the Kennedy Library, National Security Files, Countries Series, USSR, Khrushchev Correspondence. A slightly different translation is printed in Department of State *Bulletin*, May 8, 1961, p. 662, and *American Foreign Policy: Current Documents, 1961*, p. 295. The Russian-language text was transmitted as an enclosure to dispatch 747 from Moscow, May 3. (Department of State, Central Files, 611.37/5-361)

"When people are denied the right of choice, recourse to such struggle is the only means of achieving their liberties."

10. Letter From President Kennedy to Chairman Khrushchev

Washington, April 18, 1961./1/

MR. CHAIRMAN: You are under a serious mis-apprehension in regard to events in Cuba. For months there has been evident and growing resistance to the Castro dictatorship. More than 100,000 refugees have recently fled from Cuba into neighboring countries. Their urgent hope is naturally to assist their fellow Cubans in their struggle for freedom. Many of these refugees fought alongside Dr. Castro against the Batista dictatorship; among them are prominent leaders of his own original movement and government.

These are unmistakable signs that Cubans find intolerable the denial of democratic liberties and the subversion of the 26th of July Movement by an alien-dominated regime. It cannot be surprising that, as resistance within Cuba grows, refugees have been using whatever means are available to return and support their countrymen in the continuing struggle for freedom. Where people are denied the right of choice, recourse to such struggle is the only means of achieving their liberties.

I have previously stated, and I repeat now, that the United States intends no military intervention in Cuba. In the event of any military intervention by outside force we will immediately honor our obligations under the inter-American system to protect this hemisphere against external aggression. While refraining from military intervention in Cuba, the people of the United States do not conceal their admiration for Cuban patriots who wish to see a democratic system in an independent Cuba. The United States government can take no action to stifle the spirit of liberty.

I have taken careful note of your statement that the events in Cuba might affect peace in all parts of the world./2/ I trust that this does not mean that the Soviet government, using the situation in Cuba as a pretext, is planning to inflame other areas of the world. I would like to think that your government has too great a sense of responsibility to embark upon any enterprise so dangerous to general peace.

I agree with you as to the desirability of steps to improve the international atmosphere. I continue to hope that you will cooperate in opportunities now available to this end. A prompt cease-fire and peaceful settlement of the dangerous situation in Laos, cooperation with the United Nations in the Congo and a speedy conclusion of an acceptable treaty for the banning of nuclear tests would be constructive steps in this direction. The regime in Cuba could make a similar contribution by permitting the Cuban people freely to determine their own future by democratic processes and freely to cooperate with their Latin American neighbors.

I believe, Mr. Chairman, that you should recognize that free peoples in all parts of the world do not accept the claim of historical inevitability for Communist revolution. What your government believes is its own business; what it does in the world is the world's business. The great revolution in the history of man, past, present and future, is the revolution of those determined to be free.

John F. Kennedy/3/

/1/Source: Department of State, Presidential Correspondence: Lot 66 D 204. No classification marking. The source text is a press release from the Office of the White House Press Secretary, which was marked for release at 6:45 p.m. April 18. Another copy of this message is in the Kennedy Library, National Security Files, Countries Series, USSR, Khrushchev Correspondence. Also printed in *Public Papers of the Presidents of the United States: John F. Kennedy, 1961*, pp. 286-287; *American Foreign Policy: Current Documents, 1961*, pp. 296-297; and Claflin, *The President Wants To Know*, pp. 59-60.
/2/See Document 9.
/3/Printed from a copy that bears this typed signature.

"But numerous facts known to the whole world – and to the Government of the United States, of course, better than to any one else – speak differently."

11. Letter From Chairman Khrushchev to President Kennedy

Moscow, April 22, 1961./1/

MR. PRESIDENT, I have received your reply of April 18./2/ You write that the United States intends no military intervention in Cuba. But numerous facts known to the whole world — and to the Government of the United States, of course, better than to any one else — speak differently. Despite all assurances to the contrary, it has now been proved beyond doubt that it was precisely the United States which prepared the intervention, financed its arming and transported the gangs of mercenaries that invaded the territory of Cuba.

United States armed forces also took a direct part in the accomplishment of the gangster attack upon Cuba. American bombers and fighters supported the operations of the mercenaries who landed on Cuban territory, and participated in the military operations against the armed forces of the lawful Government and people of Cuba.

Such are the facts. They bear witness to direct United States participation in the armed aggression against Cuba.

In your message you took the course of justifying, and even lauding, the attack on Cuba—this crime which has revolted the entire world. You try to justify the organization of a military attack on Cuba, committed for the sole reason that the way of life chosen by its people is not to the taste of the ruling circles of the United States and the North American monopolies operating in Latin America, by talk about the United States Government's adherence to the ideals of "freedom". But, one may ask, of what freedom are you speaking?

Of freedom to strangle the Cuban people with the bony hand of hunger through the establishment of an economic blockade? Is that freedom?

Of freedom to send military planes over the territory of Cuba, to subject peaceful Cuban cities to barbarous bombing, to set fire to sugar-cane plantations? Is that freedom?

History records many cases in which, on the pretext of defending freedom, peoples have been drowned in blood, colonial wars waged, and one small nation after another taken by the throat.

In the present case, apparently, the United States Government is seeking to restore to Cuba that "freedom" under which Cuba would dance to the tune of her more powerful neighbour and foreign monopolies would again be able to plunder the country's national wealth, to wax rich on the sweat and blood of the Cuban people. But it is precisely against such "freedom" that the Cuban people accomplished their revolution when they threw out Batista, who may have loyally served the interests of his foreign masters but who was a foreign element in the body of the Cuban nation.

You, Mr. President, display concern for a handful of enemies who were expelled by their people and found refuge under the wing of those who want to keep the guns of their cruisers and destroyers trained on Cuba. But why are you not concerned about the fate of the six million Cuban people, why do you not wish to pay regard to their inalienable right to a free and independent life, their right to arrange their domestic affairs as they see fit? Where are the standards of international law, or even of simple human morality, that would justify such a position? They simply do not exist.

The Cuban people have once again expressed their will with a clarity which should have left no room for doubt, even in the minds of those who prefer to close their eyes to reality. They have shown that they not only know their interests, but can stand up for them. Cuba today is not, of course, the Cuba you identify with the handful of traitors who have come out against their people. It is the Cuba of workers, peasants and intellectuals, it is a people which has rallied round its revolutionary Government headed by the national hero, Fidel Castro. And, judging from everything, this people received the interventionists in a fitting way. Is not this convincing proof of the real will of the Cuban people?

I think it is. And since this is so, is it not time for all to draw from it the right conclusions?

As for the Soviet Union, we have stated on many occasions, and I now state again, that our Government does not seek any advantages or privileges in Cuba. We have no bases in Cuba, and we do not intend to establish any. And this is well known to you, to your generals and your admirals. If, despite this, they still try to frighten the people by fabrications about "Soviet bases" on Cuba, that is obviously designed for consumption by simpletons. But there are fewer and fewer such simpletons, and that applies also, I hope, to the United States.

By the way, Mr. President, I would like to express my opinion concerning the statements made by you and by certain other United States politicians to the effect that rockets and other weapons could be installed on Cuban territory for possible use against the United States.

The inference from this is that the United States has some alleged right to attack Cuba, either directly or through the traitors to the Cuban people whom you arm with your weapons, train on your territory, maintain with the money of United States taxpayers and transport with the resources of your armed forces, covering them from the air and the sea while they fight against the Cuban people and their lawful government.

You also refer to some United States obligations to protect the Western hemisphere against external aggression.

But what obligations can possibly apply in the present case? No one can have any obligations to defend rebels against the lawful government of a sovereign State, such as Cuba is.

Mr. President, you are setting out on a very dangerous road. Think of it. You speak of your rights and obligations, and, of course, anyone can claim this or that right. But then you will have to admit that other States, too, can base their actions in similar circumstances on similar arguments and considerations.

You allege that Cuba can lend her territory for actions against the United States. That is your supposition, but it is based on no facts. We, on the other hand, can already refer to concrete facts, not suppositions: in some countries, bordering on the Soviet Union by land and sea, there are at present Governments following a policy that is far from reasonable, Governments which have concluded military agreements with the United

States and have made their territory available for
the establishment of American military bases.
And your military say openly that these bases
are spearheaded against the Soviet Union, as if
this were not already sufficiently clear. So, if you
consider yourself entitled to take such measures
against Cuba as the United States Government
has been resorting to lately, you must admit that
other countries have no lesser grounds for acting
in the same way with regard to States whose territories are the scene of actual preparations con-
stituting a threat to the security of the Soviet
Union. If you do not want to sin against elementary logic, you must obviously concede this right
to other States. We, for our part, do not hold such
views. We consider that the arguments advanced
on this score in the United States constitute, not
merely an extremely free interpretation of international law, but, to put it plainly, open advocacy
of a treacherous policy.

A powerful State can of course always find a
pretext for attacking a weaker country, and then
justify its attack by claiming that that country
was a potential menace. But is this twentieth-cen-
tury morality? This is the morality of the colonialists, of the brigands who once pursued precisely such a policy. Today, in the second half of
the twentieth century, it is no longer possible to
take the pirate morality of the colonialists as a
guide. We all see, today, how the colonial system
is crumbling and becoming a thing of the past.
The Soviet Union, for its part, is doing everything
to promote this process, and we are proud of it.

Or take the United States actions with regard

to China. What standards of law can be invoked to justify these actions? Everyone knows that Taiwan is an inalienable part of China. This has been admitted even by the Government of the United States, whose signature appears on the Cairo Declaration of 1943. But later the United States seized Taiwan—took, in fact, the road to brigandage. The People's Republic of China announced its natural aspiration to reunite the territory of Taiwan with the rest of Chinese territory. But how did the United States react to this? It declared that it would use armed force to prevent reunification of this Chinese territory, seized by it, with the rest of China. It threatens war if China takes any steps towards the recovery of Taiwan. And this is being done by a country which has officially recognized that Taiwan belongs to China! Is not this perfidy in international relations? If such methods were to become the rule in relations between States, there would be no place left for law. Its place would be taken by lawlessness and arbitrariness.

So, Mr. President, your sympathies are one thing; but actions against the security and independence of other peoples, taken on the basis of such sympathies, are very much another. You may, of course, express your sympathy with the imperialist and colonialist countries; that does not surprise anyone. For example, you vote with them in the United Nations. This is a matter of your morality. But what has been done against Cuba is no longer morality. It is gangsterism.

I should like to stress that if the United Nations is really to become strong and fulfil the functions for which it was established—and at present this Organization, unfortunately, is a body already infected by the bacilli of colonialism and imperialism—the United Nations must resolutely condemn the banditry undertaken against Cuba. And the point here is not merely to condemn the United States. The important thing is that the condemnation of aggression should be seen to be a precedent, a lesson which other countries, too, might learn, so that aggression should never again be repeated. For if we were to take the course of approving or even, simply, condoning the morality of the aggressors, it could be adopted by other States as well, and this would inevitably lead to military conflicts, any of which might result in a third world war.

What you said in your last statement to the Press/3/ must fill the entire world with great alarm. For you simply claim, in fact, some right of yours to employ military force whenever you find it necessary, and to suppress other peoples each time you decide that their expression of their will constitutes "communism". But what right have you, what right has anyone in general, to deprive a people of the possibility of choosing their social and political system of their own free will? Have you never considered that other countries, too, might perhaps advance a demand similar to yours and might declare that you, in the United States, have a system which breeds wars and espouses an imperialist policy, the policy of threats and attacks against other countries? There is every ground for such accusations. And, proceeding from the principles which you now proclaim, one could, apparently, demand a change in the internal system of the United States. We, as you know, do not follow that road. We favour the peaceful coexistence of all States, and non-interference in the internal affairs of other countries.

You allude to Budapest. But we can tell you openly, without any allusions: it is you, the United States, that crushed the independence of Guatemala by sending your mercenaries there, as you are now trying to do with regard to Cuba. It is the United States, and no other country, that still mercilessly exploits and keeps in economic bondage the countries of Latin America and many other countries of the world. This is known to all. And if, Mr. President, your logic is to be followed, actions from without could apparently be organized against your country too, to put an end forever to this imperialist policy, the policy of threats, the policy of suppressing the freedom-loving peoples.

As for your concern for the emigres expelled by the Cuban people, I should like to add the following. You are of course well aware that there are, in many countries, emigres who are dissatisfied with the situation and the system existing in the countries from which they fled. And if the abnormal practice were introduced, in relations between States, of using these emigres, especially with arms in their hand, against the countries they had fled from, it can be openly said that this would inevitably lead to conflicts and wars. It would therefore be well to refrain from such ill-advised actions. This is a slippery and dangerous road which can lead to a new world war.

In your reply, you saw fit to touch upon certain questions unrelated to the subject of my message to you, including the question—as interpreted by you—of the historic inevitability of a communist revolution. I can only regard this as an attempt to evade the main question—that of aggression against Cuba. We are prepared, in appropriate circumstances, to exchange opinions on the question of the ways in which human society develops, although this question cannot be settled by debates between groups or individuals, however high their position may be. The question of whose system is the better will be decided by history, by the peoples themselves.

You, Mr. President, speak often and much of your desire that Cuba should be free. But that attitude is flatly contradicted by all United States actions with regard to this small country, let alone the latest armed attack upon Cuba organized with a view to changing Cuba's internal system by force. It was the United States which nearly 60 years ago imposed on Cuba the enslaving terms of the Havana Treaty and established its Guantanamo naval base on Cuban territory. Yet the United States is the most powerful country in the Western hemisphere, and no one in that hemisphere can threaten you with a military invasion. Consequently, if you continue to retain your naval base on Cuban territory against the clearly expressed will of the Cuban people and its Government, it is because this base is designed, not to serve as a defense against an attack by any external forces, but to suppress the will of the Latin American peoples. It was established to fulfill the functions of a gendarme, to keep the peoples of Latin America politically and economically dependent.

The Government of the United States is now fulminating against Cuba. But this indicates only one thing—your lack of trust in your own system, in the policy pursued by the United States. And this is understandable, as it is a policy of exploitation, a policy for the economic enslavement of under-developed countries. You have no confidence in your own system, and therefore fear that Cuba's example may prove contagious for other countries. But aggressive, bandit actions cannot save your system. In the historic process of the development of human society, each people decides, and will decide, its own destiny.

As for the Soviet Union, the peoples of our country settled this question finally and irrevocably over 43 years ago. We constitute a socialist state. Our social system is the most equitable of all that have so far existed, because in our country all the means of production are owned by those who work. That is indeed a contagious example, and the sooner the need to go over to this system is realized, the sooner will the whole of mankind achieve a really just society. By this very development, an end will be put, once and for all, to war.

You, Mr. President, did not like it when I said, in my previous message, that there can be no stable place in the world if anywhere war is aflame. But this is really so. The world is a single whole, whether we like it or not. And I can only repeat what I said: it is impossible to proceed by adjusting the situation and putting out the flames in one area, and kindling a new conflagration in another.

The Soviet State has always been a consistent defender of the freedom and independence of all peoples. We naturally, therefore, cannot concede to the United States any right to control the destinies of other countries, including the countries of Latin America. We consider that any interference by one State in the affairs of another— especially armed interference—is a violation of all international laws and of the principles of peaceful coexistence which the Soviet Union has invariably upheld since the first days of its existence.

If it is now, more than ever before, the duty of every State and its leaders not to permit actions which are capable of jeopardizing universal peace, that applies with all the more force to the leaders of the great Powers. It is this that I urge upon you, Mr. President.

The Soviet Government's position in international affairs remains unchanged. We wish to build our relations with the United States in such a way that neither the Soviet Union nor the United States, as the two most powerful countries in the world, shall engage in sabre-rattling or push their military or economic superiority to the forefront, since that would lead to an aggravation of the international situation, not to its improvement. We are sincerely desirous of reaching agreement, both with you and with other countries of the world, on disarmament and all the other questions whose solution would promote peaceful coexistence, the recognition of every people's right to the social and political systems established by it, genuine respect for the will of the peoples and non-interference in their internal affairs. Only under these conditions can one really speak of coexistence, for coexistence is possible only if States with different social systems obey international laws and recognize the maintenance of world peace as their highest aim. Only in that event will peace be based on firm foundations.

N. Khrushchev/4/

/1/Source: Department of State, Presidential Correspondence: Lot 66 D 204. No classification marking. Transmitted in telegram 2562 from Moscow, April 11. A copy of section 1 of 3 of that telegram is in the Kennedy Library, National Security Files, Countries Series, USSR, Khrushchev Correspondence. The source text was transmitted as an enclosure to despatch 1183 from Moscow, May 11, and indicates it was "translated from Russian." The Russian-language text was transmitted as an enclosure to despatch 747 from Moscow, May 3. (Department of State, Central Files, 611.37/5-361) A slightly different text is printed in Department of State Bulletin, May 8, 1961, pp. 664-667.
/2/Document 10.
/3/Reference is to President Kennedy's address before the American Society of Newspaper Editors on April 20; for text, see *Public Papers of the Presidents of the United States: John F. Kennedy, 1961*, pp. 304-306.
/4/Printed from a copy that bears this typed signature.

"... congratulations on the occasion of the unprecedented exploit of the Soviet people – the successful launching of the first human being into space."

12. Message From Chairman Khrushchev to President Kennedy

Moscow, April 30, 1961./1/

EXCELLENCY: Allow me to express to the people of the United States and to you personally gratitude for congratulations on the occasion of the unprecedented exploit of the Soviet people—the successful launching of the first human being into space./2/

I express the hope that the Soviet Union and the United States may work together on the matter of mastering the universe, considering the mastering of the universe as a part of the great task of creating peace without armaments and war.

N. Khrushchev

/1/Source: Department of State, Presidential Correspondence: Lot 66 D 204. No classification marking. The source text is a Department of State translation of a commercial telegram from Moscow. The transliterated Russian text is ibid.
/2/See Document 8.

TOP SECRET

"Recent outstanding achievements in man's conquests of the cosmos open up boundless possibilities for understanding nature, in the name of progress."

13. Telegram From Chairman Khrushchev to President Kennedy

Moscow, May 6, 1961./1/

DEAR MR. PRESIDENT:
On behalf of the people of the Soviet Union and on my own behalf I send you and all the American people sincere congratulations on the occasion of the successful launching of a rocket, with a man on board, that flew a distance of 300 miles and that, during flight, reached a height of up to 115 miles.

Recent outstanding achievements in man's conquest of the cosmos open up boundless possibilities for understanding nature, in the name of progress.

Please convey my heartfelt congratulations to the pilot, Shepard.

N. Khrushchev

/1/Source: Department of State, Central Files, 911.802/5-661. No classification marking. Another copy of this message is in the Kennedy Library, National Security Files, Countries Series, USSR, Khrushchev Correspondence. A slightly different translation is in Department of State, Presidential Correspondence: Lot 66 D 204. The Russian-language text is ibid.

". . . peaceful exploration of space is a venture undertaken on behalf of mankind as a whole."

14. Letter From President Kennedy to Chairman Khrushchev

Washington, undated./1/

DEAR MR. CHAIRMAN: The American people and I sincerely thank you for your/2/ message conveying congratulations on behalf of yourself and the Soviet people on the occasion of the flight of Commander Shepard in the first American manned exploration of space./3/

We believe that the peaceful exploration of space is a venture undertaken on behalf of mankind as a whole. In that spirit, each new step in the conquest and understanding of space, wherever made, will be an achievement in which all of us share.

Sincerely,/4/

/1/Source: Department of State, Presidential Correspondence: Lot 66 D 204. No classification marking. Drafted by Hartley (S/S-RO) on May 7 and cleared by Davis, Farley (S/AE), and McCloskey (P). The source text, titled "Suggested Reply," is double spaced.
/2/The word "kind" is crossed out at this point in the source text.
/3/See Document 13.
/4/Printed from an unsigned copy.

*"... our countries, which,
if one speaks frankly, are still
divided by a muddy stream of
mistrust and hostility born of the
'cold war.'"*

15. Telegram From the Department of State to Secretary of State Rusk at Geneva

Washington, May 16, 1961, 1:33 p.m./1/

Tosec 121. Eyes only Secretary and Ambassador Thompson. Following is unofficial translation letter from Khrushchev which Menshikov handed President at White House today:

Begin Text

DEAR MR. PRESIDENT:

I would like, although with a certain delay, to thank you for the message which was delivered to me by Ambassador Thompson in Novosibirsk on March 9./2/ I welcome the spirit of cooperation in which this message was composed, and I think I will not be wrong if I say that it cannot be a bad beginning for our personal contacts and mutual exchange of opinions. We share the considerations, which you expressed in the course of your recent conversation with the Minister of Foreign Affairs of the USSR, A.A. Gromyko,/3/ concerning the necessity of avoiding dangerous complications, creating a threat to peace, and to assure peaceful co-existence and the peaceful development of our countries.

Unfortunately, the international atmosphere has recently become somewhat heated in connection with the well-known events relating to Cuba, and a certain open falling out has taken place in the relations between our countries. There is no need to repeat now what I have already said in the name of the Soviet Government concerning the position of the USA in the Cuban events.

Speaking frankly, we regret that these events took place in general. However, we hope that the differences of opinion which have recently arisen will be eliminated with time, that the relations between the Soviet Union and the United States will improve if, of course, a mutual desire for this is demonstrated. Now, as never before, it is necessary without losing time to build and expand the bridges of mutual understanding with the help of which it would be possible to improve relations between our countries, which, if one speaks frankly, are still divided by a muddy stream of mistrust and hostility born of the "cold war."

I consider it necessary in this connection to emphasize especially our positive attitude toward the opinion, which you expressed in your message, about the necessity of deciding international problems and differences of opinion between our countries by peaceful means. I think that the bilateral exchange of opinions between the leaders of the USA and the USSR, so fruitfully carried out during the time of Franklin Roosevelt, can also now contribute to the achievement of this aim to a significant degree. We also, even as you,

Mr. President, attach great significance to this.
Indeed, the question of easing international tension and consequently the creation of favorable
conditions for deciding virtually all important
international problems depends to an enormous
extent on the improvement of Soviet-American
relations.

Ambassador Thompson explained to me your
deliberation about the expediency of a personal
meeting between us for an exchange of views on
questions of mutual interest. Your initiative concerning a meeting has found a favorable response
among us and we agree with you concerning the
usefulness of such an exchange of views. I confirm by this letter that I accept your proposal for
a meeting. The time and place of the meeting
which you have proposed, namely June 3-4 in
Vienna, are acceptable to me.

One of the problems which, as is apparent
from the exchange of views, gives rise to our
mutual concern is the situation in Laos. The
Soviet Union hopes that at the International
Conference in Geneva a peaceful and just solution
of this problem will be found. We consider that at
the present time there is every possibility to
guarantee the establishment of peace in that
region and to spare the people of Laos as well as
other peoples from the danger of the broadening
of the present conflict. For this it is necessary
only to proceed steadfastly along the indicated
correct path, and not to undertake anything
which could lead to a complication of the international situation. If, on the part of all participants of the conference there is revealed a sin-

cere desire for the creation of a truly neutral and independent Laos, I think that from the moment of our meeting with you we could with pleasure state that the settlement of the problem of Laos had become a fact.

There is also a series of other vitally important problems requiring solution. Among these, first of all, is the problem of disarmament. You, Mr. President, naturally are familiar with the views of the Soviet Government and its concrete proposals on this question. Therefore, it seems to me that there is no necessity to repeat all of these considerations in this letter. I wish only to underline that according to our firm conviction a practical implementation of disarmament is the most urgent and important problem in the sphere of international life in our time. Speaking figuratively, the solution of this problem could be compared to the seizure of the highest height which has been unattainable up to this time by mankind, after which it would be significantly easier to solve other unresolved problems. I should like to express the hope that our meeting can create the necessary premises for the success of the bilateral talks which are scheduled for June-July of this year between our countries on the problems of disarmament. We would only welcome this.

There is another international problem which urgently requires a solution. It is important both for the strengthening of peace in Europe and for the support of general peace. This is the problem of a peaceful settlement with Germany, including the question of Western Berlin. I believe that you have at your disposal complete information concerning the views of the Soviet Government in this regard. In conversations with your Ambassador, I have set forth our position in complete frankness. It is to be hoped, Mr. President, that you will approach this position with understanding: we do not demand any unilateral advantages of any sort for ourselves. We propose a peaceful settlement, which proceeds from the actually existing situation and which is directed toward the liquidation of a dangerous source of tension in the very heart of Europe. We seek only that finally the line should be drawn under the Second World War. The signature of a peace treaty with Germany, I am deeply convinced, would be a significant landmark in the improvement of relations between our countries.

In your letter, you, Mr. President, speak of the fact that we should recognize the fact that there are problems concerning which we cannot agree and concerning which in our governments there can be a different point of view. I agree with you. In the solution of international problems, large or small, there are, and will be, not a few difficulties. But it is our task, as heads of state, to strive to overcome them and to do everything possible for the attainment of agreement concerning questions which are ripe for solution.

I hope that at our forthcoming meeting we will be able to continue the exchange of views both on problems which have been touched on in our letters and on other problems and to indicate the path or, if you wish, the direction for their further examination and settlement.

Respectfully, N. Khrushchev

Chairman of the Council of Ministers, USSR./4/

May 12, 1961. *End text.*

/1/Source: Kennedy Library, National Security Files, Countries Series, USSR, Khrushchev Correspondence. Secret; Niact; Verbatim Text. Repeated to Moscow. Another copy is in Department of State, Central Files, 761.13/5-1661. A copy of the Russian-language text is ibid., Presidential Correspondence: Lot 66 D 204.
/2/See Document 7.
/3/See the March 27 memorandum of conversation in volume V.
/4/Following transmission of the text of this letter to Thompson, the Department of State informed him that he should seek an appointment with the Acting Soviet Foreign Minister to say that, subject to Austrian approval, a meeting on June 3 and 4 was agreeable. (Telegram 1980 to Moscow, May 16; Department of State, Central Files, 711.11-KE/5-1661) In a separate telegram the Department of State instructed Ambassador Matthews to ask the Austrian Government if a meeting on June 3 and 4, despite the short notice, was agreeable. (Telegram 1984 to Vienna, May 16; ibid.)

Bowles

"I would also like to express my appreciation . . . for the gold cigar chest, caviar and records."

16. Letter From President Kennedy to Chairman Khrushchev

Washington, June 10, 1961./1/

Dear Mr. Chairman: Many thanks for your kindness in presenting me with a case of beverages during our recent meeting in Vienna./2/ I would also like to express my appreciation to the Soviet Government for the gold cigar chest, caviar and records. For these courtesies I am very grateful.

Sincerely,

John F. Kennedy/3/

/1/Source: Department of State, Presidential Correspondence: Lot 66 D 204. No classification marking. Another copy of this message is in the Kennedy Library, National Security Files, Countries Series, USSR, Khrushchev Correspondence.
/2/Regarding these meetings June 3-4, see volume V.
/3/Printed from a copy that indicates the original was signed by President Kennedy.

"I want to express to you my great appreciation for your thoughtfulness in sending to me the model of an American whaler . . ."

17. Letter From President Kennedy to Chairman Khrushchev

Washington, June 21, 1961./1/

DEAR MR. CHAIRMAN: I want to express to

you my very great appreciation for your thoughtfulness in sending to me the model of an American whaler, which we discussed while in Vienna. It now rests in my office here at the White House.

Mrs. Kennedy and I were particularly pleased to receive "Pushinka." Her flight from the Soviet Union to the United States was not as dramatic as the flight of her mother, nevertheless, it was a long voyage and she stood it well. We both appreciate your remembering these matters in your busy life.

We send to you, your wife and your family our very best wishes.

Sincerely yours,

John F. Kennedy

/1/Source: Department of State, Presidential Correspondence: Lot 66 D 204. No classification marking.

"The Soviet and the American peoples by right must go down in history as the two great peoples who made a decisive contribution to the cause of ensuring permanent peace on earth."

18. Letter From Chairmen Khrushchev and Brezhnev to President Kennedy

Moscow, July 3, 1961./1/

DEAR MR. PRESIDENT, Personally and on behalf of the Soviet people we send to the American people, and to you personally, our sincere congratulations on the occasion of this important date in the life of the American people, namely, the 185th anniversary of achieving their independence. While sending our congratulations to you today, we want to express the hope that the recent Vienna meeting, and the exchange of opinions which took place there on questions of interest to both countries, will further the mutual efforts of our governments directed to the urgent solution of problems which long ago became pressing and which the last war left to us after the defeat of the aggressors. History imposed on our peoples, on their governments and on their leaders an enormous share of the responsibility for the preservation of peace, for the future of humanity. In order to carry out this great historical mission it is necessary to commence building, from both sides, enduring bridges of trust, of mutual understanding and of friendship. The Soviet Union has always striven and strives now to achieve this aim. The Soviet and the American peoples by right must go down in history as the two great peoples who made a decisive contribution to the cause of ensuring permanent peace on earth.

N. Khrushchev

L. Brezhnev/2/

/1/Source: Department of State, Presidential Correspondence: Lot 66 D 204. No classification marking. The source text is a Department of State translation. Another copy is in the Kennedy Library, National Security Files, Countries Series, USSR, Khrushchev Correspondence. Also printed in *Public Papers of the Presidents of the United States: John F. Kennedy, 1962*, p. 493, and *American Foreign Policy: Current Documents, 1961*, p. 593.

/2/Printed from a translation that indicates the original was signed by Khrushchev and Brezhnev.

"A special responsibility at this time rests upon the Soviet Union and the United States."

19. Telegram From President Kennedy to Chairmen Khrushchev and Brezhnev

Washington, July 4, 1961./1/

I wish to thank you personally and on behalf of the American people for your greetings on the occasion of the 185th Anniversary of the Independence of the United States./2/ It is a source of satisfaction to me that on our 185th Anniversary the United States is still committed to the revolutionary principles, of individual liberty and national freedom for all peoples, which motivated our first great leader. I am confident that given a sincere desire to achieve a peaceful settlement of the issues which still disturb the world's tranquillity we can, in our time, reach that peaceful goal which all peoples so ardently desire. A special responsibility at this time rests upon the Soviet Union and the United States. I wish to assure the people of your country of our desire to live in friendship and peace with them.

John F. Kennedy

/1/Source: Department of State, Central Files, 711.11-KE/7J461. Unclassified. Drafted by Davis and cleared by the White House and Rusk. Another copy of this message is ibid., Presidential Correspondence: Lot 66 D 204, and in the Kennedy Library, National Security Files, Countries Series, USSR, Khrushchev Correspondence. Also printed in *Public Papers of the Presidents of the United States: John F. Kennedy, 1961*, p. 493, and *American Foreign Policy: Current Documents, 1961*, p. 594.
/2/Document 18.

20. Editorial Note

On September 5, 1961, Cyrus Sulzberger met with Khrushchev and during an off-the-record conversation Khrushchev gave him a message for President Kennedy, emphasizing that it was off-the-record. Sulzberger transmitted the following message to the President on September 10:

"If you are personally in a position to meet President Kennedy, I wish you would tell him that I would not be loath to establishing some sort of informal contact with him to find a means of settling the crisis without damaging the prestige of the United States—but on the basis of a German peace treaty and a Free City of West Berlin.

"The President might say what is in his mind concerning ways of solving the problem—if he agrees in principle with the peace treaty and a

Free City. Otherwise, there is no use in contacts.

"If he does wish some settlement he could, through informal contacts, voice his opinion on various forms and stages and on how to prepare public opinion and not endanger the prestige of the United States or Mr. Kennedy." (Department of State, Presidential Correspondence: Lot 77 D 163) Also printed in *Last of the Giants,* pages 801-802.

". . . your informality, modesty and frankness which are not to be found very often in men who occupy such a high position."

21. Letter From Chairman Khrushchev to President Kennedy

Moscow, September 29, 1961./1/

DEAR MR. PRESIDENT, At present I am on the shore of the Black Sea. When they write in the press that Khrushchev is resting on the Black Sea it may be said that this is correct and at the same time incorrect. This is indeed a wonderful place. As a former Naval officer you would surely appreciate the merits of these surroundings, the beauty of the sea and the grandeur of the Caucasian mountains. Under this bright southern sun it is even somehow hard to believe that there still exist problems in the world which, due to lack of solutions, cast a sinister shadow on peaceful life, on the future of millions of people.

But as you will fully understand, I cannot at this time permit myself any relaxation. I am working, and here I work more fruitfully because my attention is not diverted to routine matters of which I have plenty, probably like you yourself do. Here I can concentrate on the main things.

I have given much thought of late to the development of international events since our meeting in Vienna, and I have decided to approach you with this letter. The whole world hopefully expected that our meeting and a frank exchange of views would have a soothing effect, would turn relations between our countries into the correct channel and promote the adoption of decisions which could give the peoples confidence that at last peace on earth will be secured. To my regret—and, I believe, to yours—this did not happen.

I listened with great interest to the account which our journalists Adjubei and Kharlamov gave of the meeting they had with you in Washington./2/ They gave me many interesting details and I questioned them most thoroughly. You prepossessed them by your informality, modesty and frankness which are not to be found very often in men who occupy such a high position.

My thoughts have more than once returned to our meetings in Vienna./3/ I remember you emphasized that you did not want to proceed towards war and favoured living in peace with our country while competing in the peaceful domain. And though subsequent events did not proceed in the way that could be desired, I thought it might be useful in a purely informal and personal way to approach you and share some of my ideas. If you do not agree with me you can consider that this letter did not exist while naturally I, for my part, will not use this correspondence in my public statements. After all only in confidential correspondence can you say what you think without a backward glance at the press, at the journalists.

As you see, I started out by describing the delights of the Black Sea coast, but then I nevertheless turned to politics. But that cannot be helped. They say that you sometimes cast politics out through the door but it climbs back through the window, particularly when the windows are open.

I have given careful thought to what you told our journalists in your personal talk with them and to the difficulties to which you referred. Of course, I fully understand that the questions which have now matured and require solution are not of the kind that easily lend themselves to solution. But they have a vitally important significance for our countries and for all the countries of the world. And therefore we cannot escape them. We cannot shift the burden of solving those questions onto the shoulders of others. And who else but the leaders of the two most influential and mighty States—the U.S.S.R. and the U.S.—can the nations expect to work out solutions which could form the basis for the consolidation of peace. After your meeting with Adjubei and Kharlamov I was about to write you a letter right then and, I admit, even drafted one. However, your television address in July,/4/

unfortunately, made it impossible for me to send that letter. After that speech which, putting it bluntly, was belligerent in its nature, my letter would not have been understood by you since it completely differed in spirit, content and tone from what you said. After that we not only made speeches and exchanged statements but, unfortunately, also proceeded to an exchange of actions which will not, and indeed cannot, yield any moral satisfaction either to you as President of the United States or to me as Chairman of the Council of Ministers of the U.S.S.R. Evidently both one side and the other are compelled to undertake their actions under the pressure of the various factors and conditions which exist and which—unless we exert a restraining influence— will propel the development of events in a direction in which you and I, and the more so the peoples of all countries, would not like them to be propelled. It would be most of all unwise from the standpoint of peace to enter into such a vicious circle when some would be responding with counter-measures to the measures of others, and vice versa. The whole world could bog down in such measures and counter-measures.

Lately I have had not a few meetings with eminent statesmen and political leaders of Western countries. I have talked with Mr. Fanfani, the Prime Minister of Italy. I shall not describe that talk of which I suppose he, as a representative of a State allied with you, had informed you. Recently I had a conversation with the former Prime Minister of France Mr. Paul Reynaud. He raised a number of questions to which I frankly replied. After Paul Reynaud I received Mr. Spaak, the Foreign Minister and Deputy Prime Minister of Belgium, who for a number of years was the Secretary General of NATO./5/ I listened to him with attention and tried to reply to his questions as exhaustively as possible, to expound our position and explain how we consider it best to solve those questions. I must say that in my opinion understanding can be reached on those questions which were touched upon in my talk with Mr. Spaak. To this end it is only necessary that both sides should display equal interest in settling the problems at issue on a mutually acceptable basis.

The statesmen of many countries are presently displaying great concern for the destinies of peace, they are seriously troubled by the tense situation that has taken shape and they sincerely fear that some rash actions might bring the world to disaster and to the unleashing of nuclear war. These feelings are dear to me and I understand them because, like many Soviet people, I spent the war years at the front and lived through all the horrors of war. I am against war. The Soviet Government is against war. The peoples of the Soviet Union are against war. I say this to you because I believe that you—a direct participant in the battles of the last war—take the same position.

I should like in this connection to dwell upon some of the basic problems which now preoccupy the whole world since the future of mankind depends on their solution. It can be said that in the disarmament question which is the major

question of our time there have now appeared
certain gleams./6/ I would like to see those
gleams in the fact that we have reached agreement on submitting to the United Nations General
Assembly a "Statement of Principles"/7/ as a
joint proposal of the U.S.S.R. and the U.S. so that
in subsequent negotiations a treaty on general
and complete disarmament can be elaborated on
its basis. Certainly it must not be forgotten that
so far this is an agreement in regard to the principles of disarmament. This is as yet far from the
achievement of the actual agreement on general
and complete disarmament, and the more so this
is not the practical start of such disarmament.
But it is precisely the conclusion of such an
agreement and its implementation within the
shortest possible time that all the nations are
expecting of us. For them and for all of us that
would mean great joy.

It is important to note that even understanding on the principles of disarmament which we
have succeeded in reaching after protracted and
intense effort and only after you came to the
White House, is a good thing too. Naturally such
understanding is not an end in itself. It must, so
to say, be the harbinger, the first successful step
on the road to general and complete disarmament. That is what we would like to hope.

If, Mr. President, you are striving towards that
noble goal—and I believe that is the case—if
agreement of the United States on the principles
of disarmament is not merely a diplomatic or tac-
tical manoeuvre, you will find complete understanding on our part and we shall stint no effort

in order to find a common language and reach the required agreement together with you.

The Soviet Union, as you are well aware, has always advocated the prompt implementation of general and complete disarmament. The solution of that question would, in our profound conviction, radically promote the settlement of other major international problems as well. Our position in that respect is still unchanged.

But you will agree with me, Mr. President, that the present international situation and its tension can hardly be assessed as a simple arithmetical sum total of unsolved issues. After all, the series of measures and counter-measures aimed at strengthening the armaments of both sides which have already been put into effect by our Governments in connection with the aggravation of the German question cannot be disregarded. I do not want here to engage in an argument as to who is right or wrong in this matter. Let us leave this aside for the time being. The main thing is that events are unfortunately continuing to develop in the same unfavourable direction. Instead of confidence we are turning to an even greater aggravation. Far from bringing the possibility of agreement between us on disarmament closer, we are, on the contrary, worsening the situation still further. That is another important reason why the Soviet Union is now attaching such exclusive significance to the German question. We cannot escape the fact that there has been a second world war and that the problems we have inherited from the last war—first and foremost the conclusion of a German peace treaty—require their solution.

History will not be reversed and West Berlin will not be moved to the other side of the Elbe. In that war the peoples of our two countries fought shoulder to shoulder. But if we fought together, we should indeed keep the peace together.

If you were to come to the Soviet Union now— and this incidentally is something I am hoping for—you would surely convince yourself that not a single Soviet citizen will ever reconcile himself to the peace, which was won at such great cost, being under constant threat. But that will be the case until the countries that participated in the war recognize and formalize the results of the war in a German peace treaty. Yes, that is what our people are demanding, and they are right. That is demanded by the Poles, that is demanded by the people of Czechoslovakia, that is demanded by other nations as well. They are right too. The position of the Soviet Union is shared by many. The impression is formed that understanding of the need to conclude a German peace treaty is growing in the world. I have already told you, Mr. President, that in striving for the conclusion of a German peace treaty we do not want somehow to prejudice the interests of the United States and their bloc allies. Neither are we interested in exacerbating the situation in connection with the conclusion of a German peace treaty. What need have we of such exacerbation? It is in the Western countries that they create all sorts of fears and allege that the socialist States intend well-nigh to swallow up West Berlin. You may believe my word, the word of the Soviet

Government that neither we nor our allies need West Berlin.

I do not doubt that, given good will and desire, the Governments of our countries could find a common language in the question of a German peace treaty too. Naturally in the solution of that question it is necessary to proceed from the obvious fact, which even a blind man cannot fail to see, that there exist two sovereign German States.

I was gratified to familiarize myself with the statement which, according to press reports, was made by your representative in Berlin Mr. Clay on the need to recognize that there now actually exist two Germanies. It is impossible not to appreciate such a reasonable and sober pronouncement. I recall Senator Mansfield made some statements in the same spirit. All this warrants the hope that evidently the process has started of a quest for a solution of the German question on the basis of a realistic appraisal of the obtaining situation, a solution in which the Soviet Union and the United States of America must, above all, play their part. Naturally this solution must be such as not to inflict any harm to the prestige of one side or the other.

If we fail to agree on the conclusion of one peace treaty for both German States we also have at our disposal such a course as the drafting of two treaties which would be similar in content— one for the German Democratic Republic and the other for the Federal Republic of Germany. In that case the States that were parties to the anti-Hitler coalition would have the opportunity of signing one or two peace treaties depending on their choice. Such an approach would allow of circumventing the difficulties that appear owing to the fact that not all the possible participants in a peace settlement are ready to recognize both existing German States legally and establish diplomatic relations with them.

In any event the contracting parties could assume moral obligations to assist in the unification into one entity of both German States if the Germans so desire. It goes without saying that such obligations would find reflection in the peace treaty itself. As for the achievement of agreement on the unification of Germany, that is the concern of the Governments of the two German States. I believe such a solution would be reasonable and understandable for everyone. It would be understood by the German people as well.

In signing a German peace treaty the States that participated in the war will have to unconditionally recognize the presently constituted frontiers of the German Democratic Republic and the Federal Republic of Germany. Under the peace treaty those frontiers would be legally formalized, I stress legally, because defacto they already exist and cannot be changed without a war.

We cannot turn our back on the facts and fail to see that until the existing borders of Germany are finally formalized the sluice-gates which release the West German revanchist desires remain open. The followers of Hitler and his policy who, unfortunately, still exist in no small numbers in the Federal Republic of Germany are dreaming of the long-awaited day when, exploiting the lack of a post-war settlement, they will succeed in bringing about a collision between the U.S.S.R., the U.S. and the other former opponents of Hitlerite Germany. Why then should we leave any ground for the activities of those forces which are fraught with the threat of a world conflict? I would think that the legal formalization of the State borders which have taken shape after World War Two equally meets the interests of both the U.S.S.R. and the United States. Thus the borders that have taken shape and presently exist between the two German States would be formalized as well.

There remains the question of West Berlin which must also be solved when a German peace treaty is concluded. From whatever side we approach the matter, we probably will not be able to find a better solution than the transformation of West Berlin into a free city. And we shall proceed towards that goal. If, to our regret, the Western Powers will not wish to participate in a German peace settlement and the Soviet Union, together with the other countries that will be prepared to do so, has to sign a treaty with the German Democratic Republic we shall nonetheless provide a free city status for West Berlin.

Your statements, Mr. President, as well as the statements of other representatives of Western Powers not infrequently show signs of concern as to whether freedom for the population of West Berlin will be preserved, whether it will be able to live under the social and political system of its own choosing, whether West Berlin will be safeguarded against interference and outside pressure. I must say we see no difficulties in creating such conditions, the more so since the assurance of the freedom and complete independence of West Berlin is also our desire, is also our concern. I declare this on behalf of the Soviet Government, and on behalf of the socialist countries allied with us which are interested in the solution of the German question. I wish to emphasize in particular that the German Democratic Republic and the Head of that State Walter Ulbricht are of the same opinion. I say this with full knowledge and in all responsibility.

Voices can also be heard contending that it is not enough to codify in a German peace treaty the guarantees of the freedom and independence of West Berlin since—so it is said—there is no certainty that those guarantees will be honored. The statesmen and political leaders of the Western Powers with whom I have had occasion to meet, sometimes plainly expressed the wish that such guarantees should not only be given under a peace treaty but should also be specially reinforced by the Soviet Union.

Frankly speaking it is hard to understand what such apprehensions are based on. I am convinced that the guarantees established under a peace treaty will be honored and observed by all the States which will have signed the treaty. Furthermore the Soviet Union as a party to the German peace treaty will feel itself responsible for the fulfillment of all the clauses of that treaty, including the guarantees in respect to West Berlin.

But if it is the common desire that responsibility for the observance of the status of West Berlin should be entrusted to the Soviet Union we shall be ready to assume such a responsibility. I and my colleagues in the Government have not infrequently given thought to the way in which the role of the Soviet Union in guarantees for West Berlin could be implemented in practice. If we were simply to make a statement that the Soviet Union will in some special way guarantee the immunity of West Berlin, you will agree that this could prejudice the sovereign rights of the German Democratic Republic and the other countries parties to the peace treaty. In order to prevent that, in order not to prejudice the prestige of any State—whether your ally or ours—I believe the question should be solved in the way we have already proposed, namely that token contingents of troops of the United States, the United Kingdom, France and the Soviet Union, the four great Powers which participated in the war against Hitlerite Germany, should be left in West Berlin. In my view that is the sole possibility. Naturally such a system should be introduced not for all time but for a specific period. Evidently an appropriate status for the deployment of the troops of the four Powers in West Berlin would then have to be devised which would be subject to the approval of the other countries signatories of the peace treaty.

Given every desire, we could find no other solution which to any greater degree would strengthen confidence in the reliability of guarantees for West Berlin. If you have any ideas of your own on this score we are ready to consider them.

Of course, such alternatives are also conceivable as the deployment in West Berlin of troops from neutral countries or United Nations troops. I have repeatedly expressed and now reaffirm our agreement to such a solution. We also agree to the establishment of the United Nations Headquarters in West Berlin which would in that case become an international city.

It goes without saying that the occupation regime in West Berlin must be eliminated. Under the allied agreements occupation is a temporary measure and, indeed, never in history has there been a case of occupation becoming a permanent institution. But sixteen years have already elapsed since the surrender of Germany. For how long then is the occupation regime to be preserved?

A more stable status should be created for West Berlin than existed under the occupation. If the occupation regime has lived out its time and has become a source of strife among States it means the time has come to discard it. It has completely exhausted itself, has become a burden in relationships among nations and does not meet the interests of the population of West Berlin itself. The transformation of West Berlin into a free city will create a far more durable basis for its independent existence than the regime of occupation. Furthermore the grounds for collisions among States which are generated by the preservation of the occupation regime will disappear.

Of course, no one can be satisfied with half-measures which superficially would seem to erase from the surface differences among States while in effect they would be preserving them under cover and driving them in deeper. What use would there be if we barely covered up this delayed action landmine with earth and waited for it to explode. Indeed, no, the countries which are interested in consolidating peace must render that landmine completely harmless and tear it out of the heart of Europe.

The representatives of the United States sometimes declare that the American side is not advancing its concrete proposals on the German question because the Soviet Union allegedly is not striving for agreed solutions and wants to do everything by itself regardless of what other States may say. It is hard for me to judge how far such ideas really tell on the actions of the United States Government, but they are based on a profoundly mistaken assessment of the position of the Soviet Union. The United States Government can easily verify that, if it wishes to introduce its own constructive proposals at the negotiations on a peaceful settlement with Germany incorporating the question of West Berlin.

I am closely following the meetings of our Minister of Foreign Affairs Andrei A. Gromyko with the Secretary of State of the United States Mr. Dean Rusk. I do not know how you will react to this idea, but it seems to me that it would be useful to broaden contacts between our Governments on the German question. If the United States Government, like the Soviet Government, is searching for understanding and is ready to devise conditions for peace with Germany which would be acceptable for both

sides and would not affect the interests or the
prestige of any State I believe it could be
arranged that you and I would appoint appropriate representatives for private meetings and
talks. Those representatives would elaborate for
us the contours of an agreement which we could
discuss before coming to a peace conference
where a decision on the question of a peace
treaty with Germany will be taken.

Your wish, Mr. President, that perhaps our
Ambassadors in Belgrade should be entrusted
with an informal exchange of views, was com-
municated to me./8/ In fact such meetings have
already started. Unfortunately, however, I see
from the dispatches of our Ambassador that they
are spending too much time in, figuratively
speaking, sniffing each other. If this goes on the
business will not move forward, whereas it
should be tackled with more energy.

I never met Mr. Kennan but, so far as I can
judge by the press, he is, to my mind, a man with
whom preparatory work could be done, and we
would accordingly authorize our Ambassador. But
evidently in that case our Ambassadors would
have to be given firm instructions to start talks
on concrete questions without needless procrastination and not merely indulge in tea-drinking,
not walk round and about mooing at each other
when they should talk on the substance.

The following alternative is also possible. You,
let us say, could send someone in your confidence
to Moscow under some plausible pretext and the
necessary contacts could be established there.
This method might possibly even expedite the

solution of the questions. However, let the final choice be up to you. You might perhaps prefer to charge Mr. Thompson, your Ambassador in Moscow, with that mission. Personally I have had a number of conversations with him and he gives the impression of being a man who can represent you in dealing with the problems that face us. But naturally it is not for me to give you advise in such matters. Please excuse me for intruding in the sphere of questions which are entirely within your own personal competence.

The non-aligned countries addressed messages to you, Mr. President, and to myself./9/ They suggested that we meet to discuss outstanding problems. You gave a positive reply to that appeal. We too reacted favourably to the initiative of the neutrals.

I believe a meeting between us could be useful and, given the desire of both sides, could culminate in the adoption of positive decisions. Naturally such a meeting would have to be well prepared through diplomatic or other confidential channels. And when preliminary understanding is reached, you and I could meet at any place in order to develop and formalize the results of such an understanding. This would undoubtedly be met with great satisfaction by all nations. They would see in that step an important contribution to the settlement of existing differences, to the consolidation of peace. The positive results of such a meeting would generate confidence that all issues can be solved peacefully by negotiation.

We are proposing that a German peace treaty be signed not only to eliminate the vestiges of

World War Two, but also to clear the way for the elimination of the state of "cold war" which can at any moment bring our countries to the brink of a military collision. We want to clear the way for the strengthening of friendly relations with you and with all the countries of the world which espouse peaceful coexistence.

You, yourself, understand that we are a rich country, our expanse is boundless, our economy is on the upgrade, our culture and science are in their efflorescence. Acquaint yourself with the Program of our Party which determines our economic development for twenty years to come. This is indeed a grand and thrilling Program. What need have we of war? What need have we of acquisitions? And yet it is said that we want to seize West Berlin! It is ridiculous even to think of that. What would that give us? What would that change in the ratio of forces in the world arena? It gives nothing to anyone.

I often think how necessary it is for men who are vested with trust and great power to be inspired with the understanding of what seems to be an obvious truism, which is that we live on one planet and it is not in man's power—at least in the foreseeable future—to change that. In a certain sense there is an analogy here—I like this comparison—with Noah's Ark where both the "clean" and the "unclean" found sanctuary. But regardless of who lists himself with the "clean" and who is considered to be "unclean," they are all equally interested in one thing and that is that the Ark should successfully continue its cruise. And we have no other alternative: either we should live in peace and cooperation so that the Ark maintains its buoyancy, or else it sinks. Therefore we must display concern for all of mankind, not to mention our own advantages, and find every possibility leading to peaceful solutions of problems.

When I was already closing this letter I was given the text of your address before the United Nations General Assembly./10/ It has long since become my habit, when reading statements by responsible statesmen, in the first instance to search for and find—even a grain at a time—ideas and propositions which could be useful for the building up of peaceful cooperation among States. Almost involuntarily you sift away all the accretions, all that has been said in a fit of temper, under the influence of unduly inflamed passions. If everything is replied to in the same vein such battles of words would have to be entered into that the voice of reason would be drowned out and the shoots of all that is good and hope-giving in relations among States would be nipped in the bud.

Of course, if one were to attune himself to an aggravation of relations between our countries, your speech before the Assembly could easily be evaluated as a challenge to an embittered dispute in the "cold war" spirit and no one could reproach us as being partial. That speech contains no few points in which homage is plainly felt to those who oppose the normalization of the international situation and seek to whip up a military psychosis by spreading all sorts of fables about the intentions of the Soviet Government and ascribing to it what does not even exist. Hence, evidently, the crude sallies tinted with ideological intolerance which are made against the social and public foundations of socialist society and which look to me, if the consolidation of peace is seriously contemplated, like a square peg in a round hole.

If you are fighting for the preservation of capitalism and consider it to be a more just society, we have our own opinion on that score. You speak of communism with disrespect, but I could reply in kind with regard to capitalism. But can we change each other's mind in questions affecting our outlooks? No, to carry ideological differences into relations among States is tantamount to an out-of-hand renunciation of hopes of living in peace and friendship with each other and we should certainly not take that road.

We can argue, we can disagree with one another but weapons must not be brought into play. I recall our conversation in Vienna about peaceful coexistence. I trust you will remember it and agree now, as you agreed then, that the question of the choice of a social system is for the people of each country to decide. Each one of us submits to his own principles, his own system but this should not lead to a collision between our countries. Let us allow history to judge the advantages of this or that social system.

A few words on Laos.

In your statement at the United Nations, Mr. President, you devoted attention to the situation in Laos and voiced certain alarm. I believe that in Vienna you and I worked out a fair basis for the solution of that question. The Soviet Government is doing all that depends on it in order to put into effect the understanding reached to the effect that Laos should become a truly neutral independent State. In your speech at the United Nations, speaking of Laos, you referred to the example of Cambodia and Burma. As we have repeatedly stated, we agree that Laos should take the same road.

As I understand it, you, like ourselves, the Soviet Union and our allies, agree that Prince Souvanna Phouma should become the Prime Minister of the Government of Laos. But obviously there are some difficulties in the question of the composition of the Government. As is known, it was proposed to the Laotians that they include in the Government eight followers of Souvanna Phouma, four representatives of Pathet-Lao and four representatives of Boun Oum. I was informed that the United States did not object to that. Now, however, information is coming in that the American Government seems to insist that of the eight posts given to the Souvanna Phouma group, three or four should be filled by the representatives of Vientiane.

In this connection I should like to make several remarks, and I am asking you to understand me correctly. You and I are being pushed towards engaging in the selection of the personal membership of the Laotian Government. This cannot fail to cause surprise. We would simply confuse the matter if we were to attempt to suggest to the Laotians the names of those persons who should be brought into the Government on behalf of these or those political groups. The Soviet Government is not properly familiar with Laotian public figures and, what is most important, it does not deem it possible to interfere in questions which are exclusively within the competence of the Laotians themselves. Let the three princes decide the question.

Souvanna Phouma has won a certain position in the country as a man of liberal leanings who advocates a policy of neutrality for Laos. His desire to form a stable and viable Government is natural and fully justified. Souvanna Phouma will be justified in fearing the strengthening of both the Pathet-Lao and the Boun Oum groups if they start claiming seats on the Government for their representatives at the cost of the seats provided for the group he himself leads. In our opinion, understanding should be displayed towards the desire of Souvanna Phouma to have a reliable support in the Government in order to effectively govern the country and pursue the policy of neutrality.

If we could reach an understanding with you on this question on the basis of the principle of non-interference in the internal affairs of Laos Souvanna Phouma could, without doubt, quickly form a Government. Naturally, in that case you and I could, by using our influence on the corresponding quarters in Laos, give Souvanna Phouma the necessary assistance.

I note with gratification that you and I are of the same opinion as to the need for the withdrawal of foreign troops from the territory of Laos. This is an essential condition in order to provide Laos with the possibility of consolidating itself as an independent State pursuing a policy of neutrality.

The Soviet representatives in Geneva have been given instructions in the spirit of the ideas described above. I hope your representatives will have the same kind of instructions. This would promote the prompt conclusion of the work of the Geneva Conference and the normalization of the situation in Laos.

I am now working on the preparation of two reports which I shall deliver at the Congress of our Communist Party: a progress report and a report on the Program of the Party. Naturally, in those reports I cannot pass over such questions as disarmament and the German question. These are the major questions of the day because on their solution depends the course which relations between our countries take in their development, and consequently the course world events take: that is whether they will develop towards the consolidation of peace and cooperation among States or whether they will proceed in a different direction, a dangerous one for mankind. We want to find the solutions of both these questions, we want to clear the road for an improvement of relations between our countries, for the assurance of peaceful coexistence and peace on earth.

Please convey my best wishes to your wife. I wish you and your entire family good health.

I should like to believe that by joint effort we shall succeed in surmounting the existing difficulties and in making our contribution to the solution of the international problems which preoccupy the nations. And then together with you we shall be able to celebrate the successes achieved in the strengthening of peace, and this is something that the peoples of our countries, as well as all men on earth, are awaiting impatiently.

Accept my respects,

N. Khrushchev/11/

/1/Source: Department of State, Presidential Correspondence: Lot 77 D 163. No classification marking. According to Salinger, this letter was handed to him by Bolshakov, at the Carlyle Hotel in New York on September 30, who said that it was for the President's eyes only. (*With Kennedy*, p. 198) Another copy is in the Kennedy Library, National Security Files, Countries Series, USSR, Khrushchev Correspondence. A copy of the Russian text, dated September 28, and also given to Salinger on September 30, is in Department of State, Presidential Correspondence: Lot 77 D 163. This is the first in a series of letters and messages between Kennedy and Khrushchev, transmitted through special emissaries, that subsequently became known as the "Pen Pal Correspondence."
/2/See Pierre Salinger's June 26 memorandum of conversation in volume V.
/3/See footnote 2, Document 16.
/4/For text of the President's radio and television address to the American people, July 25, 1961, see *Pubic Papers of the Presidents of the United States: John F. Kennedy, 1961*, pp. 533-540.
/5/Amintore Fanfani visited Moscow August 3-5; Paul Reynaud September 15; and Paul Henri Spaak September 19.
/6/A better translation of "gleams" might be "glimmering of light."
/7/For text of the Statement of Principles, September 20 (U.N. doc A/4879), see *American Foreign Policy: Current Documents, 1961*, pp. 1091-1094.

/8/Regarding the discussions in Belgrade between Ambassadors Kennan and Yepishev, see vol. XIV, p. 387.
/9/Regarding these messages, see American Foreign Policy: Current Documents, 1961, pp. 647-648.
/10/For text of the President's address before the U.N. General Assembly, September 25, see *Public Papers of the Presidents of the United States: John F. Kennedy, 1961*, pp. 618-626.
/11/Printed from a copy that bears this typed signature.

"For my part the contents and even the existence of our letters will be known only to the Secretary of State and a few others of my closest associates in the government."

22. Letter From President Kennedy to Chairman Khrushchev

Hyannis Port, October 16, 1961./1/

DEAR MR. CHAIRMAN: I regret that the press of events has made it impossible for me to reply earlier to your very important letter of last month./2/ I have brought your letter here with me to Cape Cod for a weekend in which I can devote all the time necessary to give it the answer it deserves.

My family has had a home here overlooking the Atlantic for many years. My father and brothers own homes near my own, and my children always have a large group of cousins for company. So this is an ideal place for me to spend my weekends during the summer and fall, to relax, to think, to devote my time to major tasks instead of constant appointments, telephone calls and details. Thus, I know how you must feel about the spot on the Black Sea from which your letter was written, for I value my own opportunities to get a clearer and quieter perspective away from the din of Washington.

I am gratified by your letter and your decision to suggest this additional means of communication. Certainly you are correct in emphasizing that this correspondence must be kept wholly private, not to be hinted at in public statements, much less disclosed to the press. For my part the contents and even the existence of our letters will be known only to the Secretary of State and a few others of my closest associates in the government. I think it is very important that these letters provide us with an opportunity for a personal, informal but meaningful exchange of views. There are sufficient channels now existing between our two governments for the more formal and official communications and public statements of position. These letters should supplement those channels, and give us each a chance to address the other in frank, realistic and fundamental terms. Neither of us is going to convert the other to a new social, economic or political point of view. Neither of us will be induced by a letter to desert or subvert his own cause. So these letters can be free from the polemics of the "cold war" debate. That debate will, of course, proceed, but you and I can write messages which will be directed only to each other.

The importance of this additional attempt to

explore each other's view is well-stated in your letter; and I believe it is identical to the motivation for our meeting in Vienna. Whether we wish it or not, and for better or worse, we are the leaders of the world's two greatest rival powers, each with the ability to inflict great destruction on the other and to do great damage to the rest of the world in the process. We therefore have a special responsibility—greater than that held by any of our predecessors in the pre-nuclear age—to exercise our power with the fullest possible understanding of the other's vital interests and commitments. As you say in your letter, the solutions to the world's most dangerous problems are not easily found—but you and I are unable to shift to anyone else the burden of finding them. You and I are not personally responsible for the events at the conclusion in World War II which led to the present situation in Berlin. But we will be held responsible if we cannot deal peacefully with problems related to this situation.

The basic conflict in our interests and approach will probably never disappear entirely, certainly not in our lifetime. But, as your letter so wisely points out, if you and I cannot restrain that conflict from leading to a vicious circle of bitter measures and countermeasures, then the war which neither of us or our citizens want—and I believe you when you say you are against war—will become a grim reality.

I like very much your analogy of Noah's Ark, with both the "clean" and the "unclean" determined that it stay afloat. Whatever our differences, our collaboration to keep the peace is as

urgent—if not more urgent—than our collaboration to win the last world war. The possibilities of
another war destroying everything your system
and our system have built up over the years—if
not the very systems themselves—are too great
to permit our ideological differences to blind us to
the deepening dangers of such a struggle.

I, too, have often thought of our meeting in
Vienna and the subsequent events which worsened the relations between our two countries and
heightened the possibilities of war. I have already
indicated that I think it unfruitful to fill this private channel with the usual charges and counter-
charges; but I would hope that, upon re-examina-
tion, you will find my television address of July
25th/3/ was more balanced than "belligerent," as
it is termed by your letter, although there may
have been statements of opinion with which you
would naturally disagree. To be sure, I made it
clear that we intended to defend our vital interests in Berlin, and I announced certain measures
necessary to such a defense. On the other hand,
my speech also made it clear that we would prefer and encourage a peaceful solution, one which
settled these problems, in the words of your letter, "on a mutually acceptable basis." My attitude
concerning Berlin and Germany now, as it was
then, is one of reason, not belligerence. There is
peace in that area now—and this government
shall not initiate and shall oppose any action
which upsets that peace.

You are right in stating that we should all
realistically face the facts in the Berlin and
German situations—and this naturally includes

72

facts which are inconvenient for both sides to face as well as those which we like. And one of those facts is the peace which exists in Germany now. It is not the remains of World War II but the threat of World War III that preoccupies us all. Of course, it is not "normal" for a nation to be divided by two different armies of occupation this long after the war; but the fact is that the area has been peaceful—it is not in itself the source of the present tension—and it could not be rendered more peaceful by your signing a peace treaty with the East Germans alone.

On the contrary, there is very grave danger that it might be rendered less peaceful, if such a treaty should convince the German people that their long-cherished hopes for unification were frustrated, and a spirit of nationalism and tension should sweep over all parts of the country. From my knowledge of West Germany today, I can assure you that this danger is far more realistic than the alleged existence there of any substantial number of Hitlerites or "revanchists." The real danger would arise from the kind of resentment I have described above; and I do not think that either of us, mindful of the lessons of history, is anxious to see this happen. Indeed, your letter makes clear that you are not interested in taking any step which would only be "exacerbating the situation." And I think this is a commendable basis on which both of us should proceed in the future.

The area would also be rendered less peaceful if the maintenance of the West's vital interests were to become dependent on the whims of the

East German regime. Some of Mr. Ulbricht's statements on this subject have not been consistent with your reassurances or even his own—and I do not believe that either of us wants a constant state of doubt, tension and emergency in this area, which would require an even larger military build-up on both sides.

So, in this frank and informal exchange, let us talk about the peace which flows from actual conditions of peace, not merely treaties that bear that label. I am certain that we can create such conditions—that we can, as you indicate, reach an agreement which does not impair the vital interests or prestige of either side—and that we can transform the present crisis from a threat of world war into a turning-point in our relations in Europe.

What is the framework for such an agreement? Detailed proposals must be a matter of allied agreement on our side; and formal discussion must wait further exploration of specific items. Your letter indicates, however, that you are concerned over how protracted formal diplomatic negotiations can become, with each side asking for the utmost at the outset, making more statements to the press and using extreme caution in feeling out the other side.

I agree with you that these letters should be able to supplement and thus facilitate such negotiations. We are both practical men and these are meant to be private, frank exchanges. I can tell you, for example, that I recognize how difficult it would be to secure your agreement on a plan to reunify Germany by self-determination in the near future (as desirable as I think that is), just as you recognize that we could not be a party to any agreement which legalized permanently the present abnormal division of Germany. That is one reason why we could not be a party to a peace treaty with the East Germans alone, even though, as I said at the UN, we do not view as a critical issue the mere signing by you of such a document. What is crucial, however, is the result which you have asserted that such a signing would have with respect to our basic rights and obligations.

I agree with the statement in your letter that our two governments must, in one framework or another, continue our "obligations to assist in the unification into one entity of both German states if the Germans so desire." While, as you point out, the method of achieving this goal is properly a subject for discussion among the Germans themselves, this does not excuse us from the responsibility we have assumed since the war to see the country peacefully unified—and this is the reason why we cannot attempt any final legalization as a formal international frontier of the present line of demarcation between the Western and Eastern zones. It also enjoins us against any action which would retard movement across this line—although, not being "blind," as you say, we cannot fail to recognize that this line does exist today as the Western limit of East German authority.

Whatever action you may take with East Germany, there is no difficulty, it seems to me, in your reserving your obligations and our rights

with respect to Berlin until all of Germany is unified. But if you feel you must look anew at that
situation, the real key to deciding the future status of West Berlin lies in your statement that the
population of West Berlin must be able to "live
under the social and political system of its own
choosing." On this basis I must say that I do not
see the need for a change in the situation of West
Berlin, for today its people are free to choose
their own way of life and their own guarantees of
that freedom. If they are to continue to be free,
if they are to be free to choose their own future
as your letter indicates in the phrase quoted
above, I take it this includes the freedom to
choose which nations they wish to station forces
there (limited in number but with unrestricted
access) as well as the nature of their own ties
with others (including, within appropriate limits,
whatever ties they choose with West Germany).
Inasmuch as you state very emphatically that
you have no designs on West Berlin—and I am
glad to have this assurance, for it makes the
prospects of negotiation much brighter—I am
sure you are not insisting on the location of
Soviet troops in that portion of the city.

Thus, although there is much in your letter
that makes me doubtful about the prospects in
Germany, there are many passages which lead me
to believe that an accommodation of our interests
is possible. But in our view the situation should be
peaceful now, and existing rights and obligations
are already clear. What is not clear is how any
change would be an improvement. Your letter and
earlier aide-memoire, and Mr. Gromyko in his con-

versations with Mr. Rusk and myself, have made clear what you would hope to gain by a change— a new status for the East German regime, a settlement of frontiers, and relief from what you regard as potential dangers in West Germany— but it is not clear how we in the West are to benefit by agreeing to such a change. It is not enough to say there will be a "free city" in a city that is already free—or that there will be guarantees of our access when the old guarantees are still binding—or that we can maintain token troops in a city when we have troops there now.

You are, as I said before, a practical man; and you can see that there is no way in which negotiations on that basis could conceivably be justified on our part. We would be "buying the same horse twice"—conceding objectives which you seek, merely to retain what we already possess. I hope you will give long and serious thought to this question—for the kind of "mutually acceptable" settlement you mention is possible only if it brings actual improvements, from the standpoints of both parties.

The alternative is so dire that we cannot give up our efforts to find such a settlement. In the weeks ahead, while we are consulting on these matters with our respective allies and you are meeting with your Party Congress, I hope these efforts can continue—both through this correspondence and through other contacts. Let us also both strive during this period to avoid any statement, incident, or other provocation in Berlin which make a proper negotiating climate impossible. For the present, I believe we can

agree on Ambassador Thompson as a very
acceptable means of continuing the conversation.
He knows of this letter; he has my complete confidence, and I am glad that this channel is satisfactory to you. He is in Washington at present,
and will return to Moscow after our inter-Allied
talks are further under way.

As for another meeting between the two of us,
I agree completely with your view that we had
better postpone a decision on that until a preliminary understanding can be reached through quieter channels on positive decisions which might
appropriately be formalized at such a meeting.
This reminds me that your letter also very gra-
ciously stated your desire to have me visit your
country. If we can reach a reasonable settlement
of Berlin and if the international atmosphere
improves, I would take great pleasure in such a
visit. I visited the Soviet Union in 1932 very
briefly, and would look forward to seeing the
great changes that have occurred since then.

Let me make it clear that I do not intend to
relegate the achievement of complete and general disarmament to a place of secondary importance. I share your conviction that nothing would
do more to promote good will among nations and
contribute to the peaceful solution of other major
disputes. Our agreement on the statement of
principles jointly submitted to the UN General
Assembly, while barely a beginning on a matter
where we remain far apart, at least holds out the
hope that we may someday achieve the final
stage of such disarmament, verified to remove
the fears of any people that devastation may ever

again be suddenly rained upon them.

At the same time, however, our attention is urgently needed on those current problems which keep the world poised on the brink of war. The situation in Laos is one example. Indeed I do not see how we can expect to reach a settlement on so bitter and complex an issue as Berlin, where both of us have vital interests at stake, if we cannot come to a final agreement on Laos, which we have previously agreed should be neutral and independent after the fashion of Burma and Cambodia. I do not say that the situation in Laos and the neighboring area must be settled before negotiations begin over Germany and Berlin; but certainly it would greatly improve the atmosphere.

It is now clear that Prince Souvanna Phouma will become the new Prime Minister if an agreement can be reached. But the composition of his government is far from settled, and without assuming either the knowledge or the power to select individual men for individual posts, you and I do have an obligation—if we are to reach our goal—to continue, in your words, "using our influence on the corresponding quarters in Laos" to make certain that Souvanna Phouma is assisted by the kind of men we believe necessary to meet the standard of neutrality. That standard is not met if the eight posts assigned to Souvanna are filled in a manner which heavily weights the scales in favor of one side or the other.

As you note, the withdrawal of foreign troops from the territory of Laos is an essential condition to preserving that nation's independence and neutrality. There are other, similar conditions, and we must be certain that the ICC has the power and the flexibility to verify the existence of these conditions to the satisfaction of everyone concerned.

In addition to so instructing your spokesmen at Geneva, I hope you will increasingly exercise your influence in this direction on all of your "corresponding quarters" in this area; for the acceleration of attacks on South Viet-Nam, many of them from within Laotian territory, are a very grave threat to peace in that area and to the entire kind of world-wide accommodation you and I recognize to be necessary. If a new round of measures and counter-measures, force and counter-force, occurs in that corner of the globe, there is no foretelling how widely it may spread. So I must close, as I opened, by expressing my concern over where current events are taking us.

My wife who is here with me reciprocates your good wishes, and we return the wish of good health to you and all your family. As I recall, I shall be seeing your son-in-law/4/ again in the not too distant future, and I look forward to talking with him.

I hope you will believe me, Mr. Chairman, when I say that it is my deepest hope that, through this exchange of letters and otherwise, we may improve relations between our nations, and make concrete progress in deeds as well as words toward the realization of a just and enduring peace. That is our greatest joint responsibility—and our greatest opportunity.

Sincerely,/5/

/1/Source: Kennedy Library, National Security Files, Countries Series, USSR, Khrushchev Correspondence. Top Secret. No drafting information appears on the source text. Another copy is in Department of State, Presidential Correspondence: Lot 77 D 163.
/2/Document 21.
/3/Reference is to a report by President Kennedy to the American people on the Berlin crisis; for text, see *Public Papers of the Presidents of the United States: John F. Kennedy, 1961*, pp. 533-540.
/4/Aleksei I. Adzhubei.
/5/Printed from an unsigned copy.

"It seems to me, that de Gaulle's position is rather accurately described by an allegory which is well known among our people."

23. Letter From Chairman Khrushchev to President Kennedy

Moscow, November 9, 1961./1/

DEAR MR. PRESIDENT: I have read your letter of October 16/2/ with great attention. It is good that you had an opportunity to write it in a quiet atmosphere, in your family circle, far from the turmoil of the capital. I received your letter on the very eve of the opening of the 22nd Congress of our Party, at a time when Moscow, and in fact all of our country—was living an especially elated and exciting life.

You have had probably an opportunity to get acquainted with the published reports on the proceedings of the Congress and you can imagine how much energy, time and attention on my part and on the part of my colleagues that work required. The Congress has adopted a program of material and spiritual development of the Soviet peoples' life—a program unprecedented in its scale.

However joyful it was to work out concrete plans for building communism in our country we could not but think of today since it is vitally important for us that these plans are carried out in the conditions of peace. That is why so much attention was given at the Congress to international problems and, first of all, to the security of peaceful coexistence of countries with different social and political systems which has now been included as a corner stone in the program of our Party. Our present struggle against the consequences of the cult of personality, is, if you wish, at the same time a struggle for a consistent realization of the principles of peaceful coexistence.

However I am not going to dwell especially on the importance of our Party's Congress. We may, of course, have a different point of view on this matter. It would seem to be more difficult for us to come to a common view on this point than on the German problem.

Now the Congress is over and my friends and I believe that it was quite a success. Now I am able to reply to your letter and express my views on the points you raised in it.

You ask what advantages the West would get if it agrees to the changes resulting from the solution of the German problem. In your letter you even gave a comparison asserting that the

Soviet Union wants to trade an apple for an orchard. I do not intend to argue that—such a comparison might be good by its picturesqueness, but in this case, I think, it is absolutely out of place.

What is the orchard which we are allegedly seeking, what is meant by that and what is the apple which, as you say, we are suggesting to trade? Let us consider it.

Let us look first at the proposals of the Soviet Union. The proposals, as you know, are—to conclude a German peace treaty and on this basis to transform West Berlin into a free city. Does the realization of these proposals require any concessions on the part of the Western powers? No, and, once again, no. The Soviet draft peace treaty is based only on the necessity to consolidate and legalize the situation created as a result of the war, to consolidate and legalize the German borders. Have another look at this draft and you will see that we suggest to consolidate by this treaty what had already been sanctified by the signatures which the leaders of our states put in their time under the Potsdam agreement. We demand no changes in these agreements.

This means that nobody gives anything and nobody takes anything from anyone, and that the only point is to fulfill the obligations which the four powers solemnly took upon themselves in Yalta and Potsdam.

Now, what is the position of the Western powers. If there is anyone who wants to get the whole orchard giving nothing in return—that is you and your allies. Let me show this with the facts.

It was stated in the Potsdam agreements that Germany should not be armed, that an end should be put forever to German militarism and revanchism. In spite of that the United States, Britain and France have made West Germany their ally, are arming it—and arming it rather intensively.

One cannot find a single line in the allied agreements which would allow to regard West Berlin and West Germany as one entity. In reality the Western powers as early as in 1948 introduced in West Berlin the West German mark and even made attempts to spread the FRG laws on this city. Together with the FRG the Western powers are now actively using West Berlin against the Soviet Union, the German Democratic Republic and other socialist countries.

These facts alone show that the Western powers in their present demands are stepping aside from the allied agreements and are seeking for themselves such advantages which would have been unthinkable 16 years ago. But the list of such facts does not end at this.

In 1945 the four powers pledged to do their utmost in order that Germany would never be able to threaten its neighbours and the world peace. But now West Germany with your assistance has acquired such strength that it is openly encroaching on the territory of neighbouring countries and starting to grasp its NATO allies by arms and feet.

It is not an exaggeration to say that the FRG hinders also the US Government in the free conduct of the policy which the latter believes to be reasonable and which corresponds to the interests of your country as well as other countries. You and I have agreed to establish and maintain contacts in order to search jointly for mutually acceptable solutions to the German problem. But actually that has not been accomplished yet. And we understand quite clearly that it is first of all Adenauer who resists it being zealously supported by French President de Gaulle.

It seems to me, that de Gaulle's position is rather accurately described by an allegory which is well known among our people. Once a peasant, so the story goes, boasted that he would go to the forest and catch a bear; he was warned that it was a dangerous undertaking, that bear is a strong beast. Never mind, I'll handle him, said the peasant, and went to the forest. Some time has passed but the peasant still has not come back. The people started looking for him. Where are you?—they cried. The peasant cried back: I am here, I have caught a bear.

—Well, bring him here.

—He won't go.

—Come here yourself.

—But he won't let me go.

More or less the same has happened to France. De Gaulle embraced Adenauer to lean on West Germany and to increase with its help the weight of France in European affairs and, maybe, even to try to conduct the events in the whole world. It is an open secret that de Gaulle considers himself to be the most qualified person to determine the political destiny of Europe and not only Europe. Actually it has turned out that West

Germany has so squeezed de Gaulle in her arms that he is not able any longer to escape from the embrace. In fact France has been forced to follow in the wake of the policy which is being carried on by Chancellor Adenauer.

That is why de Gaulle is saying now not the things which are helpful for ensuring peace and, consequently, helpful for France and other nations. But whatever pleases Chancellor Adenauer.

There seems to be no need to go back to the question of how and why it has happened that the Potsdam agreements remained to a considerable degree unfulfilled and what effect this fact had on the situation in Germany and in Europe as a whole. This has been stated more than once before. And life itself demands that we should look forward, not backward. It is important now to single out what brings us closer, what will help us to restore the spirit of cooperation and goodwill which was characteristic of the relations between the USSR and the USA during the hard years of war. In our opinion this can be easier and better achieved by a mutually agreed solution of the problem of a German peace treaty. The Western powers not only would not have to sacrifice in any way their interests, they would gain and, indeed, not less than the other states.

To use your comparison, it can be said that by the conclusion of a German peace treaty we would have planted an orchard the fruits of which would be enjoyed by all the states, all the peoples.

It is true that we have to settle this problem

in a rather unusual way. At the time when the Potsdam agreement was being signed nobody could have foreseen that two independent states, with different ways of life, would emerge on the territory of Germany. However, it has happened. What can we do? Should we use force so that Germany will again become united? But nobody seems to be anxious to fight for this. President de Gaulle told us frankly that France was not interested in reunification of Germany. And one can understand his position since he fears and, evidently, not without a reason, that a united Germany—if one has in mind the basis for its unification which is advocated by Adenauer— would be a militarist state with all its widely known distinctive habits.

The world public opinion has obviously no sympathy with the idea of reunification of Germany. Such opinion prevails in France, Britain, in wide enough circles of the USA and even in West Germany itself.

The situation existing in Germany is recognized everywhere in the West, but many persons prefer to keep silent. They do so, naturally, not because of a desire to help the reunification of Germany, but because of dislike for the way of life established in the German Democratic Republic. They do not like, of course, the social and political system not only in the G.D.R., but in other socialist countries as well, including, naturally, the Soviet Union. However just as we are not free to establish our systems in capitalist countries, the Western powers have no right to impose one or another way of development on the socialist countries.

I fully agree with you that it would be useless
to argue about the advantages of our social systems. We will not find a common language here.
That is why the Soviet Government proceeds
from the necessity of recognition of what exists
in reality; two German states and two systems in
the world—capitalist and socialist. Any other
approach would inevitably lead us to collision, to
war.

We have got an impression that you also want
to achieve a mutually acceptable solution of the
German problem which would not lead to the
deepening of the differences and, eventually, to
collision between our countries.

In my opinion we have already passed the
stage of sounding out each other's positions. We
should now start solving problems, otherwise
contacts and negotiations will lead to nothing but
marking time.

When I sent you my latest letter I hoped that
we would use this line of communication for concrete discussion of still unsettled issues and, first
of all, of the German peace treaty as the most
complex and urgent one. If both of us departed
from concrete discussion and confine ourselves to
repeating generalities our confidential correspondence could have been substantially depreciated.

In my recent letter I tried to set forth in detail
our position on concrete questions and, I will not
conceal, I expected you to do the same. There
were, it seemed to me, some grounds for that in
the light of the discussions which our Foreign
Minister had had in New York and in Washington

with you, Mr. President, and with the US Secretary of State. We understand, of course, that you needed some time to study and think over all that had been said. That is why, having found no concrete suggestions in your letter, we expected that Ambassador Thompson would state them on your instructions. So far this has not happened, either.

A certain apprehension is caused by an obvious dissonance between realistic notes which we hear while talking with American statesmen on questions of Germany, and conservative, extremely negative comments on these talks, which are published on the pages of influential newspapers in the United States.

I will not go back to a detailed statement of our position, and will dwell only on the main points. When we talked with you in Vienna you said that the question of Germany should be solved in such a way that the prestige of any of our countries was not hurt. I agreed with you then and I agree with you now. Indeed, the Soviet Union and the USA are great powers and the matter of prestige is important to them. We understand it.

But how the interests of the parties can be taken fully into account when the goal is to draw a line under the past war? It is clear—by the conclusion of a peace treaty on an agreed basis. The conclusion of a peace treaty is a natural way of the completion of war which is accepted by both—civilized and uncivilized peoples. Such a treaty makes it possible to juridically secure the cessation of the state of war and, at the same time, to legalize the changes which resulted from the war. It is in complete agreement with considerations of prestige.

The signing of a German peace treaty would help to liquidate the state of "cold war," to create better conditions for cooperation between our countries, for the development of trade, for the exchange of scientific achievements etc. On the basis of the peace treaty the question of West Berlin will be solved.

It was said that the time, suggested by us, for the conclusion of a peace treaty sounds like an ultimatum and this hurts the prestige of our partners in negotiations. We have, of course, made no ultimatum. But in order to create the best possible conditions for the achievement of an agreed settlement the Soviet Government has decided not to insist that the peace treaty be signed by the end of this year.

We do not dictate any firm terms for the solution of the German question and you probably know it well. The best way, in our opinion, would be the signing of a peace treaty between all countries which fought against Germany and the two German states which have appeared on the ruins of the Hitlerite Reich and the normalization of the situation in West Berlin on this basis. But it is also possible to sign two peace treaties—with West and East Germany, and the texts of these treaties should not necessarily be identical.

There is also a third possibility which I mentioned to Mr. Spaak—to agree before signing a peace treaty with the GDR by the Soviet Union and other powers on the status of West Berlin and on the indispensable solution of certain important questions of the post-war settlement in Europe.

What could constitute a special agreement on West Berlin which would then be annexed to a peace treaty and thus would acquire the full juridical force? There can be, certainly, only one thing in it—again the status of a free demilitarized city, in other words West Berlin must become independent politically, live in accordance with its internal laws, freely without any external interference, with the most widely developed ties with any state of any continent.

The situation which has developed in that city is absolutely abnormal. You yourself spoke about it as of a heavy heritage. Consequently it is necessary to liquidate this "heritage" lest it—as an abscess—spoil the relations between our countries and cause inflammation on a healthy body.

You do not need West Berlin if, of course, it is not considered as a base for subversive activities against the socialist countries. And even in this capacity it hardly justifies the hopes of those who would like to preserve the vestiges of World War II in the center of Europe and to thoroughly drive a wedge between great powers. Those, who think that it is possible to weaken the socialist countries by organizing subversive activities from West Berlin against them, are deceiving themselves. West Berlin does not fit for that under present circumstances—it is a rotten basis. The preservation of the situation which exists there can only generate conflicts and cause anxiety in the world.

Recently, through Mr. Robert Kennedy, you yourself let me know of your concern with regard to the situation in Berlin. I must say we were also grieved by the incidents which took place on the border between West and East Berlin during the last ten days of October and caused the tension that nobody wanted. ·

I would not like to go into polemics with you and, judging by your message, you do not pursue this aim either. I think, however, that the latest incidents could not have taken place if the American military authorities in West Berlin would have shown more desire to act with due regard to the real situation.

I cannot but agree with you that a period of relative moderation and calmness is particularly necessary now. We regard with understanding such a sober approach which will allow to concentrate on the solution of the problems related to the German peaceful settlement and not to turn away our attention to the settlement of—frankly speaking—secondary questions.

Your letter of October 16 can be understood in such a way that West Berlin is the very orchard which the Soviet Union wants to get for itself. But for us it is not an orchard, rather it is a weed of bur and nettle. We do not want to walk into this weed, we have no business there. We do not need West Berlin. Let West Berlin live and develop in the way its population wants. We are ready to do everything to this end.

If Western powers have no hidden aims with regard to West Berlin, why can we not agree, then, on transforming it into a free city?

International character could be given to the status of West Berlin as a free city by registering it at the UN. Such a solution would not be detrimental to any side since it would be based on the recognition of the existing social and political conditions in West Berlin. The balance of power which has developed between the two world systems after the war would not be changed as a result of the transformation of West Berlin into a free city, and the watershed between them would remain in the same place.

We could explain this decision to everybody and any sober-minded person would understand it because he would realize that our countries really want to liquidate the vestiges of World War II and clear the way for peaceful cooperation among all nations.

But what do Western powers suggest to us? There is only one thing behind all their statements about the adherence to the cause of freedom of West Berlin—the desire to preserve the regime of occupation there at any price. They insist that this regime should be preserved even after the signing of a peace treaty. I am not a diplomat and can be completely frank: if it means only to get a confirmation of occupation rights, then it will be difficult to expect not only agreement but even negotiations themselves, since there will be nothing to talk about. You have to understand that the Soviet Union cannot agree to preserve and recognize the regime of occupation in West Berlin, i.e. by its own hands to help Western powers violate after the conclusion of a peace treaty the sovereignty of the German

93

Democratic Republic, its ally.

In essence, the present position of the Western powers reflects the same selfish line which they followed in signing the peace treaty with Japan. At that time the Western powers considered it possible to neglect the interests of the Soviet Union and to conclude the peace treaty without it. Now they "allow" us condescendingly to sign a peace treaty with the GDR provided, however, that the regime of occupation in West Berlin remains intact. To agree to this would be not only the loss of our prestige but the complete surrender.

We would prefer to conclude a German peace treaty together with the USA and other participants of the anti-Hitlerite coalition. It is our ardent desire. But if our efforts to make the positions of the sides closer do not reach the goal, all the same we will sign a peace treaty and will do it certainly not with the purpose of securing the occupation rights of Western powers.

It would be the greatest fallacy to expect that these rights could be saved by threats, that under the pressure the Soviet Union will eventually agree to play the part of a permanent sentry guarding these rights. Despite all the threats on the part of Western powers the Soviet Union will in no case retreat from its principled position.

Certainly, if Western powers adopt unreasonable decisions, the consequences will be extremely sad. I think that not only myself but you also wish that the mankind will never taste such a bitter lot. In any case these consequences, if they were caused, would not be graver for the Soviet

Union than for the USA. For the allies of the USA, which are comparatively small countries, they will be especially tragic. Besides the voice of these countries can be heard in fact only until the guns start talking. When it comes to direct collision they will be even deprived of physical ability to influence in any way the course of events, which will take place in case the fatal line is crossed.

Let us throw away arguments of force and rely exclusively on the arguments of reason. The threats are of no use to us, and I agree with you that we should not talk the language of "cold war." Such language only prevents us from estimating the situation in the world soberly and seeking the solution of questions which are equally disturbing to both of our peoples. Let us solve these questions in such a way that dealing with them today we would know for sure that the relations between our countries will become better tomorrow and still better the day after tomorrow. This is what is expected from us, you and me— the men invested with great trust and great powers—by all peoples who value peace higher than anything else.

You ask me, who would guarantee that the rights and interests of West Berlin will not be violated and propose that reliable international guarantees should be given to the city. You, Mr. President, and your predecessors have repeatedly made such statements and, naturally, you have bound yourself by those statements before the American and West German public opinion as well as before the public opinion of other coun-

tries. But we also are not against guarantees. The
Soviet Union and the GDR have no secret plans
with regard to West Berlin, and therefore we ourselves propose that guarantees—and the most
effective ones—should be given to it.

Thus, we seem to agree with you that there
should be guarantees for West Berlin. And here
again there are two possibilities. I have already
told Mr. Spaak and you about that. The Soviet
position is known to you and the Secretary of
State also from what was said by the Minister of
Foreign Affairs of the USSR. I want to give you a
short summary of our point of view: if the USA
is interested in our guaranteeing the status of
West Berlin together, the Soviet Union is ready to
assume such obligation upon itself. But it must be
recognized that the Soviet Union will have equal
rights and equal responsibility which other powers—guarantors will have.

I have already written to you that the most
realistic way out is that of placing some symbolic contingents of troops of four great powers in
West Berlin. And if the troops of four powers are
stationed there, the Soviet Union, naturally, will
bear the responsibility with regard to guarantees
equal to that of Western powers. Such measure
will be understandable to both—the allies of the
USA and the allies of the Soviet Union. It will not
hurt the prestige of any power concerned. But if
you want to have your troops in West Berlin
while there will be no [sic] our troops there that
will not be equal terms. You want us to be guarantors on some other terms which are different
from those of others, of yours, but this is not

realistic.

I know that in the West attempts are being made to interpret our proposal on guarantees as an expression of a desire to penetrate into West Berlin and to gain a foothold there. Believe me, Mr. President, we are not intruding into West Berlin. Why should we have our troops there? I think that your troops too are not needed in West Berlin. They are guarding themselves, and somebody's shadow.

I will not, probably, make a mistake if I say that in the question of keeping troops in West Berlin prestige considerations are the main ones. Since you believe it so important to keep the troops in West Berlin we are prepared to make a concession. It is a definite concession on our part since the occupation rights cease to exist upon signing a peace treaty and discontinuing the state of war. But in order that this concession is not interpreted as a retreat of the USSR under the pressure of the USA—and not under the pressure of reason and expedience—our token troops should be also stationed in West Berlin. What kind of troops, of what size? It is not very important. It might be that the number of our troops will be substantially less but under an agreement the Soviet Union must be in an equal position with the USA. The Soviet Government wishes to take into account the prestige of the USA, but we would like you also, Mr. President, to display an understanding with regard to our prestige. We must mutually spare each other's prestige. For how long should the token troops remain in West Berlin? At present some people are not quite sure

as to how a free city would feel and whether its
relations with other countries will run smoothly.
But if all the fears that are now being expressed
allay, if it turns out that there are no grounds,
and we are sure that it is so, for concern about
the fate of West Berlin? Really, it would not be
quite clear why it is necessary to keep these
token troops in the city forever. And so we propose that an agreement on stationing token contingents of troops of the four powers in West
Berlin be concluded for a definite period of time.

If our proposal on stationing the token contingents of troops of the four powers in West Berlin
is not acceptable and if you believe that it is really necessary for guaranteeing purposes to keep
the troops in West Berlin, well, let them be the
United Nations troops. Such a solution should not
do any damage to you or to us, France and
Britain. The UN troops will see to it that the order
as defined by the status of the free city is strictly observed. This would seem to be even better
than to keep the troops of the four powers in
West Berlin.

I repeat: neither the troops of the four powers
nor the United Nations troops should perform
any occupation functions. The situation has
changed and so another regime corresponding to
the conditions of peace time is needed.

I know you are concerned with the question of
access to West Berlin. Moreover, you, it seems to
me, are inclined to consider it as one of the most
important and hard to solve questions. I do not
know whether I will be able to dispel the uncertainties but I would like to emphasize with all

clarity that neither the Soviet Government nor the Government of the GDR intend to impose any restrictions on the ties of West Berlin with the outside world or on the access to that city of these or those states by land, sea and air.

If we propose that the order of maintaining these ties and of using all kinds of communications going through the territory of the sovereign state—the German Democratic Republic—should be the same as accepted everywhere both in the socialist and in the capitalist countries, then, you will agree we do not demand anything special, any limitations or concessions. If some other order is established it would precisely mean creating a special discriminatory regime with regard to the GDR.

Those who cling to the occupation regime in West Berlin would like, evidently, the Soviet Union to assume the responsibilities of a traffic policeman securing continuous and uncontrolled transportation of military goods of the Western powers into West Berlin. Generally speaking no one objects to an access to West Berlin, but naturally, this access should be exercised with the consent of the country through whose territory the communications of West Berlin run. And if the Western powers still want the Soviet Union to perform the functions of a traffic policeman, then, they need it in order not to have simply an access to West Berlin but the access which rests on the occupation regime.

I will permit myself to give an example. At present the USA seems to intend to recognize the Mongolian People's Republic. How, one may ask,

an American Ambassador is going to reach this
Republic if he does not obtain our or the Chinese
People's Republic's consent to go through the
Soviet or Chinese territory? Is the USA going in
this case also to disregard the generally accepted
international norms and threatening with force
to demand for itself exclusive privileges?

You will say, of course, look we do not demand
it. It is true, the USA does not demand it. But
why, then, do you use a different approach with
regard to the GDR?

It seems to me that the US Government does
not want to sign a peace treaty precisely because
it feels its wrongness in the questions of the
order of access to West Berlin. It prefers, it
seems, to retain for the future such a position: we
are not participants of the peace treaty, we have
not signed this treaty and therefore we retain
with regard to West Berlin all our rights resulting from the surrender of Germany and the
establishment of the occupation regime in West
Berlin. But it will be clear to the entire world that
the Western powers are in the wrong here. The
fact alone that 16 years have passed since the
war makes groundless all the talks about further
maintenance of occupation regime in West Berlin.
Whatever turn the events might take, further
uncontrolled use of the territory of the GDR will
become impossible. And the point here is, naturally, not the observance of appearances but the
real respect for the sovereign rights of states.

At the present time most of the passenger
traffic and the overwhelming part of commercial
freightage between West Berlin and the capitalist

countries are carried out on the basis of agreements with the GDR. It does not create any difficulties or interruptions of the ties of West Berlin with the outside world. Therefore it is difficult, frankly speaking, to find reasons which would justify the belief that the situation may change for the worse after a peace treaty is concluded and a free city is created. Rather, everything speaks in favor of the opposite.

In the interests of clarity I would like to point out that in solving the question of access as well as other questions with regard to West Berlin we cannot agree that the FRG be placed in a special privileged position, and we will never agree to it. The Federal Republic of Germany should enjoy no worse and no better conditions than other states.

At present the FRG authorities are openly, without any disguise using West Berlin for subversive activities against the GDR and other socialist countries. It is first of all these illegal and dangerous intrigues that forced the socialist countries to take defensive measures. And it goes without saying that we will object to the continuation of such a hostile activity when the question of normalizing the situation in West Berlin on the basis of conclusion of a German peace treaty is being solved.

Incidentally, sometimes voices are heard— could not East Berlin be separated from the GDR. I would like to note that this kind of talk is simply not serious. The social and political system in the German Democratic Republic and in East Berlin is one and the same. East Berlin is the capital of the GDR, the seat of the government of the

Republic. Therefore, when they talk about a sep-
aration of the capital of the GDR it is not even a
preservation of status quo, but a change, a breaking of the political and social order. No one will
allow that the established state organism existing
and developing on the same social and political
basis be destroyed. And one should think that
this unreasonable proposal is being made not in
the interests of achieving an agreement.

It seems that some aspects of the access will
have to be settled anew. Whatever is said the
allies have never concluded any agreements on
commercial and civil air transportation into
Berlin and out of Berlin. Due to our oversight
such a transportation was put into effect arbi-
trarily. With the conclusion of a peace treaty that
will have to be corrected. Airlines interested in
maintaining traffic with West Berlin will have to
have a permission of the GDR to fly over its territory.

On the other hand, there are difficulties of a
technical nature. How is the air traffic with West
Berlin going now? To land or to take off from the
airfields in West Berlin planes fly over the city. It
is dangerous both for the passengers and, especially, for the population over whose houses
planes fly to land and take off. And it is not without reason that airfields are located outside city
limits in all countries of the world. Such a practice is prescribed by safety reasons. And if the
old outdated practice is still in effect in West
Berlin this is explained only by specific conditions which developed as a result of the war.

The government of the GDR is prepared to

permit planes flying to West Berlin to land and take off on its airfields located nearby which cannot be considered as worsening of the conditions of access to West Berlin. This is not a far-fetched but quite an actual task if one is to bear in mind that the intensity of air traffic will apparently be increasing year in and year out.

If the token troops of the four powers are stationed in West Berlin, then, the USA and other Western powers will probably insist on the right of free access to maintain communications and to supply their contingents. I think that if it meant flights of a small number of planes defined in an agreement of the four powers to satisfy the needs of the token contingents of troops then the GDR government could agree to that. Apparently these troops would retain those airfields which exist now.

It goes without saying that the German Democratic Republic should be given guarantees to the effect that the air traffic will not be used against its interests. An agreement could be reached that the four powers which would have token troops in West Berlin would exercise mutual control on the border over their transportation into and out of the city. The same control on a mutual basis could be established also for all other military transportation including those for the token contingents of the Soviet Union which would be stationed in West Berlin as guarantors. The GDR would, probably, be satisfied with it. Being its ally we would perform in a sense the functions of the government of the German Democratic Republic seeing to it that the communications with West Berlin related to the stationing there of the contingents of troops of the four powers should not be used in a way harmful to it.

Such a procedure, as I see it, could not do moral damage to any of the parties concerned.

I am setting forth these considerations in a preliminary strictly confidential order and I hope that they will be met with understanding on your part.

Dear Mr. President, I am writing not to argue with you or to try to play better the next fall-back position as diplomats call it. I have stated to you the first, second and third possibilities. To any of them which you would consider suitable, we are ready to agree. If you have something else to propose—also on the basis of a peaceful settlement—we would willingly exchange opinions with you. But if you insist on the preservation of inviolability of your occupation rights I do not see any prospect. You have to understand, I have no ground to retreat further, there is a precipice behind.

As an optimist, and they say an incurable one, I hope for the better and believe that eventually the solution can be found or, as you write, reconciliation of our interests is possible. And not only possible, it is necessary, for the alternative is a quarrel between the two most powerful nations.

The letter has come out a bit more extensive than I thought originally. But what can one do—the question is complicated and important. You start writing about one thing but some other thing has to be mentioned too.

104

I have already consumed much of your time therefore, probably, it would be better if I write you another letter on other questions which you raised in your letter.

I will allow myself to express again the hope that our frank, confidential correspondence will help to overcome difficulties however complicated it might seem now.

Sincerely,

N. Khrushchev/3/

/1/Source: Department of State, Presidential Correspondence: Lot 77 D 163. No classification marking. This text was delivered to Salinger at the White House at 12:15 p.m. on November 11 by Georgi Bolshakov, editor of USSR magazine. (Memorandum for the President, November 11; ibid.) Another copy of this letter is in the Kennedy Library, National Security Files, Countries Series, USSR, Khrushchev Correspondence.
/2/Document 22.
/3/Printed from a copy that bears this typed signature.

"As far as I know, the cause of the present tension in South Vietnam is the policy of merciless terror and mass reprisals carried on by the regime of Ngo Dinh Diem."

24. Letter From Chairman Khrushchev to President Kennedy

Moscow, November 10, 1961./1/

Dear Mr. President, As you know, I devoted my latest letter entirely to the German problem,/2/ and did not touch upon other questions raised in your letter of October 16./3/ Now I would like to express my thoughts concerning Laos and the situation in South Vietnam.

First of all, I must emphasize that with regard to the question of Laos I proceed from the fact that as early as in Vienna both of us agreed on the necessity to make our contribution so that Laos become a really independent and neutral state. In addition, our governments have also agreed that a coalition government should be formed in Laos headed by Souvanna Phouma, on the basis of the formula 4-8-4. Now, to all appearances, the major obstacle has arisen in connection with the solving of the task of forming the government.

Creation of the government by Souvanna Phouma on the basis of granting 8 posts to the neutralists, 4 posts to the Pathet Lao and 4 posts to the Boun Oum group would allow to have in Laos a government which would reflect the internal situation existing in the country and which would be able to pursue a neutralist policy in favor of which both the Soviet Government and the Government of the United States have spoken. The recent agreement of the King of Laos to naming Souvanna Phouma the Prime-Minister and entrusting him with forming a coalition government gave reasons to hope that the settlement of the Laotian problem is a matter of the very near future. To be frank, that was what we expected.

However recent reports from Laos indicate that the efforts of Souvanna Phouma to form a coalition government run into serious difficulties that, I would say, are hard to explain.

It has come to our knowledge that from the American side pressure is being exerted on Souvanna Phouma through the Boun Oum-Nosavan group to include representatives of the Vientiane group into the category of neutralists-supporters of Souvanna Phouma.

But, Mr. President, these are completely groundless claims and they endanger the creation of a coalition government. Now a situation has developed when a neutral Premier is denied a possibility to form a neutral government, and it appears that the agreement reached on the composition of a coalition government becomes entirely meaningless. Indeed a question arises—what sort of a neutral Premier one would make whose cabinet members are imposed upon him against his will, and what kind of a neutral government it would be if it does not include people who stand for a neutralist course in foreign policy? But this is precisely the way to which those who want to bind Souvanna Phouma by feet and hand during the formation of the government are pushing.

The composition of the Souvanna Phouma government is a strictly internal matter of Laos. We should give Souvanna Phouma every opportunity to act in such a way as he deems necessary proceeding from the agreement on the representation of the three political forces in Laos and the interests of securing true neutrality of his country.

When I was writing to you about the necessary to use your and my influence to accelerate the solution of the problem of forming the Laotian government, I did not mean at all that this influence would go so far that you and I would be choosing ministers or aides for Premier Souuvana Phouma. As I see it, our duty is to use our influence in order to bring about as soon as possible the formation of a coalition government neutral in the orientation of its policy and this in its turn would make it possible to accomplish earlier the work of the Geneva conference on Laos. In any case the Soviet representative at this conference has all necessary instructions to contribute to a successful conclusion of the conference.

Thinking over the situation that has now developed in Laos I have come to a conclusion that the speediest settlement in Laos requires now that the demand to include persons from the Vientiane group into the category of neutralist ministers in the coalition government of Souvanna Phouma be withdrawn. It is necessary to give up making pressure on Souvanna Phouma and stop interfering with his carrying out the agreement on forming a coalition government. Any other approach may only lead to an increased tension in Laos and to a renewal of the military conflict there which not only we but, judging by your repeated statements, you too do not want.

The Boun Oum group has of late not only been hindering the forming of a coalition government and refusing to hold a meeting of the three princes to solve the still unsettled questions but has been organizing constant attacks on the Souvanna Phouma troops and the Pathet Lao armed forces. I presume, Mr. President, that you are well aware of the facts in this connection. Thus, the continuous pressure on Souvanna Phouma and the activities of the Vientiane group threaten to bring to nil the results which have already been achieved in the negotiations in Geneva, turning Laos into a kind of almost permanent source of international tension which, naturally, both of us should not allow to happen.

Therefore I take the liberty to express anew the hope that you will use all your influence to prevent the above mentioned undesirable consequences.

In your message, Mr. President, you also touch upon the problem of South Vietnam.

As far as I know, the cause of the present tension in South Vietnam is the policy of merciless terror and mass reprisals carried on by the regime of Ngo Dinh Diem which has absolutely no support among the people. And this is not only our opinion. I think that you are informed even better than we are as to what kind of regime it is and how it is viewed both within the country and abroad. Realizing that it is doomed this regime resorts to force and repressions against the people, exterminating physically all those who in one way or another express their disagreement with the order introduced there. I think that looking at facts soberly you cannot but agree that the present struggle of the population of South Vietnam against Ngo Dinh Diem cannot be explained by some kind of interference or incitement from outside. The events that are taking place there are of internal nature and are connected with the general indignation of the population at the bankrupt policy of Ngo Dinh Diem and those who surround him. This and only this is the core of the matter.

In this connection I as well as many other people feel rightfully puzzled—how one can support a man like Ngo Dinh Diem with his bloody regime who completely lost the respect of the people? Yet, the United States Government supports him, giving him economic and military assistance. And what does it mean to give military assistance to such a regime? It means to assist this regime of terrorism which managed to antagonize not only the population in the South of the country but also its neighbours because of its aggressive policy. Mr. Johnson, Vice-President of the United States, paid a visit to Ngo Dinh Diem; quite recently General Taylor visited South Vietnam. Some news agencies report of the intention of the US Government to send American troops to South Vietnam. I do not think that all this could contribute to the improvement of the situation in this part of Southeast Asia. Sending troops to suppress national-liberation movement in other countries is by no means a way that corresponds to the interests of peace and, besides, what are the guarantees that the American troops would not get tied up in South Vietnam. I think that such a perspective is most real. But it is fraught with new complications, and to the difficulties that exist now in the international situation and that you and I are trying to overcome new difficulties would be added to which, it think, neither you nor I can be sympathetic.

I am writing this letter to you, Mr. President, being entirely under the impression of the results of the 22nd Congress of our Party. The Congress confirmed once again before the whole world an unshakable desire of the Soviet people to live in peace and friendship with all other peoples and to develop relations with all countries including the United States on the basis of peaceful coexistence. Guided by this we will continue to strive for peace and friendship with all the peoples and countries. It is precisely with this aim in mind that I take the liberty to frankly and straightfor-wardly express in this letter my opinion on the two problems of interest to us. I hope, Mr. President, that you will correctly understand that it is motivated only by my desire to contribute to the settlement of the urgent international problems in the interests of peace. I told you of this desire which reflects the very nature of our foreign policy during our meeting in Vienna too.

I avail myself of this opportunity to convey to you, Mr. President, to your wife and the members of your family my best wishes which are fully shared by my wife Nina Petrovna.

Sincerely,

N. Khrushchev/4/

/1/Source: Department of State, Presidential Correspondence: Lot 77 D 163. Top Secret. Another copy is in the Kennedy Library, National Security Files, Countries Series, USSR, Khrushchev Correspondence.

/2/Document 23.
/3/Document 22.
/4/Printed from a copy that bears this typed signature.

"Insofar as the United States is concerned, we view the situation in which the Republic of Vietnam finds itself with the utmost gravity . . ."

25. Letter From President Kennedy to Chairman Khrushchev

Washington, November 16, 1961./1/

DEAR MR. CHAIRMAN: I have now had a chance to study your most recent two letters on the German problem and on Laos and Vietnam./2/ I shall be writing you again about Germany and Berlin,/3/ but I do wish to give you my thoughts about Laos and Vietnam as soon as possible.

In writing to you, I am conscious of the difficulties you and I face in establishing full communication between our two minds. This is not a question of translation but a question of the context in which we hear and respond to what each other has to say. You and I have already recognized that neither of us will convince the other about our respective social systems and general philosophies of life. These differences create a great gulf in communication because language cannot mean the same thing on both sides unless it is related to some underlying common purpose. I cannot believe that there are not such common interests between the Soviet and the American people. Therefore, I am trying to penetrate our ideological differences in order to find some bridge across the gulf on which we could bring our minds together and find some way in which to protect the peace of the world.

Insofar as Laos is concerned, it has seemed to us that an agreement ought to be possible if you share our willingness to see that country genuinely neutral and independent, and are prepared to take, jointly, the necessary steps to that end. I have explained to you quite simply and sincerely that the United States has no national ambitions in Laos, no need for military bases or any military position, or an ally. You have stated your interest in a neutral and independent Laos which we assume means that you do not seek to impose a communist regime upon Laos.

Considerable progress has been made in Geneva, although there are still some points which ought to be clarified. Further progress there will depend upon the composition of the neutral government in Laos itself through negotiation among the Laotian leaders. It is true that the United States has agreed to the formation of a coalition government to be headed by Prince Souvanna Phouma, but it is not accurate as you write that the formula four-eight-four derives from any agreement between our governments. This formula was suggested by Prince Souvanna Phouma himself. I can assure you that the United States is not attempting to determine the compo-

113

sition of such a government, and that we have most certainly not been exerting pressure through the Royal Laotian Government in any respect. We have, in fact, been pressing the leadership of the Royal Laotian Government to negotiate these questions in good faith with Prince Souvanna Phouma. Our efforts in this direction, therefore, correspond to the request contained in your letter as to how we should use our influence.

I wish I could believe that Prince Souphanouvong is prepared to enter into such discussions in a spirit of negotiation with a view to the creation of a genuinely neutral government. Prince Souphanouvong has remained consistently at a distance from these discussions. We are hopeful that Prince Souvanna Phouma will show a willingness to take the initiative now incumbent upon him to search for a government which would be broadly representative of all elements in Laos and sincerely committed to a policy of nonalignment. We shall continue our efforts with the Royal Laotian Government for the achievement of this objective and I can only venture to hope that you, for your part, will likewise exert your influence in the same direction.

As to the situation in Vietnam, I must tell you frankly that your analysis of the situation there and the cause of the military action which has occurred in Southern Vietnam is not accurate. Precisely because of the visit of such Americans as Vice President Johnson and General Taylor we are, as you yourself recognize, well informed as to the situation in that country. I do not wish to argue with you concerning the government structure and policies of President Ngo Dinh Diem, but I would like to cite for your consideration the evidence of external interference or incitement which you dismiss in a phrase.

I would draw your attention to a letter sent by the Government of Vietnam to the International Control Commission concerning the North Vietnam subversion and aggression against Vietnam, dated October 24, 1961. I would urge that you should read this document very carefully since it contains evidence of a planned and consistent effort on the part of the DRV to overthrow by violence the legitimate government of South Vietnam. I would like to add that the evidence contained in this document is known to the United States to be accurate and sober. Many more incidents of the type outlined in this document could be deduced from our own experience and our own direct knowledge. I might point out here that in effect from 1954, the signature of the Geneva Accords, until 1959, the situation in Vietnam was relatively tranquil. The country was effecting a limited recovery from the ravages of the civil war from which it had just emerged. The Government enjoyed the support of the people and the prospects for the future appeared reasonably bright. However, in 1959, the DRV having failed in the elections which had been held in Vietnam and in the attempt to arouse the people against their legitimate government, turned to a calculated plan of open infiltration, subversion, and aggression. During the Third Party Congress of the Lao Dong Party the Secretary General Le Duan stated: "There does not exist any other way outside of that which consists in the overthrow of the dictatorial and Fascist regime of the American-Diemist clique in order to liberate totally South Vietnam, with a view to realizing national unity." As indicated in the document to which I have referred, you will find this statement in the Nhan Dan, Hanoi Daily Number 2362 of September 6, 1960.

It is the firm opinion of the United States Government that Southern Vietnam is now undergoing a determined attempt from without to overthrow the existing government using for this purpose infiltration, supply of arms, propaganda, terrorization, and all the customary instrumentalities of communist activities in such circumstances, all mounted and developed from North Vietnam.

It is hardly necessary for me to draw your attention to the Geneva Accords of July 20-31, 1954. The issue, therefore, is not that of some opinion or other in regard to the government of President Ngo Dinh Diem, but rather that of a nation whose integrity and security is threatened by military actions, completely at variance with the obligations of the Geneva Accords.

Insofar as the United States is concerned, we view the situation in which the Republic of Vietnam finds itself with the utmost gravity and, in conformity with our pledge made at the Geneva Conference on July 21, 1954, as one seriously endangering international peace and security. Our support for the government of President Ngo Dinh Diem we regard as a serious obligation, and we will undertake such measures as the circumstances appear to warrant. Since there is no semblance of any threat to the DRV by the Government of Vietnam, it is clear that if the DRV were honorably to discharge the obligations it undertook in the Geneva Accords, the prospects for peace would be greatly improved. I would, therefore, venture to suggest that you, as the head of a government which was a signatory to the Geneva Accords, should use all the influence that you possess and endeavor to bring the DRV to the strict observance of these Accords. This would be a great act in the cause of peace which you refer to as the essence of the policies of the Twenty-second Party Congress. If the DRV were to abide by its obligations under the Geneva Accords, there would be no need for the United States to consider, as we must at the present, how best to support the Government of Vietnam in its struggle for independence and national integrity.

I have written you frankly about Laos and Vietnam for a very simple reason. Both these countries are at a distance from our own countries and can be considered areas in which we ought to be able to find agreement. I am suggesting to you that you use every means at your disposal to insure a genuinely neutral and independent Laos, as those words are commonly understood throughout the world, and to insure that those closely associated with you leave South Vietnam alone. On our part, we shall work toward a neutral and independent Laos and will insure that North Vietnam will not be the object of any direct or indirect aggression. This would be a step toward peace; I am reluctant to believe that there is any necessary alternative to be imposed upon my country by the actions of others.

I am leaving for a few days for a visit to the western part of our country and will be in touch with you on other matters when I return.

Sincerely,/4/

/1/Source: Department of State, Presidential Correspondence: Lot 77 D 163. Top Secret. Another copy is in the Kennedy Library, National Security Files, Countries Series, USSR, Khrushchev Correspondence.
/2/Documents 23 and 24.
/3/See Document 26.
/4/Printed from an unsigned copy.

". . . what best serves peace, not merely prestige, must be our chief yard-stick."

26. Letter From President Kennedy to Chairman Khrushchev

Washington, December 2, 1961./1/

DEAR MR. CHAIRMAN: I enjoyed very much my talk with your son-in-law, Mr. Adzhubei./2/ His publication of the entire transcript of our interview was, I believe, a useful step in promoting better communications and public understanding among the citizens of our two countries. I was glad to hear from Mr. Adzhubei that you were in good health, having successfully weathered the arduous proceedings of your Party

Congress.

Having previously replied to your letter of November 10 on Laos and Vietnam, I want to reply now to your letter of November 9 concerning Germany and Berlin. Let me re-emphasize my strong desire that we not use this private and informal channel of communication to repeat the usual arguments and assertions normally reserved for public debates and propaganda. We should try instead to identify more clearly our areas of disagreement and areas of possible agreement on concrete matters presently before us.

Your son-in-law and I knew that there was little value in arguing over either our different social systems or our different views of history; and thus we largely avoided those subjects. Consequently I will save for a more appropriate time and place my comments in answer to yours as to who armed which part of Germany first, who violated the Potsdam agreements, why you ended the four-power administration of all Berlin, who is now abusing their presence in Berlin, or whether the Japanese Peace Treaty is a precedent for a "treaty" with only part of Germany. Nor am I going to engage in a characterization of personalities, a repudiation of what may have appeared in some Western newspaper, or a repetition of the evidence which shows why I believe West Germany to be incapable of threatening your security.

Let us clear aside in this exchange these differences of view that apparently cannot be changed. And let us, to the extent possible, also refrain from using labels or adjectives that each

119

of us may interpret differently—such as "occupation regime" or "free city". Let us talk about our responsibility: the actual situations we face now, and the concrete changes which might be discussed to improve those situations. That is the only way in which this correspondence can be meaningful—the only way in which we can make certain that we understand each other clearly and can prevent the tide of events from slipping beyond our control—and the only way, finally, in which we can achieve the lasting peace we both so devoutly desire.

I was very serious in telling your son-in-law that our two nations have the most to lose from war and the most to gain from peace. The program of development which you outlined at your 22nd Party Congress, which was fully described in our press, must necessarily be carried out, as you state in your letter, under conditions of peace. The same is true of the programs I am seeking from the American Congress—to improve our people's health, education, housing, recreation and welfare, for example, as well as general employment opportunities and economic growth.

So, with peace as our goal, let us examine where we stand in more concrete terms. After reading your letter I think it particularly important that you should have my views on these important matters.

(1) Western forces are in West Berlin now— and they will remain there as long as the people of West Berlin want them to remain. This is in accordance with your own position that they

must remain masters of their own fate.

(2) Soviet troops are not now in West Berlin, and would not in the future be needed there to guarantee our access any more than they are needed for that purpose now—and we could not under any circumstances agree to their being stationed there. I gather that you are not insisting on this and there does not seem to me, therefore, to be any need for us to become involved in long discussions in this matter except as a part of an all-Berlin solution.

(3) Western rights of access to West Berlin preceded and are independent of the Soviet Union's creation of the present East German regime. Their free exercise is a solemn obligation of the Soviet Government toward us. Those rights should therefore be confirmed and respected by any subsequent regime or any arrangement it purports to make. In no circumstances can we permit these rights to be subjected to the discretion of East German authorities, which might be subject to change; and surely you can understand how that would only increase the chances of unnecessary conflict.

While you may refer to these rights as "occupation" rights, our presence and access are not being imposed upon the West Berliners contrary to their will, and it is the "vanquished" population which is in a position to protest continuation of an occupation. Also, while these rights may not be consistent with your concept of a "free city," they do mean the city is and will be free in the sense that the West Berliners are free to choose their own future and their own protectors of that future. But whatever those terms may mean in our different languages, these facts remain. And no treaty or other arrangement with the East Germans can alter these facts, inasmuch as West Berlin has never been a part of East German territory.

Consequently, when you propose to conclude with the East Germans a settlement recognizing and consolidating the situation as it actually is, and as it was created as a result of the war, you must surely agree that the present status of West Berlin, including the access and presence of Western forces and the absence of Soviet forces, is one of those situations—and that any realistic settlement must therefore start with these facts.

I am certain that you, as a realist, recognize that we cannot permit West Berlin to be separated involuntarily from the forces of the Western Powers when it is wholly clear that this is what the people of that city want, that these forces constitute a threat to no one, and that you are unwilling, as stated in your letter, to permit East Berlin to be separated from what is now called East Germany.

Let us instead agree on the two principles stated in your letter:

"Let West Berlin live and develop in the way its population wants" without "any restrictions on (its) ties with the outside world or on the access to that city of these or those states by land, sea and air."

If the people of West Berlin should ever decide that the presence of Western forces was no longer necessary or desirable, those forces will

●

leave, without any loss of prestige. But should the people of West Berlin decide to the contrary, that should involve no loss of prestige for you, since you, too, have stated that they should be free to determine their own future. Nor does this "violate the sovereignty" of the East Germans, if any, inasmuch as West Berlin has, as I stated, never been a part of their territory, and therefore our rights in that city, including our rights of access and your responsibility therefor, cannot in any sense be terminated by any unilateral arrangements made with the East Germans.

I do not mean to imply by this that the Three Western Allied Powers and the Soviet Union cannot discuss a clarification and possible improvement of access rights. This is entirely proper, and should, in my opinion, be an important focus of any subsequent negotiations.

So let us avoid the dangers of unilateral actions, of dealing with one part of Germany only, and of abandoning agreements and goals to which both of us are legally committed. Instead let us explore together what we can do together—what joint actions for mutual benefit might be taken to improve the existing situation, without altering those situations that cannot now be altered, and consistent with our joint commitment to ultimate German self-determination. We have, as you point out, renounced force as a means of achieving that goal—but we cannot renounce the goal itself.

You state in your letter that I have not given you any "concrete" suggestions for the settlement of this matter.

This is possibly true in a formal sense. But I am actively exploring with our allies our preparations for useful negotiations at the proper time. To enter into negotiations when under threat or pressure is no more feasible for us than for you. In addition, to enter into negotiations that might later collapse for lack of preparation or unity would surely heighten the dangers to the peace. I think you understand moreover, that this is not merely a question of American policy, but also involves the intimate association we have with our Western European Allies.

As you undoubtedly are aware, there has been some divergence of views among the Western Powers on the form and timing of negotiations. There are those who believe, as you have read, that there is such a gap between the positions taken by the Soviet Union and the Western Powers that negotiations would inevitably fail, and thus the situation would become even more unsatisfactory and dangerous than it is today. My own view is that, while there are serious divergences of opinion in regard to those matters before us, they must be considered in serious and responsible discussion—and that we should not permit the present situation, so fraught with the possibility of an explosive incident, to continue without our taking every possible step to ease the matter. I have expressed this view to the other Western Powers.

I am, therefore, hopeful that shortly after the representatives of the Western Powers have met in Paris this month we and you will be in a position to sit down in an agreed and appropriate manner to attempt to reach a solution that is mutually satisfactory to all.

I want to emphasize again that what best serves peace, not merely prestige, must be our chief yard-stick. It is not the effect on Western prestige but the effect on peace in your proposals that cause me concern—and I am anxious, as you are anxious, that we find solutions "on a mutually acceptable basis" which will preserve for years to come the peace we now enjoy. While I regret that this letter cannot now be more precise as to detail, I am hopeful that stating our views clearly on certain matters at issue will help make such steps possible at an early date.

Sincerely,/3/

/1/Source: Department of State, Presidential Correspondence: Lot 77 D 163. No classification marking. Another copy is in the Kennedy Library, National Security Files, Countries Series, USSR, Khrushchev Correspondence.
/2/A transcript of this interview on November 25 is printed in volume V; it was published in Izvetiya on November 28 and was the first direct communication to the Soviet people by a U.S. President.
/3/Printed from an unsigned copy.

"It could sound as an ultimatum."

27. Letter From Chairman Khrushchev to President Kennedy

Moscow, December 13, 1961./1/

DEAR MR. PRESIDENT, Within a short period of time I had an opportunity to read two [of] your messages—one addressed to our country and the other, a confidential one, to me personally./2/

I want to express appreciation for those kind words and wishes which were addressed by you to me in the talk with A.I. Adzhubei. I am satisfied, as you are, that this interesting interview has taken place and would like to hope, together with you, that it will contribute to better understanding between our countries. I think you did not expect that we would agree with all your observations. Nevertheless, I would say that some of the ideas expressed by you sound encouraging.

Yes, the Soviet Union and the United States of America must live in peace with each other. They must build their relations on the basis of reason, of due regard for the real situation, and of mutual respect, on the basis of the establishing of the principle of peaceful coexistence between states with different social systems in international affairs. This is the only right and sound basis for cooperation and securing of a lasting and stable peace. It is my most ardent desire that it would not remain only a dream and not become a mirage, that creates nothing but false hopes.

But allow me to return to your letter of December 2. I read with satisfaction the words to the effect that our personal and unofficial exchange should not be used for the repetition of arguments and statements usually resorted to in public debates and propaganda. Being in a complete agreement with that I expected to find in your letter something new, not things which I saw many times on the pages of Western newspapers and magazines which are still afraid of fresh air and prefer a stuffy and poisoned atmosphere of the "cold war" but, frankly, I was disappointed because while reading the letter I was finding exactly what you, yourself, have cautioned against.

In your letter you, Mr. President, found it necessary to formulate flately the demands which must as one may understand you, be accepted without fail by the Soviet Union as a condition for negotiation on the settlement of the German problem. There is hardly any need to say whether it is proper or improper to put forward to one another any preliminary conditions for negotiations? I think there can be no two opinions here. And therefore, leaving aside this question, I would like to express frankly my opinion on the substance of these conditions.

First of all, you state that the troops of the USA, Great Britain and France "will stay in West Berlin as long as the people of West Berlin want them to stay". It could sound as an ultimatum. But even most die-hard politicians in the West understand now that one cannot speak such language with us. Then, there must be something else in it. Frankly speaking, it is not difficult to understand that an attempt to make the presence of the troops of the three powers in West Berlin dependent on "the will of the population" reflects in effect a desire to create a new basis for their presence there. Evidently, the US Government also has inwardly come to the conclusion that to try now, 16 years after the end of the war, to base its claims upon the right of occupation or the right of a victor, or, as some say in the US, upon the right of the conquest, does not meet either the norms of international law or the spirit of time.

The approach to this question advocated in the letter in all desire cannot be accepted as valid and still less as meeting the aims of the normalization of the situation in West Berlin. As a matter of fact, Mr. President, the troops of the USA, Britain and France came to West Berlin, as known, neither on the request of the population nor for its protection. The purpose of their stationing there—let us be frank with each other—was entirely different from that of which you write in your letter. You want us to recognize now all the changes which have been unilaterally made by the Western powers in West Berlin, and not only in West Berlin, and to stand obediently on guard of the present rights of the USA, Britain and France on which we have never made any agreement with you. For to call a spade a spade we are now acting as traffic cops for the movement of the NATO troops into West Berlin. I emphasize that these are the NATO troops because American, British and French troops stationed in West Berlin are part and parcel of the armed forces of this bloc. And as to the intentions of the NATO with regard to the Soviet Union and our allies we are well informed of them.

You demand that contrary to common sense we continue to be traffic cops on the roads to West Berlin, and your temporary occupational rights become permanent there. How one can count on reaching an agreement on such a basis? This is not the way things happen in life, in any case we cannot agree to this.

You yourself note that it is necessary to avoid "the danger of unilateral actions", to avoid repudiation "of agreements and goals that both of us have legally assumed". But why this wish should concern the Soviet Union only? In your letter unfortunately I couldn't find any signs of recognition of reciprocity.

It seems that it is not necessary for me to repeat what were the major points in our agreements on Germany which now—not through our fault—are actually not exercised.

Occupation of any given territory is a temporary measure—this is exactly how it was written down in the corresponding agreements on Germany. Occupational rights can naturally be valid only as long as the state of war exists. Strictly speaking already now, occupation ought to have been ended since state of war with Germany was terminated by unilateral statements. In any case there can be no place left for it after a peace treaty has been concluded.

One may think that it is a desire to have at any cost its troops in West Berlin that prevents the US from taking part in a peaceful German settlement. You should understand us, Mr. President—and I believe you do—even if the US threatens us, tests our nerves and will, we cannot and will never agree to the prolongation of occupational order, we will struggle for our rights, for a real normalization of the situation in the center of Europe. We cannot be the guards of anybody's occupational rights forever. Sometime an end must come to all that. Even enslaving agreements have times provisions, let us say, 99 years. Even matrimonial ties, confirmed by church and law, sometimes weaken with time and break. For example, your countryman Mr. Rockefeller, having lived with his wife for 30 years decided to break up the marriage. No use to go into the reasons that caused this divorce but in all probability there must have been some.

As for you, you do not set any time limit. You mean forever, though you do not use this word. Do they in Western countries expect that social-ist system in the GDR will outlive itself and then the German problem will be solved in the way these countries want? But socialism is a progres-sive vital system, it has no time. limit, it will con-stantly develop and strengthen.

One cannot count on its liquidation. And if that is the reason for the desire to keep forever the regime of occupation in West Berlin—it is a strange, separated from life philosophy.

It can rest—excuse my harsh judgements—only on the megalomania, on an intention to act from the position of strength, though at our meeting in Vienna we, it seems, came to joint con-clusion that strength and threats are not the argument which leads to mutual understanding.

True, you say that you denounce force as a means for achieving goals. I understand you did not want to say that you are displaying generos-ity otherwise it would sound humiliating. It is well known that in politics just as in physics every action causes counteraction, and applica-tion of force or repudiation of its use are con-nected, to speak in broad terms, not with the nature of character of one or another statesman but first of all with the actual state of affairs, with the balance of power which makes peaceful settlement of all disputable questions a pressing necessity now and in the future. We have always deemed it unreasonable to orient ourselves in politics on strength and we call on other governments to do the same.

In defense of your position you refer to the rights and interests of the population of West Berlin. But you, Mr. President, are certainly aware that no one of the socialist countries is infringing upon these rights and interests. We have always proceeded from the fact that it is an internal affairs of the population of one or another state to choose its social, political and economic system.

The Soviet Union is ready to declare solemnly and to confirm in a treaty, in any international act the right of the West Berlin population to be the masters of their destiny, to live without any interference from outside, the right of West Berlin for unimpeded ties with the outside world. But we cannot recognize and will not recognize any right for the West Berlin population to call foreign troops into West Berlin since this affects the security of many states. We are for safeguarding the sovereignty of West Berlin but at the same time one obviously cannot neglect the sovereignty of other countries and first of all the sovereignty of the country in the center of which West Berlin is situated, through the territory of which all its communications with the outside world run. We do not bring the solution any closer when we are carried away by one side of the matter and do not want to take into consideration the other, if we talk of the rights of the two million citizens of West Berlin and do not want at all to give due regard to the right of the citizens of the GDR.

I like your suggestion to speak of "the real situation we face". I understand it so that, proceeding from the real situation existing in Germany, in Europe and throughout the world, we should try to reach mutual understanding on the most important questions, on which it depends today whether there be peace or war on earth. But the actual situation is not what is to the liking of one side—of the United States or the Soviet Union. It has as its components the whole range of facts, notwithstanding how pleasant or unpleasant they may be. These facts are such that the question of the presence of these or other troops in West Berlin affects many countries, its solution can influence not in a small degree the direction of further development of Soviet-American relations, and all international situations.

Here, like in other questions, one should proceed from the reality of life and to act from the position of reason. In other words, one should see not only his rights and somebody's obligations but also his obligations and somebody's rights, not only defend his own interests but also take into consideration the interests of the other side if one has a desire to sincerely seek a mutually acceptable agreement.

In this connection one cannot but pay attention to the statement in your letter that "under no circumstances," that is even after the conclusion of a peace treaty, the US has no intention to recognize the sovereignty of the GDR over its own territory through which all communications of West Berlin with the outside world run. I will tell you frankly—a dangerous position for the cause of peace! In previous messages I dwelt upon this question in detail and explained the view of the Soviet Union. Here I would deem it necessary only to emphasize once again the inconsistency and unreality of such approach. It cannot contribute to a speediest finding of a right solution of the problem we face. We would still like to believe that the Western Powers will understand this and will choose another way, the way of respect for international norms and sovereignty of all states, irrespective of their social system.

Allow me now to express my opinion on another condition—on the possibility of presence in West Berlin of Soviet troops as guarantors. You know well from my messages how the Soviet Union formulates this question.

We are not seeking to have our troops in West Berlin. The Soviet Government believes that our troops have nothing to do there, just as the troops of the Western Powers. The best thing would be to have no troops in West Berlin. And if you are very interested in placing foreign troops as guarantors let us agree that these will be the UN troops.

If you do not want the Soviet Union to be a guarantor, we are not fishing for any additional obligations: we have enough work of our own. Please deal on all questions of interest to you with the German Democratic Republic. But we believe that in this case also there should be no troops of the Western Powers in West Berlin and if there still have to be some troops there these should be the UN international troops.

However, as I understand, the US continues to insist that "responsibility" should lie on the Soviet Union. You should agree, Mr. President, that we can guarantee the interests of West Berlin only on equal conditions with other states and, naturally, not to the detriment of the sovereignty of the GDR.

It is easy to say, of course: in concluding a peace treaty with the GDR make provisions for the securing of such and such rights for the Western Powers and everything will settle by itself. Firstly, I have to say again that the Western Powers cannot expect from us more than they themselves have done and are doing. Secondly, a peace treaty would hardly correspond to its purpose and even to its name if instead of liquidating the vestiges of the war and occupation it confirmed and prolonged them forever.

If there is a desire to limit the subject of the negotiation only to the confirmation of the occupation regime and the occupation rights, to a more accurate definition as to on what kilometer and how many our traffic cops should stand, then I am not sure whether there will be any sense and, which is more important, any use in such negotiation. I would like to think that in the course of our exchange a necessary degree of accord has been established between us to the effect that the purpose of the negotiation is to bring the situation in a certain area—important from the point of view of the preservation of peace—in accordance with radically changed conditions, of course, could not be precisely anticipated at its time in quadripartite agreements on Germany and Berlin.

I can express my satisfaction with your words to the effect that the main goal of the USSR and the US Governments is to ensure peace and not only care for prestige. Peace and peace treaty, I think you will agree, are extremely close terms. You are inclined to believe that the peace treaty proposed by us will increase tension. This will depend not upon the treaty but upon the actions of Western Powers. Our proposals on peaceful settlement do not contain anything which could objectively cause an aggravation of [the] situation. It is our deep belief that a peace treaty even with one German state is already a great progress since—though on a part of the territory—it draws a line through World War II, removes its vestiges which, like poisonous plants, give shoots of "cold war" every hour. How a peace treaty aimed at establishing peace among states can cause tension! If there are any other suggestions for solving the problem of liquidation of the occupational regime on the basis of a peaceful settlement, we are ready to consider them and will willingly have exchange of views.

In your letter, Mr. President, you raise a question about your troops as the "guarantors." We also know that recently in the US there have been much talk and writing in this connection. To listen to some people in the West, it looks as if only they do really care about West Berlin and its population, though it is well known that nobody threatens this city either with war or an invasion.

But let us objectively analyze the situation in West Berlin. You, of course, know very well that the Soviet Union stands firmly to guarantee to the population of this city the right to live at their own discretion. We deeply believe at the same time that West Berlin—and this is in fact the essence of the matter—must have a perspective, a belief in its future. The population of this city needs most of all a healthy economy that can ensure full employment and high standard of living, flow of orders, inflow of capital into industry, and permanently guaranteed markets. Life in West Berlin can be in full swing only when production able to compete is organized, when the city establishes normal relations with other states, including the GDR.

But is this possible under the conditions of preserving the occupational regime which would continue to be an apple of discord and the cause of tension—is this possible? Is occupation the best way to ensure the interests of the city? The more troops there will be in West Berlin, the less confidence and the more doubts about the stability of the situation. Stationing of foreign garrisons could testify only to the abnormality of the situation. Is sitting on the volcano helpful for calming down one's nerves? What practical businessman will invest his money into business where all is shaky and a lot is unknown? Who would give him longterm orders, who would seek to live in such city where real frontline atmosphere is artificially maintained?

Without the normalization of the situation, without confidence in its future West Berlin is a doomed city. But it can have future, good, prosperous future in case it ceases to be the center of "cold war", a base of subversive activities against socialist countries and would not be used to aggravate the situation, which all impedes its life and the life of the neighbouring countries. What the US is proposing now will not cure the present illness of the city but, on the contrary, will make it still worse. Before long everybody will realize that West Berlin cannot exist under the conditions in which it is placed now, its business life will die and the population, deprived of a perspective, will have to seek solutions to all these problems in one way or another.

And not by chance there is even now, as it is evident from reports by Western press, a flight of citizens of West Berlin and "a flight" of capital from West Berlin. This process will inevitably grow if we only do not agree and create a confidence for the city in its future.

If the care should really be taken for the West Berlin population living calmly, without any fear about tomorrow, then it must be firmly acknowledged that the best possible solution is to sign a peace treaty or treaties with two German states and to admit these states to the United Nations. Thus, it will be possible to clean up completely international relations from dangerous and unnecessary layers, which remained as the heritage of World War II. Is it not a tempting and noble aim for the sake of which we together should work?

In treaties or in a solemn proclamation or in a declaration we could express our ideas about the future of Germany—about the restoration of its unity. You propose to proceed in that from the right of Germans for self-determination. You are right. Let us, then—in our positions—proceed from the exact meaning of this word—self-determination. And it means that Germans should self-determine, without an interference from outside. Germans should get together with Germans, one German government—with the other German government and define on what basis and how they will solve the question of the restoration of German unity. Let other powers, on their part, state that they will not create any obstacles for Germans. All must be in the way Germans will agree.

You will probably understand in a different way many things of which I am telling you now. Well, there are reasons for that. The United States of America did not feel all burdens of World War II in such a degree as we did. And you yourself spoke of that. Even today the United States is separated from Europe by the ocean. And everything is felt not so sharp from afar as in proximity. If you really think that you can live without a German peace treaty, it is up to you. We are not going to impose terms of peaceful settlement with Germany upon anybody of our former allies, though we will regret if the US and other Western Powers refuse to sign a German peace treaty.

But let us see what can be done to lessen tension in a situation when one group of states does not consider it necessary to sign a German peace treaty while the other has stated its intention to achieve peaceful settlement even with one of the existing German states.

I have already written to you that the Soviet Government considers it possible to agree, before the conclusion of a peace treaty with the GDR, on basic questions which are of interest to both sides. Thus, it will be possible to avoid an unnecessary aggravation of relations first of all between the USSR and the US and to settle those questions to which each of our governments attaches special importance. It is possible to agree beforehand on a status of a free city of West Berlin as I spoke of that with Mr. Spaak and to make the agreement formal by a special protocol which would be annexed to a peace treaty with the GDR. Other important questions could be solved alongside in due order. If it is accomplished an entirely different situation will come into existence in Europe and especially in West Berlin, and its citizens will undoubtedly sigh with relief. To say nothing of the fact that in this case favorable opportunities for the development of economy and of public and political life will be created in West Berlin.

This is the most wise solution which is expected from the Great Powers by the peoples of the world. It will ensure better conditions for the peaceful life of the peoples of the USSR and the US which they—and I fully support your words—

equally need.

. I would further like, in the interests of clarity to emphasize once again that the conclusion of a peace treaty is not a theoretical goal but a practical one for us. From the point of view of our national interests it is one of the most important questions and we attach paramount importance to its solution.

You wrote in your recent letter—and this idea was somehow reflected in your interview with A.I. Adzhubei—about the right of the Soviet Union for due ensurance of its national security. This is a fair approach.

You can further ask: what is of particular importance for us in the German question regarding the ensurance of the national security of the Soviet Union? I shall answer in all frankness: our main goal is to exclude a possibility for an outbreak of war in Germany or because of Germany. You maintain that the FRG does not constitute a threat to peace or security of the Soviet Union or other socialist countries. We cannot agree with that because we do not have the right to ignore the hard lessons of the past. To you, Mr. President, our warnings of the revival of German militarism and revanchism look like propaganda. To the peoples of the USSR, Poland, Czechoslovakia and other European countries German militarism continues to be a real threat, and they must always have this in mind if they do not want the events to take them by surprise again.

Mr. President, is it any use for us to argue whether West Germany is a potential source of a military threat? If one wishes to do so this discussion can be endlessly prolonged for there are no such scales that can precisely weigh the arguments of each side. Wouldn't it be better for us to turn to an objective criteria—historic experience. It binds the statesmen not to dismiss the worst possibility, it demands not to let the events come out of control, and not to make our future and our very existence dependent on the outcome of struggle in Germany between the forces of good and evil. We want to be masters of our destinies. You must agree that after what happened 20 years ago, we have the right to be insured against any historic reverses of fortune.

You think that at present the US have the situation in the FRG under control. Let it be so. And what the situation will be in 5-10 years? Senator Humphrey, for example, believes that soon West Germans may demand that American, British and French troops go because they consider themselves strong enough? And in every probability the Western Powers will have to go. The US would not go to war with Bundeswehr, would it? And what else? Can one be certain that a new lunatic will not appear in the FRG who ignoring real dislocation of forces would want to put into practice what militarists-revanchists are shouting from every roof in West Germany? Then it would probably be too late to think of the creation of security system and the prevention of a threat on the part of German militarism and it might happen we will have to pay for that with millions and millions of lives?

The farther we depart in time and policy from the Allied agreements on Germany, the more difficult it will be to find joint effective guarantees against the threat of German militarism to peace and stability which as it seems have to be our joint aim. If it is difficult now to agree on a German peace treaty because of the differences between the former allies, later on it may turn out to be even more difficult.

I am frankly sharing some thoughts with you and, please, don't understand me that another attempt is made [to] agitate you for a peace treaty. I believe that deep in your heart you will agree with me that the Soviet Union after all it has suffered cannot be indifferent to what is happening in West Germany. Behind every demand of ours to secure lasting peace in Europe and prevent new German aggression—and this is exactly the reason we want to liquidate the vestiges of World War II and to conclude a German peace treaty—are millions of lives of perished Soviet people. We will do everything to have a peace treaty concluded and we cannot act otherwise. Such is our duty before mankind and our right.

With all the wish to have good relations with you personally, to have good relations with your government and the United States of America we must conclude a German peace treaty and we will conclude it even if you do not agree with this. Our most cherished goal is to solve all the problems inherited from World War II in cooperation with the US, in agreement with you. We say this honestly and openly. But I do not want to conceal it either that the USSR will sign a peace treaty with the GDR with all naturally ensuing consequences

142

without the US if there is no other way out.

Of course, in this case too we would try to avoid unnecessary aggravations. I hope that such aggravations will not happen if leading Western Powers defining their position take into consideration multi-sided experience of peaceful settlement with various countries during the post-war period, including those in the Far East.

Of course, we are far from understanding the positive moments that have already begun to show in the course of the exchange of views between the governments of the Soviet Union and the US. But one should not close his eyes to the fact that on main principal questions narrowing the differences in our positions proceeds exceedingly slowly and, may be, sometime it does not proceed at all.

I would not like you to understand my observations as an expression of desire to argue one or another thesis of your letter only because it comes from the other side. I simply thought that I had the right to state in reply to your frank statements my viewpoint without unnecessary diplomacy in this case.

I believe, Mr. President, that our governments will be able to cooperate to the benefit of all peoples, setting as their supreme goal service to peace and in determining their positions they will always have in mind that we have all the possibilities to live in good harmony and find right solutions of any controversial problems.

The Soviet Union on its part is ready for this. Any journey begins with the first step. We have to make it together and we would like that it will be directed to one and the same goal—the strengthening of peace.

Sincerely,

N. Khrushchev/3/

/1/Source: Department of State, Presidential Correspondence: Lot 77 D 163. No classification marking. Attached to the source text was a 3-paragraph letter of transmittal from Bohlen to Thompson that stated that it was a "translation as received from the Russians." Another copy of this message and the Russian-language text is in the Kennedy Library, National Security Files, Countries Series, USSR, Khrushchev Correspondence.
/2/The confidential message is Document 26; the other message is the interview with Adzhubei; see footnote 1, Document 26.
/3/Printed from a copy that bears this typed signature.

". . . history imposed a great responsibility on our peoples for the destinies of the world."

‘

28. Telegram From the Department of State to the Embassy in the Soviet Union

Washington, December 29, 1961./1/

1537. Following is unofficial translation of message sent by Khru-shchev [sic] and Brezhnev via commercial cable December 29 to President Kennedy:

"DEAR MR. PRESIDENT:

In these few last hours of the expiring 1961 we are sending to the people of the United States the sincerest wishes for peace and happiness in the new year and likewise our best wishes of personal happiness to you and to your entire family. Right now on the doorstep of the new year the nations live with new hope that the coming year will be such a threshold in the development of events when there will be undertaken efficient steps in the cause of liquidation of centers of military danger. There is no doubt that on the state of affairs in Soviet-American relations depends very much whether humanity will go towards peace or war. At the meeting in Vienna the President of the United States and Chairman of Ministers of the USSR agreed that history imposed a great responsibility on our peoples for the destinies of the world. The Soviet people regard the future optimistically. They express hope that in the coming new year our countries will be able to find ways towards closer cooperation, will be able to find a basis for concerted actions and efforts for the good of all humanity. On the part of the Soviet Union, as before, there will be no lack of resolution to do everything in its power in order to ensure durable and lasting peace on our planet.

N. Khrushchev

L. Brezhnev" [sic]

Rusk

/1/Source: Department of State, Presidential Correspondence: Lot 66 D 204. Official Use Only; Priority. Another copy is in the Kennedy Library, National Security Files, Countries Series, USSR, Khrushchev Correspondence. Also printed in *Public Papers of the Presidents of the United States: John F. Kennedy, 1961*, p. 819. The transliterated Russian text is in Department of State, Central Files, 711.11-KE/12-2961.

"The year which is ending has been a troubled one."

29. Telegram From the Department of State to the Embassy in the Soviet Union

Washington, December 30, 1961./1/

1538. Following message sent December 30 by commercial telegram from President Kennedy to President Brezhnev and Chairman Khrushchev in response Khrushchev and Brezhnev New Year's message December 29 (see separate cable):/2/

"DEAR PRESIDENT BREZHNEV AND CHAIRMAN KHRUSHCHEV:

As the year 1961 approaches its close I wish to extend to the people of the Soviet Union and to you and your families my most sincere wishes and those of the American people for a peaceful and prosperous New Year. The year which is ending has been a troubled one. It is my earnest hope that the coming year will strengthen the foundations of world peace and will bring an improvement in the relations between our countries, upon which so much depends. It is our grave responsibility to fulfill that hope. As President of the United States, I can state on behalf of the Government and the American people that we will do our best to do so.

John F. Kennedy

White House has not yet decided whether issue public release re exchange of messages.

Rusk

/1/Source: Department of State, Presidential Correspondence: Lot 66 D 204. Official Use Only; Priority. Another copy is in the Kennedy Library, National Security Files, Countries Series, USSR, Khrushchev Correspondence. Also printed in *Public Papers of the Presidents of the United States, 1961*, p. 819, and in Claflin, *The President Wants To Know*, p. 141.
/2/Document 28.

"N.S. Khrushchev hopes the President of the United States will display a correct understanding of the situation."

30. Message From Chairman Khrushchev to President Kennedy
Moscow, undated/1/

N.S. Khrushchev, the Chairman of the USSR Council of Ministers, received a communication from Robert F. Kennedy/2/ that President John F. Kennedy is concerned by a discouraging beginning of contacts on the German problem and on other problems which should be solved in the interests of the improvement of the international situation, the strengthening of peace and the development of normal relations between our countries.

N.S. Khrushchev fully shares the President's concern. He was discouraged even in a greater extent than the President when the USSR Foreign Minister had reported on the results of his first talks with the US Ambassador in Moscow.

The position of the American Government on a number of issues, as set forth by the US Ambassador, actually repeats what had been said many times by former President Eisenhower, Chancellor Adenauer and by other Western statesmen. It proceeds from completely wrong basis and therefore is absolutely unacceptable. In fact the Soviet Union is urged to immortalize by its signature that temporary, by its nature, situation which exists now, that is contribute to the preservation of the occupation regime in West Berlin.

But this is unthinkable. It would be not a step forward, but a step backward. It is understandable that the Soviet Union cannot agree to this. So far as one can judge by the statements of the US Ambassador in Moscow in his talks with the USSR Foreign Minister the United States would like nothing less than to preserve the unhealthy and rather dangerous situation in West Berlin which has been and remains a source of tension in Europe, causes friction among dozens of states, including the USSR and the USA. The Soviet Union is pursuing quite different aims. It wants to remove the hotbed of international tension and create conditions for the development of good friendly relations among nations.

What the United States Government is proposing now would in effect not only throw us all back to the days of Vienna but would have created even worse prospectives. In this respect N.S. Khrushchev agrees with the President. That is why the Chairman of the USSR Council of Ministers is also discouraged. Yes, discouraged and distressed.

N.S. Khrushchev does not consider it necessary to explain again the aims and position of the Soviet Government since they were stated fully enough at the meeting with the President of the United States in Vienna and also in his private messages to Mr. John F. Kennedy.

On the part of the head of the Soviet Government everything possible has been done to convince the President of the United States that drawing a final line through World War II and solving on this basis the question of changing the status of West Berlin by declaring it a free demilitarized city corresponds equally to the interests of all powers, to the interests of peace. The Soviet Government is not seeking any other aim. It is only deplorable that the US Government and the President are still searching for some hidden motives in the Soviet Union's position on this question. But those motives simply do not exist and therefore there is no need to search for them. Yet, what should be done now is, of course, to seek an agreement but not to push the events towards a collapse of the renewed exchange of opinions between the Governments of the USSR and the USA and towards new complications?

Now that the parties have already familiarized themselves with each others' positions it would be useful to work out jointly the bases on which a future agreement on West Berlin as well as on other questions which it is necessary to solve with the conclusion of a German peace treaty should be built. Proceeding from that the Soviet Government has worked out a draft of the main provisions of the status of a free demilitarized city of West Berlin and a draft of the protocol on guarantees which is an enclosure to this status.

These documents were given to the US Government by A.A. Gromyko, USSR Foreign Minister through Ambassador Thompson on January 12. The US Ambassador was also given a statement in which the Soviet Government's position on the question of concluding a German peace treaty and normalizing on its basis the situation in West Berlin is explained and where it is emphasized that simultaneously such questions should be solved as appropriate legalization and confirmation of the existing German borders, due respect for the sovereignty of the GDR, non-arming of the two German states with nuclear weapons and barring them from producing those weapons, conclusion of a nonaggression pact between the NATO and the Warsaw treaty member-countries.

Having familiarized himself with those docu-

150

ments the President will see that neither the Soviet Union nor the GDR are encroaching upon West Berlin and demand more than the establishment for that city of an international legal status corresponding to the conditions of the peace time. The Soviet proposals—and it is not difficult to realize—guarantee for the population of West Berlin the right to live under the social system they choose and to have free access to the outer world.

N.S. Khrushchev would like very much the President to consider with understanding the concrete proposals which are in the drafts of the main provisions of the status of a free demilitarized city of West Berlin and the protocol on the guarantees. Those proposals do not make harm to anyone, do not discriminate against anybody.

The policy which the Western powers continue to stick to might somehow have been understood in the times when it was originated. That is a policy of diktat, a policy "from the position of strength". The late Dulles did not make bones about it. But one wants to conduct this policy even now ignoring the enormous changes that have taken place in the world.

The President of the United States has himself said and everybody knows it that now the balance of power is equal. How, then, is it possible proceeding from the equal initial conditions to attempt to conduct a policy of encroachment on the interests of the USSR and its allies—socialist countries? But what the US Government is proposing is aimed precisely against our interests.

It is known that the policy "from the position

of strength" with respect to the USSR has proved bankrupt. The establishment of the military bases around the Soviet Union, the discontinuance of trade with it—all that was aimed at the isolation of the USSR and other socialist countries, at undermining their economy. Such policy has suffered a defeat.

And this is clear to every sober-minded man if he does not deliberately close his eyes to it. It is bound to go bankrupt in the future as well if one resorts to it.

The USSR economy is striding forward and prospering. Science and technology are rapidly developing. The Soviet Union has scored great successes in the exploration of outer space. The entire world including the President of the United States recognizes the achievements of our country.

Then how under these conditions one can continue to pursue the "policy from the position of strength"? It is hard to reconcile one with the other. Therefore if the Soviet Union had not complied with and rebuffed this policy in the past, the more so will it not consent to a humiliating agreement now. The USSR will struggle with all available means against any attempt to impose upon it the conditions that do not correspond to the interests of consolidating peace and it will never sign such agreements. If on its part the United States does not display an understanding of this, some time will pass and the world will witness that this policy is suffering the same and even greater defeat as before. If in the past Dulles threatened the Soviet Union relying on the atomic weapons monopoly, now there is no trace of such monopoly. The USSR and the US are equal. Therefore it would be senseless to threaten one or the other side with war. The USSR is threatening nobody, it does not want war, and all its efforts are aimed at excluding war. It is senseless to threaten war on the Soviet people which is seeking only the normalization of international situation and liquidation of the vestiges of the war. The one who tries to frighten the Soviet people and threaten them will get in response the same that he is threatening with and not in a lesser degree.

Therefore the best thing now, if to proceed from common sense and sober consideration of all facts, is to spare no effort to normalize relations, and first of all among major powers, and not to preserve the hotbeds of tension.

N.S. Khrushchev hopes that the President of the United States will display a correct understanding of the situation. N.S. Khrushchev is under the impression that the President has difficulties and the Chairman of the Council of Ministers understands that. But every leader has his difficulties. Therefore it is necessary to undertake joint efforts to overcome those difficulties and reach such agreements which would be beneficial to peoples of the Soviet Union and the United States as well as all other peoples that long for peace and tranquil life.

/1/Source: Kennedy Library, National Security Files, Countries Series, USSR, Khrushchev Correspondence. No classification marking. The source text is a Soviet translation. Another copy of the source text is in Department of State, Presidential Correspondence: Lot 77 D 163; it is attached to a brief note from Rusk to McNamara stating that Bundy had handed it to him the morning of January 18. A January 18 note from Bohlen to Rusk states that the message was received by the Attorney General and that the Russian translation was given to President Kennedy. Under cover of his note to Rusk, Bohlen forwarded a "very quick, rough translation" that is similar to but not identical to the source text. (Ibid.) In his February 15 letter to Khrushchev (Document 34), President Kennedy referred to the source text as "the message which you sent me through my brother."

/2/Not further identified.

". . . events may take their own course and erupt in a disaster."

31. Telegram From the Department of State to the Embassy in the Soviet Union

Washington, February 6, 1962, 6:42 p.m./1/

1827. You should concert immediately with UK Ambassador to ask for joint appointment on Wednesday, February 7, with Gromyko in order to deliver text following message to Khrushchev from President and Prime Minister.

Begin Verbatim Text.

Dear Mr. Chairman:
We are taking the unusual step of addressing

this message to you in order to express our own views, as well as to solicit yours, on what we can jointly do to increase the prospects of success at the new disarmament negotiations which will begin in Geneva in March.

We are convinced that a supreme effort must be made and the three of us must accept a common measure of personal obligation to seek every avenue to restrain and reverse the mounting arms race. Unless some means can be found to make at least a start in controlling the quickening arms competition, events may take their own course and erupt in a disaster which will afflict all peoples, those of the Soviet Union as well as of the United Kingdom and United States. Disarmament negotiations in the past have been sporadic and frequently interrupted. Indeed, there has been no sustained effort to come to grips with this problem at the conference table since the three months of meetings ending in June of 1960, over a year and a half ago. Before that, no real negotiations on the problem of general disarmament had taken place since negotiations came to an end in September 1957.

It should be clear to all of us that we can no longer afford to take a passive view of these negotiations. They must not be allowed to drift into failure. Accordingly, we propose that we three accept a personal responsibility for directing the part to be played by our representatives in the forthcoming talks, and that we agree beforehand that our representatives will remain at the conference table until concrete results have been achieved, however long this may take.

We propose that our negotiators seek progress on three levels. First, they should be instructed to work out a program of general and complete disarmament which could serve as the basis for the negotiations of an implementing treaty or treaties. Our negotiators could thus build upon the common ground which was found in the bilateral talks between the United States and the USSR which took place this summer, and which were reflected in the Statement of Agreed Principles of September 20, 1961. Secondly, our negotiators should attempt to ascertain the widest measure of disarmament which would be implemented at the earliest possible time whilst still continuing their maximum efforts to achieve agreement on those other aspects which present more difficulty. Thirdly, our negotiators should try to isolate and identify initial measures of disarmament which could, if put into effect without delay, materially improve international security and the prospects for further disarmament progress. We do not believe that these triple objectives need conflict with one another and an equal measure of urgency should be attached to each.

As a symbol of the importance which we jointly attach to these negotiations, we propose that we be represented at the outset of the disarmament conference by the Foreign Ministers of our three countries, who would declare their readiness to return to participate personally in the negotiations as the progress made by our permanent representatives warrants. We assume, in this case, the Foreign Ministers of other states as well will wish to attend. The status and progress of the conference should, in addition, be the subject of more frequent communications among the three of us. In order to give impetus to the opening of the disarmament negotiations, we could consider having the Foreign Ministers of our three countries convene at Geneva in advance of the opening of the conference to concert our plans.

At this time in our history, disarmament is the most urgent and the most complex issue we face. The threatening nature of modern armaments is so appalling that we cannot regard this problem as a routine one or as an issue which may be useful primarily for the scoring of propaganda victories. The failure in the nuclear test conference, which looked so hopeful and to the success of which we attached such a high priority in the Spring of 1961, constitutes a discouraging background for our new efforts. However, we must be resolved to overcome this recent setback, with its immediate consequences, and forego fruitless attempts to apportion blame. Our renewed effort must be to seek and find ways in which the competition between us, which will surely persist for the foreseeable future, can be pursued on a less dangerous level. We must view the forthcoming disarmament meetings as an opportunity and a challenge which time and history may not once again allow us.

We would welcome an early expression of your views.

End Verbatim Text.

157

Advise Department when delivery has been made.

You should tell Gromyko that we do not plan to make text letter public although we will announce Thursday in general terms, of which you are aware, that approach on this subject has been made to Soviets.

Rusk

/1/Source: Kennedy Library, National Security Files, Countries Series, USSR, Khrushchev Correspondence. Secret; Niact; Limit Distribution; Eyes Only. Another copy is in Department of State, Presidential Correspondence: Lot 66 D 204. Also printed in *Public Papers of the Presidents of the United States: John F. Kennedy, 1962*, pp. 128-129, and *Documents on Disarmament, 1962*, vol. I, pp. 25-26.

"It is a cause of satisfaction that our views go generally in the same direction."

32. Letter From Chairman Khrushchev to President Kennedy

Moscow, February 10, 1962./1/

DEAR MR. PRESIDENT: I am addressing you on a question which, as is evident from your message of February 7 last,/2/ occupies your thoughts as well.

I could not but be gratified that you also are giving some thought to the role which the recent-ly created 18-Nation Committee, which is beginning its work on March 14, 1962 in Geneva and of which our countries are members, will play in the solution of the disarmament problem. This is required if only because the Governments of the countries represented in that Committee have been entrusted, by decision of the sixteenth session of the UN General Assembly, with a matter of such vital importance to the peoples as general and complete disarmament.

There is no need to prove that the further development of the international situation will depend, to a large degree, on how the work in that Committee will progress. Will it be able to rise to a level from which the distant and difficult will appear near and real, will it cope with the great task placed on it—to work out an agreement on general and complete disarmament? Or will the new disarmament body begin, from its very first steps, to stumble over the same difficulties over which its predecessors suffered a fiasco?

These are the questions the answers to which are now being sought by everyone who is not indifferent to the future of mankind. And these questions animate the peoples all the more deeply and strongly because the arms race is ever growing, devouring the labors and the achievements of hundreds of millions of peoples, while the danger of a new war is increasing, acquiring substance in the mass of armaments.

It seems to me that all this has to be borne in mind in order correctly to evaluate the significance which the disarmament negotiations to be resumed in Geneva are acquiring under present conditions.

You will, apparently, agree with me, that certain preparatory work for these negotiations has been done. For the first time in the entire history of negotiations a disarmament body has a rather clear mandate—the basic principles of general and complete disarmament approved by the UN General Assembly. Hopes are raised also by the fact that now the composition of the disarmament body includes representatives of all of the three main groups of states existing in the world: the socialist, those belonging to Western military blocs, and the non-committed. These are undoubtedly positive factors.

At the same time all of us cannot but be aware of the fact that there still remain to be made truly Herculean efforts in order to have the disarmament negotiations bear the awaited fruits. It is sufficient to compare the Soviet program for general and complete disarmament with other proposals advanced at the sixteenth session of the UN General Assembly, which are being put forward as a counter to our program, to see clearly what mountains have yet to be moved from the path toward agreement.

The Soviet Government deems it necessary to see to it in advance that the work of the 18-Nation Committee does not become caught in the beaten track and that it not be reduced in the final analysis to debates between bureaucrats. All too often the various committees, subcommittees, and commissions on disarmament, a great number of which have been created in the past, have ceased their inglorious existence for us not to draw the necessary lessons from this.

In our opinion, the most important thing now is to have the 18-Nation Committee make a powerful and correct start in its work and obtain a good impetus which would permit it to work productively, with a high degree of efficiency.

Who is capable of bringing about such a beginning? Who can most quickly step over the routine conceptions and disagreements which, like a snowball, accumulate on disarmament negotiations as soon as these have begun? I should think that this must first of all lie on the shoulders of those who are invested with the greatest trust of the peoples and who have the full breadth of authority.

Guided by these considerations, the Soviet Government proposes that the work of the 18-Nation Committee be opened by the Heads of Government (State) of the countries represented in that Committee. For this purpose the Heads of Government would arrive in Geneva by March 14 and would themselves perform the most responsible and complex part of the work which awaits the 18-Nation Committee at the initial stage. Perhaps this idea will appear somewhat unusual, but, you will agree, it is fully justified by the greatness of the goal and by the circumstances in which the Disarmament Committee is beginning its activity.

Today, direct contacts among State leaders have firmly entered the practice of international relations: meetings, conferences, exchanges of messages, and personal participation in the work of the most representative international bodies.

And this is understandable. The more quickly distances between States are overcome and the more terrible weapons of annihilation become, the more the responsibility of State leaders increases and the more perspicacity and wisdom is required for resolving both important international problems and others, which may, at first glance, even appear to be secondary, inasmuch as they more often than not go down with their roots to the questions of war and peace. This is doubly true in respect to disarmament, which affects the most sensitive interests of States, their security interests, and requires for its solution particular circumspection, flexibility and bold exploration.

I shall not conceal the fact that I received the joint message sent by you and the United Kingdom Prime Minister at the very moment when I was working on this message to the Heads of Government of the States represented in the 18-Nation Disarmament Committee. It is a cause of satisfaction that our views go generally in the same direction. I fully share the thought you expressed about the personal responsibility of Heads of Government for the direction of disarmament negotiations and your suggestion that the state of affairs in the 18-Nation Committee be the subject of a broader exchange of views between us. However, why must we take only a half step and limit ourselves to being represented in the opening work of the Disarmament Committee by Ministers of Foreign Affairs? If one is to be consistent, then, proceeding from the considerations expressed by you, one will perforce arrive at the very proposal which is being advanced by the Soviet Government, namely, to begin the work of the Disarmament Committee at the highest level. The work of the 18-Nation Committee can be begun at the highest level even if not all the Heads of the Governments (States) members of the Committee wish or can take part; that need not be an obstacle to our participation in its work. It goes without saying that the Ministers of Foreign Affairs of our countries should also take part in the work of the 18-Nation Committee both with the Heads of Government and during the subsequent period of the work of the Committee.

Thus very many factors speak in favor of our proposal concerning participation of the Heads of Government in the work of the 18-Nation Committee. Of course, there may be people who will understand our proposal in the sense that the Soviet Union is allegedly again placing a Summit meeting on the agenda and who will begin deliberating whether or not the conditions for that meeting now exist. I should like to clarify right away that in this case it is not a matter of a Summit meeting, as it is usually understood, but rather of the Heads of State participating in the 18-Nation Committee created by the UN; nor is it a matter of considering a broad spectrum of international problems but a question of negotiating one specific problem—that of disarmament. And only one who is not at all interested in its solution can assert that conditions are not yet ripe for the consideration of the disarmament problem.

163

Obviously, one cannot reckon that the Heads
of State will be able immediately to accomplish in
Geneva such work that all that will remain will
be to sign a treaty on complete and general disarmament. But if as a result of their efforts a
proper direction to further negotiation is given
and if the contents of a treaty on general and
complete disarmament are outlined, even that
would be an enormous change for the better long
awaited by the peoples. I should think that it is
worthwhile, very much worthwhile, to undertake
such an attempt which, in the event of its success, something the Soviet Government genuinely
hopes for, promises to bring about a break-
through in international relations and bring
mankind nearer to the realization of its age-old
dream of peace.

It is no secret to anyone that frequently negotiations about increased military preparations
are being conducted at the Heads of State level.
But since this is so, then on what grounds can
one object to the holding of the initial meetings of
the 18-Nation Committee at the highest level in
order to make real efforts for the sake of such a
noble goal as disarmament! History would not
forgive us if we were to let go by the opportunity of considering the disarmament problem in
such an authoritative forum as a meeting of the
Heads of Government of 18 States especially conducted for that purpose.

I should like to hope that you will correctly
understand the motives which have prompted the
Soviet Government to propose that the work of
the 18-Nation Committee be begun at the level of

Heads of Government (State), and that you will have a positive attitude toward this proposal.

I have addressed myself with messages of a similar content to all the Heads of Government (State) of the countries represented in the 18-Nation Disarmament Committee.

Respectfully,

N. Khrushchev/3/

/1/Source: Department of State, Presidential Correspondence: Lot 66 D 204. Confidential. Another copy is in the Kennedy Library, National Security Files, Countries Series, USSR, Khrushchev Correspondence. Also printed in *Documents on Disarmament, 1962,* vol. I, p. 32.
/2/See Document 31.
/3/Printed from a copy that bears this typed signature.

". . . I was gratified you are thinking along the same lines as Prime Minister Macmillan and myself . . ."

33. Message From President Kennedy to Chairman Khrushchev

Washington, February 14, 1962./1/

DEAR MR. CHAIRMAN: In reading your letter of February 10, 1962/2/ I was gratified to see that you have been thinking along the same lines as Prime Minister Macmillan and myself as to the importance of the new disarmament negotiations which will begin in Geneva in March. I was gratified also to see that you agree that the heads of government should assume personal responsibility for the success of these negotiations.

The question which must be decided, of course, is how that personal responsibility can be most usefully discharged. I do not believe that the attendance by the heads of government at the outset of an 18-Nation conference is the best way to move forward. I believe that a procedure along the lines of that outlined in the letter which Prime Minister Macmillan and I addressed to you on February 7/3/ is the one best designed to give impetus to the work of the conference.

I agree with the statement which you have made in your letter that there exists a better basis than has previously existed for successful work by the conference. The Agreed Statement of Principles for Disarmament Negotiations which was signed by representatives of our countries on September 20, 1961 and which was noted with approval by the 16th General Assembly of the United Nations represents a foundation upon which a successful negotiation may be built.

As you have recognized, there still exist substantial differences between our two positions. Just one example is the Soviet unwillingness so far to accord the control organization the authority to verify during the disarmament process that agreed levels of forces and armament are not exceeded.

The task of the conference will be to attempt to explore this and other differences which may

166

exist and to search for means of overcoming them by specific disarmament plans and measures. This does not mean that the conference should stay with routine procedures or arguments or that the heads of government should not be interested in the negotiations from the very outset. It does mean that much clarifying work will have to be done in the early stages of negotiation before it is possible for Heads of Government to review the situation. This may be necessary in any case before June 1 when a report is to be filed on the progress achieved.

I do not mean to question the utility or perhaps even the necessity of a meeting of Heads of Government. Indeed, I am quite ready to participate personally at the Heads of Government level at any stage of the conference when it appears that such participation could positively affect the chances of success. The question is rather one of timing. I feel that until there have been systematic negotiations—until the main problems have been clarified and progress has been made, intervention by Heads of Government would involve merely a general exchange of governmental positions which might set back, rather than advance, the prospects for disarmament. It is for these reasons that I think that meetings at the highly responsible level of our Foreign Ministers as well as the Foreign Ministers of those other participating states who wish to do so would be the best instrument for the opening stages.

A special obligation for the success of the conference devolves upon our two Governments and that of the United Kingdom as nuclear powers. I therefore hope that the suggestion made in the letter of Prime Minister Macmillan and myself to you, that the Foreign Ministers of the three countries meet in advance of the conference in order to concert plans for its work, will be acceptable to the Soviet Government.

John F. Kennedy/4/

/1/Source: Department of State, Presidential Correspondence: Lot 66 D 204. No classification marking. The source text is a February 14 press release from the Office of the White House Press Secretary and is marked "immediate release." Another copy is in the Kennedy Library, National Security Files, Countries Series, USSR, Khrushchev Correspondence. Also printed in *Public Papers of the Presidents of the United States: John F. Kennedy, 1962*, pp. 132 -133; *Documents on Disarmament, 1962*, vol. I, pp. 36-38; and Claflin, *The President Wants To Know*, pp. 146-147.
/2/Document 32.
/3/See Document 31.
/4/Printed from a copy that bears this typed signature.

". . . we view the recent acts of harassment in the Berlin air corridors with very grave concern . . ."

34. Letter From President Kennedy to Chairman Khrushchev

Washington, February 15, 1962./1/

DEAR MR. CHAIRMAN: In order to permit the further development of the conversations between Ambassador Thompson and Foreign

Minister Gromyko, I have not answered directly your letter of December 13, 1961,/2/ nor the message which you sent me through my brother./3/ I had hoped that these conversations might lead to some more positive note on Germany and Berlin that could be further developed in this more direct and confidential channel.

It appears, however, that neither that series of conversations nor this channel is bringing our positions any closer together. The talks between Messrs. Thompson and Gromyko are tending to become more and more formal, with each side exchanging diplomatic messages restating their positions. Your communications to me still refer to the policy of "positions of strength" as though the West were in some way threatening the Soviet Union—and inasmuch as I am quite aware of the strength and determination of the Soviet people, and you, I am sure, are equally aware of our qualities, I would hope that we could dispense with this kind of exchange which is reminiscent of an earlier period in our relations.

It would seem today that neither of us knows very much more about the prospects for accommodation than we knew many months ago—i.e., you know that the West will not withdraw its troops from West Berlin or accept the stationing of Soviet troops there, and we know that you will not accept any arrangements for the city of Berlin as whole.

While these changes are thus not on the list of possible agreement, I should state again in this regard that it is not the Western powers who are seeking a change in the status of Berlin. While we do not consider the situation in Germany today to be satisfactory, we recognize that there is very little likelihood of effecting any basic change in the direction of Western aims, inasmuch as we exclude the employment of force to this end, and certainly prefer not to initiate any unilateral action that might provoke increased tension or fear. On the other hand, the Soviet Union also recognizes, I am sure, that it cannot unilaterally bring about a change in the existing situation which would result in damage to the rights, obligations and interests of the Allied powers and the people of West Berlin.

Both of us, therefore, however differently we may view the issues, are confronted with the same basic question: how to deal with the present state of affairs in a manner which will (1) avoid any shift favorable to one side and detrimental to the other, and (2) ensure a greater degree of stability and tranquillity in the entire German situation. I believe that if we take these two principles as a starting point, we might be able to see some light at the end of the tunnel.

Nevertheless it is increasingly clear that we hold wholly different views on what kind of solution would be best in the long run; and equally clear, therefore, that we must patiently expect the negotiations, exchanges and conferences required before agreement is reached to extend over a considerable period of time. Look how many months and years, for example, were spent in the talks on nuclear tests which, though as yet unproductive, covered an area where a potential agreement was no more urgently in the common interest of both sides. Fortunately, both you and I—or so I strongly believe—are able to take the long view, and to recognize our joint responsibility for patiently continuing the search for a joint solution—instead of taking some precipitate unilateral action that might endanger the peace that prevails in Germany now. While our negotiations should make whatever progress is possible and avoid undue delays, we should bear in mind, as I said to Mr. Adzhubei,/4/ that world conditions will look very differently to us three or five or seven years from now, as the result of evolutionary changes, or progress in disarmament or other areas.

For this reason I would hope that we would both take special pains to adhere to that principle, included in the disarmament principles on which we agreed at the UN last fall, which enjoined both sides to refrain, as the disarmament talks began, from any actions in the international field which might tend to increase tensions. As Ambassador Thompson has made clear, we view the recent acts of harassment in the Berlin air corridors with very grave concern; and it does not seem likely that serious progress could be made on these or other talks as long as one side is increasing tensions in this fashion.

I had understood, from my conversations with Mr. Adzhubei as well as my earlier talks with Mr. Gromyko, that both sides recognized the desirability of doing nothing which would increase the difficulties of peaceful negotiation. As you have stated in your letter, in politics just as in physics every action causes counteraction, so that every danger or pressure you place upon us is in effect adding to the dangers or pressures which the increased prospects of conflict signify for you. Moreover, the prospects for alleviating the other concerns which you have expressed and which I fully understand—a future excess of German nationalism and the proliferation of nuclear weapons, for example—are certain to be increased rather than diminished by each new increase in tension and pressure. I am certain that these concerns could be satisfactorily met if an understanding could be achieved—but further pressures on the West in Berlin only increase the pressure within France and the Federal Republic of Germany to build a greater military force, to secure an independent nuclear capacity and to adopt a more rigid attitude on any accommodation.

Another way to improve the prospects of an advance in these discussions would be to instruct our two representatives in Moscow to concentrate on concrete matters and avoid further generalized and repetitive statements of position. For example, Mr. Adzhubei, during our very interesting conversation of last January 30 here at the White House,/5/ suggested there might be some variation in the possibilities of an International Commission supervising access with East German participation. If further details on this possibility and other variations are forthcoming, they might be further explored by Ambassador Thompson and Foreign Minister Gromyko. This is the sort of fresh and concrete subject matter to which their time should be devoted.

I have written frankly of these matters in the

hope that you will respond in kind. I can assure you that I will continue to hold in the utmost secrecy any message or proposal sent through this channel, for I have always regarded it as a private and confidential means of communication, without all of the pressures which public communications bring to any question of this kind.

I realize that such an exchange, if successful, would represent a considerable departure from normal diplomacy. But, surely we both recognize that new situations require new methods of procedure. And I feel very strongly that we must make every effort and explore every possibility to avoid the development of a major crisis over Berlin, replete with all the dangers of war. To avoid such a development is, I know, your basic desire as well as mine; and I am convinced, as I believe you are, that if we can either find some modus vivendi in regard to Berlin or a more solid long-range agreement, this will open up the possibility of agreements on many other questions, including those mentioned in your communications through my brother—including the question of German frontiers, respect for the sovereignty of the GDR, prohibition of nuclear weapons for both parts of Germany, and the conclusion of a pact of non-aggression between NATO and the Warsaw powers.

I was particularly glad to read in your letter that you share our hopes for peace. It was in that spirit that I was pleased to talk again with your son-in-law, Mr. Adzhubei, and stress to him the importance of avoiding any threats to the peace in this area. I enjoyed meeting with him on this occasion, and I was very pleased to see your lovely daughter. I hope she enjoyed her visit, and that there will be an opportunity for similar visits in the years to come.

Sincerely,/6/

/1/Source: Department of State, Presidential Correspondence: Lot 77 D 163. No classification marking. The source text bears no drafting information, but on February 12 Bohlen had sent a "first draft" of this letter, which was the same in substance but 3 pages longer. (Ibid.) Another copy is ibid.: Lot 66 D 204, and in the Kennedy Library, National Security Files, Countries Series, USSR, Khrushchev Correspondence.
/2/Document 27.
/3/Document 30.
/4/In a conversation on January 31; see vol. XIV, pp. 780-784.
/5/According to a page attached to the source text, the rest of this paragraph was a redraft by Sorensen on February 15.
/6/Printed from an unsigned copy.

"One more step has been taken toward mastering the cosmos . . ."

35. Letter From Chairman Khrushchev to President Kennedy

Moscow, February 21, 1962./1/

DEAR MR. PRESIDENT: On behalf of the people of the Soviet Union and myself personally I congratulate you and the American people on the occasion of the successful launching of a spaceship with a man on board.

One more step has been taken toward mastering the cosmos and this time Lieutenant Colonel John Glenn, a citizen of the United States of America, has been added to the family of astronauts. The successful launching of spaceships signalizing the conquest of new heights in science and technology inspire legitimate pride for the limitless potentialities of the human mind to serve the welfare of humanity. It is to be hoped that the genius of man, penetrating the depth of the universe, will be able to find ways to lasting peace and ensure the prosperity of all peoples on our planet earth which, in the space age, though it does not seem so large, is still dear to all of its inhabitants.

If our countries pooled their efforts—scientific, technical and material—to master the universe, this would be very beneficial for the advance of science and would be joyfully acclaimed by all peoples who would like to see scientific achievements benefit man and not be used for "cold war" purposes and the arms race.

Please convey cordial congratulations and best wishes to astronaut John Glenn.

N. Khrushchev/2/

/1/Source: Department of State, Presidential Correspondence: Lot 66 D 204. No classification marking. The source text is a Department of State translation of a commercial cable from Moscow. The transliterated Russian text is ibid. Another copy of this message is in the Kennedy Library, National Security Files, Countries Series, USSR, Khrushchev Correspondence. Also printed in Department of State *Bulletin*, March 12, 1962, p. 411, and *Pravda*, February 24, 1962.

/2/Printed from a copy that bears this typed signature.

"I am instructing the appropriate officers of this Government to prepare new and concrete proposals . . ."

36. Telegram From the Department of State to the Embassy in the Soviet Union

Washington, February 21, 1962, 7:49 p.m./1/

1940. Please deliver following message immediately to Foreign Office for Khrushchev. Advise date time delivery. Message being released here 8 p.m., EST, February 21.

Begin Text.

Dear Mr. Chairman:

I thank you warmly for your message of congratulations on Colonel Glenn's successful space flight, and I welcome your statement that our countries should cooperate in the exploration of space./2/ I have long held this same belief and indeed put it forward strongly in my first State of the Union message.

We of course believe also in strong support of the work of the United Nations in this field and we are cooperating directly with many other countries individually. But obviously special opportunities and responsibilities fall to our two countries.

I am instructing the appropriate officers of this Government to prepare new and concrete proposals for immediate projects of common action, and I hope that at a very early date our representatives may meet to discuss our ideas and yours in a spirit of practical cooperation.

Sincerely,
John F. Kennedy.

End text.

Rusk

/1/Source: Kennedy Library, National Security Files, Countries Series, USSR, Khrushchev Correspondence. Official Use Only; Verbatim Text; Niact. Another copy is in Department of State, Presidential Correspondence: Lot 66 D 204. Also printed in *Public Papers of the Presidents of the United States: John F. Kennedy, 1962*, p. 158, and Department of State *Bulletin*, March 12, 1962, p. 411.
/2/Document 35.

"Frankly, I am surprised at the inconsistency in certain arguments advanced in your message."

37. Letter From Chairman Khrushchev to President Kennedy

Moscow, February 21, 1962./1/

DEAR MR. PRESIDENT: I have received your reply/2/ to the proposal of the Soviet Government that the work of the 18 Nation Disarmament Committee be initiated by the Heads of Government (State) of the countries represented in that Committee./3/ I must say frankly that I am chagrined by your negative attitude toward that proposal.

I shall not conceal that for a long time I have been hatching the thought of beginning the work of the disarmament committee at the highest level. And as I have already written, your message of February 7/4/ reached me at the very moment when I was working on a message on this question to the participants in the forthcoming negotiations, and that encouraged me even more.

However, after your reply to my message, the situation looks entirely different.

According to your message, you believe that even if participation by the Heads of Government in disarmament negotiations is possible it should be postponed until such time when definite progress has been reached in negotiations. But the legitimate question arises—who, then, can ensure with the greatest probability of success such progress, who can create a favorable situation for negotiations? Those who are vested with the full breadth of authority and who have the leading role in shaping policy or, on the other hand, those who are not vested with such responsibility and consequently are limited in their actions by previously determined instructions? It seems to me that there can be no two answers to this question. It is clear that the Heads of Government have much greater possibilities for this than anybody else.

The question may also be raised in the following manner: what is better, what will yield greater benefits—leadership exercised by the Heads of Government from a distance, or on the other hand when they themselves, having rolled up their sleeves, undertake the most difficult and give a correct orientation to the negotiations and ensure the progress of which you speak in your message.

As for me, the guiding precept of my life is to be where the main work is being done, where it is most important to obtain success. As I understand it, the position of Head of State requires this. If we remained far from Geneva, we would, whether we wanted it or not, have to consider the problems arising in the course of the disarmament negotiations merely as one among many other important matters with which officials in our position have to deal every day.

Frankly, I am surprised at the inconsistency in certain arguments advanced in your message. You agree that the Heads of Government should assume personal responsibility for the success of the disarmament negotiations to be opened in Geneva on March 14 of this year. But at the same time you propose that we wait until the Ministers of Foreign Affairs have achieved definite progress. Well, if, as was the case in the past, disarmament negotiations should fail to make progress—what then, should the Heads of State wash their hands? But then what will there be left of their personal responsibility for the course of negotiations, the importance of which you emphasize in your message? No, you can not really make these things jibe.

Nor do I find convincing your statement that before it becomes possible for the Heads of State to examine the situation arising in the disarmament negotiations there should be done a great deal of work in clarifying the positions of the sides. I shall go even further and say that your statement that something is yet to be fully clarified was extremely disappointing to me. The unfortunate thing lies precisely in the fact that so far disarmament has not gone beyond clarification of positions. How long can one continue to engage in eliciting, studying, and clarifying each other's positions, when negotiations, meetings and contacts at various levels, endless arguments and disputes, which have been going on for some fifteen years have been devoted essentially to this task.

Do we not have enough documents accumulated which give a complete schedule of the stages of disarmament, which set forth in all the details and minutia the methods of disarmament and the measures of control over it, in short, documents which quite clearly set forth the positions of the respective governments? Of course to this pile of documents more than one heap of papers could be added, but that would not reduce the existing armies even by one division or even one soldier, or armaments by a single rocket or a single bullet. The delay is caused not by the lack of clarity as to the questions where we disagree but rather as to where our views are closer together. For a long time now the problem has been not that of clarifying positions but rather of how the differences that have emerged should be overcome and how the path toward agreement should be paved. To say, then, that somebody still has to engage in clarifying positions—that is simply refusal to attempt to direct disarmament negotiations in a practical channel.

If the previous negotiations have really left certain questions unanswered, then this is apparently not at all because little effort has been made to clarify them. As I have already indicated, disarmament intrudes in the sacrosanctum of every state, in the area of ensuring their security, which, in the present world situation, everybody prefers to keep far from the eyes of others. A certain degree of trust and responsibility, without which it is impossible even to come close to the solution of disarmament problems, can therefore be reached only among those who bear the highest responsibility before the peoples of their countries for their security. And nobody else but the Heads of Government (State) bear such responsibility. Moreover, many of them would have to assume the leadership of the armed forces of their countries should times of trial occur. Nor is it necessary to prove that personal contacts among Heads of State can sooner lead to a better understanding of one another's aspirations, greater trust, and as a consequence—who knows—perhaps even new ideas.

If the experience of previous disarmament negotiations has been in any way useful, then it is primarily because it has demonstrated how few practical moves in the matter of disarmament one can expect without the most direct and businesslike participation in negotiations of officials holding the highest position. It is precisely because the positions of the participants in negotiations have been overly clarified that the conclusion arises by itself that only such officials can move the disarmament question off dead center, if, of course, all parties desire this.

Therefore neither Ministers, whatever esteem they may enjoy on the part of the governments and the peoples of their countries, nor other representatives, whatever their rank, will achieve anything if the Heads of State do not place the negotiations on a solid foundation, having demonstrated the will and desire to reach agreement on disarmament problems.

If you have no desire to head now the U.S. Delegation to the negotiations in the 18-Nation Committee and you use in explanation of your position such an artificial argument as lack of appropriate preparations, then this can only indicate that the resolution to reach agreement on disarmament questions has not yet become ripe in your mind. There unavoidably arises the question—is it not, Mr. President, because in your own mind you have already condemned the 18-Nation Committee to failure and are thinking in advance in terms of this Committee's failing to ensure the solution of the questions for which it has been created that you do not wish to go to Geneva now? It appears that the Western Powers are not yet ready for a disarmament agreement and you therefore think that for the time being it is more convenient to keep somewhat aside from the negotiations on this question. This is how all thinking people will have to assess your unwillingness to have the Disarmament Committee meet at the highest level.

To unload the work in the 18-Nation Committee on the Ministers of Foreign Affairs is to demonstrate clearly—and the Ministers will, of course, understand this—that the Heads of Government, the Heads of State do not wish to assume the responsibility for a possible failure of negotiations and prefer that all sins be charged to the Ministers.

It is easy to imagine what the situation may turn out to be in the final analysis. The Ministers of Foreign Affairs, who are busy people, transfer—and this happens quite frequently—the conduct of negotiations to persons of a somewhat lower rank and those, in turn, to officials who are another step lower on the ladder. This is how it turns out that negotiations, as a matter of fact, are finally conducted among bureaucrats. And then try to find out where that personal responsibility of the Heads of Government for negotiations, of which you now speak, actually is.

In your message of February 14, you, Mr. President, refer to the fact that there are substantial differences between our countries in the question of control of disarmament. That is correct, such differences exist, but what is their root? You seek the Soviet Union's agreement to the establishment of control not only over armed forces and armaments which are being reduced or destroyed under the agreement but also over that portion which will remain in the possession of states for the time being. It appears that the U.S. and its allies would like to have the Soviet Union place under control all of its armed forces and open up its entire defense system even before disarmament has really begun.

I must say frankly that with such an approach to the question of control you will attain nothing because to this we will not agree.

The Soviet Union is interested in the establishment of the strictest international control over the fulfillment of a disarmament agreement. If, for instance, we reach agreement on general and complete disarmament in stages, then, in our opinion, the implementation of all disarmament measures provided for each stage must be thoroughly verified. We want no less than anybody else to have assurance that the armaments and armed forces to be liquidated at a given stage are actually being liquidated or are being treated in such a manner as had been agreed in advance and recorded in the Treaty. This precisely is real, effective control over disarmament. On the other hand, you propose not control over disarmament but something entirely different.

Let us imagine that we are negotiating reduction of the armed forces of our countries by several divisions. We are prepared to agree to this.

184

But you demand that control be established not only over the disbanding of those divisions but over all of the armed forces and armaments that are at the disposal of states. This is really like the saying: "A ruble for a lamb with ten rubles for change".

In the age of rocket and nuclear weapons—and we have entered that age—masses of troops have far less significance than they had in the First and Second World Wars. Today, war would immediately assume an all-embracing universal character and its outcome would depend not on the actions of troops placed at the line dividing the belligerent parties but rather on the application of rocket and nuclear weapons, with which the deciding strike can be made even before mass armies have been mobilized and introduced into combat.

Thus, under modern conditions reduction of the armed forces of states by several divisions would in no way change the situation. Control over the military potential of states which you wish to obtain in exchange for an essentially insignificant reduction in armed forces, is another matter. The establishment of such control would yield a major strategic advantage to the state planning aggression.

The control proposed by the Western Powers, i.e., control actually before disarmament, we regard with full justification as espionage. Such control would permit an aggressive state to place its intelligence agents on the territories of peace-loving states and to collect information about their defense systems: and then to decide the question whether to agree to further disarmament or turn the course of events toward war.

We do not wish this. The Soviet Union strives for an honest agreement which would provide guarantee that neither during the process of disarmament nor after its completion a threat to the security of any state will arise. This is why we say—let us work out a treaty on general and complete disarmament under the strictest international control and let us implement the provisions of that treaty in stages so that control be commensurate with the disarmament steps undertaken. Having completed one stage of disarmament under control let us move to the implementation of the next stage, also under control. This is a sound, realistic approach to the question of control, and so far no one has been able to propose a better one.

In the initial stages of disarmament there will of course remain some armed forces and armaments which will temporarily be outside the sphere of international control. But will this change anything as compared with what we have today? After all, even now we know exactly the amounts of armaments at the disposal of the other side. Under staged disarmament we will reduce the armed forces and armaments by agreed increments and therefore the correlation of forces and the balance which has by now been established will not be disturbed. As to the amount of armed forces and armaments on which we will have no exact data after the completion of each stage, it will constantly decrease until it comes down to zero.

Where then, does this involve a threat to strategic security of states? There is no such threat and it cannot exist with this approach.

This can in no way be said about proposals of the Western Powers. In insisting that control march before disarmament the Western Powers only strengthen the suspicions that they are pursuing any possible objective other than disarmament. The impression is created that some kind of a disarmament game is being played. The peoples of the entire world demand disarmament, they want to throw off their shoulders the burden of military expenditures, to clear the horizon of the thunder clouds of war, while the Western Powers do not feel like disarming. This is why all sorts of plans appear, deliberately calculated to be rejected by the other side. All this resembles trickery which is resorted to in order to bury a live cause.

Now how else can one assess such recipes for disarmament as provide for the reduction in troops by one percent and for the extension of control over all of the other ninety-nine percent of armed forces? How else can one understand the refusal of the Western Powers to reduce the scope of their military preparations at least to some extent, for example, to liquidate the military bases in foreign territories and to withdraw their troops from Europe to the confines of their states. The Soviet Union is prepared even now to bring home its troops which are outside the country if the Western Powers do the same.

Where is there to be found here real partnership, understanding of the aspirations of the peoples, and the desire to remove the danger of a rocket and nuclear war, which would bring unbelievable disaster and suffering to all of mankind? There is not even a trace of that.

With this attitude on the part of the Governments of the Western Powers toward the cause of disarmament, where behind ostensible bustle around the questions of control there is being pushed somewhere into the backyard the main thing—disarmament of the military establishment of states, one has really to fear lest the new Committee is facing the sorry lot of its predecessors. If there is no desire to agree on a realistic basis, then obviously disarmament negotiations will amount to nothing whether the work of the Committee started with the participation of the Heads of Government or at the Foreign Minister level, or any other level.

I am not used to playing the hypocrite and hiding the truth in my pocket and therefore shall say without beating around the bush: Your reply message, Mr. President, as well as the message from Prime Minister Macmillan have generated in me the feeling that those journalists who see some special purposes in your proposal to begin the work of the 18-Nation Committee at the Foreign Minister level are perhaps right. They connect this proposal directly with the statement of the Governments of the United States and Great Britain about their intention to resume nuclear weapon tests in the atmosphere.

What is the reasoning of the journalists? They understand that the Soviet Union will not leave that aggressive action unanswered. The unrestrained desire on the part of the United States and Great Britain to increase their nuclear arsenal and to increase the destructive power of their nuclear weapons will unavoidably lead to the Soviet Union's being drawn into competition in the sphere of accumulation and perfection of nuclear weapons. It is understandable that the Soviet Union, which incidentally has conducted far fewer experimental nuclear explosions, will not wish to lag behind and will do everything to maintain its nuclear weapons at the proper level. As a result, swings will be set in motion to heights never seen before, raising the nuclear armaments race to ever-higher levels. Naturally, the peoples will place the responsibility for this on the Governments of the United States and Great Britain.

It is in connection with this that it is being said that in advancing the idea of conducting disarmament negotiations at the Ministerial level, the Governments of the United States and Great Britain sought somehow to paralyze the negative attitude of public opinion toward the planned resumption of nuclear tests and to sweeten the bitter pill by making a gesture in the direction of disarmament. This opinion became even stronger when the United States and Great Britain replied in the negative to the concrete, businesslike proposal of the Soviet Union to begin the work of the disarmament committee at the highest level with participation by the Heads of Government, a proposal that gives greater assurance of success in negotiations. As much as I would like to avoid unpleasant words—but the conclusion imposes itself that apparently there is some truth in such commentaries by journalists.

Where then is the matter going? We live in a time when science and technology are developing swiftly and new scientific and technological achievements are born literally not every day but every hour. Rocket and nuclear armaments are ever increasing and now both we and you already have thousands of units of such weapons. They are manned by many thousands of personnel and that number is ever increasing as the number of rockets increases. But the more people are assigned to the manning of lethal rockets and nuclear weapons, the greater the probability that the unexpected may occur. After all, there have already been cases in the United States where bombers on alert missions with a payload of nuclear bombs had accidents and fell to the ground causing considerable unpleasant consequences.

And is it really out of the question that something similar can happen not only with bombers but also with rockets equipped with thermonuclear warheads? In addition to all sorts of other reasons, this or that human being manning a rocket-launching site may suffer a mental breakdown and then an irreparable event would occur: A nuclear explosion would occur on the territory of another state. It would then be difficult to prove that this was the consequence of an accident and nothing more. Moreover, would there be time for any explanations or for the hearing of such explanations? The accidental launching of a rocket with a thermonuclear warhead could serve as a signal for a world-wide military catastrophe.

Hunters have a good unwritten rule: Even if you know that your gun is not loaded, never aim it in the direction of a human being, even for fun. It is not for nothing that they say that once in ten years even an unloaded gun goes off.

Comparatively recently there was a report in the press that the life of the great American writer Hemingway had been ended by an accidental shot while a shotgun was being cleaned. As great as this loss may be, still in this instance only one human being lost his life as a result of careless handling of a weapon. On the other hand an accident in handling rocket and nuclear weapons would bring about the death of millions upon millions of people, while many would be condemned to slow death as a result of radioactive contamination.

All this brings to mind once again that the leading officials of states, who bear the responsibility for the destinies of peoples, must realize the actual state of affairs which has already been brought about by the rocket and nuclear armaments race and to which this race is leading. General and complete disarmament, that is, complete destruction of all armaments, particularly nuclear, has become in our time a vitally necessary task, which stands above everything else. In the interests of the speediest solution of this task the Soviet Government has been and still is for having the 18-Nation Disarmament Committee begin its work at the highest level.

The search for agreement on disarmament problems requires that unnecessary punctiliousness be cast aside and that the interests of the cause, the interests of strengthening peace, be placed above everything else. This is why I should like to hope that you, Mr. President, have not yet said your last word concerning your participation in the negotiations in the 18-Nation Disarmament Committee.

The Soviet Government sincerely seeks to reach agreement on disarmament and has proposed with the best of intentions that the work of the 18-Nation Committee be begun at the highest level.

The Soviet Government believes that the proposals for general and complete disarmament under strict international control advanced by it provide a basis for reaching agreement without prejudice to any individual party and without advantage to any other party. Of course we are prepared to consider other proposals as well if they really will ensure the solution of the problem of general and complete disarmament.

If the Governments of the Western Powers desire agreement on disarmament problems—and the Soviet Union and the other socialist countries do wish to reach it—then one could definitely hope that negotiations with the participation of the Heads of Government will yield tangible results, and agreement will become possible. This would be a great honor to those who would have laid, at the beginning of the negotiations, the foundation for a future agreement and found ways of overcoming the existing difficulties. And what a great reward it would be for the Heads of Government, Heads of State, then to sign a treaty on general and complete disarmament and to become participants in an historic event which would remain in the memories of all mankind for ages to come.

Respectfully,

N. Khrushchev/5/

/1/Source: Department of State, Presidential Correspondence: Lot 66 D 204. No classification marking. The Russian-language text is ibid. Another copy is in the Kennedy Library, National Security Files, Countries Series, USSR, Khrushchev Correspondence. Also printed in *Documents on Disarmament, 1962,* vol. I, pp. 49-57. Soviet Charge d'Affaires Smirnovsky delivered this letter to the Department of State on February 22; for a memorandum of conversation, see vol. VII, pp. 324-325.
/2/Document 33.
/3/See Document 32.
/4/See Document 31.
/5/Printed from a copy that bears this typed signature.

"It was the resumption of testing by the Soviet Union which put this issue back into the context of the arms race . . ."

38. Telegram From the Department of State to the Embassy in the Soviet Union

Washington, February 24, 1962, 1:14 p.m./1/

1959. You should deliver following reply from Kennedy to Khrushchev's letter of February 21.

Begin Verbatim Text.

Dear Mr. Chairman:

I regret that in your message of February 21,/2/ you seem to challenge the motivations of Prime Minister Macmillan and myself in making our proposal of February 7/3/ that the forthcoming Disarmament Conference open at the Foreign Minister level. I believe that there can be a legitimate difference of opinion on the most effective and orderly way to make progress in the vitally important field of disarmament.

You have presented your own views and I do not wish to imply that they are motivated by anything other than your own conviction that the way you suggest is the best way to proceed. However, I must say that even though I have given the most careful thought to the considerations you advance, I continue to hold to my view that the personal participation in Geneva by the Heads of Government should be reserved until a later stage in the negotiations when certain preliminary work has been accomplished.

Indeed some of the statements you make reinforce my view in this respect. Your discussion of the control problem, for example, is based, in my view, on a fundamental misconception of the US position that can probably best be clarified in the light of discussion of specific verification requirements for specific disarmament measures. It is not true, as you allege, that the United States is seeking to establish complete control over national armaments from the beginning of the disarmament process. Our position is a quite simple one and it is that whatever disarmament obligations are undertaken must be subject to satisfactory verification. For example, if, as we have both proposed, there is an agreement to reduce the level of armed forces to a specified number, we must be able to ensure through proper verification mechanisms that this level is not exceeded. I do not propose here to discuss this subject at length. I wish merely to point out that this is the type of issue on which more work should be done before it can usefully be dealt with at a Heads of Government meeting.

If it were not for the existence of the Statement of Agreed Principles which was worked out so laboriously between representatives of our two countries last year, there might be greater force to your reasoning that Heads of Government should meet at the outset to set directions for the negotiations. In my view the Statement of Agreed Principles constitutes just the type of framework which would be the most that could be expected at this point from a meeting of the Heads of Government. Since this has already been done, I believe now we need to have our representatives do further exploratory work of a more detailed nature.

As I have said and as I now repeat, I think it is of the utmost importance that the Heads of Government of the major nuclear powers assume a personal responsibility for directing their countries' participation in and following the course of these negotiations. I can assure you that the Secretary of State would present my views with complete authority. Even so, I hope developments in the conference and internationally would make it useful to arrange for the personal participation of the Heads of Government before June 1. I do not, however, believe that this should be done at the outset and I must say frankly, Mr. Chairman, that I believe this view is well founded. I believe that to have such a meeting at this point would be to begin with the wrong end of the problem. The Heads of Government should meet to resolve explicit points of disagreement which might remain after the issues have been carefully explored and the largest possible measure of agreement has been worked out at the diplomatic level.

I continue to hope that you will agree to the proposed procedure which was set forth in Prime Minister Macmillan's and my initial letter of February 7. I believe that the replies which have been made by other prospective participants to your messages indicate a general support for this approach and I trust that you will give a favorable response.

I cannot conclude this letter without mentioning briefly the problem of nuclear testing. Since I assumed the office of President of the United States, the conclusion of a nuclear test agreement has been a primary objective of mine. The record of American participation in the negotiations on this subject has demonstrated fully the creative effort we made to achieve agreement. It must be understood that in the absence of an agreement which provides satisfactory assurance that all States will abide by the obligations they undertake, there is no real basis for securing a safe end to the competition in the development of nuclear weapons. It is strange for the Soviet Union, which first broke the truce on nuclear testing, now to characterize any resumption of testing by the United States as an aggressive act. It was resumption of testing by the Soviet Union which put this issue back into the context of the arms race and that consequently forced the United States to prepare to take such steps as may be necessary to insure its own security. Any such steps could not be characterized now as "aggressive acts." They would be matter of prudent policy in the absence of the effectively controlled nuclear test agreement that we have so earnestly sought.

In our February 7 message, the Prime Minister and I attempted to layout a further framework for the conduct of disarmament negotiations. We believe that in a preliminary meeting among the Foreign Ministers of the US, UK and USSR views could be exchanged and agreement reached on the three parallel approaches we suggested and on some of the procedural aspects which we might jointly recommend to guide the committee's work. Such a discussion, together with the Statement of Agreed Principles, could give a valuable direction and impetus to the committee's work.

Mr. Chairman, I think you agree that we must approach this meeting with utmost seriousness and dedication if we are to avoid a gradual drift to the same kind of aimless and propaganda-oriented talk which has characterized so much of past disarmament negotiations. This can be best achieved if we who are ultimately responsible for the positions we take, and our chief diplomatic officials, concern ourselves directly, as we are now doing, with this subject. I believe we should consider most carefully as we proceed when and how our actual participation at the conference table could be of most benefit. End Verbatim Text.

Text will be released after notice confirmation of delivery.

Rusk

/1/Source: Kennedy Library, National Security Files, Countries Series, USSR, Khrushchev Correspondence. Confidential; Priority. Repeated to USUN. Drafted by Ronald I. Spiers (ACDA), cleared by Kohler and Bohlen, and approved by Rusk. Another copy is in Department of State, Presidential Correspondence: Lot 66 D 204. Also printed in *Public Papers of the Presidents of the United States: John F. Kennedy, 1962*, p. 160, and in *Documents on Disarmament, 1962*, vol. I, p. 61.
/2/Document 37.
/3/See Document 31.

"Consequently, with your tests you will start a new stage in the race in the creation of deadly weapons."

39. Message From Chairman Khrushchev to President Kennedy

Moscow, March 3, 1962./1/

DEAR MR. PRESIDENT: I have carefully studied your message of February 25 last./2/ Having thought about the considerations advanced by you concerning the forthcoming negotiations in the 18-Nation Disarmament Committee, I continue to adhere to the conviction that personal participation of the most responsible state officials would be particularly necessary in the initial stage, and I repeat—precisely in the initial stage of negotiations, when their direction is being determined and, consequently, their outcome is being predetermined to no small degree.

You know that disarmament negotiations have been continuing for a good fifteen years, now becoming active, now dying out again, as if only to raise the hopes of peoples to destroy these hopes again. All sorts of methods of conducting such negotiations have been used: creation of various committees and subcommittees, commissions and subcommissions, discussion of disarmament questions in the halls of the UN, and exchange of views through diplomatic channels, but, as they say, the cart is still stuck.

To what conclusions, then, does this lead? First of all that it would be at least short-sighted again to rely on those methods that have already proven their uselessness in the past and, secondly that it is the direct duty of the states participating in disarmament negotiations to find new, more reliable methods for conducting such negotiations. This is what the Soviet Government did in addressing the Governments of all the countries included in the 18-Nation Committee with the suggestion that the work of that Committee be initiated at the highest level, with the participation of the Heads of State or Government.

Our proposal was dictated by only one thing: by the desire to free disarmament negotiations from the routine in which those negotiations became entangled as soon as they started and to pave the way for an agreement on general and complete disarmament. It would seem incontestable that those state leaders who are vested with the broadest authority and occupy the most responsible position in their country also have much greater possibilities of coping with these difficult tasks. Therefore we regret that our proposal to begin the work of the 18-Nation Committee at the highest level has not met with understanding on your part. The arguments advanced in your message are not capable of affecting the weighty and serious considerations which speak in favor of the fact that the course proposed by the Soviet Government is the best course.

You yourself note the necessity of approaching the forthcoming negotiations in the 18-Nation Committee with the utmost seriousness and purposefulness and have come out in favor of the leading state officials devoting undeviating attention to these negotiations. You also recognize that personal participation of the heads of state in disarmament negotiations may prove to be useful, although you adhere to the view that such participation should be deferred to a later stage in the negotiations. In this connection you express the hope that developments in the 18-Nation Committee and internationally will make it useful to arrange for the personal participation of the

Heads of Government before June 1 of this year.

Thus, as a result of the exchange of messages among the leading officials of states, general agreement has emerged with regard to the significance which the disarmament negotiations in the 18-Nation Committee are acquiring. It is no less important that everybody has now recognized the personal responsibility of the Heads of Government and State for the success of these negotiations and the necessity of direct participation by state officials of the highest level in the work of the 18-Nation Disarmament Committee. We take this as a definite step toward our position. In as much as the United States and some of our other partners in the forthcoming negotiations are not prepared for the time being to have the leading state officials participate personally in the work of the 18-Nation Disarmament Committee from the very beginning, we shall proceed, Mr. President, on the basis that we both, as well as the leading state officials of the other states members of the committee, will do that somewhat later.

The most important thing, of course, is to achieve results, to reach agreement on general and complete disarmament, and, at every stage of the negotiations, we shall do everything that depends on us in order to ensure their success. Of course, we are in favor of fully utilizing the possibilities of the Foreign Ministers, who can play their useful role if all the participants in the 18-Nation Committee demonstrate the desire to reach agreement on disarmament. The situation has developed in such a way that the ministers are to be the first to set sail after the creation of the 18-Nation Committee. Well then, let us wish them success! Of course there is no objection to the Ministers of Foreign Affairs of the United States and the United Kingdom meeting, as you have proposed, with the Minister of Foreign Affairs of the USSR before the 18-Nation Committee begins its work.

Your message also touches upon some questions relating to the substance of the disarmament problem. In this connection I would like to make some comments of my own.

First of all, a few words about verification. You believe that the considerations set forth with regard to this point in my preceding message are based on an "incorrect understanding of the United States position".

I would only be glad if the position of the United States Government on the question of control were actually to prove different from what we have understood it to be until now. Unfortunately, however, there are no facts which would provide grounds for such a conclusion.

The attitude of the Soviet Union toward the question of control has already been covered in my preceding message of February 21 last./3/ Is it really necessary to repeat that the Soviet Union is for an honest agreement on disarmament under strict international control. I can confirm once more our repeated statements to the effect that the Soviet Union is prepared to accept any proposals of the Western powers for control over disarmament if the Western powers accept our proposals for general and complete disarmament. If the United States Government is really concerned about how to reach agreement on the establishment of control over disarmament, then this readiness of ours removes a priori all difficulties, and there remains no room for substantive differences.

Now about nuclear weapon tests. Let us talk plainly. I have just familiarized myself with your statement in which you said that you had decided that the United States would conduct, beginning in the latter part of April of this year, a series of nuclear tests in the atmosphere. No matter how you try to justify this decision, there cannot be two views about the fact that it represents a new expression of the aggressive course in international affairs, a blow to the 18-Nation Committee which is just about to begin its work, and a blow to the forthcoming disarmament negotiations. No matter how much you may try to prove the contrary, the shock wave from the American nuclear tests in the Pacific Ocean will reach to the Palais des Nations at Geneva.

You state that it is absolutely necessary for the United States to conduct nuclear tests in order not to lag behind the Soviet Union. But you failed to utter even one word about the fact that the United States and its NATO allies have conducted many more nuclear test explosions than the Soviet Union. That is a fact, and everyone who does not have as his specific objective to misinform world public opinion must be aware of the fact that, if the United States and its allies add to the nuclear tests already conducted another series of such tests for the purpose of perfecting their nuclear weapons, then the Soviet Union will be faced with the necessity of conducting such tests of new types of its nuclear weapons as may be required under those conditions for the strengthening of its security and the maintenance of world peace. Several months ago the Soviet Union was already compelled to conduct such tests by the aggressive preparations of NATO states.

In asserting that the United States can in no way do without new nuclear weapons tests, you leave much unsaid. After all, the effect of the action planned by the Government of the United States cannot be limited merely to those nuclear explosions that have been planned by the United States itself or its allies in military blocs. No, you are beginning a new round of competition in the creation of ever more lethal types of nuclear weapons and you are unleashing, as it were, a chain reaction which, what is more, will become ever more violent. And this is what you called in your message a "reasonable policy!"

Where then, Mr. President, is logic? On the one hand you have repeatedly said in your statements that the United States is superior to the Soviet Union with regard to the power of nuclear weapons stockpiles. And your military are openly boasting that they can allegedly wipe the Soviet Union and all the countries of the Socialist camp from the face of the earth.

On the other hand, you now say that the United States has to conduct nuclear weapon tests for the alleged purpose of not lagging behind the Soviet Union in armaments. These two things clearly do not jibe.

Your entire logic, Mr. President, adds up to the fact that you have now announced the beginning of a new series of nuclear weapon tests by the United States. But quite recently you and the entire Western press argued—and argued correctly—how harmful such tests are. How much was said at that time about the fact that nuclear tests contaminate the air, soil, and vegetation, that radioactive fallout, together with contaminated plants reaches the organism of animals, and particularly cows, and that such fallout is transmitted through milk consumed by children.

But now it turns out that all these arguments were directed only against the Soviet Union and were used merely for the purpose of enabling the United States to preserve its superiority in certain types of armaments. And now that you yourself have come to the conclusion that you need to conduct such tests, where did those arguments go, where is that humanitarianism with which you were so generous in your statements and messages? After the United States has been accumulating huge stockpiles of nuclear weapons throughout the post-war years who is to profit from new nuclear tests? Apparently this is to the advantage of the monopolists who profit from the arms race, in whom the desire for profit outweighs all the dangers connected with the contamination of the atmosphere, the water, and the soil by radioactive fallout.

Yet the people of the United States of America, just as all the peoples of the world, are merely victims of the policy conducted in the interests of monopolistic capital. On the one hand, nuclear weapons are being produced, and the monopolies are profiting from their accumulation. On the other hand, by intimidating the world and not lastly the people of their own country with these weapons, the monopolists profit from the construction of shelters against such weapons and in this manner the monopolies trim the income of the population and mercilessly exploit the peoples.

It appears that all the talk about humanitarianism and love for one's fellow man ceases immediately as soon as the question of the monopolies' profits arises.

You and your allies in aggressive blocs justify your decision to begin new nuclear tests with references to the Soviet Union's having conducted such tests. This argument does not stand up because the whole world knows it was the United States of America which was the first to make the atom bomb and that the first nuclear tests were also conducted by the United States of America. Moreover, the United States has not only tested in the atmosphere but has also exploded atom bombs over the Japanese cities of Nagasaki and Hiroshima. It was precisely the United States and no one else who compelled the Soviet Union to embark on the creation and accumulation of nuclear weapons for the purpose of ensuring its security. Therefore, if one is to be logical and if one is to strive sincerely for mutual understanding and agreement on disarmament on the basis of equality, it is necessary to recognize that the Soviet Union should be the last to terminate nuclear weapon tests. The tests conducted by the

Soviet Union were from the very beginning merely actions in response to the nuclear arms race imposed by the Western powers.

In your statement, Mr. President, you said that the United States would begin tests in the atmosphere in the latter part of April. But in fact you have already given the order to begin tests and you are delaying them by six or eight weeks apparently only for the purpose of somehow preparing the world public to swallow this bitter pill.

Of course you yourself understand that, if the United States begins experimental explosions of nuclear weapons, then the Soviet Union, in the interest of ensuring its security and world peace, will unquestionably be compelled to respond to this too by conducting a series of new tests of its own, And we do have the technical capabilities for this, and they are at least equal to yours.

Consequently, with your tests you will start a new stage in the race in the creation of deadly weapons. But we would like to compete with the United States and other countries in the creation of better conditions for the peaceful life of mankind, and we would like to unite efforts with you in the cause of ensuring peace throughout the world.

The decision of the United States Government to conduct a new series of nuclear tests spurs on the perfecting and the stockpiling of precisely those types of modern weapons which represent the greatest danger: atomic and hydrogen bombs, nuclear warheads for rockets, and rockets themselves. But, one may ask, what is then to be negotiated in disarmament negotiations? Is it perhaps how many machine guns and rifles should be scrapped, or by how many soldiers we should reduce the guards around the arsenals where ever greater stockpiles of nuclear and rocket weapons will continue to accumulate?

Perhaps the Soviet Union is expected to give an answer as to whether it is prepared, before the United States begins its nuclear tests in April, to agree to the provisions already rejected by us—of a treaty that would, under the guise of international control over the cessation of tests, lead to the creation of a ramified system of intelligence and espionage? I hope that this is not expected of us; otherwise that would very much smack of atomic blackmail. I am sure that you yourself know full well that such methods in dealing with the Soviet Union have not yielded any results today, nor will they tomorrow.

Thus, as a result of the decision of the United States Government to conduct a new series of nuclear tests, state officials, particularly of those countries which bear the main responsibility for the preservation of peace are faced with very serious questions including the question of the prospects which await the 18-Nation Disarmament Committee. I consider it my duty to tell you frankly about all this.

I am convinced that an end can be put to the unrestrained increase in the power of nuclear weapons. It is precisely this objective that we pursue in our recent proposals for the cessation of nuclear weapons tests, with which you are familiar. It is conclusion of an agreement on the cessation of nuclear tests, not their resumption, that would be a demonstration of the reasonableness in policy of which you speak in your message.

Respectfully,

N. Khrushchev/4/

/1/Source: Department of State, Presidential Correspondence: Lot 66 D 204. No classification marking. Other copies are in the Kennedy Library, National Security Files, Countries Series, USSR, Khrushchev Correspondence, and ibid., President's Office Files, USSR. A different translation is printed in *Documents on Disarmament, 1962,* vol. I, pp. 75-81.
/2/See Document 38.
/3/Document 37.
/4/Printed from a copy that bears this typed signature.

"Our object now must be to make real progress toward disarmament and not engage in sterile exchanges of propaganda."

40. Letter From President Kennedy to Chairman Khrushchev

Washington, March 5, 1962./1/

DEAR MR. CHAIRMAN: I have received your message of March 3,/2/ and I am glad to know of your agreement that the meeting in Geneva on March 14 should be opened by Foreign Ministers. I am particularly glad that Mr. Gromyko will be able to join with Lord Home and Secretary Rusk before the meeting for preliminary discussions; our hope is that these conversations might begin on March 12. It will be the purpose of the representatives of the United States, headed by Secretary Rusk, to make every possible effort to find paths toward disarmament.

Our object now must be to make real progress toward disarmament, and not to engage in sterile exchanges of propaganda. In that spirit, I shall not undertake at this time to comment on the many sentiments in your letter with which, as I am sure you know, the United States Government cannot agree. Let us, instead, join in giving our close personal support and direction to the work of our representatives, and let us join in working for their success.

Sincerely yours,
John F. Kennedy/3/

/1/Source: Department of State, Presidential Correspondence: Lot 66 D 204. No classification marking. The source text is a March 6 press release from the Office of the White House Press Secretary and is marked "immediate release." Another copy is in the Kennedy Library, National Security Files, Countries Series, USSR, Khrushchev Correspondence. Also printed in *Public Papers of the Presidents of the United States: John F. Kennedy, 1962*, pp. 193-194.
/2/Document 39.
/3/Printed from a copy that bears this typed signature.

"The exploration of space is a broad and varied activity and the possibilities of cooperation are many."

41. Letter From President Kennedy to Chairman Khrushchev

Washington, March 7, 1962./1/

DEAR MR. CHAIRMAN: On February twenty-second [21] last/2/ I wrote you that I was instructing appropriate officers of this Government to prepare concrete proposals for immediate projects of common action in the exploration of space. I now present such proposals to you.

The exploration of space is a broad and varied activity and the possibilities for cooperation are many. In suggesting the possible first steps which are set out below, I do not intend to limit our mutual consideration of desirable cooperative activities. On the contrary, I will welcome your concrete suggestions along these or other lines.

1. Perhaps we could render no greater service to mankind through our space programs than by the joint establishment of an early operational weather satellite system. Such a system would be designed to provide global weather data for prompt use by any nation. To initiate this service, I propose that the United States and the Soviet Union each launch a satellite to photograph cloud cover and provide other agreed mete-

orological services for all nations. The two satellites would be placed in near-polar orbits in planes approximately perpendicular to each other, thus providing regular coverage of all areas. This immensely valuable data would then be disseminated through normal international meteorological channels and would make a significant contribution to the research and service programs now under study by the World Meteorological Organization in response to Resolution 1721 (XVI) adopted by the United Nations General Assembly on December 20, 1961.

2. It would be of great interest to those responsible for the conduct of our respective space programs if they could obtain operational tracking services from each other's territories. Accordingly, I propose that each of our countries establish and operate a radio tracking station to provide tracking services to the other, utilizing equipment which we would each provide to the other. Thus, the United States would provide the technical equipment for a tracking station to be established in the Soviet Union and to be operated by Soviet technicians. The United States would in turn establish and operate a radio tracking station utilizing Soviet equipment. Each country would train the other's technicians in the operation of its equipment, would utilize the station located on its territory to provide tracking services to the other, and would afford such access as may be necessary to accommodate modifications and maintenance of equipment from time to time.

3. In the field of the earth sciences, the pre-

cise character of the earth's magnetic field is central to many scientific problems. I propose therefore that we cooperate in mapping the earth's magnetic field in space by utilizing two satellites, one in a near-earth orbit and the second in a more distant orbit. The United States would launch one of these satellites, while the Soviet Union would launch the other. The data would be exchanged throughout the world scientific community, and opportunities for correlation of supporting data obtained on the ground would be arranged.

4. In the field of experimental communications by satellite, the United States has already undertaken arrangements to test and demonstrate the feasibility of intercontinental transmissions. A number of countries are constructing equipment suitable for participation in such testing. I would welcome the Soviet Union's joining in this cooperative effort which will be a step toward meeting the objective, contained in United Nations General Assembly Resolution 1721 (XVI), that communications by means of satellites should be available to the nations of the world as soon as practicable on a global and non-discriminatory basis. I note also that Secretary Rusk has broached the subject of cooperation in this field with Minister Gromyko and that Mr. Gromyko has expressed some interest. Our technical representatives might now discuss specific possibilities in this field.

5. Given our common interest in manned space flights and in insuring man's ability to survive in space and return safely, I propose that we

pool our efforts and exchange our knowledge in the field of space medicine, where future research can be pursued in cooperation with scientists from various countries.

Beyond these specific projects we are prepared now to discuss broader cooperation in the still more challenging projects· which must be undertaken in the exploration of outer space. The tasks are so challenging, the costs so great, and the risks to the brave men who engage in space exploration so grave, that we must in all good conscience try every possibility of sharing these tasks and costs and of minimizing these risks. Leaders of the United States space program have developed detailed plans for an orderly sequence of manned and unmanned flights for exploration of space and the planets. Out of discussion of these plans, and of your own, for undertaking the tasks of this decade would undoubtedly emerge possibilities for substantive scientific and technical cooperation in manned and unmanned space investigations. Some possibilities are not yet precisely identifiable, but should become clear as the space programs of our two countries proceed. In the case of others it may be possible to start planning together now. For example, we might cooperate in unmanned exploration of the lunar surface, or we might commence now the mutual definition of steps to be taken in sequence for an exhaustive scientific investigation of the planets Mars or Venus, including consideration of the possible utility of manned flight in such programs. When a proper sequence for experiments has been determined, we might share responsibility for the necessary projects. All data would be made freely available.

I believe it is both appropriate and desirable that we take full cognizance of the scientific and other contributions which other states the world over might be able to make in such programs. As agreements are reached between us on any parts of these or similar programs, I propose that we report them to the United Nations Committee on the Peaceful Uses of Outer Space. The Committee offers a variety of additional opportunities for joint cooperative efforts within the framework of its mandate as set forth in General Assembly Resolutions 1472 (XIV) and 1721 (XVI).

I am designating technical representatives who will be prepared to meet and discuss with your representatives our ideas and yours in a spirit of practical cooperation. In order to accomplish this at an early date, I suggest that the representatives of our two countries who will be coming to New York to take part in the United Nations Outer Space Committee meet privately to discuss the proposals set forth in this letter.

Sincerely,/3/

/1/Source: Kennedy Library, National Security Files, Countries Series, USSR, Khrushchev Correspondence. No classification marking. Other copies are ibid., President's Office Files, USSR, and Department of State, Presidential Correspondence: Lot 66 D 204. Also printed in *Public Papers of the Presidents of the United States: John F. Kennedy, 1962*, pp. 244-245, and Claflin, *The President Wants To Know*, pp. 154-157.
/2/See Document 36.
/3/Printed from an unsigned copy.

"But history does not always develop as the statesmen foresee."

42. Letter From Chairman Khrushchev to President Kennedy

Moscow, March 10, 1962./1/

DEAR MR. PRESIDENT, I have received your message on the German affairs/2/ and have closely studied the U.S. Government's memorandum handed by your Ambassador to the Soviet Foreign Minister on March 6./3/ I regret that after so many meetings of our representatives and in spite of our confidential communication, the negotiations on the questions relating to German peaceful settlement do not make any progress, to put it mildly. I have the impression that the American side has not got rid of the preconception that under the peaceful settlement which we seek somebody takes something, somebody gives—one takes an orchard and gives an apple, or sells the same horse twice. To be frank, I simply do not understand such an approach to the appraisal of the meaning of our negotiations.

Perhaps the reason for that is that we look at things from different angles, that we view the situation and the causes that have brought it about in a different way and consequently we have different views on the methods of eliminating the existing tension. If you could distract yourself from the notions so deeply rooted overseas and look at the situation in the way we see it after all we have lived through, you would probably see for yourself that in a German peaceful settlement nobody sells or buys anything, nobody trades unequal values.

No, from the point of view of common sense the situation here is quite clear. A terrible blood-shedding war took place. The peoples of our countries fought shoulder-to-shoulder against the common enemy—aggressive Hitlerite Germany. By a supreme effort and at a cost of countless losses we achieved the goal—defeated the enemy. By right of conquerors the four Allied Powers—the USSR, the USA, Britain and France—occupied temporarily, till the peace treaty is signed, the territory of Germany who had unleashed World War II.

As a heritage from our predecessors we have got a delimitation of our troops, which was not quite reasonable, and the division of Berlin into four parts. I was told that when at the end of the war the plans of occupation of Germany were discussed at the European Advisory Commission the British proposed to seat the Allied Control Council not in Berlin but in a small town at the juncture of the three occupation zones. That proposal motivated by practical considerations was not accepted and it was decided to seat the Control Council for symbolic reasons, in the capital of defeated Hitlerite Germany.

Nobody could then envisage, of course, that there would be two Germanies and the people acted at the time on the basis of the requirements of organization of military occupation. It may serve as a certain excuse for those who adopted decisions at that time.

217

But history does not always develop as the statesmen foresee. In reality it turned out that there exist two Germanies. Neither you, Mr. President, nor I know for how long the two German states that emerged on the ruins of the Reich will exist, if they ever unite. And our sympathies for these states are not quite the same: you sympathize with social and political system of the FRG, and I naturally sympathize with the German Democratic Republic as a socialist state.

In addition there exists West Berlin. The population of this city lives under old capitalist order while around it—on the territory of the GDR— socialist order has been established. And here we are looking for a solution—how to ensure peaceful coexistence under these circumstances.

You are well aware, Mr. President, that because of the absence of peaceful settlement and the continuation of occupation West Berlin has for many years been causing serious and dangerous frictions between us. I will not conceal that when you insist on keeping your troops in West Berlin, we understand it as an expression of a desire to preserve a NATO beachhead and military base against us inside the GDR. We entered Berlin as allies but we are not allies any longer. Moreover— we are in different military blocs—you are in the North Atlantic bloc, we are in the Warsaw Treaty Organization—organization of socialist countries. These two groups are antagonistic because the NATO countries have formed their bloc against socialist countries. To protect our interests we had to set up a defensive Warsaw Treaty Organization. What was left to be done?

You note that the present situation in Germany is not satisfactory. This is our point of view too. And what can we do now? Once upon a time, so the story goes, two goats met head to head on a narrow bridge across an abyss. They would not give the way to each other and down they fell. They were stupid and stubborn animals.

But if we fail now to show sober understanding of the situation and do not realize that we have to pass by each other in a friendly way and not to collide at the place where, as you yourself emphasized, our essential interests do not cross—then it will be difficult to take a reasonable decision which would permit both sides to live calmly.

You often call West Berlin a stumbling block and say that until recently everything was allegedly all right there. When we propose to sign a peace treaty and to create a free demilitarized city in West Berlin granting its population guarantees of free and independent life you assert that this is abnormal. It means, that situation can be considered normal only when your troops are stationed in West Berlin as occupants, when the state of war is preserved there, and you do not want to participate in concluding a peace treaty. But could it really be considered normal? This is against common sense.

The Soviet Union proceeds from the necessity to find such a solution which would not cause damage to either side; we must solve this whole problem amicably and, having solved it, not collide with each other in the future. In short, it is necessary to untie knots which create frictions between our states.

I do not know, Mr. President, what else you could suggest as a solution of this problem. My colleagues and I could not find anything better for the improvement of post-war relations other than the conclusion of a German peace treaty and the normalization of the situation in West Berlin on this basis. To use the language of your representatives, we do not sell or buy this city as a horse. We do not want to own this horse and it is not your horse after all. It belongs to none of us.

West Berlin has turned out to be a capitalist island in the midst of socialist countries. So, what! Let it remain such—we do not want to seize this island or to liquidate the capitalist order which exists on it. Let it be fixed what has been given by history.

You write in your message that two principles must be taken as a starting point: (1) to avoid any shift favorable to one side and detrimental to the other, and (2) to ensure a greater degree of stability and tranquility in the entire German situation. If one adds to this that it is also necessary to take into consideration the real situation in Germany, i.e. the existence of the two German states—then one can say that these very principles form the basis of the Soviet proposals on the conclusion of a German peace treaty. The peace treaty should fix the situation which really exists, should not allow to upset the established balance and should secure stable peace and tranquility in Europe and not only in Europe.

One of the important aspects of such solution is the respect for the sovereignty of the German

Democratic Republic. No one demands from the Western powers to do more than observe generally adopted norms of the international law and international practice with regard to the GDR. One cannot ignore the dignity and sovereign rights of a state, especially if one wants to use the routes of communications crossing its territory as well as its services, if a display of good will is expected from it. And it is impossible to achieve a peaceful solution by pushing aggressive circles of the FRG to still new aggravations of the situation in the center of Europe.

You write that both sides should refrain from actions which would burden the proceeding negotiations. This is a right idea. Unfortunately, the Western powers are still trying in everything—both in major and in minor matters—to ignore and tread on the rights of the GDR. The NATO Council—not without the US participation, one can assume—has even adopted a special decision recommending the members of this bloc to deprive the citizens of the GDR of the possibility to have normal contacts with many countries of the world. But what if the GDR in response to such a defiant decision forbade the citizens of the NATO countries to go and to fly to the GDR or anywhere through its territory? The Western powers, evidently, would not like it, but that would be the exercise by the German Democratic Republic of its sovereign right. Why, then, do the USA and its allies consider it possible to hold such a position towards the German Democratic Republic?

Or, perhaps, one should regard as a contribution to the solution of the questions discussed by us the endless and—let us call a spade a spade— provocative visits by politicians of the FRG and other NATO countries to West Berlin? I do not wish to go into polemics now and therefore I will not refer to many well known facts.

You, Mr. President, in your message, and also the US Ambassador when he called on the Minister of Foreign Affairs of the USSR touched upon the question of the flights of Soviet aircraft in the air routes leading to West Berlin over the territory of the GDR. In so doing the American side tries to create an impression as if the Soviet aircraft make "aggressive harassment" to the flights of the aircraft of the USA, Britain and France to West Berlin. I see no necessity to dwell on this question: the actual situation and our position are undoubtedly well known to the US Government. This position is based entirely on the corresponding international agreements and on the practice of use of these air routes.

There seems to be somebody's hand in this artificial heating up of the atmosphere around the Berlin air routes. To our mind, the best thing to do would be not to encourage certain hot-heads in the NATO, especially among the military, but to cool them off so that they realize at last that no instigating actions can change the situation and deprive the Soviet Union and the German Democratic Republic of what they possess. Abandoning by the Western powers of their attempts to violate the lawful interests of the GDR and the USSR would constitute that very abstention from unilateral actions, creating the danger of outbreak of serious incidents, which the US Government calls for.

Generally speaking, it is very difficult to find in the document handed by Ambassador Thompson on March 6 a desire to facilitate an agreement. There is, however, a statement in it to the effect that the US stands for the achievement of a just and peaceful settlement of disputed questions dividing our countries. This statement is correct, but, unfortunately, it is not substantiated in the negotiations in order to achieve the necessary agreement.

I would not like to leave anything unclear— one way or another we will sign a German peace treaty. I have already said in Vienna and repeat it now that if there is no other choice we will make use of the US example and the lesson which was taught us by it in case with Japan. Some hotheads occupying official positions in the USA are threatening us with various misfortunes, but I think they are more clever in their doings than in their words because only suicides can now threaten with war but suicides are always insane people. I, for myself, consider that our counterparts with whom we conduct conversation are mentally normal people and can realistically evaluate and understand what it would mean to attack the Soviet Union or another country.

Some people allege that we are attacking someone, demanding a peaceful German settlement. But no sane person can consider as an attack the talks on the conclusion of a peace treaty. And the conclusion of a peace treaty means putting an end not only to the state of war but also to the state of hostility which results from an unaccomplished peaceful settlement.

I believe that we, the men vested with great trust and responsibility by our peoples, should understand all this correctly and should oppose opinions which sometimes push us to the wrong way. To say it straight: let us not frighten each other with words. We have seen enough of frightening. You, Mr. President, participated in the World War II, I participated not only in that war. Both of us are aware what war means and as the leaders of states we know what military means are now at the disposal of the USSR and the USA. Let us not count by pieces who has more or who has fewer modern means of mass destruction. Each of our countries has already stock-piled more than enough means to inflict an irreparable devastating blow.

The Soviet Union intends to conclude a German peace treaty. If we do not find common language with you and you yourself do not want to take part in the peaceful settlement then the Soviet Union and other states will sign the peace treaty with the GDR.

My colleagues and I have much pondered— how to bring closer our positions on the questions under discussion including the problem of ensuring a free access to West Berlin. Your recent letter, in which certain ideas on this point are expressed, strengthened my intention to share with you the considerations that we have arrived at on the creation of an international organ on the access to West Berlin. I hope that the ideas that I am expressing here will be received with good will, without prejudice.

Specifically I have in mind the following:

We are prepared to meet halfway the desire expressed by you and to agree to the creation of a special international organ on the access to West Berlin for the period of time that will be defined by the agreement between us. The organ that I have in mind would act as an arbiter if difficulties appeared during the practical implementation of the agreements on free access to and from West Berlin. It would not be empowered with any administrative functions which would give it authority to directly regulate traffic or set its own regulations on the traffic routes connecting West Berlin with the outside world because this is a prerogative of the German Democratic Republic. In brief, any talk of an organ of the kind proposed by the American side at the negotiations in Moscow, which would be a kind of state within state is out of question. Such situation would be in basic contradiction with the most elementary concepts of respect for the sovereignty of states. From the remarks made by the American side you also, it seems to me, see the necessity to take this aspect of the matter into consideration.

Naturally, the creation of the international organ on the access to West Berlin that I have in mind is possible only under the condition that the troops which are now stationed there by virtue of occupation are withdrawn from West Berlin as a result of the conclusion of a peace treaty. We consider that for West Berlin itself it would be calmer and better if there were no foreign troops stationed there at all. However, you say, you have some doubts—would not some harm be done to the population of West Berlin on the part of the GDR. Although we have repeatedly explained that the GDR does not and cannot have such aims, we are nevertheless ready to agree to stationing in West Berlin for some period of time, let us say for 3-5 years, symbolic contingents of troops of the UN or neutral countries.

All this, of course, is connected with the transformation of West Berlin into a free demilitarized city and with the simultaneous achievement of an agreement on final legalization and consolidation of the existing German borders and also on other questions which are well known to you and which you mention in your message.

Such an arrangement could then be fixed in a peace treaty with the German Democratic Republic (or in an annex to it), which will be concluded by the Soviet Union and a number of other states, if the Western powers have definitively decided that at the present time they will not take part in a German peaceful settlement.

Under an agreed solution of all these problems a part of which would be an agreement on the creation of an international organ on the access to West Berlin, such access through the territory of the GDR would be exercised on the basis of agreements, that is with the observance of usual regulations and formalities which are applied to the transit through the territory of sovereign states. We know that the GDR is ready to assume in an appropriate form the obligations providing for an unimpeded access to and from West Berlin.

Should any complications or frictions in the exercise of a free access to West Berlin arise, the last word would be with the international organ—arbiter of which we have said above.

The international organ would include, first of all, the four powers—the USSR, the US, Britain and France. Thus the Soviet Union would act in capacity of a guarantor of a free and uninterrupted access to West Berlin to which, judging by everything, the Western powers attach particular importance. As to other possible participants of the international organ, this question could be solved later by the agreement of the parties.

What is the advantage of a decision that I have just outlined? In a sense this is an alloy of the two positions—American and Soviet. On one hand, the Soviet Government, though it is not so simple for us, agrees to the creation of an international organ on access. On the other hand, an agreement will be reached—if the US is not ready yet to conclude a peace treaty with both German states—that with the conclusion by the Soviet Union and by a number of other states of a peace treaty with the GDR the situation in West Berlin is normalized on this basis by transforming it into a free demilitarized city in accordance with our mutual agreement, and other questions which you know are being solved. That would be a great victory for the cause of consolidating peace and easing tension.

This is a reasonable proposal and if we could reach an agreement on its basis it would help us to take off the existing heat in international relations. Our proposal is a concession to you. We do not want to create difficulties for you, Mr. President, and your country because in your country there are hot-heads; maybe there are some among your allies too. These questions are correctly understood in our country and by our allies. Let us leave the troops of the UN or neutral countries in a free city of West Berlin for 3-5 years to allow the nerves to cool down during this period of time and then the whole situation will look in a quite different light.

I hope that the thoughts, expressed by me, will allow us to concentrate our attention in the course of the talks on the main questions and to achieve a necessary progress in the nearest future.

It was my intention to dwell upon in this message only the German peace treaty. But in the meantime I was informed about the confidential conversation with your brother, Robert Kennedy./4/

He said that since we had not achieved any progress on Berlin question, you, Mr. President, consider it necessary to make an effort to find the areas wherein the soonest achievement of an agreement with the Soviet Union is possible. And you, according to Mr. Robert Kennedy, think that such area is the disarmament problem and, first of all, the question of the nuclear test ban.

I would have understood such a position of yours, let us say, a few days ago. But, how, may I ask you, should we understand it now, when you have made a decision to resume nuclear weapon tests/5/ and especially on the eve of the conference where we are to deal with the disarmament questions. I have expressed my attitude towards your decision with full frankness in my message of March 3./6/ What was said there may seem harsh to you, but had I given another evaluation of such a step by the US Government I would have been simply insincere.

Your brother expressed the thought that our Ministers should discuss at Geneva the possibilities of an accommodation on the question of the nuclear test ban. As you already know from my recent message we have agreed that our Minister will participate in the work of 18 nation conference though I do not conceal that if you start series of nuclear explosions, it will certainly not increase chances for success in the Committee's work. We, you and I, must look at the course of events realistically.

Your brother said that you, Mr. President, would like to have a summit meeting, which could be prepared in advance by the Ministers of Foreign Affairs or through diplomatic channels. I also would believe that such a meeting with you would be useful if an accommodation on a number of questions is reached before it by our Ministers, that is if the questions are prepared for their final discussion, approval and formalizing at the meeting of the Heads of State. I am always ready for such a meeting in order to ensure a necessary accommodation. When I am speaking about such a meeting at the highest level I believe that both our peoples are equally interested in it. After all, when the fate of the mankind is at stake, we as statesmen must use all the opportunities to justify the great trust

placed upon us. It certainly happens sometimes
that efforts of Ministers alone are not enough
and then for the sake of success and in the interests of peace the heads of state and government
have to join the effort.

Our new Ambassador, A.F. Dobrynin, will soon
arrive in Washington. I recommend him to you
and I am confident that he will represent the
Soviet Union in your country well. He enjoys the
full confidence of the Soviet Government and my
full confidence. Whenever you need to convey
something to me in a confidential way he will be
able to transmit this to me personally.

I would like to thank you for your kind and
warm words passed to me through A.I. Adzhubei
and in my turn to wish you and your family success and good health.

Sincerely,

N. Khrushchev/7/

/1/Source: Department of State, Presidential
Correspondence: Lot 66 D 204. No classification marking.
Another copy is in the Kennedy Library, National Security
Files, Countries Series, USSR, Khrushchev Correspondence.
/2/Document 34.
/3/Regarding this memorandum, see vol. XIV, pp. 859-862.
/4/Not further identified.
/5/On March 2 President Kennedy had authorized the
resumption of nuclear testing.
/6/Document 39.
/7/Printed from a copy that bears this typed signature.

"Thus, Mr. President, do we conceive of—shall we say—heavenly matters."

43. Letter From Chairman Khrushchev to President Kennedy

Moscow, March 20, 1962./1/

DEAR MR. PRESIDENT: Having carefully familiarized myself with your message of March 7/2/ of this year, I note with satisfaction that my communication to you of February 21/3/ containing the proposal that our two countries unite their efforts for the conquest of space has met with the necessary understanding on the part of the Government of the United States.

In advancing this proposal, we proceeded from the fact that all peoples and all mankind are interested in achieving the objective of exploration and peaceful use of outer space, and that the enormous scale of this task, as well as the enormous difficulties which must be overcome, urgently demand broad unification of the scientific, technical, and material capabilities and resources of nations. Now, at a time when the space age is just dawning, it is already evident how much man will be called upon to accomplish. If today the genius of man has created space ships capable of reaching the surface of the moon with great accuracy and of launching the first cosmonauts into orbit around the earth, then tomorrow manned spacecraft will be able to race to Mars and Venus, and the farther they travel the wider and more immense the prospects will become for man's penetration into the depths of the universe.

The greater the number of countries making their contribution to this truly complicated endeavor, which involves great expense, the more swiftly will the conquest of space in the interests of all humanity proceed. And this means that equal opportunities should be made available for all countries to participate in international cooperation in this field. It is precisely this kind of international cooperation that the Soviet Union unswervingly advocates, true to its policy of developing and strengthening friendship between peoples. As far back as the beginning of 1958 the Soviet Government proposed the conclusion of a broad international agreement on cooperation in the field of the study and peaceful use of outer space and took the initiative in raising this question for examination by the United Nations. In 1961, immediately after the first space flight by man had been achieved in the Soviet Union, we reaffirmed our readiness to cooperate and unite our efforts with those of other countries, and most of all with your country, which was then making preparations for similar flights. My message to you of February 21, 1962 was dictated by these same aspirations and directed toward this same purpose.

The Soviet Government considers and has always considered the successes of our country in the field of space exploration as achievements not only of the Soviet people but of all mankind. The Soviet Union is taking practical steps to the end that the fruits of the labor of Soviet scientists shall become the property of all countries. We widely publish notification of all launchings of satellites, spaceships and space rockets, reporting all data pertaining to the orbit of flight, weight of space devices launched, radio frequencies, etc.

Soviet scientists have established fruitful professional contacts with their foreign colleagues, including scientists of your country, in such international organizations as the Committee for Outer Space Research and the International Astronautical Federation.

It seems to me, Mr. President, that the necessity is now generally recognized for further practical steps in the noble cause of developing international cooperation in space research for peaceful purposes. Your message shows that the direction of your thoughts does not differ in essence from what we conceive to be practical measures in the field of such cooperation. What, then, should be our starting point?

In this connection I should like to name several problems of research and peaceful use of space, for whose solution it would in our opinion be important to unite the efforts of nations. Some of them, which are encompassed by the recent U.N. General Assembly resolution adopted at the initiative of our two countries, are also mentioned in your message.

1. Scientists consider that the use of artificial earth satellites for the creation of international systems of long-distance communication is entirely realistic at the present stage of space research. Realization of such projects can lead to a significant improvement in the means of com-

munication and television all over the globe.
People would be provided with a reliable means of
communication and hitherto unknown opportunities for broadening contacts between nations
would be opened. So let us begin by specifying the
definite opportunities for cooperation in solving
this problem. As I understood from your message, the U.S.A. is also prepared to do this.

2. It is difficult to overestimate the advantage
that people would derive from the organisation of
a world-wide weather observation service using
artificial earth satellites. Precise and timely
weather prediction would be still another important step on the path to man's subjugation of the
forces of nature; it would permit him to combat
more successfully the calamities of the elements
and would give new prospects for advancing the
well-being of mankind. Let us also cooperate in
this field.

3. It seems to us that it would be expedient to
agree upon organising the observation of objects
launched in the direction of the moon, Mars,
Venus, and other planets of the solar system, by
radio-technical and optical means, through a joint
program.

As our scientists see it, undoubted advantage
would be gained by uniting the efforts of nations
for the purpose of hastening scientific progress in
the study of the physics of interplanetary space
and heavenly bodies.

4. At the present stage of man's penetration
into space, it would be most desirable to draw up
and conclude an international agreement providing for aid in searching for and rescuing space

ships, satellites, and capsules that have acciden-
tally fallen. Such an agreement appears all the
more necessary, since it might involve saving the
lives of cosmonauts, those courageous explorers
of the far reaches of the universe.

5. Your message contains proposals for cooperation between our countries in compiling charts
of the earth's magnetic field in outer space by
means of satellites, and also for exchanging
knowledge in the field of space medicine. I can
say that Soviet scientists are prepared to cooperate in this and to exchange data regarding such
questions with scientists of other countries.

6. I think, Mr. President, that the time has
also come for our two countries, which have
advanced further than others in space research,
to try to find a common approach to the solution
of the important legal problems with which life
itself has confronted the nations in the space age.
In this connection I find it a positive fact that at
the UN General Assembly's 16th session the
Soviet Union and the United States were able to
agree upon a proposal on the first principles of
space law which was then unanimously approved
by the members of the UN: a proposal on the
applicability of international law, including the
UN Charter, in outer space and on heavenly bodies; on the accessibility of outer space and heavenly bodies for research and use by all nations in
accordance with international law; and on the
fact that space is not subject to appropriation by
nations.

Now, in our opinion, it is necessary to go
further.

Expansion of space research being carried out by nations definitely makes it necessary to agree also that in conducting experiments in outer space no one should create obstacles for space study and research for peaceful purposes by other nations. Perhaps it should be stipulated that those experiments in space that might complicate space research by other countries should be the subject of preliminary discussion and agreement on an appropriate international basis.

I have named, Mr. President, only some of the questions whose solution has, in our view, now become urgent and requires cooperation between our countries. In the future, international cooperation in the conquest of space will undoubtedly extend to ever newer fields of space exploration if we can now lay a firm foundation for it. We hope that scientists of the USSR and the U.S.A. will be able to engage in working out and realizing the many projects for the conquest of outer space hand in hand, and together with scientists of other countries.

Representatives of the USSR on the UN Space Committee will be given instructions to meet with representatives of the United States in order to discuss concrete questions of cooperation in research and peaceful use of outer space that are of interest to our countries.

Thus, Mr. President, do we conceive of—shall we say—heavenly matters. We sincerely desire that the establishment of cooperation in the field of peaceful use of outer space facilitate the improvement of relations between our countries, the easing of international tension and the creation of a favorable situation for the peaceful settlement of urgent problems here on our own earth.

At the mean time it appears obvious to me that the scale of our cooperation in the peaceful conquest of space, as well as the choice of the lines along which such cooperation would seem possible, is to a certain extent related to the solution of the disarmament problem. Until an agreement on general and complete disarmament is achieved, both our countries will, nevertheless, be limited in their abilities to cooperate in the field of peaceful use of outer space. It is no secret that rockets for military purposes and spacecraft launched for peaceful purposes are based on common scientific and technical achievements. It is true that there are some distinctions here; space rockets require more powerful engines, since by this means they carry greater payloads and attain a higher altitude, while military rockets in general do not require such powerful engines— engines already in existence can carry warheads of great destructive force and assure their arrival at any point on the globe. However, both you and we know, Mr. President, that the principles for designing and producing military rockets and space rockets are the same.

I am expressing these considerations for the simple reason that it would be better if we saw all sides of the question realistically. We should try to overcome any obstacles which may arise in the path of international cooperation in the peaceful conquest of space. It is possible that we shall succeed in doing this, and that will be use-

ful. Considerably broader prospects for cooperation and uniting our scientific-technological
achievements up to and including joint construction of spacecraft for reaching other planets—the
moon, Venus, Mars—will arise when agreement
on disarmament has been achieved.

We hope that agreement on general and complete disarmament will be achieved; we are exerting and will continue to exert every effort toward
this end. I should like to believe that you also, Mr.
President, will spare no effort in acting along
these lines.

Yours respectfully,

N. Khrushchev/4/

/1/Source: Department of State, Presidential
Correspondence: Lot 66 D 204. Confidential; Limit
Distribution. The Russian-language text is ibid. Another
copy is in the Kennedy Library, National Security Files,
Countries Series, USSR, Khrushchev Correspondence.
/2/Document 41.
/3/Document 35.
/4/Printed from a copy that bears this typed signature.

*"We continue to hope that the
Soviet Government may reconsider
the position . . ."*

44. Telegram From the Department of State to the Embassy in the Soviet Union

Washington, April 7, 1962, 5:16 p.m./1/

2296. You should concert with British Embassy delivery on April 9 to Soviet Foreign Ministry final agreed text quoted below:

"Joint US/UK Statement on Nuclear Testing"

Begin Verbatim Text

Discussions among ourselves and the Soviet Union about a treaty to ban nuclear tests have been going on in Geneva for nearly a month. The Soviet representatives have rejected international inspection or verification inside the Soviet Union to determine the nature of unexplained seismic events which might be nuclear tests.

This is a point of cardinal importance to the United States and the United Kingdom. From the very beginning of the negotiations on a nuclear Test Ban Treaty, they have made it clear that an essential element of such a treaty is an objective international system for assuring that a ban on nuclear tests is being observed by all parties. The need for such a system was clearly recognized in the report of the scientific experts which was the foundation of the Geneva negotiations. For nearly three years this need was accepted by the Soviet delegation at Geneva. There was disagreement about details, but the principle of objective international verification was accepted. It was embodied in the Treaty tabled by the United States and the United Kingdom on April 18, 1961, which provides for such a system. Since the current disarmament meetings began in Geneva, the United States and the United

Kingdom have made further efforts to meet Soviet objections to the April 18 Treaty. These efforts have met with no success as is clearly shown by the recent statements of the Foreign Minister of the Soviet Union and of their representative in Geneva, Mr. Zorin, who have repeatedly rejected the very concept of international verification. There has been no progress on this point in Geneva; the Soviet Union has refused to change its position.

The ground given seems to be that existing national detection systems can give adequate protection against clandestine tests. In the pres-ent state of scientific instrumentation, there are a great many cases in which we cannot distinguish between natural and artificial seismic disturbances—as opposed to recording the fact of a disturbance and locating its probable epicenter. A treaty therefore cannot be made effective unless adequate verification is included in it. For otherwise there would be no alternative, if an instrument reported an unexplained seismic occurrence on either side, between accepting the possibility of an evasion of the Treaty or its immediate denunciation. The opportunity for adequate verification is of the very essence of mutual confidence.

This principle has so far been rejected by the Foreign Minister of the Soviet Union, and there is no indication that he has not spoken with the full approval of his Government. We continue to hope that the Soviet Government may reconsider the position and express their readiness to accept the principle of international verification. If they will do this, there is still time to reach agreement. But if there is no change in the present Soviet position, the Governments of the United States and the United Kingdom must conclude that their efforts to obtain a workable treaty to ban nuclear tests are not now successful, and the test series scheduled for the latter part of this month will have to go forward. End Verbatim Text.

For London: Department understands British will release to press text joint statement 3:30 p.m. April 10 London time when Macmillan begins speak in House. Text would be released simultaneously Washington 10:30 a.m./2/ Washington time. Please coordinate with British and confirm.

For USRO Paris: You may inform in strict confidence members NAC text joint statement on Monday, April 9, with injunction observe confidence until release to press.

For Tokyo: You may inform in strict confidence Japanese Government on Monday, April 9, with request observe press embargo.

For Geneva: You may inform non-Bloc delegations of text joint statement approximately one hour before release time on April 10 with injunction to observe embargo before release to press.

Ball

/1/Source: Department of State, Presidential
Correspondence: Lot 66 D 204. Secret; Priority; Verbatim
Text; Eyes Only. Drafted by Davis; cleared by Kohler, Beam
(ACDA), and Bromley Smith at the White House; and
approved by Ball. Repeated to Tokyo, London, Geneva, and
Paris for USRO. A copy of this statement is in the Kennedy
Library, National Security Files, Countries Series, USSR,
Khrushchev Correspondence. Also printed in *Documents on
Disarmament, 1962,* vol. I, pp. 292-293.
/2/Above 10:30 on the source text is handwritten 9:30.

"I owe you a letter of thanks . . ."

45. Letter From President Kennedy to Chairman Khrushchev

Washington, June 5, 1962./1/

DEAR MR. CHAIRMAN: I owe you a letter of
thanks for the generous hospitality which you
and your associates offered to Pierre Salinger
while he was in the Soviet Union. He has given
me a full account of his visit, with particular
emphasis on your own generosity in giving him
so much of your time./1/ I feel sure that visits
like his are helpful. Since I recognize that your
kindness to him was in part a friendly gesture to
me, I want to send you these thanks.

A letter of this sort is not the place for
extended discussion of the large issues which are
so important to the relations between our two
countries. I do want you to know, however, that
Mr. Salinger has carefully reported all that you
said to him, and that full attention will be given
to your new proposals. They present difficulties

which we have pointed out to Ambassador Dobrynin, but we shall be glad to discuss the matter further with him. All these matters relating to Berlin are currently being discussed in careful detail by Secretary Rusk and Ambassador Dobrynin, and I think it may be best to leave the discussion in their capable hands at this time. I am glad to learn again from Mr. Salinger that Ambassador Dobrynin has your confidence in unusual measure. He has already made a place for himself here in Washington as an intelligent and friendly representative of your Government.

In closing, let me say that I noticed with appreciation your friendly gesture in attending the concert offered by Benny Goodman in Moscow last week. I myself look forward to attending a performance of the Bolshoi Ballet when it comes to us in the fall.

Sincerely,

John Kennedy/3/

/1/Source: Kennedy Library, National Security Files, Countries Series, USSR, Khrushchev Correspondence. No classification marking. Other copies are in Department of State, Presidential Correspondence: Lot 66 D 204, and ibid., Central Files, 761.13/6-762. Also printed in part in Beschloss, *The Crisis Years*, p. 395.
/2/For an account of this meeting, see telegram 2935, May 13, in volume V.
/3/Printed from a copy that indicates the President signed the original.

"Good news has come from Laos."

46. Telegram From Chairman Khrushchev to President Kennedy

Moscow, June 12, 1962. /1/

DEAR MR. PRESIDENT, Good news has come from Laos. As a result of the successful completion of negotiations between the three political forces of Laos, it has been possible to form a coalition Government of National Unity headed by Prince Souvanna Phouma.

Without question, this act may become the pivotal event both in the life of the Laotian people themselves and in the cause of strengthening peace in Southeast Asia. Formation of a coalition Government of National Unity in Laos opens the way toward completing in the near future the work done at the Geneva Conference toward a peaceful settlement of the Laotian problem and giving life to the agreements worked out at that conference, which constitute a good basis for the development of Laos as a neutral and independent state.

The example of Laos indicates that provided there is a desire to resolve difficult international problems on the basis of cooperation with mutual account of the interests of all sides, such cooperation bears its fruit. At the same time, the results achieved in the settlement of the Laotian problem strengthen the conviction that success in solving other international problems which now divide states and create tension in the world can be achieved on the same road as well.

As for the Soviet Government, it has always adhered, as it does now, to this line, which in present conditions is the only correct policy in international affairs in accordance with the interests of peace.

I avail myself of the occasion to express satisfaction over the fact that the mutual understanding we achieved while meeting in Vienna last June on the support of a neutral and independent Laos is beginning to be translated into life.

Respectfully yours,

N. Khrushchev

/1/Source: Department of State, Presidential Correspondence: Lot 66 D 204. No classification marking. Published by TASS in English on June 12. A handwritten note on the source text indicates Bromley Smith was informed of publication of the message at 7 p.m. June 12. A transliterated Russian-language text is in Department of State, Central Files, 711.11-KE/6-1362. Another copy is in the Kennedy Library, National Security Files, Countries Series, USSR, Khrushchev Correspondence. Also printed in Department of State *Bulletin*, July 2, 1962, p. 12.

"I share your views that the reports from Laos are very encouraging."

47. Telegram From the Department of State to the Embassy in the Soviet Union

Washington, June 12, 1962, 9:41 p.m./1/

2825. Ambassador requested deliver following Presidential message to Khrushchev first thing Wednesday morning Moscow time.

"Dear Mr. Chairman:

I share your view that the reports from Laos are very encouraging. The formation of this Government of National Union under Prince Souvanna Phouma marks a milestone in the sustained efforts which have been put forward toward this end, especially since our meeting in Vienna.

It is of equal importance that we should now press forward with our associates in the Geneva Conference, to complete these agreements and to work closely together in their execution. We must continue also to do our best to persuade all concerned in Laos to work together to this same end. It is very important that no untoward actions be allowed to disrupt the progress which has been made.

I agree that continued progress in the settlement of the Laotian problem can be most helpful in leading toward the resolution of other international difficulties. If together we can help in the establishment of an independent and neutral Laos, securely sustained in this status through time, this accomplishment will surely have a significant and positive effect far beyond the borders of Laos. You can count on the continued and energetic efforts of the Government of the United States toward this end.

Sincerely, John F. Kennedy"

White House plans release 9:00 am Wednesday, Washington time.

Rusk

/1/Source: Department of State, Presidential Correspond-ence: Lot 66 D 204. Limited Official Use; Niact. Drafted at the White House. Another copy of this message is in the Kennedy Library, National Security Files, Countries Series, USSR, Khrushchev Correspondence. Also printed in *Public Papers of the Presidents of the United States: John F. Kennedy, 1962*, p. 479; Department of State Bulletin, July 2, 1962, p. 12; and Claflin, *The President Wants To Know*, pp. 175-176.

"On the occasion of the national holiday of the U.S.A. . . ."

48. Message From Chairmen Khrushchev and Brezhnev to President Kennedy

Moscow, July 4, 1962./1/

ESTEEMED MR. PRESIDENT: On the occasion of the national holiday of the U.S.A.— Independence Day—we send you and the entire American people sincere congratulations and best wishes from the people of the Soviet Union and from ourselves. We should like to believe that the time is beginning when congratulating one anoth-er on national holidays, we will also be able to point to the results of mutual efforts, which all peoples including the people of our country now await, for successes in the matter of removing the threat of war and for securing peace on earth.

N. Khrushchev/2/

L. Brezhnev

/1/Source: Department of State, Presidential Correspondence: Lot 66 D 204. No classification marking. The source text is marked "unofficial translation." Another copy is in the Kennedy Library, National Security Files, Countries Series, USSR, Khrushchev Correspondence.
/2/Printed from a copy that bears these typed signatures.

"Both we and you had enough time for thinking this over."

49. Message From Chairman Khrushchev to President Kennedy

Moscow, undated./1/

We are following with great attention the development of the Soviet-American exchange of opinions on German peace treaty and normalization on its basis of the situation in West Berlin and we are carefully weighing considerations being expressed by the President, the Secretary of State or on behalf of the President through unofficial channels.

On the other hand, we, naturally, cannot but take notice of the facts which indicate sharpening of the situation in West Berlin caused by activities of certain circles not interested in a German peace settlement. Other facts of recent past also support repeatedly voiced apprehensions that the absence of a final peace settlement in Germany not only keeps up the existing tension in Europe but can also cause unforeseen, undesirable consequences for European and world peace.

All this prompts the conclusion that further delay in solving the questions connected with a German peace settlement would involve such a threat to peace which must be averted already now when it is not too late.

Unfortunately in the course of the Soviet-American exchange of opinions there has not been achieved any noticeable progress since the meetings in Geneva. The whole matter has come to a standstill because of the differences in the main outstanding question—that of withdrawal of the occupation troops of the U.S., Great Britain and France from West Berlin and of abolition there of the occupation states. Motives were more than once given in detail on our side why we by no means can accept continuation of the present unsatisfactory and dangerous situation in West Berlin, the reason for which lies in the presence there of occupation troops and occupation regime covering in effect the existence of a NATO military base in the centre of the GDR territory.

We have set forth a number of concrete proposals which took into account the official position and motives of prestige of the U.S. on this main subject of disagreement. The President's considerations on the necessity to search for drawing nearer our points of view have thus been meeting with a favorable response in

Moscow. Unfortunately, however, no proposal has been put forward by the American side which would enhance the possibility for solving the question of drawing a line through World War II by abolishing the occupation regime in West Berlin and by giving it the status of a free city. The expressed considerations about some temporary settlement of the question, so far as they do not provide for abolition of the occupation regime and withdrawal of occupation troops of the three powers from West Berlin, cannot, naturally, make an agreement easier. Since the whole matter is that of eliminating the vestiges of the war it is absolutely impossible to accept mere formal changes in West Berlin without really changing the existing abnormal situation there which is fraught with possibility of a sudden explosion.

Both we and you had enough time for thinking this over. And if both of us are ready to really search for a solution then there are no reasons not to find it in the nearest future, without further procrastination. There is absolutely no sense in postponing until fall, and from fall until spring what should and can be done already now.

It can be seen from the last talk of Mr. Salinger with our Ambassador/2/ that the President shares the view that it is not expedient to postpone solution of the German problem and that he takes interest in finding a mutually acceptable solution on the main unresolved question—that of the foreign troops in West Berlin. Those proposals which we set forth before in our conviction fully correspond to the interests of both sides. But in order to speed up the solution and make a choice out of the alternatives that we face we are ready to make another effort that in the greatest possible degree takes into account the wishes of the United States on the question of the presence of its troops in West Berlin so far as those wishes are compatible with the task of completing a German peace settlement.

Our proposal is as follows.

The occupation regime in West Berlin will be abolished and during the first years the troops of the United Nations will be stationed there which will act as guarantors of independence and security of West Berlin.

Those UN troops must not, naturally, either taken as a whole or in any of their part, represent this or that military group opposing each other and their status as guarantors acting in the name of the UN should be defined on the basis of a special agreement. They would symbolize the determination of the parties to the agreement not to permit outside interference into the affairs and life of the population of West Berlin. Those troops by their nature would be police formation and not combatant troops, that should be agreed upon.

The UN police military formations, the initial strength of which should not exceed the combined strength of the troops of the three powers stationed there as of July 1, 1962, would be composed of police military formations of the U.S., Great Britain and France which combined will make one half of such U.S. formations in West Berlin; the other half of UN police military formations will consist in an equal proportion of contingents of troops of one or two neutral

states, one or two states of the Warsaw treaty
(for example, Poland, Czechoslovakia), one or two
small NATO states.

Subsequently the numerical strength of UN
police military formations in West Berlin will
gradually diminish, namely: during the first year
after the abolition of the occupation status those
UN formations will be cut by 25 per cent of their
initial strength, during the second year—by another 25 per cent and during the third year by next
25 per cent of that number. The above mentioned
gradual reduction of the numerical strength of the
UN formations will be carried on in the same proportion both with regard to the police military formations of the three powers and the formations
that will be provided by other states.

Since the sides agree that the presence of foreign troops in West Berlin should be of temporary
nature they make an arrangement that by the
end of the fourth year the remaining 25 per cent
of the UN police formations will be withdrawn
from West Berlin, and West Berlin will be free of
the presence of foreign troops. We proceed from
an assumption that after the withdrawal of those
formations the guarantees by the UN in respect
to independence of West Berlin that would guard
that city from outside interference into its domestic affairs should remain fully in force.

With the abolition of occupation status West
Berlin will be considered as an independent political entity, that is, as a free city. Subversive activities must not be carried on from West Berlin
against the GDR or other socialist countries.

Naturally, any claims by the FRG on West

Berlin must be declined for they constitute a manifestation of the policy of aggression and revanche in practice. We are generally satisfied that our positions regarding groundlessness of any claims by the FRG on West Berlin are in effect the same. An appropriate agreement will also be achieved on free access to and from West Berlin with due respect for the sovereignty of the GDR on the basis of generally established international practice. The German Democratic Republic, as it has already stated, will assume appropriate commitments on this question. We on our part again reaffirm that we have stood and continue to stand for an unimpeded access provided the requirement to respect the lawful sovereign rights of the German Democratic Republic is observed.

If differences or frictions arise on practical questions of access they will be considered by a special temporary international body—an arbitrator about which the Soviet side put forward corresponding proposals.

Simultaneously with the normalization of the situation in West Berlin and abolition there of the occupation regime other questions of a German peace settlement should be finally solved, such as: fixation and juridical formalization of the existing borders of the German states, the border between the GDR and FRG included, nonarming of the GDR and FRG with nuclear weapons (either directly, or through third countries, or through military-political groups in which they are participants), due respect for the sovereignty of the GDR, conclusion in one form or another of a nonaggression pact between the NATO and the Warsaw treaty organization. An understanding on all those questions should, naturally, be formalized in appropriate agreements.

The agreement achieved by the sides on appropriate questions will find its reflection in a peace treaty which the Soviet Union and other interested states will conclude with the German Democratic Republic.

Setting forth the new proposal on the question of foreign troops in West Berlin which we believe is paving the way to a mutually acceptable agreement and which we hope the President will duly appreciate we proceed from an assumption that as the American side has repeatedly emphasized a solution of all other questions of a German peace settlement which were discussed will not run into obstacles.

We would like the American side to correctly understand the motives and aims of this new proposal. We deem it necessary before taking steps with regard to conclusion of a peace treaty with the German Democratic Republic with all ensuing consequences which were earlier mentioned more than once to exhaust the possibilities to achieve a mutual agreement. We believe that in a question so important as that of a German peace settlement not a single unused opportunity should be left aside if, of course, all the interested sides are guided by good intentions, if they strive not for an increase of tension in Europe and in the whole world, not for encouragement of forces of revanche and aggression, not for war, but for a relaxation of tension, for peace.

The success of peaceful settlement in Laos gives all of us an encouraging example. The President once expressed an idea that if a mutually acceptable solution of the Laotian problem could be reached it would make easier for the United States to find ways to peaceful settlement of the German problem. We also believe that now it is the turn of the German problem.

In Laos we moved step by step and now it seems that we are close to a final settlement. Our proposals that were set forth above also provide for settlement of the problem of foreign troops in West Berlin during a certain transitional period, by several stages up to the complete withdrawal of those troops.

We want to draw the attention of the President that we are putting forward our proposals on problems of a German peace settlement with due regard for the considerations and position of the American side and we seriously count on the possibility of an agreement. If the President reacts positively to our new proposal, the Foreign Minister of the USSR could at a meeting with the Secretary of State in Geneva come to a final agreement. Thus a meeting between the President of the US and the Chairman of Council of Ministers of the USSR would be prepared, during which it would be possible to fix an achieved understanding and, provided there is an agreement between the parties, to sign appropriate documents.

The achievement of an agreement on the problems of a German peace settlement, including the normalization of the situation in West Berlin would have a profound impact on all the peoples as an example of effective cooperation between the powers in the field of peace in accordance with the principles of the United Nations. This would be a major victory for the policy both of the Soviet Union and the United States and, we are sure, of all those who stand for peace and condemn war. This would create a basis for a fruitful cooperation of the two powers also in the solution of other more cardinal problems relating to the main international problem of our time— that of general and complete disarmament and developing on its basis peaceful cooperation among all states and peoples.

Naturally, this would open a new chapter in the history of Soviet-American relations in which undoubtedly are vitally interested not only the peoples of our countries but also the peoples of the whole world. And the first steps of our countries along a new road could be consolidated by a state visit of the President of the United States to the Soviet Union who would be a welcome guest of the peoples and the government of our country.

/1/Source: Department of State, Presidential Correspondence: Lot 77 D 163. Secret. Handwritten notes at the top of the source text indicate it was received at the White House on July 5 and that the original and a copy of a translation were retained by Kohler, and a copy was sent to Ambassador Thompson on July 7. The source text bears no salutation or signature, but in a conversation with Rusk on July 12 (see vol. XV, pp. 215-222), Dobrynin stated that when he delivered the message to the White House on July 5, he had indicated that it was intended as a message from Khrushchev to the President. The Russian-language text is ibid. Another copy of the message is in the Kennedy Library, National Security Files, Countries Series, USSR, Khrushchev Correspondence.

/2/This conversation has not been further identified.

"I am confident that the goal of a durable peace can be achieved . . ."

50. Telegram From the Department of State to the Embassy in the Soviet Union

Washington, July 12, 1962, 8:15 p.m./1/

81. Please deliver following message from the President to President Brezhnev and Chairman Khrushchev:

"Dear Mr. President

"Dear Chairman Khrushchev

On behalf of the American people and myself I wish to thank you sincerely for your good wishes on the occasion of the 186th anniversary of the Independence of the United States of America.

I am confident that the goal of a durable peace can be achieved if, in cooperation with all other governments and peoples, we devote our best efforts to this end.

Sincerely,

John F. Kennedy"
White House

/1/Source: Department of State, Presidential Correspondence: Lot 66 D 204. Limited Official Use. Drafted by Davis and cleared by Smith at the White House. Another copy of this message is in the Kennedy Library, National Security Files, Countries Series, USSR, Khrushchev Correspondence.

"What we . . . find especially troubling in the present Soviet position is the consistent failure . . . to take in any real account of what we have made clear are the vital interests of the United States and its Allies."

51. Letter From President Kennedy to Chairman Khrushchev

Washington, July 17, 1962./1/

DEAR MR. CHAIRMAN: I am responding to the communication received through Ambassador Dobrynin on July 5, 1962./2/ Secretary of State Rusk made certain preliminary comments on this communication during his meeting with Ambassador Dobrynin on July 9th [12th],/3/ since its contents related directly to the subject of their discussion, but I should also like to take this opportunity to add my personal views. I believe that in a matter of such seriousness and potential danger to peace, we must take advantage of any legitimate channel in an effort to clarify our respective positions.

As heads of government we are naturally

interested in the welfare of our peoples, but we also have a certain obligation to history and to humanity as a whole. This dual responsibility demands that each of us make an effort to understand the position of the other and to see whether accommodations cannot be made, consistent with the basic interests of both parties, directed toward finding peaceful solutions to outstanding differences. This seems particularly important in the case of Germany and Berlin where the vital interests of great nations are involved at a major point of friction.

What we, therefore, find especially troubling in the present Soviet position is the consistent failure, even in the very formulation of the problem, to take any real account of what we have made clear are the vital interests of the United States and its Allies. For example, the Soviet Government has on a number of occasions, as in your most recent communication, complained that it has put forward a number of concrete proposals which take into account "the official position and motives of prestige of the United States," but that "unfortunately, no proposal has been put forward by the American side which would enhance the possibility of solving the question of drawing a line through World War II by abolishing the occupation regime in West Berlin and giving it the status of a free city." Such a formulation is, in effect, the very crux of the problem, because it states the issue in a way which embodies all of the Soviet premises and none of the Western premises in its evaluation of the current situation.

We have gone to some pains over the past

year to define to you what we consider to be our
vital interests in the Berlin situation. These do
not take away anything from the Soviet Union
which it now enjoys. On the contrary, we have
attempted to show that an arrangement mindful
of these interests could lead to a chain of developments of mutual benefit to both sides. The
Soviet Government, on the other hand, consistently states the problem in terms which completely ignore our vital interests and proposes an
outcome under the shadow of a threatened fait
accompli which the Western Powers can either
accept in advance or in the actual fact.

In your recent communication, you note that
the "main outstanding question is that of the
withdrawal of the occupation troops of the United
States, Great Britain and France from West
Berlin and of the abolition there of the occupation
status." To accept this formulation would be to
accept the Soviet position one hundred per cent.
We find it difficult to see even the slightest element of compromise here on the part of the
Soviet Government. The various formulae which
the Soviet Government has put forward all have
the same objective—the total withdrawal or a
severe reduction in the position of Western forces
in Berlin. Merely mixing the same ingredients
together in different proportions does not change
the basic fact that the result is impossible from
our point of view. We cannot, therefore, accept as
accurate the statement that these formulae
attempt to take into account the "official position
and motives of prestige of the United States."
They run directly counter to them. Does the

Soviet Government really believe that our acceptance of any of them, including the most recent,
would not be interpreted throughout the world as
a complete capitulation? We know that it would
be, not only by the West Berliners who would
immediately begin to abandon the city and leave
it a hollow shell, but by all governments and
informed peoples. It was for this reason that, at
our meeting in Vienna now more than a year ago,
we placed such stress on the commitment of the
United States to Berlin in terms of our national
prestige and vital interests. Nothing that has
happened since then has affected the meaning of
our remarks.

The question of Western troop presence is central. Surface changes in the Soviet position which
do not really take account of this fact do not provide a real basis for serious negotiations. Without
this recognition of our vital interests it is difficult
to see how other aspects of the situation can usefully be considered.

Having said this much about the Soviet position, I feel that I must also comment on your
description of our position. To say that the
American side has not put forward a proposal
"which would enhance the possibility of solving
the question of drawing a line through World War
II by abolishing the occupation regime in West
Berlin and by giving it the status of a free city"
is, as I have indicated, to state the problem without the most minimum elements of reciprocity.
We are not opposed to drawing a line through
World War II (though we believe it more important to avoid World War III), but drawing such a

line to us cannot mean accepting the position of
one of the victors of World War II at the complete
expense of three of the other victors. Our views
as to how appropriately to draw a line through
World War II are well known. We understand that
these views are unacceptable to the Soviet
Government. Because we know this we have not
insisted on pressing our views to the point of conflict and crisis, although we believe them to be
correct. We could not, of course, be expected to
put forward proposals eliminating ourselves from
West Berlin.

We have instead tried to be practical in our
approach and in the specific proposals we have
put forward. These have not proceeded from the
assumption that one side must be prepared to
abandon its position entirely. We have instead
been motivated by the desire to eliminate the
Berlin issue as a source of major conflict, which
it is in the interest of both sides to avoid. We have
attempted, therefore, to provide a means of dealing with the fact of disagreement in such a way
as to serve the broader common interest of both
sides in the avoidance of head-on collision and in
the preservation of peace. We have also made a
number of suggestions for relaxing the sense of
crisis in the Berlin area.

You are, of course, familiar with the informal
working paper which Secretary Rusk gave
Foreign Minister Gromyko at Geneva on March
22, 1962./4/ We have never felt that the merits
of our suggested approach have really adequate-
ly been considered by the Soviet Government or
dealt with in subsequent discussions. The lan-

guage of this paper was not meant to be sacrosanct, but it reflected a sincere effort to find points on which there seemed to be at least some agreement in terms of previous statements made by both sides. We would, therefore, hope that you would review the explanations which Secretary Rusk has given to see whether our approach does not suggest an acceptable way out of the present impasse.

In a recent speech, you pointed to the example of Laos as showing that, given a desire for agreement, ways can be found to settle the most challenging and complicated international problems. We can agree entirely with this. In the case of Berlin, there is also undoubtedly a desire for agreement. What seems to be lacking so far, however, is any common ground as to what might be required in order to achieve agreement. Desire for agreement is important as a necessary beginning, but it cannot suffice in itself unless a spirit of patience and of respect for the vital interests of the other party is also present. We feel confident that, if these factors are present, we will also be able to work out something on Berlin which will contribute a resolution satisfactory to both sides.

In your same speech you pointed out that the German question did not have a direct bearing on disarmament but was closely related to it. Here again we can agree. Even a quieting of the Berlin question on the basis of respect for the mutual interests of both sides could not help but markedly improve the entire atmosphere of relations between the Soviet Union and the United States.

As the two major nuclear powers, we have an overriding common interest, deriving from our troubling knowledge of the destructive potentialities of the new weapons, in preventing their spread into the control of other countries. We are certain that one of the major factors in recent years, not only in the general acceleration of arms preparations but also in focusing attention on nuclear weapons, has been the almost continuous crisis over Berlin since November, 1958. Further threats to Berlin and continued heightening of the crisis can only lead to additional measures in this direction.

We feel, therefore, that we have an additional strong and common interest in arriving at a solution of the Berlin problem, consistent with our mutual interests and prestige, in order to relieve the continuing pressures for an arms race including the piling up and diffusion of nuclear weapons. We might add that the enlarged U.S. military preparations which began last summer took place only after the renewal of Soviet threats against our position in Berlin. Our efforts in the military field, and those of our Allies, were a sign of the seriousness with which we all regard the defense of our vital interests in Berlin. This military build-up, however, was not something we wanted, or something which would have happened in the absence of the developments of last summer. If it is true that the threats to our position in Berlin remain a serious source of difference between our two countries, it is just as obvious that some satisfactory arrangement on Berlin would greatly improve the atmosphere and remove an important motive for increased Western effort in the armaments field. This is a consideration to which we hope you will give deep personal thought. Further pressures on Berlin can only exacerbate the situation and enhance the danger of an arms race which we assume neither of us basically desires.

We undoubtedly live in a climactic age. Science has now given man a capacity for destruction which, for the first time, could threaten the very existence of the race itself. This fact makes it imperative that, as rational men, we attempt to resolve our differences rather than move step-by-step towards a major confrontation. In reading the history of past wars and how they began, we cannot help but be impressed how frequently the failure of communication, misunderstanding and mutual irritation have played an important role in the events leading up to fateful decisions for war. In the nuclear age, we cannot be resigned to passive acceptance of a chain of causation which seems to determine the course of history from the outset. We know from your own willingness to discuss these matters that you do not hold to the view that what is happening now is predetermined, and cannot be effected by the decisions which our governments take. I write with this in mind, and urge that you give serious thought to the reflections and suggestions which this communication contains. I have not tried here to deal with every aspect of your communication, but have limited our comment to what seems to be the heart of the issue between us. We would not, however, want silence on these other points to be interpreted as complete agreement on our part with your formulation of the problems and suggested solutions.

If I may summarize, the following lines of approach have seemed to us to be open in seeking a satisfactory resolution of the German and Berlin question:

1. We might join in a real attempt to draw a line through World War II by agreeing on a German settlement based on the freely expressed wish of the German people. As you know, this is in our view the best solution to the problems of Germany and Berlin. We have not pressed in these private exchanges for your agreement to this solution because you have emphasized that it is unacceptable to you—as unacceptable as your proposals for the removal of our troops from Berlin are to us.

2. Short of an all-German settlement, we might agree on new and improved arrangements for all of Berlin.

3. We might deal with the present situation as a factual matter, including the fact of the Western presence in West Berlin. This could mean proceeding on the basis of our informal working paper of March 22, 1962. It would essentially reflect a recognition that there are basic elements in the Berlin situation on which there cannot now be agreement. With such recognition, steps might be taken to ease tensions in the immediate area of Berlin, and it might perhaps be less difficult thereafter to deal with other aspects of the Berlin question while moving ahead with the reduction of tensions in other fields. We have in mind here

particularly steps toward disarmament.

It is now expected that our Foreign Ministers will be meeting shortly in Geneva to sign an agreement on Laos. They will undoubtedly find the occasion to discuss further the question of Berlin. We hope that Foreign Minister Gromyko will come to Geneva with a position embodying genuine elements of reciprocity and taking account of our vital interests in the Berlin situation. If this should prove to be the case, we feel certain that much progress can be made in removing a major source of contention—an accomplishment which would surely have a remarkable and heartening effect in improving the atmosphere and making possible progress in other related areas.

Sincerely,

John F. Kennedy/5/

/1/Source: Kennedy Library, National Security Files, Countries Series, USSR, Khrushchev Correspondence. No classification marking. Another copy is in Department of State, Presidential Correspondence: Lot 66 D 204.
/2/Document 49.
/3/For a memorandum of this conversation, see vol. XV, pp. 215-222.
/4/For text, see vol. XV, pp. 69-71.
/5/Printed from a copy that indicates the President signed the original.

"I send to you and to the Soviet people the heartiest congratulations of the people and the government of the United States . . ."

52. Memorandum From the President's Special Assistant for National Security Affairs (Bundy) to the Executive Secretary of the Department of State (Brubeck)

Washington, August 15, 1962./1/

Will you please have the following message sent in the fastest way possible, and notify my office of the approximate time of delivery.

"Dear Mr. Chairman:

I send to you and to the Soviet people the heartiest congratulations of the people and government of the United States in the outstanding joint flights of Major Nikolayev and Colonel Popovich. This new accomplishment is an important forward step in the great human adventure of the peaceful exploration of space. America's astronauts join with me in sending our salute to Major Nikolayev and Colonel Popovich.

John F. Kennedy"

McGeorge Bundy

/1/Source: Department of State, Presidential Correspondence: Lot 66 D 204. No classification marking. Another copy
is in the Kennedy Library, National Security Files, Countries
Series, USSR, Khrushchev Correspondence. Also printed in
Claflin, *The President Wants To Know,* p. 192.

"The positions of our sides on the question of cessation of nuclear tests are well known."

53. Informal Communication From Chairman Khrushchev to President Kennedy

Moscow, September 4, 1962./1/

We have familiarized ourselves with the statement which you and the Prime Minister of Great
Britain Mr. Macmillan made August 27,/2/ concerning the latest Anglo-American proposals on
the cessation of nuclear tests.

Now I would like to address myself to you to find
out whether we can reach at last a practical agreement on this important problem even though it
may not solve the whole problem completely.

The positions of our sides on the question of
cessation of nuclear tests are well known. We
believe that it would be in the interests of peace
to put an end to all nuclear tests with an appropriate control by the national means of states to
be established. You still express doubts with
regard to this position of ours. At the same time
you appeal to us to accept your proposals on the
cessation of nuclear tests in all environments on

such conditions which in our deep conviction do not have any justification and are absolutely unacceptable to us for the reasons to which we have pointed out more than once. I think you yourself understand that too. Perhaps that is why the Anglo-American proposals contain also an alternative version. You propose to conclude an agreement on the cessation of nuclear tests in the atmosphere, in outer space and under water and leave aside underground tests.

We are ready to take into account your position. Let us immediately sign an agreement on the cessation of nuclear tests in the atmosphere, outer space and under water but at the same time let us agree that with regard to underground tests negotiations will go on with an aim to reach an agreement on the underground tests as well. However we are of the opinion that the peoples would be extremely disappointed if the underground tests continue even at the time when negotiations are in progress on the possibility of an agreement on this problem. We believe that the governments of nuclear powers would act with honor if they agreed, and fixed that in the agreement as well, that the negotiations on the cessation of underground nuclear tests must go on and that during those negotiations and henceforth until an agreement banning also underground nuclear tests is reached, nuclear powers shall refrain from conducting such tests.

We think that an agreement on such basis, though in our opinion it is not satisfactory in every respect, would, nevertheless, be a major step forward.

I will tell you frankly that [in] accepting such an agreement we make a step to meet your position which we cannot justify since we are convinced that there is every possibility to conclude already now a comprehensive agreement on the cessation of all nuclear tests, but which we are ready to take into consideration.

You may say that there is not much new in what I have said. May be. But we are convinced that such a solution and such an agreement do not give either us or you any unilateral advantage, but benefits arising out of them for all nuclear powers and for the cause of peace in general are obvious.

And, finally, the last consideration: it is not clear from your and Mr. Macmillan's statement what role France as nuclear power shall play. We proceeded earlier and proceed now from an assumption that under any international agreement on the cessation of nuclear weapons tests France should assume commitments analogous to those of the USSR, the US and Britain.

I await with great interest your reaction to the considerations I have expressed. If you react to them positively then our representatives could, evidently without great difficulty, work out the text of an appropriate international treaty.

/1/Source: Department of State, Presidential Correspondence: Lot 66 D 204. Secret; Eyes Only. Other copies are ibid.: Lot 77 D 163, and in the Kennedy Library, National Security Files, Countries Series, USSR, Khrushchev Correspondence. Copies were sent to Robert Kennedy, Bundy, Fisher (ACDA), Tyler, and Rusk.

/2/Reference is to the joint statement made by Prime Minister Macmillan and President Kennedy on ending nuclear testing; for text, see Department of State *Bulletin,* September 17, 1962, pp. 403-404.

"I wish to thank you . . ."

54. Message From Chairman Khrushchev to President Kennedy

Moscow, September 4, 1962./1/

DEAR MR. PRESIDENT: I wish to thank you for the felicitations which you sent on behalf of the people and the government of the United States of America to the Soviet people on the occasion of the historic group flight of the spaceships "Vostok-3" and "Vostok-4."/2/ The peoples of the Soviet Union consider their achievements in the cosmos to be an important contribution to the noble cause of universal peace and progress.

The Soviet people join in those greetings and best wishes for peace and happiness which Major Nikolayev and Lieutenant Colonel Popovich sent to the American people from the cosmos.

N. Khrushchev/3/

/1/Source: Department of State, Presidential Correspondence: Lot 66 D 204. No classification marking. The source text is a Department of State translation of a commercial telegram from Moscow. Another copy is in the Kennedy Library, National Security Files, Countries Series, USSR, Khrushchev Correspondence.
/2/See Document 52.

/3/Printed from a copy that bears this typed signature.

"There is still time to put an effective end to this threat."

55. Message From President Kennedy to Chairman Khrushchev

Washington, September 15, 1962./1/

I am happy to note your suggestion that you are prepared to negotiate a treaty banning nuclear tests in the atmosphere, in outer space and under water in the immediate future./2/ Now that the subcommittee on nuclear test ban is continuing in session throughout the recess in the 18-Nation Disarmament Conference, I think we should make a serious effort to work out such an agreement in time to meet the target date of January 1, 1963, which both sides have mentioned in the Geneva negotiations. We have prepared such a treaty,/3/ and our representatives and those of the United Kingdom will be working with yours in the subcommittee to get the earliest possible agreement on a final text.

While we are negotiating toward a limited ban of this type we should at the same time be negotiating towards a treaty for banning nuclear weapons tests in all environments. As part of this effort we could be working to eliminate the difference of view as to a question of scientific fact which has so far kept our negotiators apart. Our scientists advise me that although substantial progress has been made in detecting and identifying nuclear explosions on the basis of instrumentation, it is not possible to do so on a basis which renders the requirement of on-site inspections unnecessary. Your delegation has taken the opposing view but has not supplied any scientific information which may have led your government to hold this view. A joint working party of your scientists together with ours and scientists from the United Kingdom might be able, finally, to dispel the differences which have so far blocked our efforts to obtain agreement.

I believe that when we have prepared and put into effect a treaty banning tests in the atmosphere, in outer space and under water, we can then look at the problem of continued testing under ground and take such steps as we may then determine seem most likely to be helpful in arriving at a comprehensive treaty in the light of the progress which has been made at that time.

In your message you mention the role that France should play in the treaty. Of course, our comprehensive treaty draft provides that the United States, the United Kingdom, and the Soviet Union shall cooperate in encouraging other states to become parties to the treaty. For its part, the United States would work in close consultation with France and would hope that France would adhere to the treaty. Indeed, both you and we have a great interest in assuring the adherence to the treaty of all states or authorities capable of conducting a nuclear weapons test. Without their adherence the treaty could not endure.

A test ban agreement, together with an agreement on the nondissemination of nuclear weapons of the kind which Secretary Rusk had discussed with Ambassador Dobrynin,/4/ would have a powerful effect in deterring the spread of nuclear weapons capabilities to other countries. I firmly believe that obtaining this objective is in our mutual interest. It cannot be in the security interest of any of us if the present small number of nuclear powers is expanded, for, to the extent this is the case, the possibilities of war by accident or by design can only increase.

There is still time to put an effective end to this threat./5/

/1/Source: Kennedy Library, National Security Files, Countries Series, USSR, Khrushchev Correspondence. Secret; Eyes Only. Also printed in Claflin, *The President Wants To Know*, pp. 201-203.
/2/See Document 53.
/3/Reference is to ENDC/59, submitted to the Eighteen-Nation Disarmament Committee on August 27; for text, see Documents on Disarmament, 1962, vol. II, pp. 804-807.
/4/Memoranda of conversations on August 8 and 23 are in vol. VII, pp. 541-547 and 556-559.
/5/Printed from an unsigned copy.

"What is the way out?"

56. Message From Chairman Khrushchev to President Kennedy

Moscow, September 28, 1962./1/

I studied with interest your reply to my considerations forwarded through Ambassador

Dobrynin on the question of cessation of nuclear weapon tests./2/

It is said in your reply that a serious effort should be made to work out by January 1, 1963 an agreement on the question of cessation of nuclear weapon tests. Well, I can say quite definitely that we will not make you wait. The Soviet Union in the course of many years has been pressing for concluding an agreement on cessation of all nuclear weapon tests and we are prepared to make new efforts in this direction for the sake of achieving this aim.

The Soviet Government is convinced that national means of detecting nuclear explosions now at the disposal of the states are quite adequate to ensure strict control over the fulfillment by all states of their commitments with regard to cessation of nuclear weapon tests in the atmosphere, in outer space and under water as well as underground. And the U.S. too recognizes this now with respect to three types of tests—in the atmosphere, in outer space and under water— and no longer insists on establishing international control over the cessation of these tests. Thus there seems to be no difference between us on this point any longer. There remains the question of underground tests. In the U.S. doubts are still being expressed as to the adequacy of national means for detecting underground tests. We do not have such doubts. Nevertheless we are prepared to use every opportunity to come to an agreement on this question on a mutually acceptable basis, on such a basis that would remove your doubts.

I do not know whether you have noticed a suggestion of British scientists Bullard and Penney put forward at the recent Pugwash conference of scientists/3/ concerning the use of automatic seismic stations working without any personnel. As we understood, the idea of this suggestion is that automatic seismic stations help with their records to determine what is the cause of this or that underground tremor—underground nuclear blasts or ordinary earthquakes. It would be a sort of mechanical control without men. After thinking this suggestion over we came to the conclusion that it can be accepted if this would make it easier to reach an agreement. In this case it could be provided in the treaty banning all nuclear weapon tests that automatic seismic stations be set up both near the borders of the nuclear states and 2-3 such stations directly on the territory of the states possessing nuclear weapons—in the areas most frequently subjected to earthquakes.

The Soviet Government agrees to this only because it seeks a mutually acceptable basis for an agreement. We do not intend to violate the commitment that we assume regarding cessation of tests but we also want to make you and the public opinion of the U.S. to feel confident that all sides will display an honest approach in fulfilling this commitment.

If you agree to this then we could without much difficulty come to an agreement on cessation of all nuclear weapon tests.

I would like to view as an encouraging sign the fact that the American scientists who took part in the Pugwash conference—and as I was told, very

prominent ones—approved of the suggestion
about the use of automatic seismic stations for
the purposes of control. The Soviet scientists—
participants in the Pugwash conference—also
approved of this suggestion. So it appears that
the scientists are already in agreement. Then
there is a possibility to move ahead quickly. And
as for us, we would like very much to put an end
to all that and reach, at last, an agreement on
cessation of nuclear tests of all kinds. There have
been enough—both for us and for you—of experimental blasts carried out in the atmosphere and
underground.

If we can come now to the conclusion of an
agreement on cessation of all nuclear weapon
tests we will make good for the peoples of our
countries and for the peoples of the entire world.

We prefer to conclude now a treaty on cessation of all nuclear weapon tests. But if the
Western powers are not yet prepared for that
even taking into account the suggestions put forward at the Pugwash conference we, as I have
already told you, are ready in this case also to
make a step toward the Western powers and to
conclude at this time a treaty on cessation of
nuclear weapon tests in three environments: in
the atmosphere, in outer space and under water.

It would be incorrect in doing that to leave
open the question of underground nuclear tests.
For it would create a false impression with the
world public opinion, a kind of illusion, that an
agreement on cessation of tests has seemingly
been concluded and that the competition among
states in perfecting nuclear arms in coming to an

end whereas in fact this competition would continue. The weapons already created would be remodeled on the basis of new scientific data obtained as a result of experimental underground blasts, that is the states would replenish their arsenals with ever more perfect, ever more destructive types of nuclear weapons. With that we cannot agree. I must say frankly and openly that it is impossible to agree to conclude an agreement on the basis of tests in the atmosphere, in outer space and under water if the United States intends to continue underground nuclear explosions. Since in this case we too would face a necessity to carry out experimental nuclear weapon tests and we would conduct those tests, as we are doing now, in the atmosphere.

What is the way out? From our previous exchange of opinion you know how we propose to overcome this difficulty—to agree that after a treaty banning nuclear tests in the atmosphere, in outer space and under water is signed, negotiations on cessation of underground tests as well should be continued and while these suggestions are in progress and until the agreement is reached all nuclear powers should refrain from conducting such tests.

But some people in the West do not want even to hear about any commitment by the states to refrain from conducting nuclear tests. And on the part of some statesmen and in the American press assertions are made from time to time that the Soviet Union has allegedly violated some agreement on moratorium on nuclear tests. However those who make such statements have neither proof nor ground to support them.

And what are the facts? No international agreement on moratorium on underground or any other nuclear tests ever existed and nobody ever signed such an agreement. It can be reminded that as early as March 31, 1958 the Soviet Union unilaterally discontinued tests of all kinds of atomic and hydrogen weapons and called upon the Western powers to follow its example. But the U.S. and Britain responded then to that proposal of ours with an unprecedented in scope new series of tests of nuclear bombs. In subsequent period since the end of 1958 neither the United States or Britain nor the Soviet Union conducted nuclear weapon tests, but they acted so not because of any obligations coming from an international agreement but because of their own unilateral decisions. However, as early as December 29, 1959 your predecessor President Eisenhower clearly and definitely stated that the U.S. did not consider itself any longer bound by its statement that it had no intention to conduct nuclear tests. As for France—a NATO ally of the U.S. and Britain—it was even at that time conducting one nuclear explosion after another.

All this is perfectly known and he who nevertheless claims that the Soviet Union allegedly violated some moratorium on nuclear tests either has a short memory or simply seeks to torpedo the conclusion of an agreement on cessation of nuclear weapon tests.

I would like to note with satisfaction that now you seem to agree in principle that along with the conclusion of a treaty on the ban of nuclear weapon tests in the atmosphere, in outer space and under water a moratorium with regard to underground explosions be accepted. If this is so, then it opens certain prospects.

You believe at the same time, as I have understood, that there should be no unlimited moratorium on underground tests. But we do not put the question that way. We do not propose to declare an unlimited moratorium on underground explosions. We suggest to declare such moratorium for a certain period of time, while the negotiations on banning underground tests of nuclear weapons are in progress. For how long those negotiations will go on—it is of course, impossible to say. But we do not think that much time is needed to conclude a final agreement on underground tests, provided, of course, that both sides display interest in reaching such an agreement promptly.

Anyway we are ready to agree on a term for the course of which the states will assume commitments not to conduct underground nuclear explosions, if an agreement banning nuclear tests only in the atmosphere, in outer space and under water is reached. We agree, for instance, on a 5-year term. And during the five years it will certainly be possible to agree on a final solution of the question of banning also underground nuclear explosions though, I repeat, I am convinced that it could be done much faster, especially if the idea of use for the purposes of control of automatic seismic stations is acceptable to you. During this period of time, one should assume, all American scientists too will get convinced that the national means of detection of nuclear explosions are quite adequate for assuring a foolproof control over cessation of nuclear tests, underground tests included.

If, however, even during that term an agreement is not reached—what to do in this case? Then the whole question of banning nuclear weapon tests will have to be reconsidered anew. And if the American side then insists on renewing underground nuclear tests, then—I want to say this already now and in plain terms—the Soviet Union will consider itself free from assumed obligations not to conduct nuclear tests in the atmosphere, in outer space and under water.

These are considerations which came to my mind in connection with your reply on the question of cessation of nuclear weapon tests. Giving you these considerations I think of nothing else but how to move from the dead point, and out of deadlock, the question of cessation of nuclear weapon tests.

If you being concerned about the same are in agreement with our considerations let me know and then the Soviet representatives in Geneva will at once be given instructions to get down together with your and British representatives to practical work of preparing a draft agreement.

One cannot doubt that an agreement on cessation of nuclear weapon tests would be greeted with tremendous joy by all mankind. The peoples wherever they live—in Europe or America, in Africa, Asia or Australia—desire peace, a lasting peace, they want an end to the nuclear arms race, they want the threat of nuclear war be eliminated.

During his meeting with Ambassador Dobrynin Robert Kennedy referring to you, Mr. President, confidentially touched upon the problem of Soviet-American relations. He said in particular that you are concerned with the worsening of these relations. We ourselves are very much upset about that but we would like to draw your attention to the fact that the aggravation of relations between the Soviet Union and the United States was not sown by us and it was not we who started it. We have sincerely sought and continue to seek to do everything for the normalization of our relations and not only for normalization but for their radical betterment. But that is being hindered by the hot-beds of international tension which are a source of constant friction between our countries. They should be removed and, first of all, the abnormal situation in West Berlin should be done away with.

I believe that you, Mr. President, like me realize that until a reasonable solution is reached on West Berlin this source will always make our relations feverish. And under present circumstances we do not see any other way out but to sign a German peace treaty. On this basis it would be possible with no loss to the prestige of either side to solve the problem of West Berlin too, to guarantee, as you say, the freedom of the population of West Berlin by stationing there for some not very long time a certain number of symbolic troops under the UN flag. It would seem, what can be more reasonable, if there is a desire to actually reach an agreement and eliminate the hot-beds that from time to time make our relations feverish and sometimes bring them to the red-hot glow.

If there is somebody who is interested in preserving those hot-beds then such interest stems from nothing else but a desire to prevent by all means the normalization of relations between the Soviet Union and the U.S. And I say straightforwardly that it is, of course, Adenauer who is interested in that in the first place. By no means he is motivated by good intentions. The Hitlerite Germany lost the war with all the ensuing consequences. Its plans to expand "Lebensraum" at the expense of other states ended in failure. This should be recognized once and for all. In fact, that is what the United States, Britain, France, the Soviet Union and other countries fought for against the Hitlerite Germany. Why then should you and we now reckon with the revanchist strivings of the FRG and even encourage them delaying indefinitely the conclusion of a German peace treaty and preserving the present indefinite situation, fraught with danger? After all it is the absence of a peace treaty that feeds the hopes of aggressive revanchist circles in West Germany for a possibility to revise the results of World War II.

Now in all countries there are more and more people who think of and are concerned with the destinies of the world and who seek not to let it escalate to war. They more and more clearly understand that it is impossible to postpone any further the conclusion of a German peace treaty and to preserve the present dangerous situation.

During my conversations on all those questions with your Ambassador Thompson I told him that we are ready to take into consideration the circumstances that you are finding yourself in in connection with preparation for congressional elections. Such, evidently, are "traditions" in the United States that in the course of election struggle they forget, carried away by passions, about common sense and begin playing with fire, competing in saying more and louder absurd things that sow danger of world war. In order not to play in such conditions a role of some third force breaking from outside into this struggle between the competing parties we decided to put the German problem, so to say, on ice until the end of the elections. We had in mind that after elections we would resume the dialogue. We were under the impression that we would meet an understanding on the part of the American side, all the more that on many questions relating to German peace settlement a certain rapprochement of our positions has already been achieved that gives hope for a possibility of an agreement.

The only question on which the difference between us still remains is, as we believe, that of the presence of foreign troops in West Berlin. And even not the question of the presence of troops as such because on that we have already made a step in your direction, but only the question—the troops of what countries will be stationed there. You insist that the occupation troops of the U.S., Britain and France continue to stay in West Berlin. But that would not normalize the situation even after the signing of a peace treaty because the main source of friction between our countries—the use of West Berlin under the cover of occupation regime as a NATO base—would remain unremoved. That is why we considered and continue to consider that the best thing under the circumstances would be to station in West Berlin the UN troops. To stabilize the situation in Europe it would be also reasonable to have both German states—the GDR and the FRG—admitted to the UN, so that they normalize at last relations between each other and with other states—members of the UN.

Such is our position. I stated it in detail to Ambassador Thompson who, evidently, informed you about it.

Recently I had a talk with your Secretary of the Interior Mr. S. Udall./4/ He made a good impression on me. Our conversation was friendly. And I never expected that at the time I talked with him you would take a decision to request from the Congress an authority to call up 150.000 reservists. Motivating that step of yours you referred to the red-hot state of international atmosphere and to a necessity for you in that connection to react promptly to the dangers that may arise in any part of "the free world". Everybody understands that when the President of the U.S. demands an increase in armed forces and explains that demand by an aggravation of the situation, it means that he considers that the situation is aggravated by the other side, that is by us, the Soviet Union. But we haven't done anything that could give a pretext for that. We did not carry out any mobilization, and did not make any threats.

I must tell you straightforwardly, Mr. President, that your statement with threats against Cuba is just an inconceivable step. Under present circumstances, when there exist thermonuclear weapons, your request to the Congress for an authority to call up 150.000 reservists is not only a step making the atmosphere red-hot, it is already a dangerous sign that you want to pour oil in the flame, to extinguish that red-hot glow by mobilizing new military contingents. And that, naturally, forces the other side to respond in kind. What could it lead to, all the more that you consider that the U.S. has the right to attack Cuba whenever it wishes? But nowadays is not the Middle Ages, though even at the time it was considered brigandage, and measures were taken against such actions. And in our time such actions are absolutely unthinkable. That is what made us to come out with the TASS statement and later at the session of the UN General Assembly to qualify your act, to remind of the norms of international law and to say about West Berlin.

If there were no statement by you on Cuba, we, naturally, as Ambassador Thompson and Mr. Udall were told, would not say anything on West Berlin. Your statement forced us to do so.

We regret that this dangerous line is being continued in the United States now. What is going on, for example, in the U.S. Congress? How can one, for example, fail to notice the decision of the House of Representatives to stop giving U.S. aid to any country that trades with Cuba or whose ships are used for trading with Cuba. Isn't that an act of an unpermissible arbitrariness against freedom of international trade, an act of crude interference into domestic affairs of other countries?

Very serious consequences may have the resolution adopted by the U.S. Senate on the Cuban question. The contents of that resolution gives ground to draw a conclusion that the U.S. is evidently ready to assume responsibility for unleashing thermonuclear war. We consider that if what is written in that resolution were actually carried out it would mean the beginning of war because no country can agree with such interpretation of rights, with such arbitrariness. Then there would be no U.N., everything would collapse and roll into abyss as it happened once when the League of Nations collapsed. Who wrecked it then? Japan and Hitler, who quit the League of Nations to untie their hands and start war. And they did start it. Could it be that the US wants to embark on such road?

We would greatly regret if it were so. We still do not lose hope that we will be able to normalize our relations. But this can be achieved only when the United States and its allies will strictly adhere to the generally recognized norms of international law and will not interfere into the domestic affairs of other states, will not threaten other countries. This is the main thing. And this is the coexistence of which we spoke more than once. You spoke of it too. But what kind of coexistence is this if the United States would attack countries whose government or socio-political system are not to its liking? In our time the world has split into two camps—capitalist and socialist: you have neighbours whom, as you say, you do not like while we have neighbours whom we do not like, but they are your friends and allies. How can one, especially under these circumstances, consider it to be one's right to attack another country merely because its government and internal order are not to your liking? If we conduct such a policy, where this will lead to—to world war.

The most reasonable and the only right policy in our time if we want to ensure peace and to live in peace is the policy of coexistence. And coexistence is first of all recognizing for every people the right to choose its socio-political system and noninterference by states into internal affairs of others. This also directly follows from the U.N. Charter—the Charter which was adopted by our countries who, moreover, are the founding members of the U.N. To interfere into the internal affairs of other states means to undermine the very foundation on which the whole structure of the U.N. is based. One should not wreck the international building which has been created for the task of ensuring peace and peaceful coexistence.

On the state of Soviet-American relations I would also like to express some other considerations.

I spoke, for instance, to Ambassador Thompson of the buzzing of our ships by American planes. On what grounds this buzzing of the ships sailing in international waters is carried on? Moreover, U.S. Navy ships demand that our ship report to them where they go and what cargo they carry. One U.S. Navy ship even attempted to stop our vessel. I told then Mr.

Thompson to convey to you, that we protest against this. Soviet ships which follow on the course given to them by the Government have instructions not to yield to any pirate demands in international waters and to proceed on their course even if they are threatened with opening fire. I said then and I repeat—let them try to stop and sink our ships—this will be the beginning of war because we will answer in kind. We have enough of submarines which can defend the honor of the motherland. Our state possesses other means too. You also have similar means. Why then should such provocations be staged, why should we threaten each other?

I was pleased to receive from you, Mr. President, your assurance that you had given strict instructions not to allow buzzing of our ships. But whether you know it or not the assurance you gave me is not being kept. Your planes even now go on buzzing our ships. I can tell you: in August there were 140 cases of such buzzing.

It has just become known that the Puerto-Rican but actually American authorities detained a British ship and arrested the Soviet cargo aboard that ship—sugar that we have bought in Cuba. If such arbitrariness is not stopped, you yourself realize what it can lead to.

Another unpleasant incident took place in connection with which we had to officially and publicly protest—an intrusion into our air space of a U-2 reconnaissance plane in the area of Sakhalia. You explained that it happened by incident. We took this explanation with understanding. Now it is clear that it did not happen by incident because a U-2 plane also appeared over China. Whom does it belong to? They say—to Chiang Kai-shek. But what is Chiang Kai-shek? Chiang Kai-shek is an affiliate of the U.S. Chiang Kai-shek could not purchase the planes because he himself is on the payroll of the U.S. Therefore those were also the actions of the United States.

Evidently, the same line appears in this case showing that the U.S. has taken a dangerous course. This makes us apprehensive and we are now compelled to take appropriate measures. We did not carry out mobilization and we do not think of one but we have been compelled to order our armed forces to be in peak combat readiness. You forced us to do that by your mobilization and by other measures that you have taken recently.

It may be that all this is being done in connection with pre-election situation in your country. But this is very dangerous. This already goes beyond the limits of the situation within one country because such actions make the international situation red-hot, create a dangerous situation which cannot but cause deep anxiety on the part of the peoples of all countries for the destinies of peace.

It is not pleasant for me, Mr. President, to tell you about it. It would be better, of course, to talk about more pleasant things. But nothing can be done—my position obliges me to give due appraisal of those actions which are now being taken by the United States. We cannot close our eyes and pretend that we do not notice it or do not understand it.

Therefore I would ask you to correctly understand our anxiety and not to do anything that could further aggravate the atmosphere and even expose the world. We on our part again say to you that we will do nothing with regard to West Berlin until the elections in the U.S. After the elections, apparently in the second half of November, it would be necessary in our opinion to continue the dialogue. Of great importance for finding the ways to solve both this problem and other pressing international problems are personal contacts of statesmen on the highest level. I think that if we, persons entrusted with great confidence and bearing enormous responsibility, constantly feel this responsibility, we will have to come to the realization of the necessity of reaching an agreement on West Berlin to eliminate this dangerous hot-bed which spoils our relations all the time./5/

/1/Source: Department of State, Presidential Correspondence: Lot 77 D 163. No classification marking. Kennedy's response of October 8 (Document 58) indicates this message was dated September 28 although no date appears on the source text. Other copies are ibid.: Lot 66 D 204, and in the Kennedy Library, National Security Files, Countries Series, USSR, Khrushchev Correspondence.
/2/Documents 55 and 53.
/3/Reference is to Sir Edward Bullard and Sir William Penney and the 10th Pugwash Conference on Science and World Affairs held in London September 3-7.
/4/Reported in telegram 616 from Moscow, September 7; for text, see volume V.
/5/Printed from an unsigned copy.

"... I am happy to congratulate you and the American people ..."

57. Message From Chairman Khrushchev to President Kennedy

Moscow, October 4, 1962./1/

ESTEEMED MR. PRESIDENT, On behalf of the Soviet people and myself personally, I am happy to congratulate you and the American people on the occasion of the successful completion of the flight of the space ship "Sigma-7" with Cosmonaut W. Schirra. Please convey cordial greetings and very best wishes to Cosmonaut-Airman Walter Schirra.

N. Khrushchev/2/

/1/Source: Department of State, Presidential Correspondence: Lot 66 D 204. No classification marking. The source text is a translation of the Russian-language text, which is ibid. Another copy is in the Kennedy Library, National Security Files, Countries Series, USSR, Khrushchev Correspondence. Also printed in *Public Papers of the Presidents of the United States: John F. Kennedy, 1962*, p. 433. /2/Printed from a copy that bears this typed signature.

"I thank you and the Soviet people ..."

58. Telegram From the Department of State to the Embassy in the Soviet Union

TOP SECRET

Washington, October 6, 1962, 12:25 p.m./1/

826. Following message for delivery soonest to Khrushchev from the President:

Begin Verbatim Text:

Dear Mr. Chairman:
I thank you and the Soviet people on behalf of the American people for your congratulations on Commander Schirra's successful space flight./2/ Your greetings and best wishes have been conveyed to Commander Schirra.

John F. Kennedy.

End Verbatim Text.

Time of release of this message by White House not decided.

Ball

/1/Source: Kennedy Library, National Security Files, Countries Series, USSR, Khrushchev Correspondence. Limited Official Use. Drafted by Owen (SOV) and cleared by Bromley Smith. Another copy of this telegram is in Department of State, Presidential Correspondence: Lot 66 D 204. Also printed in *Public Papers of the Presidents of the United States: John F. Kennedy, 1962*, p. 433.
/2/Document 57.

"So I continue to think that we are within striking distance of a treaty banning nuclear tests in the atmosphere, in outer space and under water."

59. Message From President Kennedy to Chairman Khrushchev

Washington, October 8, 1962./1/

I am giving careful consideration to your communication of September 28th,/2/ and I am glad that we can continue to use this channel as a means of communicating privately and frankly.

I shall want to comment separately on other aspects of your letter, but because of the imminent discussions in the UN I want you to have my views promptly on the subject of nuclear testing. I believe that we are nearer to agreement on this issue than on others, and I believe that we should keep at it to see if we cannot promptly reach the understanding which the world wants and needs.

With respect to this topic, I am encouraged by the areas in which we are in accord and by your statement that the Soviet Union is prepared to make "new efforts" in order to conclude an early agreement. Certainly it would seem we are agreed in our approach to three types of tests—in the atmosphere, in outer space and under water.

With respect to underground tests, I am inclined to agree with you that the recent Pugwash conference of scientists brought forth

some interesting suggestions, particularly those
of British scientists Bullard and Penney. I must
comment that we interpret those suggestions in
somewhat different light than your letter indicates you do. Nonetheless the suggestions certainly are worthy of intensive development. The
development of automatic unmanned seismic
mechanisms might very well, if properly worked
out, facilitate agreement on the means of actually detecting underground explosions—although
my scientists indicate that it would require much
more than the two or three such stations you
mentioned as being located directly in the areas
most frequently subjected to earthquakes. Of
course, these mechanical devices would still have
to be supplemented by a modest number of on-
site inspections—for scientists agree that the
data gathered by these machines would still leave
doubt as to the cause of the explosion in a number of cases. Surely, considering the great value
for international relations and the general security and tranquility of the world which the comprehensive agreement on the cessation of nuclear
tests would entail, we can agree on the number of
such inspections which would be necessary to
identify the nature or cause of these explosions.
Once that is done, with the number of unmanned
stations worked out scientifically, and the method
for international coordination established, we can
conclude a treaty which will enable all peoples of
the world to rest easier.

In the meantime, you suggest that the agreement we can more promptly reach on the cessation of tests in the atmosphere, in outer space

and under water be accompanied by a five year moratorium on underground explosions. But surely it will not take five years to reach agreement—if agreement is ever to be reached—on banning underground tests, particularly in view of our mutual interest in the role of automatic seismic stations for detecting explosions. I would not feel justified in submitting to the Senate, moreover, a treaty on tests in other environments which would be discarded if agreement was not reached on testing under ground. It is nuclear explosions in the atmosphere, in outer space and under water which increase the percentage of fall-out and are the cause of grave concern to all peoples of the world. Such a treaty, in short, would be in itself a great step forward, both for humanitarian and political reasons.

So I continue to think that we are within striking distance of a treaty banning nuclear tests in the atmosphere, in outer space and under water. I believe we should try to work out such an agreement in time to meet the target day of January 1, 1963, and I think also that in the meanwhile we should be working intensively to make progress as rapidly as possible on the remaining problem of testing under ground. I believe that our negotiators should return to their labors in an intense effort to reach agreement on the questions that still divide us, and I hope very much that they will be able to make real and rapid progress in the meetings now scheduled to resume on November 12th.

JFK/3/

/1/Source: Department of State, Presidential Correspondence: Lot 66 D 204. Top Secret. Other copies are ibid.: Lot 77 D 163, and in the Kennedy Library, National Security Files, Countries Series, USSR, Khrushchev Correspondence.
/2/Document 56.
/3/Printed from a copy that bears these initials in an unidentified hand.

"I have not assumed that you or any other sane man would, in this nuclear age, deliberately plunge the world into war . . ."

60. Letter From President Kennedy to Chairman Khrushchev

Washington, October 22, 1962./1/

DEAR MR. CHAIRMAN: A copy of the statement I am making tonight concerning developments in Cuba and the reaction of my Government thereto has been handed to your Ambassador in Washington./2/ In view of the gravity of the developments to which I refer, I want you to know immediately and accurately the position of my Government in this matter.

In our discussions and exchanges on Berlin and other international questions, the one thing that has most concerned me has been the possibility that your Government would not correctly understand the will and determination of the United States in any given situation, since I have not assumed that you or any other sane man would, in this nuclear age, deliberately plunge the world into war which it is crystal clear no country could win and which could only result in catastrophic consequences to the whole world, including the aggressor.

At our meeting in Vienna and subsequently, I expressed our readiness and desire to find, through peaceful negotiation, a solution to any and all problems that divide us. At the same time, I made clear that in view of the objectives of the ideology to which you adhere, the United States could not tolerate any action on your part which in a major way disturbed the existing over-all balance of power in the world. I stated that an attempt to force abandonment of our responsibilities and commitments in Berlin would constitute such an action and that the United States would resist with all the power at its command.

It was in order to avoid any incorrect assessment on the part of your Government with respect to Cuba that I publicly stated that if certain developments in Cuba took place, the United States would do whatever must be done to protect its own security and that of its allies.

Moreover, the Congress adopted a resolution expressing its support of this declared policy./3/ Despite this, the rapid development of long-range missile bases and other offensive weapons systems in Cuba has proceeded. I must tell you that the United States is determined that this threat to the security of this hemisphere be removed. At the same time, I wish to point out that the action we are taking is the minimum necessary to remove the threat to the security of the nations of this hemisphere. The fact of this minimum response should not be taken as a basis, however, for any misjudgment on your part.

I hope that your Government will refrain from any action which would widen or deepen this already grave crisis and that we can agree to resume the path of peaceful negotiations.

Sincerely,

JFK/4/

/1/Source: Department of State, Presidential Correspondence: Lot 66 D 204. Eyes Only. At 7:41 p.m. on October 21 the Department of State had sent Ambassador Kohler the first draft of this message. (Telegram 961 to Moscow; ibid.: Lot 77 D 163) Subsequent changes and additions resulted in only the second and final paragraphs remaining as originally drafted. The message was delivered to the Foreign Ministry at about 6 p.m. Washington time. Another copy of this letter is in the Kennedy Library, National Security Files, Countries Series, USSR, Khrushchev Correspondence. Also printed in Department of State *Bulletin,* November 19, 1973, pp. 635-636, and Claflin, The *President Wants To Know,* pp. 205-206. This letter and the letters and messages exchanged through December 14 (Document 84) were published in English and Russian in United States Information Agency, *Problems of Communism,* Special Edition, Spring 1992.
/2/For text of the President's October 22 radio and television report to the American people on the Soviet arms buildup in Cuba, see *Public Papers of the Presidents of the United States: John F. Kennedy, 1962,* pp. 806-809. A 3-paragraph memorandum of Rusk's conversation with Dobrynin at 6 p.m., during which the Secretary of State gave the Soviet Ambassador copies of the President's address and this message is in Department of State, Central Files, 611.61/10-2262.
/3/For text of this resolution, October 3, see *American Foreign Policy: Current Documents, 1962,* pp. 389-390.
/4/Printed from a copy that bears these initials in an unidentified hand.

"I hope that Government of United States will show prudence and renounce actions pursued by you, which could lead to catastrophic consequences for peace throughout the world."

61. Telegram From the Embassy in the Soviet Union to the Department of State

Moscow, October 23, 1962, 5 p.m./1/

1042. Policy. Embtel 1041./2/ Embassy translation follows of Khrushchev's letter of October 23 to President. Kuznetsov informed me letter would not be published "for time being."

Begin Text. Mr. President.

I have just received your letter, and have also acquainted myself with text of your speech of October 22 regarding Cuba./3/

I should say frankly that measures outlined in your statement represent a serious threat to peace and security of peoples. United States has openly taken path of gross violation of Charter of United Nations, path of violation of international norms of freedom of navigation on high seas, path of aggressive actions both against Cuba and against Soviet Union. Statement of Government of United States America cannot be evaluated in any other way than as naked interference in domestic affairs of Cuban Republic, Soviet Union, and other states. Charter of United Nations and international norms do not give right to any state whatsoever to establish in international waters control of vessels bound for shores of Cuban Republic.

It is self-understood that we also cannot recognize right of United States to establish control over armaments essential to Republic of Cuba for strengthening of its defensive capacity.

We confirm that armaments now on Cuba, regardless of classification to which they belong, are destined exclusively for defensive purposes, in order to secure Cuban Republic from attack of aggressor.

I hope that Government of United States will show prudence and renounce actions pursued by you, which could lead to catastrophic consequences for peace throughout world.

Viewpoint of Soviet Government with regard to your statement of October 22 is set forth in statement of Soviet Government, which is being conveyed to you through your Ambassador in Moscow./4/

N. Khrushchev.

End Text.

Original of letter being airpouched today.

Kohler

/1/Source: Kennedy Library, National Security Files, Countries Series, USSR, Khrushchev Correspondence. Secret; Eyes Only; Niact; Elite. Passed to the White House at 11:05 a.m. October 23. A Department of State translation of this message is in Department of State, Presidential Correspondence: Lot 66 D 204, along with the Russian-language text. Also printed in Department of State *Bulletin*, November 19, 1973, pp. 636-637.
/2/Dated October 23. (Department of State, Central Files, 611.3722/10-2362)
/3/Document 60 and footnote 2 thereto.
/4/For text of this statement, see *The New York Times*, October 14, 1962.

"I think you will recognize that the steps which started the current chain of events was the action of your Government in secretly furnishing offensive weapons to Cuba."

62. Telegram From the Department of State to the Embassy in the Soviet Union

Washington, October 23, 1962, 6:51 p.m./1/

985. You should deliver following letter addressed by the President to Chairman Khrushchev immediately. This replaces message contained Deptel 982./2/

"Dear Mr. Chairman:

I have received your letter of October twenty-third./3/ I think you will recognize that the steps which started the current chain of events was the

303

action of your Government in secretly furnishing
offensive weapons to Cuba. We will be discussing
this matter in the Security Council. In the meantime, I am concerned that we both show prudence
and do nothing to allow events to make the situation more difficult to control than it already is.

I hope that you will issue immediately the necessary instructions to your ships to observe the
terms of the quarantine, the basis of which was
established by the vote of the Organization of
American States this afternoon, and which will go
into effect at 1400 hours Greenwich time October
twenty-four.

Sincerely, JFK."

Rusk

/1/Source: Department of State, Presidential Correspondence: Lot 66 D 204. Confidential; Niact; Eyes Only. Drafted
and approved by Ball and cleared by Bundy. Other copies of
this message are ibid.: Lot 77 D 163, and in the Kennedy
Library, National Security Files, Countries Series, USSR,
Khrushchev Correspondence. Also printed in Department of
State *Bulletin,* November 19, 1973, p. 636.
/2/Not printed. (Department of State, Presidential
Correspondence: Lot 66 D 204)
/3/See Document 61.

"In presenting us with these conditions, you, Mr. President, have flung a challenge at us."

63. Letter From Chairman Khrushchev to President Kennedy

Moscow, October 24, 1962./1/

DEAR MR. PRESIDENT: I have received your letter of October 23,/2/ have studied it, and am answering you.

Just imagine, Mr. President, that we had presented you with the conditions of an ultimatum which you have presented us by your action. How would you have reacted to this? I think that you would have been indignant at such a step on our part. And this would have been understandable to us.

In presenting us with these conditions, you, Mr. President, have flung a challenge at us. Who asked you to do this? By what right did you do this? Our ties with the Republic of Cuba, like our relations with other states, regardless of what kind of states they may be, concern only the two countries between which these relations exist. And if we now speak of the quarantine to which your letter refers, a quarantine may be established, according to accepted international practice, only by agreement of states between themselves, and not by some third party. Quarantines exist, for example, on agricultural goods and products. But in this case the question is in no way one of quarantine, but rather of far more serious things, and you yourself understand this.

You, Mr. President, are not declaring a quarantine, but rather are setting forth an ultimatum and threatening that if we do not give in to your demands you will use force. Consider what you are saying! And you want to persuade me to agree to this! What would it mean to agree to these demands? It would mean guiding oneself in one's relations with other countries not by reason, but by submitting to arbitrariness. You are no longer appealing to reason, but wish to intimidate us.

No, Mr. President, I cannot agree to this, and I think that in your own heart you recognize that I am correct. I am convinced that in my place you would act the same way.

Reference to the decision of the Organization of American States cannot in any way substantiate the demands now advanced by the United States. This Organization has absolutely no authority or basis for adopting decisions such as the one you speak of in your letter. Therefore, we do not recognize these decisions. International law exists and universally recognized norms of conduct exist. We firmly adhere to the principles of international law and observe strictly the norms which regulate navigation on the high seas, in international waters. We observe these norms and enjoy the rights recognized by all states.

You wish to compel us to renounce the rights that every sovereign state enjoys, you are trying to legislate in questions of international law, and you are violating the universally accepted norms of that law. And you are doing all this not only out of hatred for the Cuban people and its government, but also because of considerations of the election campaign in the United States. What morality, what law can justify such an approach by the American Government to international affairs? No such morality or law can be found, because the actions of the United States with regard to Cuba constitute outright banditry or, if you like, the folly of degenerate imperialism. Unfortunately, such folly can bring grave suffering to the peoples of all countries, and to no lesser degree to the American people themselves, since the United States has completely lost its former isolation with the advent of modern types of armament.

Therefore, Mr. President, if you coolly weigh the situation which has developed, not giving way to passions, you will understand that the Soviet Union cannot fail to reject the arbitrary demands of the United States. When you confront us with such conditions, try to put yourself in our place and consider how the United States would react to these conditions. I do not doubt that if someone attempted to dictate similar conditions to you—the United States—you would reject such an attempt. And we also say—no.

The Soviet Government considers that the violation of the freedom to use international waters and international air space is an act of aggression which pushes mankind toward the abyss of a world nuclear-missile war. Therefore, the Soviet Government cannot instruct the captains of Soviet vessels bound for Cuba to observe the orders of American naval forces blockading that Island. Our instructions to Soviet mariners are to observe strictly the universally accepted norms of navigation in international waters and not to retreat one step from them. And if the American side violates these rules, it must realize what responsibility will rest upon it in that case.

Naturally we will not simply be bystanders with regard to piratical acts by American ships on the high seas. We will then be forced on our part to take the measures we consider necessary and adequate in order to protect our rights. We have everything necessary to do so.

Respectfully,

N. Khrushchev/3/

/1/Source: Kennedy Library, President's Office Files, Cuba. No classification marking. This "official translation" prepared in the Department of State and an "informal translation" from the Embassy in Moscow (transmitted in telegram 1070, October 25; Department of State, Presidential Correspondence: Lot 66 D 304) are printed in Department of State *Bulletin,* November 19, 1973, pp. 637-639.
/2/See Document 62.
/3/Printed from a translation that indicates that Khrushchev signed the original Russian-language text.

"The sequence of events is clear."

64. Telegram From the Department of State to the Embassy in the Soviet Union

Washington, October 25, 1962, 1:59 a.m./1/

997. Ref Embtel 1070./2/ Signed original following message from President to Khrushchev delivered to Soviet Embassy 1:45 a.m. Washington time October 25. Please deliver to highest ranking Soviet official immediately available.

October 25, 1962

"Dear Mr. Chairman:

I have received your letter of October 24,/3/ and I regret very much that you still do not appear to understand what it is that has moved us in this matter.

The sequence of events is clear. In August there were reports of important shipments of military equipment and technicians from the Soviet Union to Cuba. In early September I indicated very plainly that the United States would regard any shipment of offensive weapons as presenting the gravest issues. After that time, this Government received the most explicit assurances from your Government and its representatives, both publicly and privately, that no offensive weapons were being sent to Cuba. If you will review the statement issued by Tass in September, you will see how clearly this assurance was given.

In reliance on these solemn assurances I urged restraint upon those in this country who were urging action in this matter at that time. And then I learned beyond doubt what you have not denied—namely, that all these public assurances were false and that your military people had set out recently to establish a set of missile bases in Cuba.

I ask you to recognize clearly, Mr. Chairman, that it was not I who issued the first challenge in this case, and that in the light of this record these activities in Cuba required the responses I have announced.

I repeat my regret that these events should cause a deterioration in our relations. I hope that your Government will take the necessary action to permit a restoration of the earlier situation.

Sincerely yours, John F. Kennedy."

Please report time delivery.

Rusk

/1/Source: Department of State, Presidential Correspondence: Lot 66 D 204. Confidential; Niact; Eyes Only. Drafted at the White House. Another copy is ibid.: Lot 77 D 163, and in the Kennedy Library, National Security Files, Countries Series, USSR, Khrushchev Correspondence. Also printed in Department of State *Bulletin,* November 19, 1973, p. 639.
/2/See the source note, Document 63.
/3/Document 63.

"What would a war give you?"

65. Telegram From the Embassy in the Soviet Union to the Department of State

Moscow, October 26, 1962, 7 p.m./1/

1101. Policy. Embassy translation follows of letter from Khrushchev to President delivered to Embassy by messenger 4:43 p.m. Moscow time October 26, under cover of letter from Gromyko to me.

Begin Text.

Dear Mr. President:

I have received your letter of October 25./2/ From your letter, I got the feeling that you have some understanding of the situation which has developed and (some) sense of responsibility. I value this.

Now we have already publicly exchanged our evaluations of the events around Cuba and each of us has set forth his explanation and his understanding of these events. Consequently, I would judge that, apparently, a continuation of an exchange of opinions at such a distance, even in the form of secret letters, will hardly add anything to that which one side has already said to the other.

I think you will understand me correctly if you are really concerned about the welfare of the world. Everyone needs peace: both capitalists, if they have not lost their reason, and, still more, Communists, people who know how to value not only their own lives but, more than anything, the lives of the peoples. We, Communists, are against all wars between states in general and have been defending the cause of peace since we came into the world. We have always regarded war as a calamity, and not as a game nor as a means for the attainment of definite goals, nor, all the more, as a goal in itself. Our goals are clear, and the means to attain them is labor. War is our enemy and a calamity for all the peoples.

It is thus that we, Soviet people, and, together with US, other peoples as well, understand the questions of war and peace. I can, in any case,

311

firmly say this for the peoples of the Socialist countries, as well as for all progressive people who want peace, happiness, and friendship among peoples.

I see, Mr. President, that you too are not devoid of a sense of anxiety for the fate of the world/3/ understanding, and of what war entails. What would a war give you? You are threatening us with war. But you well know that the very least which you would receive in reply would be that you would experience the same consequences as those which you sent us. And that must be clear to us, people invested with authority, trust, and responsibility. We must not succumb to intoxication and petty passions, regardless of whether elections are impending in this or that country, or not impending. These are all transient things, but if indeed war should break out, then it would not be in our power to stop it, for such is the logic of war. I have participated in two wars and know that war ends when it has rolled through cities and villages, everywhere sowing death and destruction.

In the name of the Soviet Government and the Soviet people, I assure you that your conclusions regarding offensive weapons on Cuba are groundless. It is apparent from what you have written me that our conceptions are different on this score, or rather, we have different estimates of these or those military means. Indeed, in reality, the same forms of weapons can have different interpretations.

You are a military man and, I hope, will understand me. Let us take for example a simple cannon. What sort of means is this: offensive or defensive? A cannon is a defensive means if it is set up to defend boundaries or a fortified area. But if one concentrates artillery, and adds to it the necessary number of troops, then the same cannons do become an offensive means, because they prepare and clear the way for infantry to attack. The same happens with missile-nuclear weapons as well, with any type of this weapon.

You are mistaken if you think that any of our means on Cuba are offensive. However, let us not quarrel now. It is apparent that I will not be able to convince you of this. But I say to you: You, Mr. President, are a military man and should understand: Can one attack, if one has on one's territory even an enormous quantity of missiles of various effective radiuses and various power, but using only these means. These missiles are a means of extermination and destruction. But one cannot attack with these missiles, even nuclear missiles of a power of 100 megatons because only people, troops, can attack. Without people, any means however powerful cannot be offensive.

How can one, consequently, give such a completely incorrect interpretation as you are now giving, to the effect that some sort of means on Cuba are offensive. All the means located there, and I assure you of this, have a defensive character, are on Cuba solely for the purposes of defense, and we have sent them to Cuba at the request of the Cuban Government. You, however, say that these are offensive means.

But, Mr. President, do you really seriously think that Cuba can attack the United States and that even we together with Cuba can attack you from the territory of Cuba? Can you really think that way? How is it possible? We do not understand this. Has something so new appeared in military strategy that one can think that it is possible to attack thus. I say precisely attack, and not destroy, since barbarians, people who have lost their sense, destroy.

I believe that you have no basis to think this way. You can regard us with distrust, but, in any case, you can be calm in this regard, that we are of sound mind and understand perfectly well that if we attack you, you will respond the same way. But you too will receive the same that you hurl against us. And I think that you also understand this. My conversation with you in Vienna gives me the right to talk to you this way.

This indicates that we are normal people, that we correctly understand and correctly evaluate the situation. Consequently, how can we permit the incorrect actions which you ascribe to us? Only lunatics or suicides, who themselves want to perish and to destroy the whole world before they die, could do this. We, however, want to live and do not at all want to destroy your country. We want something quite different: To compete with your country on a peaceful basis. We quarrel with you, we have differences on ideological questions. But our view of the world consists in this, that ideological questions, as well as economic problems, should be solved not by military means, they must be solved on the basis of peaceful competition, i.e., as this is understood in capitalist society, on the basis of competition. We have proceeded and are proceeding from the fact that the peaceful co-existence of the two different social-political systems, now existing in the world, is necessary, that it is necessary to assure a stable peace. That is the sort of principle we hold.

You have now proclaimed piratical measures, which were employed in the Middle Ages, when ships proceeding in international waters were attacked, and you have called this "a quarantine" around Cuba. Our vessels, apparently, will soon enter the zone which your Navy is patrolling. I assure you that these vessels, now bound for Cuba, are carrying the most innocent peaceful cargoes. Do you really think that we only occupy ourselves with the carriage of so-called offensive weapons, atomic and hydrogen bombs? Although perhaps your military people imagine that these (cargoes) are some sort of special type of weapon, I assure you that they are the most ordinary peaceful products.

Consequently, Mr. President, let us show good sense. I assure you that on those ships, which are bound for Cuba, there are no weapons at all. The weapons which were necessary for the defense of Cuba are already there. I do not want to say that there were not any shipments of weapons at all. No, there were such shipments. But now Cuba has already received the necessary means of defense.

I don't know whether you can understand me and believe me. But I should like to have you believe in yourself and to agree that one cannot give way to passions; it is necessary to control them. And in what direction are events now developing? If you stop the vessels, then, as you yourself know, that would be piracy. If we started to do that with regard to your ships, then you would also be as indignant as we and the whole world now are. One cannot give another interpretation to such actions, because one cannot legalize lawlessness. If this were permitted, then there would be no peace, there would also be no peaceful coexistence. We should then be forced to put into effect the necessary measures of a defensive character to protect our interests in accordance with international law. Why should this be done? To what would all this lead?

Let us normalize relations. We have received an appeal from the Acting Secretary General of the UN, U Thant, with his proposals. I have already answered him. His proposals come to this, that our side should not transport armaments of any kind to Cuba during a certain period of time, while negotiations are being conducted—and we are ready to enter such negotiations—and the other side should not undertake any sort of piratical actions against vessels engaged in navigation on the high seas. I consider these proposals reasonable. This would be a way out of the situation which has been created, which would give the peoples the possibility of breathing calmly. You have asked what happened, what evoked the delivery of weapons to Cuba? You have spoken about this to our Minister of Foreign Affairs. I will tell you frankly, Mr. President, what evoked it.

We were very grieved by the fact—I spoke about it in Vienna—that a landing took place, that an attack on Cuba was committed, as a result of which many Cubans perished. You yourself told me then that this had been a mistake. I respected that explanation. You repeated it to me several times, pointing out that not everybody occupying a high position would acknowledge his mistakes as you had done. I value such frankness. For my part, I told you that we too possess no less courage; we also acknowledged those mistakes which had been committed during the history of our state, and not only acknowledged, but sharply condemned them.

If you are really concerned about the peace and welfare of your people, and this is your responsibility as President, then I, as the Chairman of the Council of Ministers, am concerned for my people. Moreover, the preservation of world peace should be our joint concern, since if, under contemporary conditions, war should break out, it would be a war not only between the reciprocal claims, but a world wide cruel and destructive war.

Why have we proceeded to assist Cuba with military and economic aid? The answer is: We have proceeded to do so only for reasons of humanitarianism. At one time, our people itself had a revolution, when Russia was still a backward country. We were attacked then. We were the target of attack by many countries. The USA participated in that adventure. This has been recorded by participants in the aggression against our country. A whole book has been written about this by General Graves, who, at that time, commanded the US Expeditionary Corps.

Graves called it "The American Adventure in Siberia."

We know how difficult it is to accomplish a revolution and how difficult it is to reconstruct a country on new foundations. We sincerely sympathize with Cuba and the Cuban people, but we are not interfering in questions of domestic structure, we are not interfering in their affairs. The Soviet Union desires to help the Cubans build their life as they themselves wish and that others should not hinder them.

You once said that the United States was not preparing an invasion. But you also declared that you sympathized with the Cuban counter-revolutionary emigrants, that you support them and would help them to realize their plans against the present Government of Cuba. It is also not a secret to anyone that the threat of armed attack, aggression, has constantly hung, and continues to hang over Cuba. It was only this which impelled us to respond to the request of the Cuban Government to furnish it aid for the strengthening of the defensive capacity of this country.

If assurances were given by the President and the Government of the United States that the USA itself would not participate in an attack on Cuba and would restrain others from actions of this sort, if you would recall your fleet, this would immediately change everything. I am not speaking for Fidel Castro, but I think that he and the Government of Cuba, evidently, would declare demobilization and would appeal to the people to get down to peaceful labor. Then, too, the question of armaments would disappear, since, if there is no threat, then armaments are a burden for every people. Then too, the question of the destruction, not only of the armaments which you call offensive, but of all other armaments as well, would look different.

I spoke in the name of the Soviet Government in the United Nations and introduced a proposal for the disbandment of all armies and for the destruction of all armaments. How then can I now count on those armaments?

Armaments bring only disasters. When one accumulates them, this damages the economy, and if one puts them to use, then they destroy people on both sides. Consequently, only a madman can believe that armaments are the principal means in the life of society. No, they are an enforced loss of human energy, and what is more are for the destruction of man himself. If people do not show wisdom, then in the final analysis they will come to a clash, like blind moles, and then reciprocal extermination will begin.

Let us therefore show statesmanlike wisdom. I propose: We, for our part, will declare that our ships, bound for Cuba, will not carry any kind of armaments. You would declare that the United States will not invade Cuba with its forces and will not support any sort of forces which might intend to carry out an invasion of Cuba. Then the necessity for the presence of our military specialists in Cuba would disappear.

Mr. President, I appeal to you to weigh well what the aggressive, piratical actions, which you have declared the USA intends to carry out in international waters, would lead to. You yourself know that any sensible man simply cannot agree with this, cannot recognize your right to such actions.

If you did this as the first step towards the unleashing of war, well then, it is evident that nothing else is left to us but to accept this challenge of yours. If, however, you have not lost your self-control and sensibly conceive what this might lead to, then, Mr. President, we and you ought not now to pull on the ends of the rope in which you have tied the knot of war, because the more the two of us pull, the tighter that knot will be tied. And a moment may come when that knot will be tied so tight that even he who tied it will not have the strength to untie it, and then it will be necessary to cut that knot, and what that would mean is not for me to explain to you, because you yourself understand perfectly of what terrible forces our countries dispose.

Consequently, if there is no intention to tighten that knot and thereby to doom the world to the catastrophe of thermonuclear war, then let us not only relax the forces pulling on the ends of the rope, let us take measures to untie that knot. We are ready for this.

We welcome all forces which stand on positions of peace. Consequently, I expressed gratitude to Mr. Bertrand Russell, too, who manifests alarm and concern for the fate of the world, and I readily responded to the appeal of the Acting Secretary General of the UN, U Thant.

There, Mr. President, are my thoughts, which, if you agreed with them, could put an end to that tense situation which is disturbing all peoples.

These thoughts are dictated by a sincere desire to relieve the situation, to remove the threat of war.

Respectfully yours,

/s/ N. Khrushchev

October 26, 1962.

End Text.

Original of letter being air pouched today under transmittal slip to Executive Secretariat.

Kohler

/1/Source: Kennedy Library, National Security Files, Countries Series, USSR, Khrushchev Correspondence. Secret; Eyes Only; Niact; Verbatim Text. Passed to the White House at 9:15 p.m. October 26. Other copies of this message are in Department of State, Presidential Correspondence: Lot 66 D 204, and ibid.: Lot 77 D 163. A copy of the Russian-language text is in the former. This "informal translation" and an "official translation" prepared by the Department of State are printed in Department of State *Bulletin,* November 19, 1973, pp. 640-645.
/2/See Document 64.
/3/Garble in the source text. It was subsequently corrected to read "not without an".

"I therefore make this proposal: We are willing to remove from Cuba the means which you regard as offensive."

66. Letter From Chairman Khrushchev to President Kennedy

Moscow, October 27, 1962./1/

DEAR MR. PRESIDENT, I have studied with great satisfaction your reply to Mr. Thant concerning measures that should be taken to avoid contact between our vessels and thereby avoid irreparable and fatal consequences./2/ This reasonable step on your part strengthens my belief that you are showing concern for the preservation of peace, which I note with satisfaction.

I have already said that our people, our Government, and I personally, as Chairman of the Council of Ministers, are concerned solely with having our country develop and occupy a worthy place among all peoples of the world in economic competition, in the development of culture and the arts, and in raising the living standard of the people. This is the most noble and necessary field for competition, and both the victor and the vanquished will derive only benefit from it, because it means peace and an increase in the means by which man lives and finds enjoyment.

In your statement you expressed the opinion that the main aim was not simply to come to an agreement and take measures to prevent contact between our vessels and consequently a deepening of the crisis which could, as a result of such contacts spark a military conflict, after which all negotiations would be superfluous because other forces and other laws would then come into play—the laws of war. I agree with you that this is only the first step. The main thing that must be done is to normalize and stabilize the state of peace among states and among peoples.

I understand your concern for the security of the United States, Mr. President, because this is the primary duty of a President. But we too are disturbed about these same questions; I bear these same obligations as Chairman of the Council of Ministers of the U.S.S.R. You have been alarmed by the fact that we have aided Cuba with weapons, in order to strengthen its defense capability—precisely defense capability—because whatever weapons it may possess, Cuba cannot be equated with you since the difference in magnitude is so great, particularly in view of modern means of destruction. Our aim has been and is to help Cuba, and no one can dispute the humanity of our motives, which are oriented toward enabling Cuba to live peacefully and develop in the way its people desire.

You wish to ensure the security of your country, and this is understandable. But Cuba, too, wants the same thing; all countries want to maintain their security. But how are we, the Soviet Union, our Government, to assess your actions which are expressed in the fact that you have surrounded the Soviet Union with military bases; surrounded our allies with military bases; placed military bases literally around our country; and stationed your missile armaments there? This is no secret. Responsible American personages openly declare that it is so. Your missiles are located in Britain, are located in Italy, and are aimed against us. Your missiles are located in

Turkey.

You are disturbed over Cuba. You say that this disturbs you because it is 90 miles by sea from the coast of the United States of America. But Turkey adjoins us; our sentries patrol back and forth and see each other. Do you consider, then, that you have the right to demand security for your own country and the removal of the weapons you call offensive, but do not accord the same right to us? You have placed destructive missile weapons, which you call offensive, in Turkey, literally next to us. How then can recognition of our equal military capacities be reconciled with such unequal relations between our great states? This is irreconcilable.

It is good, Mr. President, that you have agreed to have our represent-atives meet and begin talks, apparently through the mediation of U Thant, Acting Secretary General of the United Nations. Consequently, he to some degree has assumed the role of a mediator and we consider that he will be able to cope with this responsible mission, provided, of course, that each party drawn into this controversy displays good will.

I think it would be possible to end the controversy quickly and normalize the situation, and then the people could breathe more easily, considering that statesmen charged with responsibility are of sober mind and have an awareness of their responsibility combined with the ability to solve complex questions and not bring things to a military catastrophe.

I therefore make this proposal: We are willing to remove from Cuba the means which you regard as offensive. We are willing to carry this out and to make this pledge in the United Nations. Your representatives will make a declaration to the effect that the United States, for its part, considering the uneasiness and anxiety of the Soviet State, will remove its analogous means from Turkey. Let us reach agreement as to the period of time needed by you and by us to bring this about. And, after that, persons entrusted by the United Nations Security Council could inspect on the spot the fulfillment of the pledges made. Of course, the permission of the Governments of Cuba and Turkey is necessary for the entry into those countries of these representatives and for the inspection of the fulfillment of the pledge made by each side. Of course it would be best if these representatives enjoyed the confidence of the Security Council as well as yours and mine— both the United States and the Soviet Union—and also that of Turkey and Cuba. I do not think it would be difficult to select people who would enjoy the trust and respect of all parties concerned.

We, in making this pledge, in order to give satisfaction and hope of the peoples of Cuba and Turkey and to strengthen their confidences in their security, will make a statement within the framework of the Security Council to the effect that the Soviet Government gives a solemn promise to respect the inviolability of the borders and sovereignty of Turkey, not to interfere in its internal affairs, not to invade Turkey, not to make available our territory as a bridgehead for such an invasion, and that it would also restrain those who contemplate committing aggression against Turkey, either from the territory of the Soviet Union or from the territory of Turkey's other neighboring states.

The United States Government will make a similar statement within the framework of the Security Council regarding Cuba. It will declare that the United States will respect the inviolability of Cuba's borders and its sovereignty, will pledge not to interfere in its internal affairs, not to invade Cuba itself or make its territory available as a bridgehead for such an invasion, and will also restrain those who might contemplate committing aggression against Cuba, either from the territory of the United States or from the territory of Cuba's other neighboring states.

Of course, for this we would have to come to an agreement with you and specify a certain time limit. Let us agree to some period of time, but without unnecessary delay—say within two or three weeks, not longer than a month.

The means situated in Cuba, of which you speak and which disturb you, as you have stated, are in the hands of Soviet officers. Therefore, any accidental use of them to the detriment of the United States is excluded. These means are situated in Cuba at the request of the Cuban Government and are only for defense purposes. Therefore, if there is no invasion of Cuba, or attack on the Soviet Union or any of our other allies, then of course these means are not and will not be a threat to anyone. For they are not for purposes of attack.

If you are agreeable to my proposal, Mr. President, then we would send our representatives to New York, to the United Nations, and would give them comprehensive instructions in order that an agreement may be reached more quickly. If you also select your people and give them the corresponding instructions, then this question can be quickly resolved.

Why would I like to do this? Because the whole world is now apprehensive and expects sensible actions of us. The greatest joy for all peoples would be the announcement of our agreement and of the eradication of the controversy that has arisen. I attach great importance to this agreement in so far as it could serve as a good beginning and could in particular make it easier to reach agreement on banning nuclear weapons tests. The question of the tests could be solved in parallel fashion, without connecting one with the other, because these are different issues. However, it is important that agreement be reached on both these issues so as to present humanity with a fine gift, and also to gladden it with the news that agreement has been reached on the cessation of nuclear tests and that consequently the atmosphere will no longer be poisoned. Our position and yours on this issue are very close together.

All of this could possibly serve as a good impetus toward the finding of mutually acceptable agreements on other controversial issues on which you and I have been exchanging views. These issues have so far not been resolved, but they are awaiting urgent solution, which would clear up the international atmosphere. We are prepared for this.

These are my proposals, Mr. President.

Respectfully yours,

N. Khrushchev/3/

/1/Source: Department of State, Presidential Correspondence: Lot 66 D 204. No classification marking. Other copies
of this letter are ibid.: Lot 77 D 163, and in the Kennedy
Library, National Security Files, Countries Series, USSR,
Khrushchev Correspondence. This "official translation" prepared by the Department of State and an "informal translation" from the Embassy in Moscow are printed in
Department of State Bulletin, November 19, 1973, pp. 646-
649. A note on the source text indicates a copy was sent to
Acting Secretary General U Thant. *Problems of Communism*
reports that this message was broadcast over Moscow radio
at 5 p.m., the same time the Russian text was delivered to
the Embassy.
/2/Regarding this message, see vol. XI, Document 59.
/3/Printed from a translation that indicates Khrushchev
signed the original Russian-language text.

"We, on our part, would agree . . . to give assurances against an invasion of Cuba."

67. Telegram From the Department of State to the Embassy in the Soviet Union

Washington, October 27, 1962, 8:05 p.m./1/

1015. Following message from President to
Khrushchev should be delivered as soon as possible to highest available Soviet official. Text has
been handed Soviet Embassy in Washington and

has been released to press:

"Dear Mr. Chairman:

I have read your letter of October 26th/2/ with great care and welcomed the statement of your desire to seek a prompt solution to the problem. The first thing that needs to be done, however, is for work to cease on offensive missile bases in Cuba and for all weapons systems in Cuba capable of offensive use to be rendered inoperable, under effective United Nations arrangements.

Assuming this is done promptly, I have given my representatives in New York instructions that will permit them to work out this weekend—in cooperation with the Acting Secretary General and your representative—an arrangement for a permanent solution to the Cuban problem along the lines suggested in your letter of October 26th. As I read your letter, the key elements of your proposals—which seem generally acceptable as I understand them—are as follows:

1) You would agree to remove these weapons systems from Cuba under appropriate United Nations observation and supervision; and undertake, with suitable safeguards, to halt the further introduction of such weapons systems into Cuba.

2) We, on our part, would agree—upon the establishment of adequate arrangements through the United Nations to ensure the carrying out and continuation of these commitments—(a) to remove promptly the quarantine measures now in effect and (b) to give assurances against an

329

invasion of Cuba. I am confident that other nations of the Western Hemisphere would be prepared to do likewise.

If you will give your representative similar instructions, there is no reason why we should not be able to complete these arrangements and announce them to the world within a couple of days. The effect of such a settlement on easing world tensions would enable us to work toward a more general arrangement regarding 'other armaments', as proposed in your second letter which you made public./3/ I would like to say again that the United States is very much interested in reducing tensions and halting the arms race; and if your letter signifies that you are prepared to discuss a detente affecting NATO and the Warsaw Pact, we are quite prepared to consider with our allies any useful proposals.

But the first ingredient, let me emphasize, is the cessation of work on missile sites in Cuba and measures to render such weapons inoperable, under effective international guarantees. The continuation of this threat, or a prolonging of this discussion concerning Cuba by linking these problems to the broader questions of European and world security, would surely lead to an intensification of the Cuban crisis and a grave risk to the peace of the world. For this reason I hope we can quickly agree along the lines in this letter and in your letter of October 26th.

/s/ John F. Kennedy"

Rusk

/1/Source: Kennedy Library, National Security Files, Countries Series, USSR, Khrushchev Correspondence. Unclassified; Niact. Drafted and cleared by Brubeck. Other copies of this letter are in Department of State, Presidential Correspondence: Lot 66 D 204, and ibid.: Lot 77 D 163. Also printed in *Public Papers of the Presidents of the United States: John F. Kennedy, 1962*, p. 813; *Documents on Disarmament, 1962*, vol. II, pp. 990-991; and Claflin, *The President Wants To Know*, pp. 209-210.
/2/See Document 65.
/3/Document 66.

"We are not threatening.
We want nothing but peace.
Our country is now on the upsurge."

68. Letter From Chairman Khrushchev to President Kennedy

Moscow, October 28, 1962./1/

DEAR MR. PRESIDENT: I have received your message of October 27./2/ I express my satisfaction and thank you for the sense of proportion you have displayed and for realization of the responsibility which now devolves on you for the preservation of the peace of the world.

I regard with great understanding your concern and the concern of the United States people in connection with the fact that the weapons you describe as offensive are formidable weapons indeed. Both you and we understand what kind of weapons these are.

In order to eliminate as rapidly as possible the conflict which endangers the cause of peace, to

331

give an assurance to all people who crave peace, and to reassure the American people, who, I am certain, also want peace, as do the people of the Soviet Union, the Soviet Government, in addition to earlier instructions on the discontinuation of further work on weapons construction sites, has given a new order to dismantle the arms which you described as offensive, and to crate and return them to the Soviet Union.

Mr. President, I should like to repeat what I had already written to you in my earlier messages—that the Soviet Government has given economic assistance to the Republic of Cuba, as well as arms, because Cuba and the Cuban people were constantly under the continuous threat of an invasion of Cuba.

A piratic vessel had shelled Havana. They say that this shelling was done by irresponsible Cuban emigres. Perhaps so, however, the question is from where did they shoot. It is a fact that these Cubans have no territory, they are fugitives from their country, and they have no means to conduct military operations.

This means that someone put into their hands these weapons for shelling Havana and for piracy in the Caribbean in Cuban territorial waters. It is impossible in our time not to notice a piratic ship, considering the concentration in the Caribbean of American ships from which everything can be seen and observed.

In these conditions, pirate ships freely roam around and shell Cuba and make piratic attacks on peaceful cargo ships. It is known that they even shelled a British cargo ship. In a word, Cuba was under the continuous threat of aggressive forces, which did not conceal their intention to invade its territory.

The Cuban people want to build their life in their own interests without external interference. This is their right, and they cannot be blamed for wanting to be masters of their own country and disposing of the fruits of their own labor.

The threat of invasion of Cuba and all other schemes for creating tension over Cuba are designed to strike the Cuban people with a sense of insecurity, intimidate them, and prevent them from peacefully building their new life.

Mr. President, I should like to say clearly once more that we could not remain indifferent to this. The Soviet Government decided to render assistance to Cuba with the means of defense against aggression—only with means for defense purposes. We have supplied the defense means which you describe as offensive means. We have supplied them to prevent an attack on Cuba—to prevent rash acts.

I regard with respect and trust the statement you made in your message of October 27, 1962, that there would be no attack, no invasion of Cuba, and not only on the part of the United States, but also on the part of other nations of the Western Hemisphere, as you said in your same message. Then the motives which induced us to render assistance of such a kind to Cuba disappear.

It is for this reason that we instructed our officers—these means as I had already informed you earlier are in the hands of the Soviet officers—to take appropriate measures to discontinue construction of the aforementioned facilities, to dismantle them, and to return them to the Soviet Union. As I had informed you in the letter of October 27,/3/ we are prepared to reach agreement to enable United Nations Representatives to verify the dismantling of these means.

Thus in view of the assurance you have given and our instructions on dismantling, there is every condition for eliminating the present conflict.

I note with satisfaction that you have responded to the desire I expressed with regard to elimination of the aforementioned dangerous situation, as well as with regard to providing conditions for a more thoughtful appraisal of the internal situation, fraught as it is with great dangers in our age of thermonuclear weapons, rocketry, spaceships, global rockets, and other deadly weapons. All people are interested in insuring peace.

Therefore, vested with trust and great responsibility, we must not allow the situation to become aggravated and must stamp out the centers where a dangerous situation fraught with grave consequences to the cause of peace has arisen. If we, together with you, and with the assistance of other people of good will, succeed in eliminating this tense atmosphere, we should also make certain that no other dangerous conflicts which could lead to a world nuclear catastrophe would arise.

In conclusion, I should like to say something about a detente between NATO and the Warsaw

Treaty countries that you have mentioned. We have spoken about this long since and are prepared to continue to exchange views on this question with you and to find a reasonable solution.

We should like to continue the exchange of views on the prohibition of atomic and thermonuclear weapons, general disarmament, and other problems relating to the relaxation of international tension.

Although I trust your statement, Mr. President, there are irresponsible people who would like to invade Cuba now and thus touch off a war. If we do take practical steps and proclaim the dismantling and evacuation of the means in question from Cuba, in so doing we, at the same time, want the Cuban people to be certain that we are with them and are not absolving ourselves of responsibility for rendering assistance to the Cuban people.

We are confident that the people of all countries, like you, Mr. President, will understand me correctly. We are not threatening. We want nothing but peace. Our country is now on the upsurge.

Our people are enjoying the fruits of their peaceful labor. They have achieved tremendous successes since the October Revolution, and created the greatest material, spiritual, and cultural values. Our people are enjoying these values; they want to continue developing their achievements and insure their further development on the way of peace and social progress by their persistent labor.

I should like to remind you, Mr. President, that military reconnaissance planes have violated the

borders of the Soviet Union. In connection with
this there have been conflicts between us and
notes exchanged. In 1960 we shot down your U-
2 plane, whose reconnaissance flight over the
USSR wrecked the summit meeting in Paris. At
that time, you took a correct position and
denounced that criminal act of the former U.S.
Administration.

But during your term of office as President
another violation of our border has occurred, by
an American U-2 plane in the Sakhalin area. We
wrote you about the violation on 30 August. At
that time you replied that that violation had
occurred as a result of poor weather, and gave
assurances that this would not be repeated. We
trusted your assurance, because the weather was
indeed poor in that area at that time.

But had not your planes been ordered to fly
about our territory, even poor weather could not
have brought an American plane into our airspace. Hence, the conclusion that this is being
done with the knowledge of the Pentagon, which
tramples on international norms and violates the
borders of other states.

A still more dangerous case occurred on 28
October, when one of your reconnaissance planes
intruded over Soviet borders in the Chukotka
Peninsula area in the north and flew over our
territory. The question is, Mr. President: How
should we regard this. What is this: A provocation? One of your planes violates our frontier
during this anxious time we are both experiencing, when everything has been put into combat
readiness. Is it not a fact that an intruding

American plane could be easily taken for a nuclear bomber, which might push us to a fateful step? And all the more so since the U.S. Government and Pentagon long ago declared that you are maintaining a continuous nuclear bomber patrol.

Therefore, you can imagine the responsibility you are assuming especially now, when we are living through such anxious times.

I should like to express the following wish; it concerns the Cuban people. You do not have diplomatic relations. But through my officers in Cuba, I have reports that American planes are making flights over Cuba.

We are interested that there should be no war in the world, and that the Cuban people should live in peace. And besides, Mr. President, it is no secret that we have our people in Cuba. Under such a treaty with the Cuban Government we have sent there officers, instructors, mostly plain people: specialists, agronomists, zoo technicians, irrigators, land reclamation specialists, plain workers, tractor drivers, and others. We are concerned about them.

I should like you to consider, Mr. President, that violation of Cuban airspace by American planes could also lead to dangerous consequences. And if you do not want this to happen, it would [be] better if no cause is given for a dangerous situation to arise.

We must be careful now and refrain from any steps which would not be useful to the defense of the states involved in the conflict, which could only cause irritation and even serve as a provocation for a fateful step. Therefore, we must display sanity, reason, and refrain from such steps.

We value peace perhaps even more than other peoples because we went through a terrible war with Hitler. But our people will not falter in the face of any test. Our people trust their Government, and we assure our people and world public opinion that the Soviet Government will not allow itself to be provoked. But if the provocateurs unleash a war, they will not evade responsibility and the grave consequences a war would bring upon them. But we are confident that reason will triumph that war will not be unleashed and peace and the security of the peoples will be insured.

In connection with the current negotiations between Acting Secretary General U Thant and representatives of the Soviet Union, the United States, and the Republic of Cuba, the Soviet Government has sent First Deputy Foreign Minister V. V. Kuznetsov to New York to help U Thant in his noble efforts aimed at eliminating the present dangerous situation.

Respectfully yours,

N. Khrushchev/4/

/1/Source: Department of State, Presidential Correspondence: Lot 66 D 204. No classification marking. Other copies of this letter are ibid.: Lot 77 D 163, and in the Kennedy Library, National Security Files, Countries Series, USSR, Khrushchev Correspondence. The Russian-language text is in Department of State, Presidential Correspondence: Lot 66 D 204. Also printed in *Documents on Disarmament, 1962,* vol. II, pp. 995-999. This "informal translation" and an "official translation" prepared by the Department of State are printed in Department of State *Bulletin,* November 19, 1973, pp. 650-654. According to a footnote in the *Bulletin* this message was broadcast in English over Moscow radio at 5 p.m. Moscow time, October 28, and a Russian text delivered to the Embassy at 5:10 p.m. the same day.
/2/See Document 67.
/3/Document 66.
/4/Printed from a translation that indicates Khrushchev signed the original Russian-language text.

"Perhaps now, as we step back from danger . . ."

69. Telegram From the Department of State to the Embassy in the Soviet Union

Washington, October 28, 1962, 5:03 p.m./1/

1020. Following is text President's reply to Khrushchev letter of October 28 for delivery to highest available Soviet official. Text has been handed to Soviet Embassy and released by White House at 4:35 PM.

Begin text.

Dear Mr. Chairman:

339

I am replying at once to your broadcast message of October twenty-eight/2/ even though the official text has not yet reached me because of the great importance I attach to moving forward promptly to the settlement of the Cuban crisis. I think that you and I, with our heavy responsibilities for the maintenance of peace, were aware that developments were approaching a point where events could have become unmanageable. So I welcome this message and consider it an important contribution to peace.

The distinguished efforts of Acting Secretary General U Thant have greatly facilitated both our tasks. I consider my letter to you of October twenty-seventh/3/ and your reply of today as firm undertakings on the part of both our governments which should be promptly carried out. I hope that the necessary measures can at once be taken through the United Nations as your message says, so that the United States in turn can remove the quarantine measures now in effect. I have already made arrangements to report all these matters to the Organization of American States, whose members share a deep interest in a genuine peace in the Caribbean area.

You referred in your letter to a violation of your frontier by an American aircraft in the area of the Chukotsk Peninsula. I have learned that this plane, without arms or photographic equipment, was engaged in an air sampling mission in connection with your nuclear tests. Its course was direct from Eielson Air Force Base in Alaska to the North Pole and return. In turning south, the pilot made a serious navigational error which carried him over Soviet territory. He immediately made an emergency call on open radio for navigational assistance and was guided back to his home base by the most direct route. I regret this incident and will see to it that every precaution is taken to prevent recurrence.

Mr. Chairman, both of our countries have great unfinished tasks and I know that your people as well as those of the United States can ask for nothing better than to pursue them free from the fear of war. Modern science and technology have given us the possibility of making labor fruitful beyond anything that could have been dreamed of a few decades ago.

I agree with you that we must devote urgent attention to the problem of disarmament, as it relates to the whole world and also to critical areas. Perhaps now, as we step back from danger, we can together make real progress in this vital field. I think we should give priority to questions relating to the proliferation of nuclear weapons, on earth and in outer space, and to the great effort for a nuclear test ban. But we should also work hard to see if wider measures of disarmament can be agreed and put into operation at an early date. The United States Government will be prepared to discuss these questions urgently, and in a constructive spirit, at Geneva or elsewhere.

/s/ John F. Kennedy

End text.

Rusk

/1/Source: Kennedy Library, National Security Files, Countries Series, USSR, Khrushchev Correspondence. Unclassified; Niact. Repeated to Paris, London, and USUN. Other copies of this message are in Department of State, Presidential Correspondence: Lot 66 D 204, and ibid.: Lot 77 D 163. Also printed in *Public Papers of the Presidents of the United States: John F. Kennedy, 1962*, pp. 814-815; Department of State *Bulletin*, November 19, 1963, pp. 654-655; *Documents on Disarmament, 1962*, vol. II, pp. 654-655; and Claflin, *The President Wants To Know*, pp. 211-212.
/2/See Document 68.
/3/See Document 67.

"The crisis that we have gone through may repeat again."

70. Letter From Chairman Khrushchev to President Kennedy

Moscow, October 28, 1962./1/

DEAR MR. PRESIDENT, Ambassador Dobrynin has apprised me of his conversation with Robert Kennedy which took place on October 27. In this conversation Robert Kennedy said that it is somewhat difficult for you at the present time to publicly discuss the question of eliminating the US missile bases in Turkey because of the fact that the stationing of those bases in Turkey was formalized through a NATO Council decision.

Readiness to agree on this issue that I raised in my message to you of October 27/2/ was also emphasized. In this context Robert Kennedy said that removal of those bases from Turkey would take 4 to 5 months. Furthermore, a wish was

342

expressed that exchanges of views on this matter between you and I should continue through Robert Kennedy and the Soviet Ambassador, and that these exchanges should be considered confidential.

I feel I must state to you that I do understand the delicacy involved for you in an open consideration of the issue of eliminating the US missile bases in Turkey. I take into account the complexity of this issue and I believe you are right about not wishing to publicly discuss it. I agree that our discussion of this subject be pursued confidentially through Robert Kennedy and the Soviet Ambassador in Washington. You may have noticed that in my message to you on October 28, which was to be published immediately, I did not raise this question—precisely because I was mindful of your wish conveyed through Robert Kennedy. But all the proposals that I presented in that message took into account the fact that you had agreed to resolve, [sic]/3/ the matter of your missile bases in Turkey consistent with what I had said in my message of October 27 and what you stated through Robert Kennedy in his meeting with Ambassador Dobrynin on the same day./4/

I express my great appreciation to you for having instructed your brother R. Kennedy to convey those thoughts.

I hope, Mr. President, that agreement on this matter, too, shall be a no small step advancing the cause of relaxation of international tensions and the tensions between our two powers. And that in turn can provide a good impetus to resolving other issues concerning both the security of

Europe and the international situation as a whole.

Mr. President, the crisis that we have gone through may repeat again. This means that we need to address the issues which contain too much explosive material. Not right away, of course. Apparently, it will take some time for the passions to cool down. But we cannot delay the solution to these issues, for continuation of this situation is frought [sic] with many uncertainties and dangers.

Sincerely,

N. Khrushchev/5/

/1/Source: *Problems of Communism*, Special Edition—Spring 1992, pp. 60-62. The Russian-language text is ibid. This letter was forwarded by Ambassador Dobrynin to Robert Kennedy on October 29. The Attorney General studied the letter over night before asking Dobrynin to come to his office on October 30 and take it back because it involved a quid pro quo. For an account of this incident, see Arthur M. Schlesinger, Jr., *Robert Kennedy and His Times,* p. 546. No record of the meeting has been found. The version of the letter printed here is an unofficial translation prepared by the Russian Embassy for publication in *Problems of Communism*.
/2/Document 66.
/3/These and following brackets are in the source text.
/4/For a memorandum of this meeting, see vol. XI, Document 96.
/5/Printed from a copy that bears this typed signature.

". . . I believe that you as a military man, and your military people understand that we were not preparing for war when we delivered means of defense to Cuba."

71. Letter From Chairman Khrushchev to President Kennedy

Moscow, October 30, 1962./1/

DEAR MR. PRESIDENT, I want to convey to you confidentially some considerations which, if you agree with them, could serve, in my opinion, our common cause, that is, prompt elimination of the remnants of the dangerous crisis which you and we have in the main liquidated. This would help to finalize the settlement more quickly so that life would resume its normal pace.

First of all, I would like to express a wish that you already now remove the quarantine without waiting for the procedure for the inspection of ships on which an agreement has been reached to be put into effect. It would be very reasonable on your part. You yourself realize that the quarantine will in fact accomplish nothing since those ships that are now heading for Cuba naturally, after we have agreed on the removal of our missiles from Cuba, do not carry not only any offensive weapons, but as I have already stated it publicly and informed you confidentially, any weapons at all. Immediate lift of the quarantine would be a good gesture. It would be appreciated

345

both by us and world public opinion as a major step to speed up liquidation of the aftereffects of the crisis. For all practical purposes the quarantine is of no use to you, but being a manifestation of the crisis, it continues to poison relations among states, relations between you and us and Cuba and produces a depressing effect on world public which would like to see a complete relaxation. You would lose nothing but you would score a gain as far as public opinion is concerned.

On the other hand, immediate lift of the quarantine would give us an opportunity to use our ships that are approaching Cuba to take out the weapons which are being dismantled now and, I think, have been already dismantled. After the ships are unloaded the dismantled weapons could be loaded on them and shipped to the Soviet Union.

Naturally, after the elimination of the crisis it is impossible to continue the blockade and discrimination in trade and communications. All this must be done away with. But you, as we know, undertook measures and put pressure on your allies and other countries so that even flights of civilian passenger planes be not permitted. Do you really think that IL-28 carries any means of destruction? This is laughable.

All this is being done not to ensure security, but as pinpricks and cannot but cause irritation and worsening of our relations. Why should it be done? Who needs it? It serves only the aggressive forces to strain nerves and thus to reach their goal which is to push the world into the abyss of a thermonuclear war.

Therefore I believe that you, Mr. President, will understand me correctly and will draw appropriate conclusions aimed at clearing the way for bettering the relations between our states.

Next question. I do not know what you will think about it but if you were prepared already now to proclaim the liquidation of your base in Guantanamo, this would be an act which would give world public opinion real satisfaction and would contribute to the easing of tension. I think that you yourself realize what significance the base in Guantanamo may have now after your statement that you do not pursue the aim of invading Cuba. Then the question arises: at whom this base is aimed, what purposes does it serve, from whom can it guard the approaches to America? I do not see forces that can threaten America from that direction. Therefore the base in Guantanamo is only a burden for your budget, and what is the main thing, it is a great burden of a moral nature for political leaders in the USA. And everybody realizes that the functions of the base in Guantanamo—and this is in fact the case—are aggressive, not defensive.

You know our position with regard to the bases. We are against military bases in general and that's why we liquidated those our bases that we had in Finland and China and we think that we acted rightly. That was an act that manifested our good intentions in ensuring peaceful coexistence. By that we did not diminish our defensive capability but raised our moral prestige among the peoples of all the world. The more true it is now when there are perfect means of war, the range and destructive power of which are so great that no bases could in any degree replace them.

This would be a good preparation to an agreement between you and us on the liquidation of all military bases in general since military bases have lost now their importance. Those are not my words. I think, you yourself said and even stated it publicly that you want to reduce the number of your military bases. Of this spoke Bowles and others, and they spoke correctly.

Such your step would be highly appreciated by world public.

I would like also to tell you my following consideration.

My colleagues and I consider that both sides have displayed restraint and wisdom in liquidating the military conflict which might have resulted in a world thermonuclear war. I take the liberty to think that you evidently held to a restraining position with regard to those forces which suffered from militaristic itching. And we take a notice of that. I don't know, perhaps I am wrong, but in this letter I am making the conclusion on the basis that in your country the situation is such that the decisive word rests with the President and if he took an extreme stand there would be no one to restrain him and war would be unleashed. But as this did not happen and we found a reasonable compromise having made mutual concessions to each other and on this basis eliminated the crisis which could explode in the catastrophe of a thermonuclear war, then, evidently, your role here was restraining. We so believe, and we note and appreciate it.

Our systems are different and my role was simpler than yours because there were no people around me who wanted to unleash war. My efforts aimed at eliminating the conflict were supported by both our military men and my colleagues in the leadership of the party and government.

Mr. President, we have now conditions ripe for finalizing the agreement on signing a treaty on cessation of tests of thermonuclear weapons. We fully agree with regard to three types of tests or, so to say, tests in three environments. This is banning of tests in atmosphere, in outer space and under water. In this respect we are of the same opinion and we are ready to sign an agreement.

But there are still some differences with regard to underground explosions. Therefore it would be good if you gave instructions to find a compromise in the decision on the underground test ban, but without inspection. We shall not accept inspection, this I say to you unequivocally and frankly. Of course, if one aims at delaying or torpedoing an agreement then there is sense in insisting on the inspection of underground explosions.

We do not carry on underground tests, we did it but once and we are not going to do it anymore. Maybe such a necessity will arise sometime in future, but in any case I do not envisage it.

It would be very useful to agree on ending tests after such strain when people lived through great anxiety. It would be a great reward for the nervous strain suffered by the peoples of all countries. I think that your people felt as much

anxiety as all other peoples expecting that thermonuclear war would break out any moment.
And we were very close to such war indeed. That
is why it would be good to give satisfaction to the
public opinion. This would contribute to easing
the tension.

We appreciate it very much that you took the
initiative and in such a moment of crisis stated
your readiness to conduct negotiations with the
purpose of signing a non-aggression treaty
between the two military blocs. We responded and
supported it. We are prepared to come to an
agreement on this question confidentially or
through diplomatic channels and then make it
public and start negotiations. This also would contribute to lessening tension. The world public
would learn with satisfaction that in the moment
of crisis not only declarative statements were
made but certain commitments with signatures
affixed were taken as well.

But the best thing to do would be—I do not
know how you will look upon it—to disband all
military blocs. We are not coming up with this
now though we spoke of this before; however we
believe now too that this would be most reasonable. But if you and your allies are not ready yet
for that we are not pressing. However I must say
that in the interests of the same elimination of
tension this would be greatly useful.

We have eliminated a serious crisis. But in
order to forsee and forestall appearance of a new
crisis in future which might be impossible to cope
with everything in our relations capable of gen-
erating a new crisis should be erased now. It

would seem that now when we possess thermonuclear weapons, rocket weapons, submarine fleet and other means the situation obliges all states, every state to adhere to such norms of conduct which would not generate conflicts, to say nothing of wars. From our point of view, this is quite obtainable. This would be a big step forward at a time when we in effect have not yet disarmed. I think that this would be not a loss but a gain for the supporters of peaceful coexistence, a mutual benefit which the peoples of the U.S. and other countries participating in military blocs would enjoy. It can also be said with confidence that this would be highly appreciated by all peoples and would give great reassurance and satisfaction to people interested in securing peace. More efforts should be made already now to solve the problem of disarmament. To do it with regard not to one stage but to a real solution of the whole problem.

In our proposals on general and complete disarmament which we have made we have taken into consideration your wishes as well. Our recent proposals on this point were expressed by the USSR Foreign Minister A.A. Gromyko at the XVII session of the U.N. General Assembly. In those proposals of ours adjustments we made to take into account your wishes. What we considered to be reasonable we took into consideration.

And of course, Mr. President, I am again reminding you of the necessity to solve the German question because next crisis, possibly of no lesser danger, can be caused by the German question. And the main thing is that that crisis will be foolish as all crises are.

There was war, two German states emerged, or actually three states, which are in existence since the end of World War II. Specific relations among them have already developed. But these relations—economic and political—exist because the German Democratic Republic regulates traffic through its territory on the basis of some substitutes for treaties though in reality, daily life, in practice such treaties are already operative.

Besides, we and you, our Foreign Minister and your Secretary of State, have agreed on all questions. And the only question which remains unsolved is that the presence of troops in West Berlin and in effect not even of the troops but under what flag those troops will be and of what states, naturally within certain period of time.

Could not we both understand it? And who needs that the present unsolved situation continue? Not you and not your people. This is not in our or your interests, and not in the interests of our or your allies. This is only—and I repeat again—in the interests of revanchist forces who do not want to recognize the borders and conditions emerged as a result of the defeat of the Hitlerite Germany. Only they benefit from that. Nobody else.

Who expresses such policy now—Adenauer or somebody else—that is of no particular importance to me or to you. But if one takes a realistic view, if you, Mr. President, analyze the situation then you in your heart will undoubtedly agree with me. What you say publicly is another matter. But that comes not from how you personally understand the situation but, so to say, from political expedience, from desire "not to offend" your ally. However it would be better to be guided by a desire not to offend the public opinion and to give satisfaction to it, to give satisfaction to all peoples, the American people included—to eliminate the hotbed of international tension in the center of Europe. And we would be able to eliminate it. If you and we come to an agreement on this question—and we do want it—this would be a great joy for all peoples because this would mean consolidation of peace.

There would remain many unsettled matters in the world but the main thing after that—and I would like to tell you about it—is the question of China. It is anomalous that China is not having her seat in the U.N. Similar anomalies already existed in history and were overwhelmed by life. When the Revolution broke out and won in America and Russian Emperor showed stubbornness and did not recognize America for 26 years. But America did not cease to exist because of that. So, that was a foolish policy. The United States answered with the same lack of cleverness. But that happened, however, in different times. Therefore the U.S. acted unreasonably for roughly half that time: the Russian Emperor—for 26 years, you—for 16 years. But then the U.S. realized that it was unwise, and your great President Roosevelt took the courage and responsibility and displayed wisdom.

You would greatly raise your prestige, personal and that of your country, in the eyes of the peoples if you take an attitude facilitating China taking its lawful seat in the U.N. This is possible only if it is understood that there cannot be two Chinas. No state which respects itself can agree to a part of its territory, a part of its population being cut off, it applies even more strongly to a great power. This is an internal question of China and let the Chinese decide it among themselves. When China participated in the creation of the U.N. and when it was made a permanent member of the Security Council, then it was one China. And that one China exists now. If China occupies again its lawful seat in the U.N., if you understand the necessity of it—and I think that you do understand it—then it would be good, it would be a great contribution to the cause of peace.

It is impossible to come to an agreement on disarmament without China. There are countries with population of half a million and even less which are members of the U.N. and have voice in this international organization. Iceland, for instance has the population of 180 thousand people. China has 650 million people and does not have such voice. We have respect for the people of Iceland and their will as well as for all peoples. But from the point of view of ensuring peace—even if there seems to be a contradiction here—the contribution of a given people and that of another people, the real contribution to the cause of ensuring peace may be different.

Therefore it would be proper to solve the question of the restoration of China's rights in the U.N.; the peoples are waiting for it. And this will happen, it is only a matter of time. Therefore in order not to prolong this time, if you understood now the necessity for such a step, then, it would in effect be possible to solve this problem at the present session of General Assembly. What satisfaction it would give to the world public opinion, you would see from the expression of feelings of all peoples because it would be a real step, indeed, towards stabilization and strengthening of peace all over the world.

We, the Soviet people and the peoples of Asian and Europe countries, saw war. War often rolled through our territory. America participated in the two wars but it suffered very small losses in those wars. While huge profits were accumulated as result of the wars. Of course, it was monopolists who benefited but workers, working people got something out of it, too. War did not touch the soil of the United States. The American people did not experience destruction, sufferings, they only received notifications about deaths of their kin. Now during this crisis war was knocking at the gates of America.

These, in effect, are my considerations after the crisis situation. I want to tell you that in this crisis, as our saying goes, there is no evil without good. Evil has brought some good. The good is that now people have felt more tangibly the breathing of the burning flames of thermonuclear war and have a more clear realization of the threat looming over them if arms race is not stopped. And I would say that what has just happened will serve especially good the American people.

Mr. President, I believe that you as a military man, and your military people understand that

we were not preparing for war when we delivered
means of defense to Cuba. Those means were not
meant against the U.S., but were the means to
ensure the security of Cuba. Do you really think
that we are so narrow-minded in our understanding of military matters that in preparing for
war against the U.S. we picked up Cuba as a
bridgehead for such a war? And the means
there—a certain number of missiles. This is foolish. For Cuba is no good as a bridgehead for a big
war and it cannot be used for those purposes
and, of course, nobody ever contemplated that.
Those were the means for deterring aggressor, to
use the language of the late Dulles.

It is our opinion that the crisis has been eliminated on the compromise basis through reciprocal concessions. We are satisfied with it. We also
appreciate your cooperation in the elimination of
the crisis and your understanding of the necessity for reciprocal concessions and compromise so
that the conflict be prevented from going beyond
the limits that might really break into a thermonuclear war. All the peoples of the world, the
peoples of the United States and the Soviet Union
as well as the peoples of all countries, are interested in eliminating this conflict. In particular, I
think, it will be highly appreciated by the people
of Cuba who have now been assured that their
borders will be respected and there will be no
threat of invasion of their land on the part of
stronger states. In other words, the Cuban people
will have the long-awaited opportunity to enjoy
the benefits of their labor and they will have the
guarantee of their independence on the basis of

the U.N. Charter which provides for non-interference into internal affairs of other states and respect for sovereignty and integrity of state.

These are the considerations, Mr. President, which I wanted to express to you. I understand that I listed a great number of questions. Therefore, if we started after breakfast we would not have finished solving them before dinner. It would require more time but they have to be solved. They face the world. And the more we delay the solution of these questions, the more of unknown will appear which can prove to be fatal in a future crisis. Therefore, the sooner we clear away the roadblock, the windfallen wood, which has piled up in the international relations, and make clear the roads to correct mutual understanding the better it would be.

Mr. President, you lived through this crisis yourself. For us too, it presented the Rubicon: whether to agree to a compromise, whether to make concessions. Indeed, from the point of view of the legal standards your claims had no grounds whatsoever. Therefore there was a great trial and there were hesitations. We still believed, however, that you might have difficulties too since how could it be that you could not know that the unjustified demands of the USA exposed the world to the hazards of catastrophe. However, we decided to make a compromise proposal which would suit both you and us. We received your assurances that you would not invade Cuba and would not permit others to do it and on this condition we withdrew the weapons which you called offensive. As a result, there has been practically achieved the purpose which had been intended to be achieved through the shipments of means of defense. Now this question is solved on these compromise and reciprocal concessions.

And we consider it to be reasonable. Having eliminated this crisis we gave each other mutual satisfaction: you promised not to attack and not to permit attack against Cuba on the part of others, and we moved forward to make the USA feel confident that we do not contemplate anything bad against it and that there is no threat against the USA on our part. You certainly possess means of destruction. But you know that we also have these means and they are of a different nature than those that were in Cuba. Those were trifles there. Our means were brought to the state of combat readiness, they were of a more serious nature and they were pointed at the USA and your allies.

To our mutual satisfaction we maybe even sacrificed self-esteem. Apparently, there will be such scribblers who will engage in hair-splitting over our agreement, will be digging as to who made greater concessions to whom. As for me, I would say that we both made a concession to reason and found a reasonable solution which enabled us to ensure peace for all including those who will be trying to dig up something.

Such is our understanding of this whole question.

I would like to sum up the above said and express in conclusion the following considerations on the questions touched upon in this letter.

I think it would be possible to pick up from the

questions listed by me those which are more ripe and which should, perhaps, be prepared for taking decisions on them. Then it would be possible to meet, maybe, at the U.N. or may be at a specially arranged meeting. I repeat, I have in mind a meeting in case questions are prepared for taking decisions on them so that the appropriate agreements could be signed during the meeting. It would be a good gift for the peoples of the whole world.

We have a different understanding of the mentioned questions. Therefore I would like to know your considerations as to whether you believe that some or other of the questions raised by me are ripe for decision. If you do not consider them ripe, then there should be no meeting because a meeting in such conditions would not only fail to justify hopes of the peoples, but would distress them.

Sincerely,

N. Khrushchev/2/

/1/Source: Department of State, Presidential Correspondence: Lot 77 D 163. Confidential. Another copy is in the Kennedy Library, National Security Files, Countries Series, USSR, Khrushchev Correspondence. The source text appears to be a translation by the Soviet Embassy in Washington.
/2/Printed from a copy that bears this typed signature.

"Premier Castro has announced his opposition to measure of verification on the territory of Cuba."

72. Letter From President Kennedy to Chairman Khrushchev

Washington, November 3, 1962./1/

DEAR MR. CHAIRMAN: I wish to thank you for your letter of October 30./2/ I am commenting now only on a problem raised in your letter which relates to the Cuban affair.

With respect to the quarantine on shipments to Cuba, I am hopeful that arrangements can be worked out quickly by the United Nations which would permit its removal. We were happy to agree to your suggestion that the International Committee of the Red Cross undertake responsibility for inspection. You are, of course, aware that Premier Castro has announced his opposition to measures of verification on the territory of Cuba. If he maintains this position this would raise very serious problems. So far as incoming shipments are concerned, I understand that efforts are being made to have the International Red Cross carry out the necessary measures at sea and I hope that these will be successful. In the meantime, perhaps the existence of the quarantine can be of assistance to Mr. Mikoyan in his negotiations with Premier Castro. I should also like to point out that in an effort to facilitate matters, I instructed our delegation in New York to inform your representative there, Mr. Kuznetsov, that for the next few days any Soviet ships in the quarantine area would be passed without inspection and only the hailing procedure which was carried out in the case of your vessel, the Bucharest, would be applied.

I am hopeful we can dispose of this pressing matter quickly so that we can go on in a better atmosphere to the broader questions. We both must make our best efforts to this end.

Sincerely,/3/

/1/Source: Kennedy Library, National Security Files, Countries Series, USSR, Khrushchev Correspondence. Secret. Another copy is in the Department of State, Presidential Correspondence: Lot 77 D 163.
/2/Document 71.
/3/Printed from an unsigned copy.

"... missiles which you called offensive should be removed from Cuba. We agreed to that."

73. Letter From Chairman Khrushchev to President Kennedy

Moscow, undated./1/

DEAR MR. PRESIDENT, I have just received information from Mr. V. Kuznetsov, our representative at the negotiations in New York for liquidation of the tense situation around Cuba, that Mr. Stevenson handed him a list of weapons which your side calls offensive./2/ I have studied the list and, I must confess, the approach of the American side to this matter has seriously worried me. In such a move, I will say frankly, I see a wish to complicate the situation, because it is impossible indeed to place into the category of "offensive" weapons such types of weapons which have always been referred to as defensive weapons even by a man uneducated militarily—by a common soldier, not to say of an officer.

It is hard for us to understand what aim is being pursued by the introduction of that list, by setting forth such a demand—in any case it must be some other aim, but not a desire for a speediest clearing of the atmosphere. And it is being done at a moment when we have already agreed with you on the main questions and when we on our part have already fulfilled what we agreed upon—have dismantled rocket weapons, are loading them now on ships and these weapons will be soon shipped from Cuba. That is why I feel greatly concerned with the advancing of such demand by the American side, concerned with its possible consequences, if necessary reasonableness is not displayed.

The demand which has been set forth is evidently pursuing, as I have already said, some other aims and that—I would wish, Mr. President, that you understand me correctly—can lead not to the betterment of our relations but, on the contrary, to their new aggravation. We should understand the position each side is in and take it into consideration but not overburden, not complicate our relations, especially at such an important

moment when measures are being taken to eliminate the acute tension and bring these relations
to a normal state.

That is why I would ask you, Mr. President, to
meet our anxiety with understanding, to take
measures on your side in order not to complicate
the situation and to give your representatives a
directive to eliminate the existing tension on the
basis upon which both of us have agreed by having exchanged public messages. You spoke to the
effect that missiles which you called offensive
should be removed from Cuba. We agreed to that.
You in your turn gave assurances that the so-
called "quarantine" would be promptly removed
and that no invasion of Cuba would be made, not
only by the U.S. but by other countries of the
Western hemisphere either.

Let us then bring the achieved understanding
to a completion, so that we could consider that
each side has fulfilled its pledges and the question has been settled. If, however, additional
demands are made, then that means only one
thing—the danger that the difficulties on the way
to eliminating tension created around Cuba will
not be removed. But that may raise then new
consequences.

I think that you will understand me correctly.
For you and I will evidently have to deal not only
with elimination of the remnants of the present
tension—there lies ahead for you and me a great,
serious talk on other questions. Why then start
now complicating the situation by minor things.
Maybe there exist some considerations, but they
are beyond our comprehension. As for us, we

view the introduction of additional demands as a wish to bring our relations back again into a heated state in which they were but several days ago.

Sincerely,

N. Khrushchev/3/

/1/Source: Kennedy Library, National Security Files, Countries Series, USSR, Khrushchev Correspondence. No classification marking. According to *Problems of Communism* the Russian text was transmitted by the Soviet Foreign Ministry to the Soviet Embassy in Washington on November 4. A note on the source text indicates it was received on November 5. Other copies are in Department of State, Presidential Correspondence: Lot 77 D 163, and ibid.: Lot 66 D 204.
/2/Transmitted in telegram 1606 from USUN, November 2. (USUN Files: NY FRC 84-84-001, Outgoing Telegrams, 1953-1963)
/3/Printed from a copy that bears this typed signature.

"These recent events have given a profound shock to relations between our two countries."

74. Letter From President Kennedy to Chairman Khrushchev

Washington, November 6, 1962./1/

DEAR MR. CHAIRMAN: I am surprised that in your letter, which I received yesterday,/2/ you suggest that in giving your representative in New

York a list of the weapons we consider offensive there was any desire on our part to complicate the situation. Our intention was just the opposite: to stick to a well-known list, and not to introduce any new factors. But there is really only one major item on the list, beyond the missiles and their equipment, and that is the light bombers with their equipment. This item is indeed of great importance to us.

The solution of the Cuban affair was established by my letter to you of October twenty-seventh and your reply of October twenty-eighth./3/ You will recall that in my letter of October twenty-seventh, I referred to "all weapons systems in Cuba capable of offensive use." You will also recall that in my broadcast address of October twenty-second,/4/ in addition to medium-range ballistic missiles, I mentioned specifically "jet bombers capable of carrying nuclear weapons," as "an explicit threat to the peace and security of all the Americas." Finally, my proclamation of October twenty-third entitled "Interdiction of the Delivery of Offensive Weapons to Cuba"/5/ specifically listed bomber aircraft. These facts were all known at the time of our exchange of letters on Cuba, and so it seems clear to me that our exchange of letters covers the IL-28s, since your undertaking was to remove the weapons we described as offensive.

Your letter says—and I agree—that we should not complicate the situation by minor things. But I assure you that this matter of IL-28s is not a minor matter for us at all. It is true, of course, that these bombers are not the most modern of

365

weapons, but they are distinctly capable of offensive use against the United States and other Western Hemispheric countries, and I am sure your own military men would inform you that the continued existence of such bombers in Cuba would require substantial measures of military defense in response by the United States. Thus, in simple logic these are weapons capable of offensive use. But there is more in it than that, Mr. Chairman. These bombers could carry nuclear weapons for long distances, and they are clearly not needed, any more than missiles, for purely defensive purposes on the island of Cuba. Thus in the present context their continued presence would sustain the grave tension that has been created, and their removal, in my view, is necessary to a good start on ending the recent crisis.

I am not clear as to what items you object to on the list which Ambassador Stevenson handed to Mr. Kuznetsov. I can assure you I have no desire to cause you difficulties by any wide interpretation of the definitions of weapons which we consider offensive and I am instructing my representative in New York to confer promptly with Mr. Kuznetsov and to be as forthcoming as possible in order to meet any legitimate complaints you may have in order to reach a quick solution which would enable our agreement to be carried to completion. I entirely agree with your statement that we should wind up the immediate crisis promptly, and I assure you that on our side we are insisting only on what is immediately essential for progress in this matter. In order to make our position clear, I think I should go on to give you a full sense of the very strong feelings we have about this whole affair here in the United States.

These recent events have given a profound shock to relations between our two countries. It may be said, as Mr. Kuznetsov said the other day to Mr. McCloy, that the Soviet Union was under no obligation to inform us of any activities it was carrying on in a third country. I cannot accept this view; not only did this action threaten the whole safety of this hemisphere, but it was, in a broader sense, a dangerous attempt to change the world-wide status quo. Secret action of this kind seems to me both hazardous and unjustified. But however one may judge that argument, what actually happened in this case was not simply that the action of your side was secret. Your Government repeatedly gave us assurances of what it was not doing; these assurances were announced as coming from the highest levels, and they proved inaccurate.

I do not refer here only to the TASS article of September, but also to communications which were addressed to the highest levels of our Government through channels which heretofore had been used for confidential messages from the highest levels of your Government. Through these channels we were specifically informed that no missiles would be placed in Cuba which would have a range capable of reaching the United States. In reliance upon these assurances I attempted, as you know, to restrain those who were giving warnings in this country about the trend of events in Cuba. Thus undeniable photographic evidence that offensive weapons were being installed was a deep and dangerous shock, first to this Government and then to our whole people.

In the aftermath of this shock, to which we replied with a measured but necessary response, I believe it is vital that we should re-establish some degree of confidence in communication between the two of us. If the leaders of the two great nuclear powers cannot judge with some accuracy the intentions of each other, we shall find ourselves in a period of gravely increasing danger—not only for our two countries but for the whole world.

I therefore hope that you will promptly recognize that when we speak of the need to remove missiles and bombers, with their immediate supporting equipment, we are not trying to complicate the situation but simply stating what was clearly included in our understanding of October twenty-seventh and twenty-eighth. I shall continue to abide fully by the undertakings in my letter of October twenty-seventh, and specifically, under the conditions stated in that letter I will hold to my undertaking "to give assurances against an invasion of Cuba." This undertaking has already come under attack here and is likely to become increasingly an object of criticism by a great many of my countrymen. And the very minimum that is necessary in regard to these assurances is, as we agreed, the verified removal of the missile and bomber systems, together with real safeguards against their reintroduction.

I should emphasize to you directly, Mr.

Chairman, that in this respect there is another problem immediately ahead of us which could become very serious indeed, and that is the problem of continuing verification in Cuba. Your representatives have spoken as if this were entirely a problem for the Castro regime to settle, but the continuing verification of the absence of offensive weapons in Cuba is an essential safeguard for the United States and the other countries of this hemisphere, and is an explicit condition for the undertakings which we in our turn have agreed to. The need for this verification is, I regret to say, convincingly demonstrated by what happened in Cuba in the months of September and October.

For the present we are having to rely on our own methods of surveillance, and this surveillance will surely have to be continued unless, as we much prefer, a better and durable method can be found. We believe that it is a serious responsibility of your Government to insure that weapons which you have provided to Cuba are not employed to interfere with this surveillance which is so important to us all in obtaining reliable information on which improvements in the situation can be based. It was of great importance, for example, for me last week to be able to announce with confidence that dismantling of missiles had begun.

Finally, I would like to say a word about longer range matters. I think we must both recognize that it will be very difficult for any of us in this hemisphere to look forward to any real improvement in our relations with Cuba if it continues to be a military outpost of the Soviet Union. We have limited our action at present to the problem of offensive weapons, but I do think it may be important for you to consider whether a real normalization of the Cuba problem can be envisaged while there remains in Cuba large numbers of Soviet military technicians, and major weapons systems and communications complexes under Soviet control, all with the recurrent possibility that offensive weapons might be secretly and rapidly reintroduced. That is why I think there is much wisdom in the conclusion expressed in your letter of October 26th, that when our undertakings against invasion are effective the need for your military specialists in Cuba will disappear. That is the real path to progress in the Cuban problem. And in this connection in particular, I hope you will understand that we must attach the greatest importance to the personal assurances you have given that submarine bases will not be established in Cuba.

I believe that Cuba can never have normal relations with the other nations of this hemisphere unless it ceases to appear to be a foreign military base and adopts a peaceful course of non-interference in the affairs of its sister nations. These wider considerations may belong to a later phase of the problem, but I hope that you will give them careful thought.

In the immediate situation, however, I repeat that it is the withdrawal of the missiles and bombers, with their supporting equipment, under adequate verification, and with a proper system for continued safeguards in the future, that is essential. This is the first necessary step away from the crisis to open the door through which we can move to restore confidence and give attention to other problems which ought to be resolved in the interest of peace.

Sincerely,/6/

/1/Source: Kennedy Library, National Security Files, Countries Series, USSR, Khrushchev Correspondence. Top Secret; Eyes Only for the Secretary. Another copy is in Department of State, Presidential Correspondence: Lot 77 D 163. Also printed in Claflin, *The President Wants To Know*, pp. 217-221.
/2/Document 73.
/3/Documents 67 and 68.
/4/See footnote 1, Document 60.
/5/For text, see *Public Papers of the Presidents of the United States: John F. Kennedy, 1962*, pp. 809-811.
/6/Printed from an unsigned copy.

"And I would like to inform you that our obligations with regard to dismantling and removal of both missiles and warheads have already been fulfilled."

75. Message From Chairman Khrushchev to President Kennedy

Moscow, undated./1/

DEAR MR. PRESIDENT, I would like to express my satisfaction that the mutual obligations taken in accordance with the exchange of messages between us are being carried out both by your side and our side. One can say that certain favourable results are already seen at this time. We appreciate your understanding of the situation and your cooperation in carrying out the obligations taken by our side. We, on our part, will as always honor our obligations. And I would like to inform you that our obligations with regard to dismantling and removal of both missiles and warheads have already been fulfilled.

We appreciate that we have come to an agreement with you regarding the mutually acceptable means for your side to ascertain that we really carry out our obligations. What has already been achieved in the course of negotiations between our representatives—Kuznetsov, McCloy and Stevenson—and the cooperation reached in the process of these negotiations is a good thing. The same should be said about the cooperation between captains of our ships, which were taking our missiles from Cuba, and corresponding U.S. ships. This is very good, this has created an impression that your side also wishes to cooperate in eliminating the remnants of the tension which only yesterday was very dangerous both for our two peoples and for the peoples of the whole world.

Thus, if we proceed from our understanding which was expressed in your message of October 27 and in our reply of October 28,/2/ then we, the Soviet side, have carried out our obligations and thereby have created possibility for complete elimination of tension in the Caribbean. Consequently, now it is your turn, it is for your side to carry out precisely your obligations. We

have in mind that apart from the long term obligations that the United States itself will not
attack Cuba and will restrain other countries of
the Western Hemisphere from doing that, the
most important thing which is required today is
to give moral satisfaction to world public opinion
and tranquillity to peoples. And what is required
from your side to that end is to lift the so-called
quarantine and of course to stop violating the territorial waters and air space of Cuba. If this continues confidence in your obligations will thus be
undermined which can only grieve world public
and throw us back to the positions to which we
must not return after the liquidation of such a
dangerous situation. To say nothing of the fact
that it would hamper us in the future.

At present, we must—and we are convinced in
that—look forward and draw necessary conclusions from what has happened up till now and
from the good which followed due to the efforts of
both sides. Therefore, we believe that conditions
are emerging now for reaching an agreement on
the prohibition of nuclear weapons, cessation of
all types of nuclear weapon tests and on all other
questions which are ripe and require solution.
You have already ended your tests and we shall
probably also end our tests in November or at
least before the end of this year.

Now it is also necessary to think of some real
measures with regard to the question of ensuring
more stable security in the world. In this connection we attach great importance to your statement that the US is ready to support idea of a
non-aggression pact between NATO and the

Warsaw treaty countries. But the basic question, of course, remains that of disarmament, of destroying the whole war machine of states. To give more assurance on the first stage it might be expedient to return to the proposals forwarded by us some time ago on the establishment of observation posts on mutual basis at airfields, in major seaports, at railway junctions, on highways. This would exclude a possibility of a surprise attack if any side does not behave honestly, if it wants to concentrate military equipment and its troops for an attack. Precisely this is pursued by the suggestion made recently by Mr. Thant.

It goes without saying that the question of a German peace treaty still remains and we can not escape from solving it. Moreover what we and you have lived through makes a speediest solution of this question still more imperative.

I do not name other unresolved questions, we have plenty of them, I name only the main problems, on the solution of which the destinies of the world largely depend.

Now about the matter that, as you state, worries you today—about the IL-28 planes which you call an offensive weapon. We have already given you our clarification on this point and I think you can not but agree with us. However, if you do not agree—and this is your right—ask your intelligence after all and let it give you an answer based not on guesswork but on facts. If it really knows anything it must tell you the truth and namely that it is long since the IL-28's have been taken out of production and out of use in our armed forces. And if some planes still remain now—and a certain number of them have been brought by us to Cuba—that was done as a result of your action last year when you increased the budget and called up reservists. We on our part had to take measures in response at that time, having postponed taking those planes out of use as well.

Had there been no such action on your part we would not have IL-28's in existence because they would have been used for scrap. Such is this "formidable offensive" weapon. If your intelligence is objective it must give a correct appraisal of these 12-year old planes and report to you that they are incapable of offensive actions. We brought them to Cuba only because they can be used as a mobile means of coastal defense under the cover of anti-aircraft fire from their own territory. They can not however fly beyond the limits of that cover since they will be immediately destroyed either by modern anti-aircraft means or by simple conventional artillery; not to speak of interceptors before which they are entirely defenseless. But all this must be known not only to the intelligence but to all engaged in military matters.

Nevertheless we regard your concern with understanding though on our part we share the desire of the Government of Cuba to possess defensive weapons which would permit to defend the territorial integrity of its country.

Therefore if you met this with understanding and if we agreed with you on solving other questions in implementing the mutually assumed obligations then the question of IL-28 bombers would be solved without difficulties.

In what way should this cooperation, in our understanding, find its expression and what would facilitate the solution of this question?

We state to you that these bombers are piloted solely by our fliers. Consequently you should not have any fears that they can be used to do harm to the United States or other neighbouring countries in Western Hemisphere. And since you and your allies in Western Hemisphere have taken an obligation not to invade Cuba then it would seem this weapon should not pose any threat for you. Moreover, we are aware of what military means are in your possession. If the enemy were threatening us with such weapon we would ignore that threat completely for it would cause us no anxiety whatsoever.

But because you express apprehension that this weapon can be some sort of threat to the US or other countries of Western Hemisphere which do not possess adequate defensive means we state to you as a guarantee that those planes are piloted by our fliers and therefore there should be no misgivings that they could be used to the detriment of any state.

As you ascertained yourself we have removed the missiles, we also removed everything else related to missiles, all the equipment necessary for their use and recalled the personnel manning those missiles. Now that the missiles are removed the question of IL-28's is an incomprehensible argument because that weapon as I have already said is of no value as a combat weapon at present, to say nothing of the future. Let us come to an agreement on this question as well, let us do away with tension, let us fulfil the mutual pledges made in our messages. We will not insist on permanently keeping those planes on Cuba. We have our difficulties in this question. Therefore we give a gentleman's word that we will remove the IL-28 planes with all the personnel and equipment related to those planes, although not now but later. We would like to do that some time later when we determine that the conditions are ripe to remove them. We will advise you of that.

I think that an agreement on such basis will enable us to complete the elimination of all the tension that existed and will create conditions for life to resume its normal course, that is the blockade would be immediately removed; the pledges of the sides would be registered in the appropriate documents in the United Nations Organization; non-invasion of Cuba and strict observance of her sovereignty guaranteed; the UN posts established in the countries of the Caribbean so that neither one nor the other side would indeed undertake any unexpected actions to the detriment of another state.

This would be the best solution which can be anticipated especially having in mind the tension that we lived through and the abyss we came to. And I believe, Mr. President, that you yourself understand that we were very close to that abyss. But you and we soberly and wisely appraised the situation and maintained self-control. Let us now give a complete satisfaction to the public.

What happened should now prompt us to make new great efforts so that no repetition of

such events should be allowed because if we succeeded in finding a way out of a dangerous situation this time, next time we might not safely
untie the tightly made knot. And the knot that we
are now untying has been tied rather tightly,
almost to the limit.

We displayed an understanding with regard to
the positions of each other and came out of a critical situation through mutual concessions to the
satisfaction of all peoples of the world. Let us now
give joy to all peoples of the world and show that
this conflict really became a matter of yesterday,
let us normalize the situation. And it would be
good if on your part efforts were made to make
the normalization a complete, real normalization
and it is necessary to do this in the interests of
all peoples and this is within our power.

Sincerely,/3/

/1/Source: Department of State, Presidential Correspondence: Lot 77 D 163. Top Secret. *According to Problems of
Communism* the Russian text was transmitted to the Soviet
Embassy in Washington on November 11 and was given to
Robert Kennedy the following day. A note at the top of the
source text reads "1st oral" and a note at the
 indicates it was received on November 12. Another copy is
in the Kennedy Library, National Security Files, Countries
Series, USSR, Khrushchev Correspondence.
/2/Documents 67 and 68.
/3/Printed from an unsigned copy.

76. Editorial Note

At 8:30 p.m., on November 12, 1962, Robert
F. Kennedy went to the Soviet Embassy's recep-

tion for the Bolshoi Ballet. The Attorney General gave Ambassador Dobrynin an oral message. According to a typed note with a handwritten note by Bromley Smith, the message was: "If the Soviet Union will at once give the order to start removing IL-28's and complete the removal in 30 days we would be prepared immediately to announce the removal of the quarantine." (Kennedy Library, National Security Files, Countries Series, Cuba, General, 11/11/62-11/15/62)

The Ministry of Foreign Affairs of the former Soviet Union has made available the following version of what Robert Kennedy proposed to Dobrynin:

"During the second meeting with A.F. Dobrynin on the evening of November 12, R. Kennedy, under instruction from the President, formulated the US proposal in this way:

'N.S. Khrushchev and the President agree in principle that the IL-28 aircraft shall be withdrawn within a certain period of time. Following this agreement the US will immediately, even tomorrow, lift all quarantine, without waiting for the completion of the aircraft pullout. The US side would, of course, prefer that the agreed time period for withdrawing the IL-28 aircraft were made public. However, if the Soviet side has any objections to making it public, the President will not insist. N.S. Khrushchev's word would be quite suffice. As for the period of time, it would be good if the aircraft were withdrawn within, say, 30 days.'" (Unofficial translation from the Russian Foreign Ministry Files)

". . . those planes will be removed from Cuba . . ."

77. Message From Chairman Khrushchev to President Kennedy

Moscow, November 14, 1962./1/

I have read with great satisfaction the reply of the President of the United States/2/ and I agree with the considerations expressed by the President. It is of particular pleasure to me that we seem to have the same desire to liquidate as soon as possible the state of tension and normalize the situation so that to untie our hands for normal work and for solving those questions that are awaiting their solution. And this depends in the main on agreement between us—the two greatest powers in the world with whom special responsibility for ensuring peace lies to a greater degree than with other countries.

The question of the withdrawal of the IL-28's within mentioned 30 days does not constitute any complicated question. Yet this period will probably not be sufficient. As I already said in my oral message/3/ I can assure the President that those planes will be removed from Cuba with all the equipment and flying personnel. It can be done in 2-3 months. But for me, for our country it would be a great relief if the state of tension that evolved in the Caribbean were liquidated as soon as possible. I have in mind what I have already said, namely: to lift immediately the quarantine that is blockade; to stop the flights of the US planes over Cuba; to write down the mutual commitments ensuing from the messages of the President and mine of October 27 and 283 to which end your representatives and ours have to prepare with the participation of the UN Acting Secretary General U Thant an appropriate document. This is the main thing now.

You understand that when we say that it is necessary to announce now the withdrawal of the IL-28's at the time when your planes are flying over Cuba it creates for us no small difficulties. I have no doubt that you will understand—and the Cuban Government understands this—that such actions constitute violation of sovereignty of the Cuban state. Therefore it would be a reasonable step to create in this respect also conditions for the normalization of the situation and this in a great degree would make it easier to meet your wish of expediting the withdrawal of the IL-28 planes from Cuba.

If we attain all that now and if this were announced, then more favourable conditions would be created for our country to solve the question of timetable for the withdrawal of IL-28 planes.

Now our main difficulties lie precisely in the fact that, as it is well known to everybody and it is being rightfully pointed out to us, we have removed from Cuba missiles and warheads, that is, we have fulfilled our commitments while the US is not carrying out its commitments—the quarantine continues, the US planes continue to fly over Cuba and there is no agreement that would register the pledges of the US. And all this

finds ears that are listening and listening attentively. It is difficult for us to give explanations to
such unjustifiable state of affairs. Therefore to
carry out the final procedure after the missiles
and warheads have been removed, already now
the quarantine must be lifted, the flights of the
American planes over Cuba must be stopped and
mutual commitments of the sides must be written
down in an appropriate document with the participation of the UN.

It is hard to say for me what specific agreement is possible on the question of UN observation posts. But we as well as the Government of
Cuba have already expressed a desire to come to
terms on this question. If the question of the
observation posts is of interest to the US—and I
think it must be of interest—then I consider it
wise to come to an agreement on this. I think that
the Government of Cuba will not object to the UN
posts, of course on the condition of respect for
the sovereignty of Cuba, on the condition of treating her as equal which must mean that on the
territory of other countries of the Caribbean and
in a corresponding region of the US there will be
also set up similar UN posts, that is on the condition that reciprocity will be observed in this
question.

You understand, Mr. President, that no country can assume unilateral commitments, and it
would be wise to make them mutual.

I have already said that perhaps it will be necessary for us in the negotiations on disarmament
between our countries at the first stage to return
to our proposals providing for the establishment

of posts at airfields, in major sea-ports, at railway junctions, on highways in order to give guarantees to all the countries of the world that no
country will be able to secretly concentrate
troops and get prepared for an attack against or
invasion of another country. It is wise, it appeals
to us.

If you would give your representatives—
McCloy, Stevenson and others—appropriate
instructions on the question of UN posts in the
Caribbean region and adjoining regions of the
US—and our representatives have such instructions—and if they would come to an agreement
then all this could be made public. Then there
would be removed the difficulties connected with
making a public announcement on the withdrawal of IL-28 planes and we would name then specific dates. These dates will be probably much
closer than those which I name and maybe even
closer than those which were named by you.

That is why we should make a final step in
this direction. Then we would really cut the knot
which was tied tightly enough and having cut it
we would create normal relations between our
countries to which our people aspire and which
your people, we are sure of that, also want.

I will allow myself to express some other considerations and I believe you will not take offence
and will not consider that I intrude too much into
the sphere of your internal affairs. Voting in the
elections to the Senate, the House of
Representatives and in gubernatorial elections
which just took place has resulted in the defeat of
your former rival who was clearly preparing for

the next presidential elections. It is significant that as a result of the elections precisely those candidates were defeated who, if I may use such an expression, were making most frenzied bellicose speeches.

This indicates that the American people already begin to feel that if the arms race continues further, if a reasonable solution is not found and an understanding is not achieved between our countries then our peoples will feel still more strongly the threat of the dreadful catastrophe of a thermonuclear war.

Let us then not keep people of peace all over the world in suspense, let us give them joyous satisfaction. Having cut the knot in the Caribbean we would thereby immediately create better conditions and would reinforce peoples' hope for coping with other questions which are now awaiting their solution. Peoples expect wisdom from us, first of all from our two states. Of course our two states can not do everything, but all that depends on us in the sense of reaching an understanding will be of decisive importance. Needless to prove that other states would be also satisfied. And he who was especially displeased will have to agree after this understanding is reached that there is no other way, that the way to peace is the wisest and the only way of meeting the aspirations of all states, all peoples.

Sincerely,/S/

/1/Source: Kennedy Library, National Security Files, Countries Series, USSR, Khrushchev Correspondence. No classification marking. The date is handwritten on the source text. According to *Problems of Communism* the Russian text was transmitted to the Soviet Embassy in Washington on November 14, and Dobrynin was instructed to convey Khrushchev's message to President Kennedy to Robert Kennedy. The source text is apparently a Soviet translation. Another copy is in Department of State, Presidential Correspondence: Lot 77 D 163.
/2/Apparent reference to Document 74.
/3/Document 75.
/4/Documents 67 and 68. (*Footnote reference not indicated in text.—T. Fensch)*
/5/Printed from an unsigned copy.

"... we undertook to agree to remove the quarantine ...."

78. Message From President Kennedy to Chairman Khrushchev

Washington, November 15, 1962./1/

I am glad to learn of your assurance of agreement that the IL-28s should be withdrawn./2/ All that remains is to reach understanding on the timing.

Let me review the undertakings in my letter of October twenty-seventh and your letter of October twenty-eighth./3/ You agreed to remove the weapons systems we described as offensive and with suitable safeguards to halt the further introduction of such weapons into Cuba. On our side, we undertook to agree to remove the quarantine measures in effect and to give assurances

385

against an invasion of Cuba. There were two conditions attached to our undertaking. The first was that the weapons systems would be removed "under appropriate United Nations observation and supervision," and, second, that there would be established "adequate arrangements through the United Nations to ensure the carrying out and continuation of these commitments."

I cannot agree with your statement that you have fulfilled your commitments and that we have not fulfilled ours. Let us recall what, in fact, has occurred. You have removed a certain number of missiles from Cuba—not under United Nations supervision—but you did cooperate in arrangements which enabled us to be reasonably sure that forty-two missiles were in fact taken out of Cuba. There has been no United Nations verification that other missiles were not left behind and, in fact, there have been many reports of their being concealed in caves and elsewhere, and we have no way of satisfying those who are concerned about these reports. The IL-28's are still in Cuba and are of deep concern to the people of our entire Hemisphere. Thus, three major parts of the undertakings on your side— the removal of the IL-28's, the arrangements for verification, and safeguards against introduction—have not yet been carried out.

We suppose that part of the trouble here may be in Cuba. The Secretary General of the United Nations was not allowed to make arrangements for the experts he took with him to Cuba to verify removal of the offensive weapons; the Cuban Government did not agree to International Red

Cross inspection at ports; they have refused the Secretary General's suggestion that the Latin American Ambassadors in Havana undertake this verification; they have rejected a further suggestion of the Secretary General concerning the use of various non-aligned Chiefs of Mission in Havana for this purpose. It is difficult for me to understand why the Cubans are so resistant to the series of reasonable proposals that have been made to them by U Thant unless, for reasons of their own, they are determined to see the crisis prolonged and worsened. We both have means of influencing the Cuban government and I do not believe that we can allow that government to frustrate the clear understandings our two governments have reached in the interests of peace.

In these circumstances we have so far been patient and careful, as we have been, indeed, at every stage. As you know from your own reports, we have always applied the quarantine with care and with regard for the position of others, and in recent days we have relied on the oral assurances of the masters of your ships and other ships. Moreover I myself held back orders for more forceful action right to the limit of possibility during the week of October 27th and 28th. But we cannot make progress from here—or avoid a return of danger to this situation—if your side now should fall into the mistake of claiming that it has met all its commitments, and refusing to help with the real business of carrying out our purpose of untying the Cuban knot.

What, in these circumstances, should be done? We are entitled to insist on removal of the IL-28's and on safeguards against reintroduction of offensive weapons before we lift the quarantine or give assurances of any sort. But we are interested in making rapid progress, step-by-step, and that is why we have proposed an arrangement more favorable from your standpoint: that as soon as you give the order for the removal of the IL-28's and their men and equipment, to be completed within thirty days, (and I am glad you say the length of time is not the real problem) we will announce the lifting of the quarantine. That is more than we agreed to on October twenty-seventh and twenty-eighth, but we wish to end this crisis promptly.

Beyond that, we are quite willing to instruct our negotiators in New York to work closely with yours in order to reach agreement on other matters affecting this problem. We believe, again, that these matters should follow the removal of offensive weapons systems, but just as we have been able to discuss other matters while a number of missiles were leaving, we believe the urgently needed talks can and should go forward while the bombers are leaving. We do not insist that everything wait its exact turn—but only that the essential first steps be clearly going forward.

But what is most urgent, after we can agree that offensive weapons are leaving, and after the quarantine is lifted, is to make some real progress on continuing observations and verification. It will be essential to have such arrangements—and this again is clear in the letters of October 27 and 28—before our assurances can be more formally stated. Our undertaking on this point remains firm and clear, and we want nothing better than to be able to give our assurances, just as we said we would, when the necessary conditions exist.

In the absence of any arrangements under the United Nations or otherwise for international verification or safeguards, we have of course been obliged to rely upon our own resources for surveillance of the situation in Cuba, although this course is unsatisfactory. Just today we learned of new threats by Castro against this necessary surveillance. I should make it very clear that if there is any interference with this surveillance, we shall have to take the necessary action in reply, and it is for just this reason that it is so urgent to obtain better safeguards.

We note with interest that in your last message the arrangement of observation and verification is enlarged from Cuba to include certain other areas. This is a substantial change from the terms of our exchange of messages, and as we see it any such wider arrangements would necessarily require careful discussion. For example, if we move outside Cuba to observe what is happening in other countries which have been involved in the recent tensions, there might have to be observation posts at the appropriate ports in the Soviet Union from which weapons could be shipped to Cuba, as well as in appropriate places in the United States. This is a matter which deserves close study and it may offer a chance of real progress in the long run, but for the immediate future it seems to us better to work within the framework of our understanding of October

27 and 28.

We also think that Brazilian proposal for a verified Denuclearized Zone in Latin America/4/ could, with the cooperation of Cuba and if acceptable to the other Latin American countries, in the long run offer an acceptable means for a broader approach. However, the immediate problem is, I repeat, the carrying out of our understanding with regard to verification that offensive weapons have in fact been removed from Cuba and the establishing of safeguards against their reintroduction pending the coming into effect of longer-term arrangements. Even apart from our understanding, given the history of this matter, I am sure, Mr. Chairman, that you can understand that this is a real necessity if we are to move to the settlement of other matters.

But the first step is to get the bombers started out, and the quarantine lifted—for both are sources of tension. Meanwhile discussion can continue on other aspects of the problem.

/1/Source: Kennedy Library, National Security Files, Countries Series, USSR, Khrushchev Correspondence. No classification marking. This message was considered an "oral" exchange, but a written copy was given to Dobrynin. Copies of this message went to Thompson, McNamara, and McCone.
/2/See Document 77.
/3/Documents 67 and 68.
/4/Draft U.N. Resolution A/C.1/L.312. A revised version of it, U.N. doc. A/C.1/L.312/Rev.2, was submitted to the First Committee of the United Nations by Bolivia, Brazil, Chile, and Ecuador on November 15. For text, see *Documents on Disarmament, 1962,* vol. II, pp. 1056-1057.

*"As for the rumours alleging
that the missiles may have been
left in Cuba somewhere in the caves,
one can say we do not live in
the cave-man age . . ."*

79. Message From Chairman Khrushchev to President Kennedy

Moscow, November 20, 1962./1/

I have studied attentively your considerations which were forwarded through our Ambassador in Washington in the evening of November 15./2/ I wish first of all to express satisfaction with regard to your statement that the United States is also interested in the achievement of a rapid progress in untying the Cuban knot. This is our great desire too. It is good that you have confirmed once again that the U.S. commitment to give assurance of non-invasion of Cuba, which was agreed upon in the exchange of messages on October 27 and 28/3/ remains firm and clear. I fully share also the thought expressed by you about the necessity to act with caution, to take into consideration the position of others. Now when we speak of eliminating the remnants of the crisis this is as important as at any of its past stages.

I always believed and believe now that both of us are guided by the realization of the immense responsibility for the peaceful settlement of the crisis over Cuba being completed. The basis for such settlement already exists: the sides have achieved an agreement and have taken upon themselves certain obligations. It is precisely where we proceed from.

What have we agreed upon? In brief our agreement has come to the following.

The Soviet Union removes from Cuba rocket weapons which you called offensive and gives a possibility to ascertain this. The United States of America promptly removes the quarantine and gives assurances that there will be no invasion of Cuba, not only by the US but also by other countries of the Western Hemisphere. This is the essence of our agreement.

Later on you raised the question of removal of IL-28 planes from Cuba. I think you could not but feel the precariousness of that request. Now, of course, there may appear those who would wish to rummage in the wordings and to interpret them in different ways. But you and we do know well what kind of weapons they were that set the forest on fire, they were missiles. It was not accidental, indeed, that in our and your messages of October 27 and 28 there was not a single mention of bomber planes and specifically of IL-28's. At the same time those messages have direct reference to rocket weapons.

By the way, you yourself refer not to direct obligations of the sides but to the understanding implied by the American side in the expression "offensive weapons" mentioned in the messages and in this connection you recall your TV address of October 22 and your proclamation of October 23./4/ But you will agree, Mr. President, that messages that fix the subject of agreement and unilateral statements of the U.S. Government are two different things indeed.

I informed you that the IL-28 planes are twelve years old and by their combat character-istics they at present cannot be classified as offensive types of weapons. In spite of all this, we regarded your request with understanding. We took into consideration that you made certain statements and therefore the question of removal of IL-28 planes assumed for you as President a certain significance and probably created certain difficulties. We grant it. Since you might really have your difficulties in this question we moved in your direction having informed you of our con-sent to remove these planes from Cuba. What is the situation now if to summarize it in short and to speak of the main?

We have dismantled and removed from Cuba all the medium range ballistic missiles to the last with nuclear warheads for them. All the nuclear weapons have been taken away from Cuba. The Soviet personnel who were servicing the rocket installations have also been withdrawn. We have stated it to your representatives at the negotia-tions in New York too.

The U.S. Government was afforded the possi-bility to ascertain the fact that all 42 missiles that were in Cuba have really been removed.

Moreover, we expressed our readiness to remove also the IL-28 planes from Cuba. I inform you that we intend to remove them within a month term and may be even sooner since the term for the removal of these planes is not a matter of principle for us. We are prepared to remove simultaneously with the IL-28 planes all the Soviet personnel connected with the servicing of these planes.

What can be said in connection with the commitments of the American side? Proper consideration through the U.N. of the commitment not to invade Cuba—and it is the main commitment of your side—so far is being delayed. The quarantine has not been lifted as yet. Permit me to express the hope that with receipt of this communication of mine you will issue instructions to the effect that the quarantine be lifted immediately with the withdrawal of your naval and other military units from the Caribbean area.

Furthermore, your planes still continue to fly over the Cuban territory. It does not normalize the situation but aggravates it. And all this is taking place at the time when we have removed the missiles from Cuba, have given you the possibility to ascertain it through appropriate observation and when we declare our intention to remove the IL-28 planes from Cuba.

I will not conceal that lately I have to hear more and more often that we are too trustful with regard to the statements of the U.S. readiness to carry out its part of the agreement on Cuba and that the American side will under various pretexts evade the fulfilment of the obligations which it assumed. I do not want to believe this and I proceed from something different: the President has given his word and he will keep it as well as we keep our word. But in such an acute and delicate question which we face there cannot but exist the limits beyond which the trust begins losing its value if it is not being strengthened with practical steps towards each other. All this should be mutually taken into consideration to sooner crown with success our efforts in settling the conflict.

I understand, of course, that some time is needed to formalize through the U.N. the agreement on the settlement of the conflict in the Caribbean area, including commitments of non-invasion of Cuba. But this time should be measured by days, not by weeks and, of course, not by months.

Of all the commitments based on the agreement achieved between us in the course of the exchange of messages you declare of your readiness to remove the quarantine immediately as soon as we agree on the term for the removal of IL-28's, without waiting for their removal.

Moving in your direction and taking the decision on the removal of IL-28 planes from Cuba, we presume that we have grounds to count on similar understanding on your part also in the questions of the flights of American planes over Cuba and in promptest formalizing through the U.N. of the U.S. commitments.

As for the discontinuance of flights of American planes over Cuba you yourself can see better how this should be done. In my opinion, actual discontinuance of such flights over Cuba would already be a major step forward and would bring about a great easing in the situation, the more so that our missiles have been removed and your side has ascertained this.

They say that so far as it is a matter of formalizing the commitments through the U.N. it is difficult for the American side to accept the form of a protocol we are suggesting in which the commitments of the sides are to be fixed. We do not attach decisive significance to a form. Other forms are not excluded either. For instance, a declaration (or declarations) which would be confirmed by the U.N. It is the contents of the document which is important and also that the commitments of the sides be formalized through the U.N. without delay.

I heard that Americans have a rule: in any business each side should approach with the same standard the fulfilment of both its own obligations and the obligations of its counterpart and not use "double standard"—one for itself and another for the others. This is a good rule and if it is observed this promises a prompt settlement of the Cuban conflict. Let us follow this good American rule.

Now about the conditions which you set forth with regard to carrying out the verification and measures of further observation.

Yes, we really agreed to the effect that U.N. representatives could ascertain the removal from Cuba of rocket weapons which you called offensive. But we stipulated however that this question can be solved only with the consent of the Government of Cuba. We could not take an obligation for the Government of Cuba and your reference, Mr. President, that we allegedly took such an obligation, of course, does not reflect the real situation. I believe that you see for yourself the weakness of such a reference.

But what is the main thing in connection with the question of verification with regard to the missiles removed by us that is evaded in your communication? The main thing is that under agreement with you we gave you the possibility to carry out verification of the removal of our rockets in the open sea. We did that and that was an act of goodwill on our part. You will agree that we took this step in the circumstances when no promise had been made by us with regard to this matter in our messages. We did something more in comparison with what had been said by us in the message with regard to verification.

It is clear that the said verification of the removal of the missiles conducted in accordance with the arrangement between us substitutes the verification of which you spoke in your message and I would say, in a more effective form at that, because the American side was observing the missiles we were shipping out, so to say, at the final stage of their removal. While even verification of the dismantling would mean observing only the first stage of their removal from Cuba.

As a result the American side, as it itself so declared, had every opportunity to count the missiles put on our ships, to photograph them and to ascertain their removal.

Thus a way out was found and not a bad one, and the question of the verification must, of course, belong to the past. Now no one can doubt that we have carried out our commitment with regard to the dismantling and shipping of the missiles from Cuba which were a subject in our correspondence. The fact of the removal of those missiles has been officially confirmed also by the U.S. Department of Defense./5/

As for the rumours alleging that the missiles may have been left in Cuba somewhere in the caves, one can say that we do not live in the cave-man age to attach great significance to the rumours of this sort. If someone is spreading rumours of this kind he is doing that deliberately to create difficulties in the negotiations.

As far as the question of the American side ascertaining our removing the IL-28 planes from Cuba is concerned, we do not see any problem here. In this respect you and we have the paved way and let us take that way. We have no objections against applying also to this case the procedure agreed upon between us for observation of the removal of the missiles though, speaking frankly, one could do without it. But if you want your naval vessels and helicopters to spend several hundred tons of fuel sailing and somersaulting around our ships carrying the IL-28 planes, let us then consider that such possibility exists.

I will tell you frankly that it was part of our plans, and we believe that we will do it at a proper time, to ship out of Cuba those groups of our military personnel which although were not directly involved in servicing the rocket weapons now removed, still had something to do with guarding those installations. We will do this upon the arrival of our ships. But I must say that the strength of those groups in Cuba is not significant.

You raise the question as to what to do next, how to ensure that those types of weapons on the removal of which we have agreed are not brought back to Cuba. I believe that with respect to non-introduction of such weapons in the future you and I do not have any differences. We are prepared to give firm assurances with regard to this matter.

However, you speak not only about this. You now want some permanent supervision to be established, in Cuba or over Cuba. But where was it taken from that we gave our consent to permanent supervision? The question has never been put that way in the exchange of messages. And generally, how one can take as a normal thing an establishment, and without any reciprocity at that, of some permanent supervision over a sovereign state?

If we are to show serious concern that no unexpected steps are taken on either side to the detriment of each other, then as I already said, the proposal of the U.N. Acting Secretary General U Thant on the so-called "presence of the U.N.," i.e. on establishing U.N. posts in the countries of the Caribbean area would meet this task. This proposal of U Thant was also supported as is known by the Government of the Republic of Cuba. We believe it to be a reasonable basis on which it is possible to come to an agreement. And it would be good if that idea was accepted by you and put into life.

To tell the truth, I am somewhat surprised that in connection with the idea of "presence of the U.N." in the Caribbean area you are talking for some reason about setting up observation posts at the ports of the Soviet Union. May be you have in mind the proposal which we submitted during the negotiations on the problem of disarmament and on the problem of prevention of surprise attack in 1955 and 1958. But those proposals had nothing to do and cannot have anything to do with the question of Cuba since that question simply did not exist at the time. Incidentally, I have already told you that in our opinion it would be useful to get back to considering the proposals to set up on a mutual basis the observation posts at airfields, major seaports, railway junctions and auto routes. We have given our representatives at the negotiation on disarmament in Geneva the necessary instructions. I repeat—we would like to come to an agreement on this question and if you give such instructions to your representatives at the negotiations on disarmament we will only greet that.

Such is our viewpoint on the three questions raised by you: on the removal of the IL-28 planes, on organizing the verification and on non-introduction to Cuba of such weapons which in accordance with the agreement are removed from Cuba.

How should we deal with the matter now so that we and you could soon bring joy to humanity with the news that the crisis over Cuba is completely liquidated?

The Government of the USA in view of the agreement reached on the IL-28 planes should immediately remove the quarantine which corresponds to your own statement as well.

It is necessary to stick to generally recognized international norms and rules fixed in the U.N.

Charter—not to violate the territorial waters and air space of sovereign states and stop the flights of American aircraft over Cuba. I will tell you frankly, Mr. President, that I met with some relief the report that during the last one-two days the flights of American planes over Cuba did not take place. It is good if it promises maintaining of such wise decision in the future as well.

Let both of us agree, Mr. President, also that our representatives in New York be given at once the instructions to immediately proceed with working out an agreed document (or documents) that would formalize through the U.N. the commitments of the sides.

As we see the matter this will require only a few days if, of course, all the sides want to have speediest liquidation of the aftermath of a tense and dangerous situation evolved in the Caribbean area, the situation that really brought humanity to the brink of thermonuclear war.

One more point. I have read V. Kuznetsov's report on his talk with A. Stevenson from which I learned that the American side is going to give us a draft of its document stating the U.S. commitments of non-invasion of Cuba./6/ Our draft of the document on settling the conflict has been already forwarded to your representatives.7 Naturally, we will study your document with utmost attention. Let us hope that as a result of the negotiations we will manage to formalize the achieved agreement so that it satisfies all the sides.

Your brother Robert Kennedy through our Ambassador Dobrynin in Washington and Mr.

McCloy through our representatives in New York
expressed a desire to get promptly our answer to
the considerations expressed by you on the question of the removal of IL-28 planes from Cuba.
Well, I think, this answer of mine gives you not
bad material for your statement at your press
conference./8/ However, I hope, Mr. President,
that your statement will not be one-sided but will
respond to mutual understanding of the situation
with regard to immediate steps to remove the
quarantine and to discontinue the flights of
American planes over Cuba as well as with
regard to the immediate formalizing through the
U.N. of the commitments of the sides on the final
liquidation of the crisis evolved in the Caribbean
area.

In conclusion I wish to stress that much time
has already passed since an agreement was
reached between us and it is not in the interests
of our countries, not in the interests of peace to
delay the fulfilment of the agreement that has
been reached and the final settlement of the
Cuban crisis. Such is our conviction.

[Here follow, on a separate page, 2 paragraphs
apparently added by Dobrynin regarding Cuba
and the President's upcoming press conference;
for text, see volume XI, Document 196.]

/1/Source: Kennedy Library, National Security Files,
Countries Series, USSR, Khrushchev Correspondence. No
classification marking. For Robert Kennedy's account of
how this message was delivered by Dobrynin, see
Schlesinger, *Robert Kennedy and His Times,* p. 550.
Another copy is in Department of State, Presidential
Correspondence: Lot 77 D 163.
/2/Document 78.

/3/Documents 67 and 68.
/4/Regarding the President's October 22 address, see footnote 1, Document 60. For text of the proclamation, see
*Public Papers of the Presidents of the United States: John
F. Kennedy, 1962,* pp. 809-811.
/5/For text, see *American Foreign Policy: Current
Documents, 1962,* p. 458.
/6/Stevenson's account of this meeting, transmitted in
telegram 1818 from USUN, November 15, is printed in
vol. XI, Document 183.
/7/The text was transmitted in telegram 1798 from USUN,
November 15. (Department of State, Central Files,
737.00/11-1562)
/8/For text of the President's press statement, see *Public
Papers of the Presidents of the United States: John F.
Kennedy, 1962,* pp. 830-838.

80. Editorial Note

At 5 p.m., November 20, 1962, 1 hour before
President Kennedy's press conference, Ambassador at Large Thompson transmitted the following
message through Soviet Ambassador Dobrynin:

"In addition to what he intends to announce at
the press conference, he has also ordered a lower
state of alert for the US armed forces, that had
been introduced in the beginning of the Cuban
events. Simultaneously, those air squadrons that
had been called to active duty during the Cuban
crisis have been ordered back into reserve."

(Unofficial translation from the Soviet Foreign
Ministry)

"I regret that you have been unable to persuade Mr. Castro to accept a suitable form of inspection . . ."

81. Message From President Kennedy to Chairman Khrushchev

Washington, November 21, 1962./1/

DEAR MR. CHAIRMAN: I have been glad to get your letter of November 20,/2/ which arrived in good time yesterday. As you will have seen, I was able to announce the lifting of our quarantine promptly at my press conference, on the basis of your welcome assurance that the IL-28 bombers will be removed within a month.

I am now instructing our negotiators in New York to move ahead promptly with proposals for a solution of the remaining elements in the Cuban problem. I do not wish to confuse the discussion by trying to state our present position in detail in this message, but I do want you to know that I continue to believe that it is important to settle this matter promptly and on reasonable terms, so that we may move on to other issues. I regret that you have been unable to persuade Mr. Castro to accept a suitable form of inspection or verification in Cuba, and that in consequence we must continue to rely upon our own means of information. But, as I said yesterday,/3/ there need be no fear of any invasion of Cuba while matters take their present favorable course./4/

/1/Source: Department of State, Presidential Correspondence: Lot 77 D 163. Confidential. Another copy is in the Kennedy Library, National Security Files, Countries Series, USSR, Khrushchev Correspondence. Also printed in Claflin, *The President Wants To Know*, p. 222.
/2/Document 79.
/3/In a statement at his press conference on November 20; for text, see *American Foreign Policy: Current Documents, 1962*, pp. 461-463.
/4/Printed from an unsigned copy.

"I express great satisfaction. I fully trust the statement made in that message too that the United States confirms its commitment not to invade Cuba . . ."

82. Letter From Chairman Khrushchev to President Kennedy

Moscow, November 22, 1962./1/

DEAR MR. PRESIDENT, I have received your message./2/ I express great satisfaction. I fully trust the statement made in that message too that the United States confirms its commitment not to invade Cuba which you also confirmed in your statement at the news conference.

In my confidential messages to you I have already laid down our understanding of the questions and of those steps which are needed to normalize the situation in the Caribbean area after the great and dangerous tension we and you have lived through.

No less important questions are facing us now, that must be solved to avoid recurrence of the situation which has just been eliminated through our mutual efforts.

You say that I was not able to convince Prime-Minister Fidel Castro about something. In general you are partly right. But it should be taken into consideration that Cuba is a young republic, the Cuban leaders being very able and devoted to their people are however young, expansive people—Spaniards in a word, to use it far from pejorative sense. But one should understand the position they are in as the leaders of Cuba. The Republic of Cuba is a small country having for its neighbour a big and powerful state—the United States of America, a state which has been unfriendly to her since the first day the Cuban revolution was born. Moreover, one should not forget either that there was an invasion of Cuba.

That is what has to be taken into consideration in order to correctly assess and understand the situation and, if you wish, the state of mind of the leaders of Cuba. I even think that Prime-Minister Fidel Castro may have looked upon some questions with a great sense of understanding but he probably also correlated his steps with the feelings of the Cuban people who are taken by a great patriotic upsurge and desire to defend their independence. The Cuban people and their desire are worthy of respect.

Of course, you and we have a different appraisal of the Cuban revolution and of the events which developed around Cuba and of the position of the Cuban leaders. But this is another matter. The different appraisal must not after all prevent us from finding agreed solutions in the interest of peace. That is what the peaceful coexistence is. One should treat both sides with understanding and take into account the actual state of things—in this case the situation in Cuba which has chosen the way for its development in accordance with the will of its people.

We have been doing with understanding and patience everything that was needed and that was within our power to ensure the achievement of agreement on the elimination of the remnants of the crisis. A great work has been done in Cuba on our instructions by our representative, my first deputy A.I. Mikoyan. Incidentally, he will come back soon because we have given him appropriate instructions to this effect.

I understood your message in a sense that you yourself regard with understanding the difficulties that still remain. I would wish that we having accomplished the main thing, having given relief to the world public and having given orders to the armed forces contributing to the normalization of the situation—and we gave such order at once as soon as we learned that analagous steps were taken on your side—that we would take speedy measures to complete the settlement of the questions that would crown all our efforts.

It would be necessary that appropriate instructions be also given to your representative, Mr. McCloy, for whom we and I personally, after my meeting with him in Pitsunde last year, have respect, despite the fact that he, as I told him half seriously and half-jokingly, is a representative of

Wall Street. True, he tried to convince me that Wall Street was not so terrible a thing as I imagined. He even promised when I happen to be in New York to take me to Wall Street to try to convince me that this is so. I do not lose hope that one fine day Mr. McCloy will fulfil his promise, that is, will take me to Wall Street. But generally, as you understand, [that] is just a digression.

As for us, in connection with the completion of the questions which have not been completed yet, we on our part have already given instructions to Kuznetsov regarding proposals to that effect which, as far as I know, have already been forwarded to the attention of your representatives in New York. We consider these proposals to be constructive, and we were guided by a desire to facilitate the completion of our agreement.

Now I would like to express the following wish: it would be extremely useful if while working on the proposals no steps are made on your part that would be pin-pricks for the other participants in the negotiations and that would create hooks capable of causing scratches to national pride and prestige of these other participants. The main thing has been achieved indeed and at the final stage it would be necessary to create good, reliable relations so that, relying on common sense, on reason and on the understanding of all the responsibility that lies upon you and us, to reach a final solution on a firm reasonable basis and thus to create conditions for a good, stable situation in the Caribbean area.

In this message of mine I do not raise any questions of substance since the questions that must be completed are known to you. Let us then make a joint effort to complete the remaining questions as well. This may serve as a good omen for both our sides in working out an approach for the solution of other not less important questions that we face. After all the question that you and we are struggling with is, though important, but a particular one. Meanwhile there are questions the solution of which is extremely important for destinies of peace and they must be solved in order to really stabilize the situation and secure lasting peace on earth.

Sincerely yours,

N. Khrushchev/3/

/1/Source: Kennedy Library, National Security Files, Countries Series, USSR, Khrushchev Correspondence. No classification marking. Another copy is in Department of State, Presidential Correspondence: Lot 77 D 163. The Russian-language text is ibid. The source text is apparently a Soviet translation.
/2/Document 81.
/3/Printed from a copy that bears this typed signature.

". . . we and you were already prepared to fight and this would lead to a thermonuclear war."

83. Message From Chairman Khrushchev to President Kennedy

Moscow, December 11, 1962./1/

DEAR MR. PRESIDENT, It would seem that you
and we have come now to a final stage in the elimination of tension around Cuba. Our relations are
already entering now their normal course since
all those means placed by us on the Cuban territory which you considered offensive are withdrawn and you ascertained that to which effect a
statement was already made by your side.

That is good. We appreciate that you just as we
approached not dogmatically the solution of the
question of eliminating the tension which evolved
and this enabled us under existing conditions to
find also a more flexible form of verification of the
withdrawal of the above mentioned means.
Understanding and flexibility displayed by you in
this matter are highly appreciated by us though
our criticism of American imperialism remains in
force because that conflict was indeed created by
the policy of the United States with regard to Cuba.

More resolute steps should be taken now to
move towards finalizing the elimination of this
tension, i.e. you on your part should clearly confirm at the U.N. as you did at your press conference and in your messages to me the pledge of
non-invasion of Cuba by the United States and
your allies having removed reservations which
are being introduced now into the U.S. draft declaration in the Security Council and our representatives in New York should come to terms
with regard to an agreed wording in the declarations of both powers of the commitments undertaken by them.

I believe that you already had an opportunity
to familiarize yourself with the text proposed by

us/2/ of a brief declaration of the Soviet Government in which the Soviet Union's main commitments resulting from the exchange of messages between us are formulated. We proceed from the assumption that an analogous brief declaration should be made by the U.S. Government and that the main U.S. commitments resulting from the exchange of messages will also be fixed in it. Have a look, Mr. President, at this proposal submitted by us through your representatives in New York.

But notwithstanding what the agreement on the concrete texts of our declarations at this concluding stage will be, anyway the basic goal has been achieved and tension removed. I will tell you frankly that we have removed our means from Cuba relying on your assurance that the United States and its allies will not invade Cuba. Those means really had the purpose of defending the sovereignty of Cuba and therefore after your assurance they lost their purpose. We hope and we would like to believe—I spoke of that publicly too, as you know—that you will adhere to the commitments which you have taken, as strictly as we do with regard to our commitments. We, Mr. President, have already fulfilled our commitments concerning the removal of our missiles and IL-28 planes from Cuba and we did it even ahead of time. It is obvious that fulfilment by you of your commitments cannot be as clearly demonstrated as it was done by us since your commitments are of a long-term nature. But it is important to fulfil them and to do everything so that no doubts are sown from the very start that they will not be fulfilled. I already told you at one time that our friends, especially those of them who regard us with certain lack of understanding, are trying to convince us that imperialism cannot be trusted, that is that you cannot be trusted, as a representative of such capitalist state as the United States of America.

It goes without saying that you and I have different understanding of these questions. I shall not go into details as to what my understanding is because in this regard you and I cannot have common opinion since we are people representing different political poles. But there are things that require common understanding on both sides and such common understanding is possible and even necessary. This is what I would like to tell you about.

Within a short period of time we and you have lived through a rather acute crisis. The acuteness of it was that we and you were already prepared to fight and this would lead to a thermonuclear war. Yes, to a thermonuclear world war with all its dreadful consequences. We took it into account and, being convinced that mankind would never forgive the statesmen who would not exhaust all possibilities to prevent catastrophe, agreed to a compromise although we understood—and we state it now—that your claims had no grounds whatsoever, had no legal basis and represented a manifestation of sheer arbitrariness in international affairs. We agreed to a compromise because our main purpose was to extend a helping hand to the Cuban people in order to exclude the possibility of invasion of Cuba so that Cuba could exist and develop as a free sovereign state. This is our main purpose today, it remains to be our main purpose for tomorrow and we did not and do not pursue any other purposes.

Therefore, Mr. President, everything—the stability in this area and not only in this area but in the entire world—depends on how you will now fulfil the commitments taken by you. Furthermore, it will be now a sort of litmus paper, an indicator whether it is possible to trust if similar difficulties arise in other geographical areas. I think you will agree that if our arrangement for settling the Cuban crisis fails it will undermine a possibility for manoeuvre which you and we would resort to for elimination of danger, a possibility for compromise in the future if similar difficulties arise in other areas of the world, and they really can arise. We attach great significance to all this, and subsequent development will depend on you as President and on the U.S. Government.

We believe that the guarantees for non-invasion of Cuba given by you will be maintained and not only in the period of your stay in the White House, that, to use an expression, goes without saying. We believe that you will be able to receive a mandate at the next election too, that is that you will be the U.S. President for six years, which would appeal to us. At our times, six years in world politics is a long period of time and during that period we could create good conditions for peaceful coexistence on earth and this would be highly appreciated by the peoples of our countries as well as by all other peoples.

Therefore, Mr. President, I would like to express a wish that you follow the right way, as we do, in appraising the situation. Now it is of special importance to provide for the possibility of an exchange of opinion through confidential channels which you and I have set up and which we use. But the confidential nature of our personal relations will depend on whether you fulfil—as we did—the commitments taken by you and give instructions to your representatives in New York to formalize these commitments in appropriate documents. This is needed in order that all the peoples be sure that tension in the Caribbean is a matter of yesterday and that now normal conditions have been really created in the world. And for this it is necessary to fix the assumed commitments in the documents of both sides and register them with the United Nations.

You, Mr. President, do not want to agree with the five conditions put forward by Prime Minister of the Republic of Cuba Fidel Castro./3/ But, indeed, these five principles correspond fully to the provisions of the United Nations Charter which is a legal basis for the relations among states, a sort of foundation for securing peace and peaceful coexistence. I will tell you frankly that such position of yours is surprising. Maybe you have some difficulties. But, Mr. President, we who occupy such responsible position in the world and who are endowed with high trust have to overcome those difficulties. The peoples will appreciate that because for them it means insuring lasting peace on earth.

I would like to express to you my disapproval

of certain things. We read now various articles by your columnists and correspondents and we are concerned that in those articles they are widely commenting on the confidential exchange of opinion and it is being done by the people who as it would seem have no relation to confidential channels set up between us. Judging by the contents of these articles it is clear that their authors are well informed and we get an impression that this is not a result of an accidental leak of the confidential information but a result of benevolence for those people into whose hands gets the information they make public. This evidently is done for the purpose of informing the public in a one-sided way.

Frankly speaking, if we use the confidential communications this way, it will be far from facilitating confidence in those channels. You yourself realize that if your side begins to act in the way that our exchange of opinion by way of confidential channels will leak through fingers these channels will cease to be of use and may even cause harm. But this is up to you. If you consider that those channels have outlived themselves and are of no use any longer, then we also will draw appropriate conclusions in this respect. I tell you this straightforwardly and I would like to know your opinion on this matter. I have been denouncing American imperialism. But on the other hand I consider it useful for us to continue to maintain the possibility of confidential exchange of opinion because a minimum of personal trust is necessary for leading statesmen of both countries and this corresponds to the inter-

ests of our countries and peoples, to the interest
of peace all over the world.

Let us, Mr. President, eliminate promptly the
consequences of the Cuban crisis and get down to
solving other questions, and we have them in
number. As far as nuclear test ban is concerned
this is a minor question on the whole. I am going
to address to you a confidential letter/4/ and proposals on this question and I hope that we will
overcome difficulties existing in this question.
The problem of disarmament is a different matter; it is a major and difficult question now.

But, of course, the main question is the
German question and it is an easy and at the
same time difficult one. I say that it is an easy
and at the same time difficult question. But this
is really so. It is easy because our proposals for
concluding a peace treaty do not demand any
concessions from either side, neither do they
demand any losses from either side. These proposals only fix the situation which has developed
as a result of World War II.

After the talks that our Minister of Foreign
Affairs A. Gromyko had with your Secretary of
State D. Rusk, only one question in effect
remained unresolved—that of troops in West
Berlin: troops of what countries, for what term
and under what flag will be stationed there.

I would like you to understand me correctly on
this question. Let us solve it. We will not escape
the necessity to solve this question anyway. To
tell the truth, this question is not worth an
eggshell if a realistic approach is employed in
appraising the situation in Germany where two

sovereign German states have developed and if a course followed is aimed at an agreement on West Berlin and not at leaving it to remain a dangerous hot-bed of collision between states. Should really you and we—two great states—submit, willingly or unwillingly, our policy, the interests of our states to the old-aged man who both morally and physically is with one foot in grave? Should we really become toys in his hands? By concluding peace treaty we would lose nothing but we would gain a possibility to strengthen friendly relations between our states, would untie the knot in Europe which is fraught with danger for the whole world only because most extreme aggressive militarist forces in West Germany are interested in this.

Please, excuse me for my straightforwardness and frankness but I believe as before that a frank and straightforward exchange of opinion is needed to avoid the worst.

Please, convey to your wife and your family wishes of good health from myself, my wife and my entire family./5/

/1/Source: Kennedy Library, National Security Files, Countries Series, USSR, Khrushchev Correspondence. No classification marking, but the Department of State classified the message Top Secret and Eyes Only. (Department of State, Presidential Correspondence: Lot 77 D 163)
/2/Transmitted in telegram 2179 from USUN, December 6; see vol. XI, Document 234.
/3/In Prime Minister Castro's October 28 letter to U Thant; for text, see *American Foreign Policy: Current Documents, 1962*, pp. 447-448.
/4/Document 85.
/5/Printed from an unsigned copy.

"We are also hopeful that once the Cuban crisis is behind us, we shall be able to tackle the other problems confronting us and find the path to their solution."

84. Letter From President Kennedy to Chairman Khrushchev

Washington, December 14, 1962./1/

DEAR MR. CHAIRMAN: I was glad to have your message of December 11th/2/ and to know that you believe, as we do, that we have come to the final stage of the Cuban affair between us, the settlement of which will have significance for our future relations and for our ability to overcome other difficulties. I wish to thank you for your expression of appreciation of the understanding and flexibility we have tried to display.

I have followed with close attention the negotiations on the final settlement of the Cuban question between your representative, Mr. Kuznetsov, and our representatives, Ambassador Stevenson and Mr. McCloy, in New York. In these negotiations we have tried to understand your position and I am glad to note that Mr. Kusnetsov has also shown effort to understand our problems. It is clearly in the interest of both sides that we reach agreement on how finally to dispose of the Cuban crisis. To this end, Ambassador Stevenson and Mr. McCloy presented on Wednesday a new draft of a joint statement

418

which by now has certainly reached you./3/ I wish to assure you that it is our purpose to end this affair as simply and clearly as possible.

You refer to the importance of my statements on an invasion of Cuba and of our intention to fulfill them, so that no doubts are sown from the very start. I have already stated my position publicly in my press conference on November 20th, and I am glad that this statement appears to have your understanding; we have never wanted to be driven by the acts of others into war in Cuba. The other side of the coin, however, is that we do need to have adequate assurances that all offensive weapons are removed from Cuba and are not reintroduced, and that Cuba itself commits no aggressive acts against any of the nations of the Western Hemisphere. As I understand you, you feel confident that Cuba will not in fact engage in such aggressive acts, and of course I already have your own assurance about the offensive weapons. So I myself should suppose that you could accept our position—but it is probably better to leave final discussion of these matters to our representatives in New York. I quite agree with you that the larger part of the crisis has now been ended and we should not permit others to stand in the way of promptly settling the rest without further acrimony.

With regard to your reference to the confidential channels set up between us, I can assure you that I value them. I have not concealed from you that it was a serious disappointment to me that dangerously misleading information should have come through these channels before the recent

crisis. You may also wish to know that by an accident or misunderstanding one of your diplomats
appears to have used a representative of a private television network as a channel to us. This
is always unwise in our country, where the members of the press often insist on printing at some
later time what they may learn privately.

Because our systems are so different, you may
not be fully familiar with the practice of the
American press. The competition for news in this
country is fierce. A number of the competitors
are not great admirers of my Administration, and
perhaps an even larger number are not wholly
friendly to yours. Here in Washington we have
1200 reporters accredited to the White House
alone, and thousands more in other assignments.
Not one of them is accountable to this government for what he reports. It would be a great
mistake to think that what appears in newspapers and magazines necessarily has anything to
do with the policy and purpose of this government. I am glad to say that I have some friends
among newspapermen, but no spokesmen.

But let me emphasize again that we do indeed
value these confidential channels. I entirely
share your view that some trust is necessary for
leading statesmen of our two countries; I believe
that it is important to build the area of trust
wherever possible. I shall of course continue to
hold and to express my convictions about the relative merits of our systems of government, and I
will not be surprised if you do the same.

In particular, we have been very glad to have
opportunities for private exchanges with and

through Mr. Bolshakov, and I am sorry to learn that he is returning to Moscow. It is our impression that he has made a real effort to improve communications and understanding between our two governments, and we shall miss him very much.

I appreciate your writing me so frankly, and in return I have tried to be as straightforward, for I agree with you that only through such frank exchanges can we better understand our respective points of view. Partly for this reason I refrained in my last press conference from commenting on certain aspects of your speech before the Supreme Soviet with which you realize, of course, we could not agree.

We also are hopeful that once the Cuban crisis is behind us, we shall be able to tackle the other problems confronting us and to find the path to their solution.

I cannot refrain from commenting briefly on your reference to the German question, though I do not think that it would be useful in this message to expound our full position once again. But your suggestion that the interests of our two countries are toys in the hands of Chancellor Adenauer seems to me to miss entirely the true nature of the problem which confronts us in Central Europe. For here the vital interests of many states are involved—on your side as well as ours. If this is recognized, then I am confident that a way can be found which will accommodate these interests and which will lead to a peaceful settlement. I cannot quite agree with you that Mr. Rusk and Mr. Gromyko have settled everything on Berlin but one issue. They are skillful and experienced diplomats, but I do not think we should give them too much credit yet. Still it is quite true, as you say, that the main issue which seems to separate us on Berlin is that of the presence of allied troops in West Berlin. I am confident that if you could begin from an understanding of our position on this vital point, our chances of making progress would be greatly improved.

I look forward to receiving your confidential letter and proposals on the test ban question, and I think there is every reason to keep working on this problem. I hope that in your message on this subject you will tell me what you think about the position of the people in Peking on this question. It seems to me very important for both of us that in our efforts to secure an end to nuclear testing we should not overlook this area of the world.

Thank you for your expressions of good wishes to me and my family, and let me in turn send you and your wife and family our personal good wishes for the coming year./4/

/1/Source: Department of State, Presidential Correspondence: Lot 77 D 163. No classification marking. Another copy is in the Kennedy Library, National Security Files, Countries Series, USSR, Khrushchev Correspondence. Printed in part in Claflin, *The President Wants To Know*, pp. 227–229.
/2/Document 83.
/3/Transmited in telegram 1593 to USUN, December 11; see vol. XI, Document 243.
/4/Printed from an unsigned copy.

*". . . that time has now come
to put an end once and for all
to nuclear tests . . . ."*

85. Letter From Chairman Khrushchev to President Kennedy

Moscow, December 19, 1962./1/

DEAR MR. PRESIDENT, In our recent correspondence related to the events in the Caribbean area we have touched on the question of cessation of nuclear weapon tests. Today I would like to come back again to that problem and to set forth my views concerning possible ways of its speediest solution which would be mutually acceptable to both our sides.

It seems to me, Mr. President, that time has come now to put an end once and for all to nuclear tests, to draw a line through such tests. The moment for this is very, very appropriate. Left behind is a period of utmost acuteness and tension in the Caribbean. Now we have untied our hands to engage closely in other urgent international matters and, in particular, in such a problem which has been ripe for so long as cessation of nuclear tests. A certain relaxation of international tension which has emerged now should, in my view, facilitate this.

The Soviet Union does not need war. I think that war does not promise bright prospects for the United States either. If in the past after every war America used to increase its economic potential and to accumulate more and more wealth, now war with the use of modern rocket—nuclear weapons will stride across seas and oceans within minutes. Thermonuclear catastrophe will bring enormous losses and sufferings to the American people as well as to other peoples on earth. To prevent this we must, on the basis of complete equality and with just regard for each other's interests, develop between ourselves peaceful relations and solve all issues through negotiations and mutual concessions.

One of such questions with which the governments of our countries have been dealing for many years is the question of concluding a treaty banning all tests of nuclear weapons.

Both of us stand on the same position with regard to the fact that national means of detection are sufficient to control banning experimental nuclear explosions in outer space, in the atmosphere and under water. So far, however, we have not succeeded in finding a mutually acceptable solution to the problem of cessation of underground tests. The main obstacle to an agreement is the demand by the American side of international control and inspection on the territories of nuclear powers over cessation of underground nuclear tests. I would like to believe that you yourself understand the rightness of our arguments that now national means are sufficient to control also this kind of tests and be sure that agreement is observed by any side. But so far you do not want to recognize openly this actual state of things and to accept it as a basis for concluding without delay an agreement on cessation of tests.

Striving to find a mutually acceptable basis for agreement the Soviet Union has made lately an important step toward the West and agreed to installing automatic seismic stations. This idea, as is known, was put forward not by us. It was introduced by British scientists during the recent meeting in London of the participants of Pugwash movement. Moreover, it is well known to us, that when this idea was proposed, it was not alien to your scientists who were in London at that time.

We proposed to install such stations both near the borders of nuclear powers and directly on their territories. We stated our agreement that three such stations be installed on the territory of the Soviet Union in the zones most frequently subjected to earthquakes. There are three such zones in the Soviet Union where these stations can be installed: Central Asian, Altaian and Far Eastern.

In the opinion of Soviet scientists the most suitable places for locating automatic seismic stations in the Soviet Union are area of the city of Kokcnetav for Central Asian zone of the USSR, area of the city of Bodaibo for Altaian zone and area of the city of Yakutsk for Far Eastern zone. However, should, as a result of exchange of opinion between our representatives, other places be suggested for locating automatic seismic stations in these seismic zones, we will be ready to discuss this question and find mutually acceptable solution.

Beside the above said zones there are two more seismic zones in the Soviet Union— Caucasian and Carpathian. However these zones are so densely populated that conducting nuclear tests there is practically excluded.

Of course, delivery to and from international center of appropriate sealed equipment for its periodic replacement at automatic seismic stations in the USSR could well be made by Soviet personnel and on Soviet planes. However if for such delivery of equipment to and from automatic seismic stations participation of foreign personnel were needed we would agree to this also, having taken, if necessary, precautionary measures against use of such trips for reconnaissance. Thus our proposal on automatic seismic stations includes elements of international control. This is a major act of good will on the part of the Soviet Union.

I will tell you straightforwardly that before making this proposal I have consulted thoroughly the specialists and after such consultation my colleagues in the Government and I came to a conclusion that so far as the Soviet Union is concerned the above said considerations on the measures on our part are well founded and, it seems to us, they should not cause objections on the part of the American side.

You, Mr. President, and your representatives point out that without at least a minimum number of on-site inspections you will not manage to persuade the U.S. Senate to ratify an agreement on the cessation of tests. This circumstance, as we understand, ties you and does not allow you to sign a treaty which would enable all of us to abandon for good the grounds where nuclear weapons are tested. Well, if this is the only difficulty on the way to agreement, then for the noble and humane goal of ceasing nuclear weapon tests we are ready to meet you halfway in this question.

We noted that on this October 30, in conversation with First Deputy Foreign Minister of the USSR V.V. Kuznetsov in New York, your representative Ambassador Dean stated that, in the opinion of the U.S. Government, it would be sufficient to carry on 2-4 on-site inspections each year on the territory of the Soviet Union. According to Ambassador Dean's statement, the United States would also be prepared to work out measures which would rule out any possibility of carrying on espionage under the cover of these inspection trips including such measures as the use of Soviet planes piloted by Soviet crews for transportation of inspectors to the sites, screening of windows in the planes, prohibition to carry photo-cameras, etc.

We took all this into account and, in order to overcome the deadlock and to arrive at least at a mutually acceptable agreement, we would agree, in those cases when it would be considered necessary, to 2-3 inspections a year on the territory of each of the nuclear powers in the seismic areas where some suspicious earth's tremors might occur. It goes without saying that the basis of control over an agreement on underground nuclear test ban would be the national means of detection in combination with automatic seismic stations. On-site inspections could be carried on with the precautions mentioned by Ambassador Dean against any misuse of control for purposes of espionage.

We believe that now the road to agreement is straight and clear. Beginning from January 1 of the new year of 1963 the world can be relieved of the roar of nuclear explosions. The peoples are waiting for this—this is what the UN General Assembly has called for. With the elimination of the Cuban crisis we relieved mankind of the direct menace of combat use of lethal nuclear weapons that impended over the world. Can't we solve a far simpler question—that of cessation of experimental explosions of nuclear weapons in the peaceful conditions? I think that we can and must do it. Here lies now our duty before the peoples of not only our countries but of all other countries. Having solved promptly also this question—and there are all the preconditions for that—we shall be able to facilitate working out an agreement on disarmament and with even more confidence proceed with solving other urgent international problems, which we and you unfortunately are not short of.

Sincerely,

N. Khrushchev/2/

/1/Source: Department of State, Presidential Correspondence: Lot 66 D 204. No classification marking. The Russian-language text is ibid.: Lot 77 D 163. The source text is apparently a Soviet translation. Other copies of this message are ibid., and in the Kennedy Library, National Security Files, Countries Series, USSR, Khrushchev Correspondence. Also printed in *Documents on Disarmament, 1962,* vol. II, pp. 1239-1242, and *American Foreign Policy: Current Documents, 1962,* pp. 1306-1308.
/2/Printed from a copy that bears this typed signature.

"... it is not expected that the Polaris missiles which he agreed to make available for a small British submarine force ... will become operational before 1969 or 1970."

86. Memorandum for the Files

Washington, December 22, 1962./1/

By direction of the President, I made the following statement to Ambassador Dobrynin today:

"The President wants the Chairman to know that it is not expected that the Polaris missiles which he has agreed to make available for a small British submarine force to be assigned to NATO will become operational before 1969 or 1970. The President's chief concern in making these missiles available was to prevent, or at least delay, the development of national nuclear capabilities. Failure on his part to provide a substitute for Skybolt missile would have meant a serious rift in British/American relations and would undoubtedly have resulted in British efforts to create their own missile, not tied into NATO controls.

"The British might have been obliged, because of costs, to have cooperated with the French in such efforts and there might have developed a separate German effort to do the same.

"The President believes his action in this matter has kept open the possibility of agreement on the non-proliferation of nuclear weapons and has gained time for our further efforts in the field of disarmament. It is clear that real progress in disarmament would take priority over any such arrangements which were made in the absence of a disarmament agreement."

/1/Source: Department of State, Presidential Correspondence: Lot 77 D 163. Secret. Prepared by Thompson.

". . . we must find ways for reducing or removing the recurring waves of fear and suspicion which feed on ignorance, misundrestanding or what appear to one side or the other as broken agreements."

87. Message From President Kennedy to Chairman Khrushchev

Washington, December 28, 1962./1/

DEAR MR. CHAIRMAN: I was very glad to receive your letter of December 19, 1962,/2/ setting forth your views on nuclear tests. There appear to be no differences between your views and mine regarding the need for eliminating war in this nuclear age. Perhaps only those who have the responsibility for controlling these weapons fully realize the awful devastation their use would bring.

Having these considerations in mind and with respect to the issue of a test ban, I therefore sincerely hope that the suggestions that you have made in your letter will prove to be helpful in starting us down the road to an agreement. I am encouraged that you are prepared to accept the principle of on-site inspections. These seem to me to be essential not just because of the concern of our Congress but because they seem to us to go to the heart of a reliable agreement ending nuclear testing.

If we are to have peace between systems with far-reaching ideological differences, we must find ways for reducing or removing the recurring waves of fear and suspicion which feed on ignorance, misunderstanding or what appear to one side or the other as broken agreements. To me, the element of assurance is vital to the broader development of peaceful relationships.

With respect to the question of on-site inspections I would certainly agree that we could accept any reasonable provision which you had in mind to protect against your concern that the on-site inspectors might engage in "espionage" en route to the area of inspection. In a statement at the United Nations, Ambassador Stevenson suggested that the United States would accept any reasonable security provision while the inspectors were being taken to the site, so long as they had reasonable provision for satisfying themselves that they were actually at the intended location and had the freedom necessary to inspect the limited designated area.

With respect to the number of on-site inspections there appears to have been some misunderstanding. Your impression seems to be that

431

Ambassador Dean told Deputy Minister Kuznetsov that the United States might be prepared to accept an annual number of on-site inspections between two and four. Ambassador Dean advises me that the only number which he mentioned in his discussions with Deputy Minister Kuznetsov was a number between eight and ten. This represented a substantial decrease in the request of the United States as we had previously been insisting upon a number between twelve and twenty. I had hoped that the Soviet Union would match this motion on the part of the United States by an equivalent motion in the figure of two or three on-site inspections which it had some time ago indicated it might allow.

I am aware that this matter of on-site inspections has given you considerable difficulty although I am not sure that I fully understand why this should be so. To me, an effective nuclear test ban treaty is of such importance that I would not permit such international arrangements to become mixed up with our or any other national desire to seek other types of information about the Soviet Union. I believe quite sincerely that arrangements could be worked out which would convince you and your colleagues that this is the case.

But in this connection, your implication that on-site inspections should be limited to seismic areas also gives us some difficulty. It is true that in the ordinary course we would have concern about events taking place in the seismic areas. However, an unidentified seismic event coming from an area in which there are not usually earthquakes would be a highly suspicious event. The United States would feel that in such a circumstance the U.S.S.R. would be entitled to an on-site inspection of such an event occurring in our area and feels that the United States should have the same rights within its annual quota of inspections.

Perhaps your comment would be that a seismic event in another area designated for inspection might coincide with a highly sensitive defense installation. I recognize this as a real problem but believe that some arrangement can be worked out which would prevent this unlikely contingency from erecting an insuperable obstacle.

Your suggestion as to the three locations in the Soviet Union in which there might be unmanned seismic stations is helpful but it does not seem to me to go far enough. These stations are all outside the areas of highest seismicity and therefore do not record all of the phenomena within those areas. These stations would be helpful in increasing the detection capability of the system but I doubt that they would have the same value in reducing the number of suspicious seismic events by identifying some as earthquakes. For this purpose unmanned seismic stations should be in the areas of highest seismicity, not outside them. To achieve this result there would be need for a number of stations in the vicinity of the Kamchatka area and a number in the Tashkent area. It might be possible, of course, to reduce somewhat the number actually in the Soviet Union by arranging stations in Hokkaido, Pakistan, and Afghanistan. If the stations on Soviet territory were sited in locations free from local disturbances and could be monitored periodically by competent United States or international observers who took in portable seismometers and placed them on the pedestals it would be very helpful in reducing the problem of identification.

You have referred to the discussion of the "black box" proposal at the Tenth Pugwash Conference in London in September of this year/3/ as a United Kingdom proposal to which the United States has agreed. I do not believe that this was the situation. This proposal was reported to me as a Soviet proposal which was discussed with some United States scientists. Of the United States scientists who signed the statement none represented the United States Government or had discussed the matter with responsible officials. All were speaking as individuals and none were seismologists. Their agreement does not signify anything other than that this was an area which justified further study. The United States Government has given it that study and the results have been the conclusions which I have indicated above.

Notwithstanding these problems, I am encouraged by your letter. I do not believe that any of the problems which I have raised are insoluble but they ought to be solved. I wonder how you think we might best proceed with these discussions which may require some technical development. It occurs to me that you might wish to have your representative meet with Mr. William C. Foster, the Director of our Arms Control and Disarmament Agency, at a mutually convenient place, such as New York or Geneva. I will be glad to have your suggestions. After talks have been held we will then be in a position to evaluate where we stand and continue our work together for an effective agreement ending all nuclear tests./4/

/1/Source: Department of State, Presidential Correspondence: Lot 66 D 204. No classification marking. Other copies are ibid.: Lot 77 D 163, and in the Kennedy Library, National Security Files, Countries Series, USSR, Khrushchev Correspondence. Also printed in *Documents on Disarmament, 1962, vol. II, pp. 1277-1279*, and in *American Foreign Policy: Current Documents, 1962*, pp. 1310-1212.
/2/Document 85.
/3/See footnote 3, Document 56.
/4/Printed from an unsigned copy.

"We are sorry that the essence of the question on which you informed me is still armament . . . ."

88. Message From Chairman Khrushchev to President Kennedy

Moscow, December 29, 1962./1/

DEAR MR. PRESIDENT, I am grateful to you for your wish to clarify the considerations by which, as you tell us, the U.S. Government was guided in taking the decision regarding making Polaris missiles available for the disposal of Britain./2/ You note that the Polaris missiles will be given to small British submarine forces which will be assigned to NATO and that these missiles are not expected to be operational before 1969-70.

I took notice of your words that the President's chief concern in making the decision on availability for transfer of the Polaris missiles was to prevent or at least delay the development of national nuclear capabilities and that you seek to gain time for further efforts in the field of disarmament. I would like to regard what you said with understanding. But in your turn, please regard with understanding those thoughts which cannot but come to our mind in connection with the step which you are taking.

If one is to appraise this step objectively, i.e. not only from the point of view of its effect on the relations between the U.S. and Britain, between the U.S. and its other allies in NATO, not only from the point of view of what type of destructive weapons is more suitable or costs less for them to manufacture, then the conclusion can be only one—this still is a matter of expansion of armaments of states. Yes, the agreement regarding the Polaris missiles reached on the Bahamas is one more effort in the implementation of the plans for nuclear armament, armament that is, while the peoples are awaiting from statesmen and governments efforts in a completely different direction—to scrap the war machine of states, to destroy all means of annihilation of people.

We are sorry that the essence of the question on which you informed me is still armament. Measures on which you inform us lead not to creating conditions facilitating general and complete disarmament, not to clearing road to agreement but to further intensification of arms race. This can only grieve all those people who see in general and complete disarmament a really reliable guarantee of peace.

In the messages which we exchanged the two of us expressed more than once our desire to seek mutually acceptable solutions to the questions of disarmament. Unfortunately, however, in those U.N. committees and subcommittees where negotiations on disarmament are conducted, in particular, in the 18 Nation Committee in Geneva they do not yet go beyond declarations of readiness for disarmament.

I do not think that in this message I should touch more in detail on the negotiations on disarmament. I touched on this topic because I cannot but express my concern that every meeting of statesmen of the Western powers regardless of the level of these meetings is devoted first of all to working out new armament programs.

I was informed that you consider interesting the proposal concerning nuclear test ban which was contained in my recent message to you. This makes me hopeful.

I send you, your wife and your entire family good wishes and New Year's greetings from myself and my family./3/

/1/Source: Department of State, Presidential Correspondence: Lot 77 D 163. No classification marking. The Russian-language text is ibid. Another copy is in the Kennedy Library, National Security Files, Countries Series, USSR, Khrushchev Correspondence.
/2/See Document 86.
/3/Printed from an unsigned copy.

> *"Now the peoples of the world
> expect from us energetic efforts
> aimed at the solution of urgent
> problems fraught with the rise
> of new crises . . ."*

89. Message From Chairmen Khrushchev and Brezhnev to President Kennedy

Moscow, December 30, 1962./1/

DEAR MR. PRESIDENT: On the eve of the new year we extend to the American people and also to you and your family New Year's congratulations and very best wishes from the Soviet people and from us personally. The year of 1962 now passing into history witnessed events, the fatal development of which it was possible to avert thanks to the fact that the (two) sides showed a sensible approach and reached a compromise. Now the peoples of the whole world expect from us energetic efforts aimed at the solution of urgent problems fraught with the threat of the rise of new crises in order to assure reliable conditions for peaceful life and constructive labor on the earth. There is no doubt that the people of the United States are no less interested in this than are the Soviet people. May the new year be a year of a turn for the better in relations between our countries, a year of joint efforts for a decisive improvement of the international situation in the interest of all humanity.

⸙ N. Khrushchev

L. Brezhnev/2/

/1/Source: Department of State, Presidential Correspondence: Lot 66 D 204. No classification marking. A note on the
source text indicates it is an unofficial translation by Henry
and Ramsey of SOV. Another copy is in the Kennedy
Library, National Security Files, Countries Series, USSR,
Khrushchev Correspondence.
/2/Printed from a copy that bears these typed signatures.

". . . no opportunity will be missed to promote world peace . . ."

90. Telegram From the Department of State to the Embassy in the Soviet Union

Washington, December 30, 1962, 10:46 p.m./1/

1367. Please deliver following message from President:

"Dear Chairman Khrushchev and Chairman Brezhnev:

On behalf of the American people and myself I extend best wishes for the New Year to the Soviet people and to you and your families.

The American people look forward to the coming year with the deepest desire that the cause of peace be advanced. For our part, I assure you that no opportunity will be missed to promote world peace and understanding among all peoples.

John F. Kennedy"

Rusk

/1/Source: Department of State, Presidential Correspondence: Lot 66 D 204. Unclassified; Priority. Drafted by Henry
and Ramsey. Another copy of this message is in the
Kennedy Library, National Security Files, Countries Series,
USSR, Khrushchev Correspondence.

*". . . the USA has by no means
removed all of its military personnel
from Laos, but (merely) dressed
some of them in civilian clothes and
left them in the country."*

91. Oral Statement by Chairman Khrushchev to President Kennedy

Moscow, January 4, 1963./1/

Upon his return from the USA, A.I. Mikoyan told me that during your talk with him you took up, among other problems, the question of Laos.

We reached an agreement with you in Vienna that Laos would be neutral and independent. The subsequent exchange of views on the Laos question, which took place unofficially between us after Vienna, in my opinion, also was held in a spirit of necessary mutual understanding and contributed to the success of the Geneva conference on Laos.

What was accomplished as a result of the

activity of this international conference is highly important. The Geneva agreements on Laos not only reestablished peace in that country and created the bases for its development along the path of neutrality and independence but also showed that, when the countries concerned desire settlement, all kinds of international problems can be resolved, especially if the USSR and the USA join forces in the interest of clearing up centers of tension. It is now important that the agreements on Laos be fully implemented.

As a result of the protracted civil war, the Laos of today has inherited a series of internal problems which must be settled between the three political forces of the nation. We proceeded, and are proceeding, from the premise that these internal problems must be resolved by the Laotians themselves, without any interference from outside. However, it must be recognized that the difficulties in resolving certain Laotian internal problems complicate considerably the full implementation of the Geneva agreements on Laos.

It is true that some success has now been achieved in settling the internal problems in Laos. Specifically, the recent agreement reached by the three factions in Laos on the subject of the unification of their armed forces and police is an indubitable step forward. However, such progress has not been noted in all the problems that require solution. The main obstacle on this path is still the unsurmounted distrust among the factions in Laos, which arose during the period of hostilities in that country. During the period of

the armed struggle such a large amount of suspicion and mutual distrust accumulated that to
remove it will require time and appropriate
efforts and not only on the part of the Laotians.

You implied that the Democratic People's
Republic of Viet-Nam had not withdrawn all its
troops from Laos. But the Government of the
Democratic People's Republic of Viet-Nam
informed us that all the Vietnamese personnel
had been completely withdrawn from Laos and
that there are no Vietnamese troops there now. In
this connection, I should like also to call your
attention to the joint Laos-Viet-Nam communique,
issued after the stay in Hanoi of the Laos
Government delegation, headed by General
Nosavan. In this communique it was stated that,
in accordance with the Geneva agreement, the
Government of the Democratic People's Republic
of Viet-Nam had withdrawn from Laos all of its
military personnel which was sent there at the
request of the government of Prince Souvanna
Phouma. The Laos Government delegation
declared its satisfaction with the policy of the
Government of the Democratic People's Republic
of Viet-Nam, as outlined above, and expressed its
trust in it.

At the same time, our friends say that up to
now the USA has by no means removed all of its
military personnel from Laos, but [merely]/2/
dressed some of its military personnel in civilian
clothes and left them in that country. They also
point out that in the territory of Laos there are
still some adherents of Chiang Kai-shek. They
report that American aircraft after the conclu-

sion of Geneva agreements still continue to fly without the permission of the Laos Government over the territory of Laos and drop guerilla groups and arms.

The absence of a settlement of a series of internal problems and the distrust still prevailing engender undesirable incidents such as, for example, the loss of an American airplane in the Plaine des Jarres. Certainly, that was a sad incident, it cost men's lives, it brought sorrow to their families. It demonstrates once more the necessity of creating in Laos a situation in which such incidents could not take place.

I think that a great deal in this connection depends on all the countries party to the Geneva agreements on Laos, including the USA, contributing to their implementation by observing their conditions exactly and thus making it possible for the Laotians to resolve their internal problems.

In so far as the Soviet Union is concerned, I must tell you that our Government is doing everything possible to ensure the implementation of the Geneva agreements. In conversations with Souvanna Phouma, with Prince Souvanavong and, quite recently, with General Nosavan, all of whom at various times came to the Soviet Union, we tried to emphasize the necessity of their getting along with each other and of finding a common language. We insistently recommended to them that they faithfully carry out the Geneva agreements, that they quickly resolve their internal political problems on the basis of the political program of the coalition government, which pro-

gram they themselves approved, that they not
permit violation of the peace in Laos, and that
they show the necessary restraint.

In view of the urgent need of Laos to rebuild
its economy which was wrecked by the war, the
Soviet Government complied with the request of
the coalition Government of Laos and decided to
grant it certain economic assistance in accordance with the principles of the Geneva agreements. You undoubtedly are aware that we trans-
ferred to the coalition Government of Laos our
planes which carried freight from the Democratic
People's Republic of Viet-Nam to Laos.

I think that you will agree that the strengthening of peace in Laos is indissolubly bound up
with the situation in the neighboring countries.
But I want to tell you frankly that the policy the
USA is now following in South Viet-Nam in no way
promotes the normalization of the situation in
Laos. I have in mind the presence and extensive
use of American troops in South Viet-Nam. The
tension on the Cambodian borders should also be
given consideration.

Guided by our desire to improve the situation
in Southeast Asia, we, for example, supported the
proposal of Prince Norodom Sihanouk to convene
an international conference for the purpose of
concluding an agreement that would guarantee
the independence, neutrality, and territorial
integrity of Cambodia. I have learned that this
proposal of Prince Sihanouk has not yet met with
the support of the USA.

These are the considerations that I wanted to
express in connection with what A.I. Mikoyan

said to you about Laos. Our earnest desire is that Laos be a peaceful, neutral, and independent nation and that the Geneva agreements on Laos be observed, which we consider would constitute great progress toward maintaining peace in Southeast Asia and a good example of how, if all interested nations strive to reach the same goal, that of peace, they can always find a common language and come to an agreement.

/1/Source: Department of State, Presidential Correspondence: Lot 77 D 163. No classification marking. The source text is a Department of State translation. The Russian-language text is ibid. Another copy of this message is in the Kennedy Library, National Security Files, Countries Series, USSR, Khrushchev Correspondence.
/2/Brackets in the source text.

". . . the Soviet Union is prepared to seek a mutually acceptable solution also in the question of location of automatic seismic stations."

92. Letter From Chairman Khrushchev to President Kennedy

Moscow, January 7, 1963./1/

DEAR MR. PRESIDENT, I received your reply to my message of December 19, 1962./2/ I am satisfied that you have appraised correctly the Soviet Government's proposals set forth in that message as directed to securing in the very near future a ban on all tests of nuclear weapons.

We understand your answer as meaning that you do not object that national means of detection together with automatic seismic stations should be the basis for control over an agreement banning underground nuclear tests. We note your agreement that installation of automatic seismic stations will prove useful from the point of view of increasing the effectiveness of control over cessation of underground nuclear explosions. During the Geneva talks it was justly observed, also by your representatives, that installation of such seismic stations would serve as good means of verifying the correctness of functioning of national seismic stations. It is precisely by these considerations that the Soviet Government was guided in proposing that the idea of installing automatic seismic stations put forward at the Pugwash meeting of scientists be utilized.

In my message of December 19, 1962, I indicated those three areas where in the opinion of our scientists automatic seismic stations should be set up on the territory of the Soviet Union. Those areas were selected after a thorough study with comprehensive consideration being given to geological and seismic conditions in those places.

In the areas of Kokchetav and Bodaibo automatic seismic stations would be located, according to our suggestion, at the exposures of crystalline rocks while in the Yakutsk area—in the zone of eternal congelation [permafrost]. As is known on crystalline rocks and on grounds frozen deep down always only minor seismic hindrances are noticed which facilitate reliable detection of underground nuclear explosions. In combination with seismic stations abroad, on territories adjacent to the seismic zones in the Soviet Union automatic stations located in the above mentioned points will be adequate means capable of removing possible doubts of the other side with regard to the correctness of functioning of the national seismic station network.

You did not make any comments on the location of an automatic seismic station for the Altai zone in the region of the city of Bodaibo, and thus we could consider this question as agreed upon.

However, you have doubts as to the location of automatic seismic stations for the other seismic zones in the Soviet Union—Far Eastern and Central Asian ones. As far as those zones are concerned, in your opinion, it would be expedient to place such stations in the Kamchatka area and in the area of Tashkent. In the opinion of Soviet scientists placing automatic seismic stations in the areas of Tashkent and Kamchatka would be a worse variant as compared to the one that we propose because in those areas functioning of automatic stations will be seriously handicapped by seismic hindrances. But if you believe it more expedient to relocate those stations we will not object to that. In my message to you I have already pointed out that the Soviet Union is prepared to seek a mutually acceptable solution also in the question of location of automatic seismic stations. We would agree to relocate the automatic seismic station for Central Asian zone of the USSR to the Tashkent area placing it near the city of Samarkand and for the Far Eastern zone— to place the automatic station at Seimchan which is part of the Kamchatka seismic area.

Location of an automatic seismic station on the Kamchatka peninsula itself seems, in the opinion of Soviet scientists, clearly unacceptable in view of strong hindrances caused by the proximity of the ocean and strong volcanic activity in the peninsula itself which will inevitably hamper normal functioning of a station. It appears to us that thus we could consider as agreed upon also the question of the location of automatic seismic stations for the Central Asian and Far Eastern zones of the USSR.

The Soviet Government having consulted its specialists came to the conclusion that it is quite enough to install three automatic seismic stations on the territory of the Soviet Union. The more so that in your message, Mr. President, a possibility is envisaged of setting up automatic seismic stations on territories adjacent to the seismic zones in the Soviet Union—on the Hokkaido, in Pakistan and Afghanistan, naturally with the consent of respective governments.

The Soviet Government has named definite areas for the location of automatic seismic stations on the territory of the USSR. Moreover, Mr. President, taking into account your wishes we agree to relocate two stations to new places. We are entitled to expect therefore that your side also will name definite areas where such stations should be set up on the territory of the U.S. and that in reaching an agreement on the sites where stations are to be placed the American side will take into account our wishes.

Mr. President, we are convinced that all conditions exist now for reaching an agreement also on the question of inspection. It is known that all the recent time we heard not once from the Western side—agree in principle to inspection and then the road to agreement will open. We believed and we continue to believe now that, in general, inspection is not necessary and if we give our consent to an annual quota of 2-3 inspections this is done solely for the purpose of removing the remaining differences for the sake of reaching agreement.

As you see we have made a serious step in your direction. The quota of inspections on the territory of each of the nuclear powers that we propose is sufficient. Indeed, in the negotiations your representatives themselves recognized that there is no need to verify all or a greater part of a significant suspicious phenomena to restrain the states from attempts to violate the treaty. And they gave figures of annual inspections practically equaling the quota proposed by us. Naturally it is most reasonable to carry out inspection in seismic areas where the biggest number of unidentified seismic phenomena may occur. However if you consider it necessary we have no objection to inspection being carried out also in non-seismic areas provided such inspections are conducted within the annual quota indicated by us.

I noticed that in your reply you agree with the necessity of taking reasonable measures of precaution which would exclude a possibility of using inspection trips and visits to automatic seismic stations for the purpose of obtaining intelligence data. Of course, in carrying out on-site inspection there can be circumstances when in the area designated for inspection there will be some object of defense importance. Naturally, in such a case it will be necessary to take appropriate measures which would exclude a possibility to cause damage to the interests of security of the state on the territory of which inspection is carried out. In this respect I fully agree with the considerations expressed in your message.

Mr. President, in your message you suggest that our representatives meet in New York or in Geneva for a brief preliminary consideration of some of the problems you touched upon. We have no objections to such meeting of our representatives. The Soviet Government for that purpose appointed N.T. Fedorenko, USSR Permanent Representative to the U.N., and S.K. Tsarapkin, USSR Representative to the 18-Nation Disarmament Committee, who could meet with your representative Mr. William C. Foster in New York on January 7-10. We proceed here from the assumption that meetings of our representatives should lead already in the very near future to agreement on questions still unsettled so that upon the reopening of the 18-Nation [Disarmament] Committee Session our representatives could inform it that the road to the conclusion of agreement banning all nuclear weapons tests is open.

Sincerely,

N. Khrushchev/3/

/1/Source: Department of State, Presidential Correspondence: Lot 66 D 204. No classification marking. The Russian-
language text is ibid.: Lot 77 D 163. Other copies are ibid.,
and in the Kennedy Library, National Security Files,
Countries Series, USSR, Khrushchev Correspondence. Also
printed in *Documents on Disarmament, 1963*, pp. 1-4, and
American Foreign Policy: Current Documents, 1963, pp.
940-942.
/2/See Documents 87 and 85.
/3/Printed from a copy that bears this typed signature.

". . . one cannot fail to note that the continuing armed attacks on the Cuban coast could not have taken place, and this is clear to everyone, unless they had been encouraged in the USA."

93. Message From the Soviet Ministry of Foreign Affairs to the Soviet Ambassador to the United States (Dobrynin)

Moscow, April 1 1963./1/

You should meet with R. Kennedy and, referring to your last conversations with him on
[date left blank],/2/ give voice to the following
considerations:

"First. In past conversations we have spoken
in a fairly detailed manner about the situation
around Cuba. As we understand from statements
coming from Washington, President Kennedy is
convinced that implementation of the agreement
reached during resolution of the Caribbean crisis

is the course to be followed. We accord statements such as this an appropriate degree of respect, especially when they express the opinion of the President. For my part, I can confirm that N.S. Khrushchev is also convinced that this course is correct.

It would of course be good if we could bring our discussions on the Cuban question to an end by means of an exchange of mutual assurances. But it seems that the time for that has not yet arrived—neither of us can say that everything here has turned out well. I would like to add, so to speak in hot pursuit of this theme, a few words about recent incidents along the Cuban coast—attacks on Cuban ports by armed vessels of emigrant Cuban riff-raff and gunfire from these vessels aimed at the Soviet merchant ships L'gov and Baku.

The Soviet Government has already expressed in diplomatic notes its views on these piratic attacks. It is nevertheless appropriate to dwell on this question in our present discussion, for, as we both know, contacts through confidential channels played a significant role in the resolution of certain aspects of the Caribbean crisis.

First of all, one cannot fail to note that the continuing armed attacks on the Cuban coast could not have taken place, and this is clear to everyone, unless they had been encouraged in the USA.

It is true that it can be said that the Government of the United States does not approve of such actions and that they take place almost without its knowledge. I thus expect that you will now refer to statements by the Department of State in this regard. We are of course already aware of them. But what is the primary idea behind these statements? Apparently that the USA is against 'brief attacks on Cuba' because they are said to be 'ineffective.' Those who have read these documents could interpret them to mean that if the attacks on Cuba were more solidly prepared and more 'effective,' that would not be at all bad.

We also cannot fail to point out that all statements and explanations made by representatives of the Government of the United States after the attacks on our ships and on the Cuban ports contain efforts to deny U.S. responsibility for these criminal attacks.

Allow me to say to you, however, that the U.S. cannot evade this responsibility. The whole world knows that the bases of the Cuban emigrant counter-revolutionaries are in Florida and Puerto Rico, and that, as before, the Central Intelligence Agency provides sustenance and all their needs to these renegades. The political ground for these bandit-like strikes is prepared by calls similar to those that rang out, in particular, during a parade by traitors to the Cuban people last December in Miami. The attacks on the Soviet vessels L'gov and Baku have revealed, more than anything else in the recent past, the grave danger these policies pose for world peace.

As one who is embroiled on a daily basis with the political life of the American capital, I cannot overlook an obvious fact. When the State Department issued its statement on March

19,/3/ the leaders of the Cuban counter-revolutionaries held a press conference, here in Washington, in which they boasted about having carried out armed raids on the Cuban coast and their objective as having been the killing of Soviet military personnel. As far as we are aware, you, as Attorney General, have responsibility for the investigation of the circumstances surrounding this matter. It is to be hoped that as a result those guilty will receive due punishment in order to discourage others who might plot new and dangerous adventures.

It is perhaps not superfluous to remind you that even during the most difficult moments of the crisis around Cuba there were no shots fired on Soviet vessels, for everyone understood well where that could take the world. One should think that that understanding is not lost on today as well.

Of course, the Soviet Government and N. S. Khrushchev personally have taken note of the joint statement by the

Departments of State and Justice on March 30 concerning several measures in regard to Cuban emigrants./4/ If these measures are in fact aimed at putting an end to the bandit-like provocations of these dangerous adventurists, then that will deserve a positive evaluation. The future will show if that is the case and if these measures are those that should be carried out to prevent new tensions in the Caribbean.

In our previous discussions you touched on several aspects of the Cuban question which you said complicated the President's situation in light of the approaching election campaign. You know that we take into account, to the degree we can, the President's situation, and in a number of instances we have accommodated his wishes. The Soviet Government not only faithfully and strictly is carrying out the agreement on the Caribbean crisis, but has undertaken steps which go even further than required by the responsibilities it has assumed. You yourself noted that the Government of the U.S. understands that the Soviet Government is acting in a spirit of good will in matters which have been agreed with the U.S. or about which the U.S. has been informed.

But it is necessary to emphasize that pressure and threats are not appropriate means with which to achieve any result; they produce only a counterreaction. Take only the following question: we are removing our military personnel from Cuba, in considerable numbers, but we are doing that not because the U.S. is exerting pressure on us but rather because we consider for our troops to remain in Cuba would not be to put them to effective use. We have removed several times more people than the figures bandied about in the U.S. press. We have not given you a specific number, for if we had done so, you would have immediately presented that as our giving you an accounting. You would have blared out through all channels that you had forced us to do so. We respond adversely to such methods, which you have tried to use in similar circumstances. We reject them.

To be frank, as we are as a matter of principle in these confidential contacts, it seems some-

what one-sided when the problems and difficulties the President encounters in carrying out his
policy toward Cuba are blamed on the Soviet
Union or on the Republic of Cuba. But in fact the
roots of these problems, as we have repeatedly
emphasized, lie elsewhere—in a policy which
announces that its objective is to remove, by any
means necessary, overt or covert, the new social
structure which has established itself in Cuba,
although the right to establish order in one's own
home belongs only to the people of that nation
and to no one else.

On the one hand, we hear assurances that the
President of the U.S. intends to uphold the agreement reached during resolution of the crisis in the
Caribbean, and that despite pressures on him to
do so he will not allow himself to be pushed onto
the dangerous road of possible military confrontation with the Soviet Union. On the other, in
addition to the continuing attacks on the Cuban
coast I already mentioned, measures are being
taken to suffocate the economy of Cuba, break off
its commercial trade, and erect some sort of police
line around Cuba that would fence Cuba off from
the other countries of the western hemisphere.

I will try to explain our understanding of why
the President is experiencing the difficulties you
mentioned by use of the following example. When
we shot down the U-2 piloted by the airman
Powers, then-President Eisenhower experienced
substantial difficulties both domestically and in
the international arena. And what was the primary cause of Eisenhower's 'difficulties'? If he
had not dispatched American aircraft on spy

flights over the territory of a sovereign nation—
in this instance the Soviet Union—he would have
been spared the 'difficulties' of that time.

If I speak now of these quite sensitive issues,
I do so only because you yourself introduced
them. Of course, I will not debate with you, by
dint of your position the top lawyer in the U.S.,
matters of flexibility or precision in statements
of this nature. What I wish to do is to emphasize
a fairly simple idea, that the truest path to ensuring that no 'complications' arise in connection
with Cuba is strict and conscientious implementation of the United Nations Charter; that is, carrying out a policy of non-interference in the
affairs of other states and respect for their sovereignty and independence.

It is indeed in strict implementation by our
Governments of the Charter of the U.N. as well as
of the additional obligations we assumed during
resolution of the crisis in the Caribbean that lies
a good opportunity, in our view, to create conditions, day by day and step by step, for a strengthening of trust and mutual understanding between
the Soviet Government and the Government of
the U.S., and personally between N.S. Khrushchev
and President J. Kennedy, the necessity of which
you, as a person close to the President, have
often discussed in our meetings.

Second. In our previous discussions we did not
avoid, as you will remember, the issue of a ban on
nuclear weapon tests. This problem, it is true,
occupies the minds not only of government officials but also that of the common man; for even
if the latter is far from the making of policy, he

is nevertheless concerned about the air he breathes and that his children and grandchildren will have to breathe.

Your comments that the President sincerely wants an agreement banning nuclear tests, and that he has children whom he loves, were transmitted, as you asked, to N.S. Khrushchev. I can say in reply that N.S. Khrushchev fully understands motives of a purely personal nature, which, naturally, should strengthen the resolve of every government official to do everything possible to end test explosions of atom and hydrogen bombs. As you of course know, N.S. Khrushchev has children, grandchildren, and even great-grandchildren, and personal motives are no less close to his heart.

You have said that President Kennedy considers, in principle, that a treaty banning nuclear tests is a very important step toward normalization of the international situation and bettering relations between the Soviet Union and the U.S. You know that the Soviet Government and personally N.S. Khrushchev share this view. It followed from what you have said that the President is ready to use all his authority in the country to achieve ratification of such a treaty, and that it would be more convenient for the President were the treaty considered by the present session of Congress. Such an effort would of course meet a most positive response from us. We in fact propose such an approach, which would make it possible to bring negotiations on a cessation of nuclear tests to a rapid conclusion.

You must understand us and our position. We

understand your position well. N.S. Khrushchev asked me to tell you that. Throughout the world, many people, and especially those who are professionally involved in nuclear weapons and their testing, know that national means are adequate to confirm that any nuclear explosion has taken place. And that has been proven in practice; whenever explosions have taken place in the Soviet Union you registered that fact and immediately made it public. We ascertain when you or other countries carry out explosions. One therefore asks, why is it not possible to come to an agreement banning all nuclear tests and to sign a corresponding treaty?

You explain this as caused by the internal conditions and specific problems existing in your country. We increasingly have to listen to you say that a treaty banning nuclear tests is facing an almost impassable barrier in the U.S. Senate if we do not make further concessions to the United States. You essentially put the problem that way in your statements. But is it not too much to expect from the Soviet Union that it agree to adjust its positions in the nuclear test ban negotiations in April to suit the bad mood of a Senator from Connecticut and in May that of a Senator from Arizona? We have in that way already conceded a great deal to the U.S. on verification of a test ban, taking into account the President's comments that were passed to us confidentially. But you must understand that in international negotiations it is states that participate, not individuals whose views for some reason may differ from the point of view of the participating governments. If governments are not able to raise themselves above narrow group interests expressed by unreasonable politicians within their own country, then they have totally deprived themselves of any chance of concluding international agreements, the usefulness of which they seem to recognize.

An analysis of the specific problems you mention shows that they are nothing more than two parties competing for the White House who are arguing whether to poison the air by nuclear explosions or not to poison it. And you want us to help one of the contesting sides, and to do so by making concessions. But why should we reward you for signing a test ban which, it would seem, should be in the interests of both sides equally, by allowing you, at the expense of Soviet interests, to engage in espionage on Soviet territory?

How are we to understand this, Mr. Kennedy? What kind of partnership is that? You want us to help you in this matter. Well, what if we do not do so, what harm will come to the Soviet Union if we reach no agreement? No more than to the U.S. If we conceded this to you we would in reality gain nothing, only lose. You would gain that which we lost, in addition to the opportunity to carry out espionage on the territory of the USSR, and plus the moral satisfaction of knowing that you pressured us from a position of strength and forced us to make further concessions.

Understand us, we cannot do that. We have already agreed to a minimum, and that in fact is not a minimum but rather a substantial maximum—2-3 inspections. And that, of course, we could not agree to interpret in such a manner that under the guise of these 2-3 inspections intelligence information-gathering could be carried out all over the territory of the Soviet Union, above ground and underground, in and on water, and by aerial observation to boot. These activities are not at all made necessary by the requirements for inspections. No, these demands are dictated by completely different intentions—the same ones that governed President Kennedy's predecessor, Eisenhower, when he demanded the right to flights around the borders of the Soviet Union and to send U-2 spy planes into our air space.

What kind of policy is that? The Soviet Union, after all, is no weaker than you, and U.S. Government officials have more than once in their statements recognized that we are equally powerful. But if you consider the Soviet Union an equal, then why carry out such a policy, why make such demands on us? Such demands can only be made by the strong from the weak, based not on right, but on force.

And the time has also passed when colonial powers could, using force, seize colonies. The colonial powers are still more powerful than the countries over whom they once held sway, but, as a result of changing conditions in the world—and they themselves would have to admit this—they have had to leave them while in one piece, because if they had not they would have left them not in the best of health.

Examples of this were demonstrated in Vietnam, and in Algeria. Now the struggle is being joined in other countries, particularly in the Indonesian region. One can point out many such examples which have shown that the departure of the colonial powers was not voluntary, but rather was made to avoid a kick in a certain area.

And you wish to talk to us in this manner and pressure us to make concessions that do not correspond to the balance of forces between us, to the present times nor to the position we occupy in the world. How is it possible to expect that we would agree to your demands? We cannot agree to them.

You said that your brother does not want to go down in history as a second Wilson if the Senate does not ratify a treaty banning nuclear tests, basing its action on the number of inspections the Soviet Union has offered. Neither do we wish for J. Kennedy to become a second Wilson, and we are exercising maximum good will in the matter of a test ban. We sincerely wish that your brother enter history as the President of the United States of America who was able to place above all else the need for statesmanlike wisdom, and as the government official who, together with N.S. Khrushchev, wrote his name in the great book of peace.

If the President in fact wants to do something useful and establish a claim for his presidency to be noted by history, he will have to work against aggressive circles within the country, against all who urge irrational and aggressive policies. We are convinced that all people of sound mind in America want to live, to raise their children, and want good for themselves and their children, just as you contend do you and the President. Why then do you think that the American people will not support such healthy undertakings against that Rockefeller? The people can only gain from this, for that bunch of shameless people, or as you call them, crazies, is a small group, and in their overwhelming majority Americans are a healthy people that want to live, and can live for their children in the world together with other peoples. Why does the President not want to take advantage of this opportunity?

You in fact are moving the opposite way, trying to get from us even more significant concessions. You want us with our own concessions to satisfy Rockefeller and the other crazies who carry out a frantic and aggressive propaganda campaign against the Soviet Union. Understand us, we cannot do that, and N.S. Khrushchev asks that you pass that message to the President.

Can you, are you ready to move on a sound, equitable basis toward conclusion of a treaty, taking into account the concessions we have already made, though they were not required and had as their sole objective making it easier for the President to move the treaty through Congress? That was a sacrifice by our side, and we cannot, I repeat, do more.

The test ban treaty may or may not be signed. Whether or not really is of no significance to limitation of the arms race, for enough test explosions have already been carried out to perfect nuclear weapons. And as far as the future is concerned, new tests will add nothing, or almost nothing. But you should be clear on what will happen if there is no test ban agreement. You are now carrying out nuclear weapons tests at your test ranges in Nevada even after we have finished our series of nuclear explosions. And now the roar of a nuclear explosion has been heard in the Sahara. It is true, as they say, that in recent times dissimilarities in the architectural styles of the Elysee Palace and the White House have become more noticeable, but fact remains fact; France is your ally, and she is exploding her own nuclear devices. So, if there is no agreement and NATO countries continue testing, and if under these circumstances our scientists and military find it necessary to put the question of carrying out new tests in the Soviet Union before the Soviet Government, they of course will have to be allowed to do so.

. It is clear that any new nuclear tests harm the people living on this earth. But what can we do? It is not our fault. Responsibility for that rests on your government. The fate of the agreement banning nuclear weapon tests rests today in the hands of the U.S. Government. What turn further negotiations now take depends on it, and on no one else: will they be swept away by a new wave of nuclear test explosions or crowned by the conclusion of a treaty the people have long waited for.

Third. I would like to touch on a question at this point that has already been the subject of a confidential exchange of opinion between N.S. Khrushchev and the President, and which in light of latest events is worthy of further attention. I refer to various plans for creating nuclear forces within the NATO framework which would include also states that at present do not have nuclear weapons.

We remember the explanations which were passed to us unofficially in the name of the President after his meeting in Nassau with Prime Minister Macmillan. The President assured us that his main concern in deciding the Polaris transfer was to prevent, or at least delay, the development of national nuclear forces. It was also emphasized that practical implementation of this plan lay far in the future, and that it was necessary to win time for further efforts in the disarmament area.

We immediately gave our views on the Nassau agreement. As you know, President Kennedy was informed that N.S. Khrushchev considered this agreement as yet another effort in the implementation of plans for nuclear weapons—weapons, mind you, when peoples expect from their governments and statesmen efforts in quite the opposite direction—to destroy national military machines and all means of killing people.

Events since Nassau have not only not lessened the accuracy of this evaluation but on the contrary have brought new confirmation of the danger these plans pose to peace. Whatever label is pasted on these planned nuclear forces of NATO—'multilateral' or 'multinational', or both at the same time—the fact of the matter does not change. Whether the USA wants that to be the case or not, that is the nature of any plans that allow the 'unconsecrated' to get their hands on nuclear weapons; their implementation prepares the ground for other NATO members, and especially West German revanchists, to break their way into the nuclear club. That is not only our opinion. Many people in other countries share that view. Even, apparently, some statesmen in NATO states themselves are not spared these concerns.

If only one country strays from the path along which the nuclear powers have traveled, and in one manner or another provides nuclear weapons to any one of its allies, then the nuclear arms race will embrace new countries and regions in a powerful surge, and it will be difficult to say where it will stop.

The West is now doing its calculations on how many additional fingers can be on nuclear weapon launch buttons, and at the same time is trying to prove that the risk of outbreak of a nuclear war will not increase. But arithmetic here can deceive. The danger of unleashing a thermonuclear war will steadily rise, and it will rise not just in proportion to the additional fingers on the launch triggers; it will be multiplied many times over by a thirst for revenge and perhaps by irresponsibility on the part of someone.

We would like to trust the statements of U.S. Government leaders that proliferation of nuclear weapons is not in U.S. interests. But they are difficult to reconcile with the fact that emissaries of the U.S. Government are now traveling from one NATO capital to another strongly promoting plans to create a NATO nuclear force.

You have said that the U.S. Government is fulfilling its promise to withdraw missiles from Turkey and Italy and that that would be completed during the first half of April. We of course greet liquidation of these bases. But put yourself in our place, and you will understand that from the standpoint of the security of the Soviet Union this is not liquidation of missile bases, but rather exchanging old weapons for more advanced. In place of having missiles aimed at us from land we will now have missiles of the latest model aimed at us from the seas that wash the shores of that land. That is how it will be if the Mediterranean, as is now being planned, is filled with nuclear submarines and surface vessels, armed with 'Polaris' missiles and cruising along the coasts of Italy and Turkey.

Fourth. N.S. Khrushchev asked that the President be informed that he is now becoming skeptical that any reasonable agreement can be reached with the United States. During resolution of the crisis in the Caribbean, N.S. Khrushchev in an exchange with President Kennedy, expressed the view—and the President shared his hope—that after the crisis was over efforts would be continued to resolve issues that are key to a liquidation of tension in the world and normalization of relations between our governments. But as soon as that crisis was over the President apparently forgot what he wanted, and now the United States, in the person of the President, is beginning, judging by all evidence, to test our resistance and to put pressure on us. We indignantly reject such policies. For this reason, we do not want to hear discussions about our having troops where it would be better if we did not have them, and we reject, with considerable displeasure, any claims of that sort. Our opportunities in the world should be equal to yours.

Why are your troops scattered throughout the world and you regard that as your right and obligation? Why do you consider that locating one country's military instructors in another country is a violation of international norms? On what right does that understanding turn? In any case not on the UN Charter, and not on international law.

If you want really good relations—and we want that very much—then let us proceed from the assumption, as N.S. Khrushchev told the President in Vienna, that our states are equally powerful and that we should have the same opportunities.

We long ago proposed and continue to propose that all troops be withdrawn from foreign territories to within their own borders. We propose that we conclude an agreement on that basis. We would greet such an agreement, and then we would have no troops or instructors beyond our own borders. Now, when we sell or transfer armaments, we also send troops to give instruction on how to handle these weapons. But we are ready to agree even not to do that if you take upon yourself a similar obligation.

In a word, do not try to pressure us or urge us to do anything that you yourselves do not do, because that insults us. We are very sensitive about such matters.

We have frequently heard judgments that we should not leave surface-to-air missiles in Cuba, for the Cubans may shoot down an American intelligence-gathering aircraft and then something untoward will happen. Tell the President that if that occurs, then the improbable will have occurred. You want us to understand your pressuring us to allow you to penetrate Cuban air space with your intelligence-gathering aircraft, but we react to this with indignation, for you are violating elementary norms of international relations and the UN Charter. You want us to recognize your right to violate that Charter and international norms, but we cannot do that. We can only confirm to you that we are carrying out the obligations and assurances we undertook before, and gave to, the Cuban Government that in the case of an attack on Cuba we would support her with the means at our disposal. It can be no other way. You yourselves are forcing us to make that statement, and we would rather not make it, because it will not make normalization of our relations easier. We would like to improve them, make them good. But that depends on you.

Do not try to force us to accept your policies, for that will produce a counterreaction—that is, you will receive the same in reply.

The most reasonable thing for the President to do—and N.S. Khrushchev would like the President to consider this if he really wants to benefit mankind—is to stop flights over Cuban territory before the Cubans shoot down an aircraft, for if they continue they will surely do so. If the President wants a crisis, and has in mind using the downing of an American intelligence aircraft as an excuse for an attack on Cuba, then that course of events is apparently unavoidable, for the present situation regarding the flights cannot continue.

N.S. Khrushchev does not believe it is in the interests of the United States to carry out a policy that may return us to a crisis we have already once survived. But if a new crisis is unleashed it may be impossible this time to reach the reasonable resolution that we found then, for the basis on which the agreement was reached last year has been shaken. All this has to be taken into account.

And we are not even addressing the question, a minor one for us from the material standpoint but one of great significance as a matter of principle in international relations, of pressure by the United States on its allies in regard to trade with the Soviet Union. Your representative in NATO insists that sale of steel pipe to the Soviet Union be halted. Is that important for the Soviet Union? Not at all. And what did you get for your efforts? Only West Germany obeyed you, and that only because you support their position in the German question, particularly in regard to West Berlin. But for that reason only. Not selling us pipe is not in their interest. It is no accident that even your own allies did not support you. You pressured them to ignore their own interests, knowing that it was advantageous for them to trade with us.

Even your allies do not understand your policies. Where is good will, where are good relations or any indication of a reasonable approach to righting relations between our states? We do not see them.

If you really want to improve relations, we are ready. Let us sign a treaty banning nuclear weapon tests on the basis of findings approved and confirmed by scientists free from outside pressure.

Let us at long last finally liquidate the remains of World War II, resolve the issue of a German peace treaty, and on that basis normalize the situation in West Berlin. We do not expect any acquisitions as a result, and no harm will come to you. The situation in West Berlin should be normalized by recognizing existing circumstances—and nothing more. We do not even demand withdrawal of foreign troops, but want only that their presence be on another basis, that the troops be of a different composition and that they be under the UN flag.

However, you do not want to do this, even though you lose nothing and we gain nothing. But if we could conclude such an agreement it would have a big payoff—the whole world would gain, and better conditions would be created for disarmament negotiations. After all, without resolution of the German question—you know this yourself, and I ask you to pass this to the President from N.S. Khrushchev—no reasonable resolution to the problem of disarmament will be found. As long as remnants of World War II are preserved that constantly remind us of their presence, we and you will have to pay for our military forces and increase our ability to destroy each other. How, under such circumstances, can we reach an agreement on disarmament? An agreement on disarmament must be based above all on trust.

And what kind of trust can there be when McNamara and Malinovsky take turns speaking, each time annihilating each other? Why do that? Malinovsky has no choice, because McNamara speaks, and not only McNamara. You have now alot of these orators, the so-called specialists in military affairs. We have to reply, but who stands to gain? The militarists and monopolists making millions on the production of armaments. Only they stand to gain.

But if you do not now understand that all of this must be brought to an end, well, then we will continue to live this way. Of course, no good agreement will be reached in such a situation. One side cannot produce that which depends on two.

In Vienna we were told that the President had just come into the White House. A year has passed, two—and now you say that the election campaign has begun. So, the first two years, the President was a newcomer in the White House, learning the ropes, and the next two years are devoted to preparation for new elections. So it turns out that in the first two years the President cannot decide key, vitally important questions and in the following two years he cannot decide them because he might otherwise, we are told, lose the election campaign.

This is a tragedy, but it is the essence of capitalism, of a classical capitalist contradiction. And it is America that appears to us as the glaring example, in our Marxist understanding of things. We do not force this understanding on you; we simply express it.

But we take into account the times in which we live, and understand what the situation now is. One will have to live in this manner until better times come, and we are certain that better times will come, and then we will have mutual understanding.

Fifth. In a recent conversation you touched on the possibility of a meeting between Chairman of the Council of Ministers of the USSR N.S. Khrushchev and President Kennedy. Our point of view regarding the significance of summit meetings is well known. The Soviet Government is a convinced advocate of those methods of carrying out foreign policy that promise the best results in resolving current problems. And reason demands that these problems, some of which you mentioned last time, be resolved at the negotiating table.

As before, we proceed from the assumption that such meetings can be useful if both sides are equally interested in a positive result. We do not believe that one can somehow separate the interest of the two sides in such a meeting, suggesting that, for example, the U.S. is less interested in it than the Soviet Union, or vice versa. And therefore it would seem inappropriate for either side to put forward any considerations which could be construed as preconditions for such a meeting. Interest in such a meeting can only be shared and inseparable, of course, if both sides actually strive to unite their forces in the interest of strengthening peace.

We for quite some time now have not given answers to questions which have remained open during the course of our discussions, and have ourselves not taken initiative in our confidential messages to the President, because American actions are already causing us to lose confidence in the usefulness of this channel. We wanted you to know that. If, nevertheless, we again decide to turn to this opportunity for confidential transmission of our ideas to the President, we will do so in the hope that it will result in better understanding by the President of the position of the Soviet Union and its leader, N.S. Khrushchev."

Decide for yourself, taking into account the actual situation in which your discussion with R. Kennedy is to take place, how best to carry out this conversation: whether to make the statement all at once or do it part by part. In either case you should leave a copy of the text with R. Kennedy.

Confirm delivery by telegram.

A.B./5/

/1/Source: Russian Ministry of Foreign Affairs, Department of History and Records. Secret. The Department of History and Records made the Russian text available to the Department of State in September 1995; the text was translated by Senior Foreign Service Officer Michael Joyce. There are no copies of the message in Department of State or White House Files. On April 3, 1963, Ambassador Dobrynin handed an English translation of this message to Robert Kennedy, who read it, returned it to Dobrynin, and summarized its contents and his reasons for returning it in an April 3 memorandum to President Kennedy (Document 94). Although the message was directed to Robert Kennedy, it was clearly intended that he pass it along to President Kennedy.
/2/Brackets in the source text.
/3/For text of this statement, see Department of State *Bulletin*, April 8, 1963, pp. 520-521.
/4/For text of the joint statement, see ibid., April 22, 1963, pp. 600-601.
/5/The initials on the source text appear to be "A.B.", but cannot be further identified.

"There could be no secret testing without the other country knowing about it. We knew everything the Soviet Union tested as they knew everytime we tested."

94. Memorandum From Attorney General Kennedy to President Kennedy

Washington, April 3, 1963./1/

Mr. Markov of the Russian Embassy/2/ called this morning and said that the Russian Ambassador wished to come by and see me. I arranged for him to come in at 3:30 p.m.

We exchanged some pleasantries. He told me that Norman Cousins had asked to see Khrushchev and he had arranged it./3/ What was Cousins' relationship to the President? Then, as is his custom, he handed me a so-called "talking paper."/4/ This document was particularly long—approximately 25 pages. It was ostensibly to me from the Ambassador but in fact it was from Khrushchev to the President.

The paper made five or six major points, among which were the following:

Mr. Khrushchev knew that President Kennedy has children and is concerned about the future. He, Mr. Khrushchev, has children, grandchildren and great-grandchildren. He is also concerned about the future. It should be clearly understood, however, that the Soviet Union will not go above their offer of two or three inspection sites. There was absolutely no need to go above that figure as our scientists had clearly demonstrated.

There could not be secret testing without the other country knowing about it. We knew everytime the Soviet Union tested as they knew everytime we tested.

As for obtaining the approval of the United States Senate for a treaty which contained provisions for only two or three sites, if President Kennedy wanted to put his prestige on the line and make the necessary effort, ratification could be obtained. Mr. Khrushchev was tired of hearing first about objections from the Senator from Connecticut and then objections from the Senator from Arizona.

The United States is run by capitalists who are interested only in war profits. They are the ones that were dictating policy. If President Kennedy was not as concerned about the Rockefellers and these capitalists then he would take this step for world peace.

Further, who did we think we were in the United States trying to dictate to the Soviet Union? All that was needed were two or three inspection sites and we were trying to obtain a greater number in order to commit espionage. In these efforts we were treating the Soviet Union as inferiors—as if we could dictate to them. The United States had better learn that the Soviet Union was as strong as the United States and did not enjoy being treated as a second class power. (Virtually, these same words were repeated later on in the letter. This was the thread or theme that ran through the whole document.)

Another point that was made was a sharp and bitter criticism about the raids that had taken place against Russian ships. These were piratical acts and the United States must take responsibility for them. It isn't possible to believe that if we really wanted to stop these raids that we could not do so. They were glad to hear of the steps that are being taken lately but in the last analysis the specific acts, namely, the arrests that we made would be the criteria by which they would judge our sincerity. The Soviet Union questions whether in fact we wish to end these attacks for our criticism of them has been not that they were wrong but that they were ineffective. The clear implication was that if the raids had been effective they would have had our approval.

Further, our efforts to isolate Cuba, to build a virtual wall around it, was a barbaric act. Our actions to stifle Cuba's commerce and to create economic difficulties and isolate her from her neighbors in Latin America were completely unwarranted. The support given to counter-revolutionaries and the statements to the barbaric mercenaries in Miami by the President were also bitterly criticized.

The document also stated that the President should understand the continued pressure on the Soviet Union for the withdrawal of troops from Cuba was not going to be effective. The Soviet Union does not respond to pressure. As a matter of fact, they had already withdrawn twice as many troops as the largest number that had appeared in the newspapers here in the United States. However, he said that he was going to refuse to give the actual number that had been withdrawn because then public statements would be issued that they had been withdrawn because of pressure by the United States and "trumpets would have been blown" by us.

This letter took note of the criticism of the fact that the Russian SAM sites remained within Cuba. The author of the letter wanted us to know that those ground-air missiles were going to stay in Cuba for the protection of Cuban people.

The overflights that were taking place were deeply resented by the Soviet Union and by Cuba. He then went on to say clearly and distinctly that these U-2 planes would be shot down and that this had better be clearly understood in the United States. The U-2 plane that Eisenhower sent over the Soviet Union was shot down and they had better understand the same thing would be done in those flights over Cuba.

The document then returned to the theme that we were treating the Soviet Union as inferiors; that this could not be continued; that the statements McNamara and Malinovski were making were not contributing to peaceful understanding; that Malinovski's statements were brought about by McNamara's warlike pronouncements. The United States was interested only in making profits from munitions, building up their efforts to dominate the world through counterrevolutionary activity. We were run by capitalists and we should understand that we could not push the Soviet Union around. He also expressed deep concern about the deployment of the Polaris submarines in the Mediterranean, replacing the

Jupiter missiles in Turkey and Italy.

At the end of the document it said that Mr. Khrushchev had felt in the past that this confidential exchange had been helpful but he said it had not been used lately because of the provocative statements that had been made by representatives of the United States Government which were offensive to the Soviet Union. However if President Kennedy wanted to reopen this area of contact he would be glad to accept it. He also said that as far as a meeting between Khrushchev and President Kennedy he thought that that might be helpful. This was, however, left in rather enigmatic terms.

After I read the document I returned it to Dobrynin. I pointed out to him that I had met with him frequently and that he had never talked like this before. He said that was correct. I asked what was the explanation for this document and he said that I should understand that it came from the Soviet Union. I said it demonstrated a complete lack of understanding of the United States and President Kennedy and that I thought it was so insulting and rude to the President and to the United States that I would neither accept it nor transmit its message. I said if they had a message of that kind to deliver it should be delivered formally through the State Department and not through me. I said that during our conversations in the past we attempted to work out matters on a mutually satisfactory basis. I said we might disagree but I never insulted or offended him or his country or Mr. Khrushchev. I said I felt that was the only basis for any kind of relationship. I said I thought this kind of document did not further that effort or our mutual interests and I repeated that if they intended to transmit that kind of message that it should be done through the State Department. He said he could understand my position. He was obviously embarrassed./5/

/1/Source: Department of State, Presidential Correspondence: Lot 77 D 163. Top Secret. The source text indicates that Rusk saw it. A copy was sent to McGeorge Bundy.
/2/Petr I. Markov, Attache, Soviet Embassy.
/3/Editor of the *Saturday Review* who met with Khrushchev on April 12 to discuss the nuclear test ban treaty.
/4/See Document 93.
/5/Llewellyn Thompson prepared an April 3 memorandum to Rusk, suggesting possible causes and motives for Khrushchev's message of April 3. (Department of State, Presidential Correspondence: Lot 77 D 163)

". . . the continued presence of Soviet forces in Cuba can never be regarded with equanimity by the people of this Hemisphere . . ."

95. Message From President Kennedy to Chairman Khrushchev

Washington, April 11, 1963./1/

DEAR MR. CHAIRMAN: It has been some time since I have written you directly, and I think it may be helpful to have some exchange of views in this private channel. As we have both earlier agreed, it is of great importance that we should try to understand each other clearly, so that we can avoid unnecessary dangers or obstacles to progress in the effort for peaceful agreements.

On the negotiations for a nuclear test ban, I fear that there may have been an honest misunderstanding between us. You and your representatives, on a number of occasions, have made clear your belief that on our side there had been some indication last year of a readiness to accept the number of inspections which you proposed in your message of December 19./2/ I know that the United States Government never adopted any such position, and I have the most direct assurances from all my senior representatives that no such American position was ever indicated by them. But I have respect for your representatives, too, and so believe that there was an honest misunderstanding on this point. I can assure you that we are not engaged in any effort to impose a one-sided or arbitrary view on this matter. We continue to believe that an agreement to end nuclear testing is deeply in the interest of our two countries. Prime Minister Macmillan and I hope to be able to make new suggestions to you on this matter very soon.

A closely connected question is the spread of nuclear weapons, and on this question the American position remains as it has been. We are strongly against the development of additional national nuclear capabilities, and the plans and proposals which we are considering for the future management of the nuclear forces of the

North Atlantic Treaty Organization are all based
upon this principle. I regret that the formal communication which Mr. Gromyko passed to
Ambassador Kohler a few days ago/3/ reaches
quite different conclusions as to the meaning of
these events. I shall not reply to that paper here,
but let me say clearly that you can rely upon our
continued and determined opposition to the
spread of national nuclear forces.

Neither the multinational nor the multilateral
forces we are considering will increase the dangers of diffusion. Both are intended to reduce
those dangers. The plan for a multinational
nuclear force implies no change in present
arrangements for the ultimate political control of
existing nuclear weapons systems, and it is a
fundamental principle in our support for a new
multilateral force that no such force could ever be
used without the consent of the United States.
The concept of this force is therefore exactly
opposite to that of independent national nuclear
forces, and the opposition to it in the West comes
precisely from those who would prefer the
expansion of independent nuclear forces.

Although together we found workable
arrangements for ending the very dangerous crisis which was created when strategic weapons
were introduced into Cuba last year, I am sure we
can agree that the situation in that island is not
yet satisfactory or reassuring to those who care
for the peace of the Caribbean. Although the
recent withdrawal of a number of your forces has
been an important contribution to the reduction
of tension, the continued presence of Soviet

forces in Cuba can never be regarded with equanimity by the people of this Hemisphere and therefore further withdrawals of such forces can only be helpful.

Meanwhile, we on our side have been endeavoring to reduce tension in this area in a number of ways. For example, the fundamental justification of our practice of peaceful observation of Cuba is precisely that it is necessary to prevent further increase in tension and a repetition of the dangers of last fall. Without such peaceful observation in 1962, this Hemisphere would have been confronted with intolerable danger, and the people of the Hemisphere could not now accept a situation in which they were without adequate information on the situation in Cuba. It is for this reason that this peaceful observation must continue, and that any interference with it from Cuba would necessarily evoke whatever response was necessary to retain it.

We are also aware of the tensions unduly created by recent private attacks on your ships in Caribbean waters; and we are taking action to halt those attacks which are in violation of our laws, and obtaining the support of the British Government in preventing the use of their Caribbean islands for this purpose. The efforts of this Government to reduce tensions have, as you know, aroused much criticism from certain quarters in this country. But neither such criticism nor the opposition of any sector of our society will be allowed to determine the policies of this Government. In particular, I have neither the intention nor the desire to invade Cuba; I consid-

er that it is for the Cuban people themselves to
decide their destiny. I am determined to continue
with policies which will contribute to peace in the
Caribbean.

Another area in which there has been a flare-
up of danger in recent days is Laos. My representatives will be in touch with yours on this
problem, and I am sure that we both have a clear
interest in preventing the breakdown of the
agreement worked out so carefully last year. We
continue to put great reliance on your own pledge
of support for a neutral and independent Laos.
Neither of us can wish for a direct test of force
in that remote country, and in the instance it
appears that the provocation has come from a
side in which your influence can be more effective than ours.

There are other issues and problems before
us, but perhaps I have said enough to give you a
sense of my own current thinking on these matters. Let me now also offer the suggestion that it
might be helpful if some time in May I should
send a senior personal representative to discuss
these and other matters informally with you. The
object would not be formal negotiations, but a
fully frank, informal exchange of views,
arranged in such a way as to receive as little
attention as possible. If this thought is appealing
to you, please let me know your views on the
most convenient time.

In closing, I want again to send my warm personal wishes to you and all your family. These
are difficult and dangerous times in which we
live, and both you and I have grave responsibili-

ties to our families and to all of mankind. The pressures from those who have a less patient and peaceful outlook are very great—but I assure you of my own determination to work at all times to strengthen world peace./4/

/1/Source: Department of State, Presidential Correspondence: Lot 77 D 163. Top Secret; Eyes Only. Another copy is in the Kennedy Library, National Security Files, Countries Series, USSR, Khrushchev Correspondence.
/2/Document 85.
/3/The note, April 8, was transmitted in telegram 2527 from Moscow, April 8. (Department of State, Central Files, DEF MLF 6)
/4/Printed from an unsigned copy.

"We have a duty to consider what are the needs of security; but we also have a duty to humanity."

96. Telegram From the Department of State to the Embassy in the Soviet Union

Washington, April 15, 1963, 9 p.m./1/

2191. Following is text of joint letter from President and Prime Minister Macmillan:

Begin verbatim text.

"Dear Mr. Chairman,

1. You will recall that in February and March, 1962, we had some correspondence about the

Geneva disarmament conference, and in particular about the possibility of reaching agreement on the text of a treaty to ban nuclear tests. Both President Kennedy/Mr. Macmillan and I pledged ourselves to take a personal interest in the progress of this conference on which so many of the hopes of mankind have been fixed. Last October we both indicated in messages to you our intention to devote renewed efforts to the problem of disarmament with particular reference to the proliferation of nuclear weapons and the banning of nuclear tests.

2. Since then the Geneva meeting has continued but it has not reached the point of definite agreement. Nevertheless, some encouraging advance has been made. For example, your acceptance of the principle of on-the-spot verification of unidentified events has been of great value. Equally, the Western countries have been able to reduce the number of annual inspections for which they felt it essential to ask, from about twenty down to seven. The difference remaining is of course real and substantial, if only because it presents in practical form the effects of two different lines of reasoning. At the same time the actual difference between the three inspections which you have proposed and the seven for which we are asking, important though this is, should not be impossible to resolve. As regards the automatic seismic stations, the difference between us appears to be fairly narrow.

3. We all have a duty to consider what are the needs of security; but we also have a duty to humanity. President Kennedy/Mr. Macmillan and

I therefore believe that we ought to make a further serious attempt by the best available means to see if we cannot bring this matter to a conclusion with your help.

4. We know that it is argued that a nuclear tests agreement, although valuable and welcome especially in respect of atmospheric tests, will not by itself make a decisive contribution to the peace and security of the world. There are, of course, other questions between us which are also of great importance; but the question of nuclear tests does seem to be one on which agreement might now be reached. The mere fact of an agreement on one question will inevitably help to create confidence and so facilitate other settlements. In addition, it is surely possible that we might be able to proceed rapidly to specific and fruitful discussions about the non-dissemination of nuclear power, leading to an agreement on this subject. Such an agreement, if it was reasonably well supported by other countries, would seem to us likely to have a profound effect upon the present state of tension in the world. If it proved possible to move promptly to an agreement on nuclear weapons and on the proliferation of national nuclear capability, an advance to broader agreements might then open up.

5. The practical question is how best to proceed. It may be that further discussions would reveal new possibilities from both sides as regards the arrangements for the quota of inspections. But if we attempted to reach this point by the present methods both sides may feel unable to make an advance because this would

appear to be surrendering some point of substance without obtaining a final agreement on a
definite treaty in exchange. It may be that we
could make some progress on this question of
numbers by exploring an idea which has been
mentioned by the neutral nations in Geneva—the
idea that a quota of on-site inspections might be
agreed upon to cover a period of several years,
from which inspections could be drawn under
more flexible conditions than an annual quota
would permit.

5. (a) But at the moment it is not only the
question of numbers which holds us up, we also
have to agree on the final content of the draft
treaty and in particular to decide certain important questions as to how inspection is to be carried out. You have taken the view that once the
quota is agreed the other matters can easily be
settled, whereas we feel that the final agreement
about the number of inspections is unlikely to be
possible unless most of the other matters have
been first disposed of. Thus we have reached an
impasse.

6. We should be interested to hear your suggestions as to how we are to break out of this.
For our part we should be quite prepared now to
arrange private tripartite discussions in whatever seemed the most practical way. For example,
our chief representatives at Geneva could conduct discussions on the questions which remain
to be settled. Alternatively, or at a later stage,
President Kennedy/Prime Minister Macmillan
and I would be ready to send in due course very
senior representatives who would be empowered

to speak for us and talk in Moscow directly with you. It would be our hope that either in Geneva or through such senior representatives in Moscow we might bring the matter close enough to a final decision so that it might then be proper to think in terms of a meeting of the three of us at which a definite agreement on a test ban could be made final. It is of course obvious that a meeting of the three of us which resulted in a test ban treaty would open a new chapter in our relations as well as providing an opportunity for wider discussions.

7. We sincerely trust that you will give serious consideration to this proposal. We believe that the nuclear tests agreement and what may follow from it is the most hopeful area in which to try for agreement between us. The procedure which we have suggested seems to us the most practical way of achieving a result which would be welcome all over the world.

Sincerely,

John F. Kennedy

Harold Macmillan

End verbatim text.

Rusk

/1/Source: Department of State, Presidential Correspondence, Lot 66 D 204. Secret; Verbatim Text; Operational Immediate; Eyes Only. Drafted and approved by James E. Goodby of ACDA and cleared by Bundy, Foster (ACDA), and Davis (EUR). Repeated to Geneva and London. This message was delivered to Khrushchev by Kohler on April 24; see vol. VII, pp. 685-686. Another copy of this message is in the Kennedy Library, National Security Files, Countries Series, USSR, Khrushchev Correspondence.

"I have become most concerned over recent developments in Laos."

97. Telegram From the Department of State to the Embassy in the Soviet Union

Washington, April 23, 1963, 3:24 p.m./1/

2273. Eyes only Ambassador and Harriman. Following is text of message for Harriman to deliver to Khrushchev:

"Dear Mr. Chairman:

I have become most concerned over recent developments in Laos. As you know, I have always regarded our mutual commitment in Vienna to bring peace to that unhappy country as an important milestone in Soviet/American relations. If we could work successfully together to make Laos neutral, we could, I have thought, make progress in resolving other matters which are at issue between us.

It is because of this concern that I have asked

Governor Harriman to make a special trip to confer with you as my representative on this particular aspect of our relations./2/ You and your colleagues have known him well and I put great
hope in the results of his discussions with you. I
will be awaiting Governor Harriman's report with
keen interest.

Sincerely"

Rusk

/1/Source: Department of State, Presidential Correspondence: Lot 66 D 204. Secret; Operational Immediate. Drafted
and approved by Thompson and cleared in draft by Rusk
and at the White House. Repeated to London. Another copy
of this message is in the Kennedy Library, National Security
Files, Countries Series, USSR, Khrushchev Correspondence.
/2/For a memorandum of Harriman's conversation with
Khrushchev, see vol. XXIV, pp. 1000-1005.

*". . . the word of the song do not
leave you but because we rightfully
prided ourselves on the fact that the
Soviet and American peoples . . .
wrote their words in the general
hymn of victory over Hitlerite
Germany and militarist Japan."*

98. Message From Chairman Khrushchev to President Kennedy

Moscow, undated./1/

DEAR MR. PRESIDENT: I have with interest acquainted myself with your message of April 11./2/ If my impression is correct as to its principal motive, namely to seek out new possibilities for the cooperation of our countries in the resolution of questions which are ripe for settlement, then it is fully responsive to my thoughts. I, like you, consider as formerly that it is extremely important to us to understand each other clearly in order to avoid unnecessary dangers or obstacles to progress in the achievement of peaceful agreements. Everything which proceeds to the advantage of mutual understanding and trust between our countries and between us personally will always meet on my part a most favorable response.

My colleagues and I frequently ponder over how relations are developing between our two countries. Yes, and could it be otherwise if by virtue of the position occupied by the USSR and the USA on earth, Soviet-American relations had become a political meridian of their own sort from which one as a matter of fact takes a reading of prognoses and hopes for the peaceful future of peoples. Probably I shall be close to your frame of mind if I say that the crisis in the region of the Caribbean Sea has given many people a new stimulus for reflection on this account.

In fact not so long ago both you and I were in the ranks of allied armies acting against the aggressors. These times come to memory not because, as they say, the words of the song do not leave you but because we rightfully prided ourselves on the fact that the Soviet and American peoples each in their own way wrote their words in the general hymn of victory over Hitlerite Germany and militarist Japan. No, I mentally return to that tragic and at the same time heroic period because it clearly demonstrated the possibility of the establishment between the Soviet Union and the USA of such relations as when their mutual interests decidedly outweigh the differences of views on the remainder. Unfortunately, shortly after the war relations between our countries were upset and rolled down an inclined plane.

We did not wish to accept such a position and undertook practical efforts in order to find some sort of general basis which would permit a return to relations between our countries in a better direction. In proposals following this aim, we appealed both to you and your predecessors in the Office of President and here we were talking about a wide circle of international questions: disarmament, security in Europe, direct Soviet-American relations and many other things. Now, one way or another it must be recognized that the track in which relations between our countries found themselves under Franklin Roosevelt, now remains empty. We refuse to believe that the sole path which remained for the two mightiest powers was a slide along that inclined plane from one international crisis to another still more dangerous one. There is another perspective: given the mutual desire of the parties—and as for us we say "Yes"—it is possible to raise our countries to the highway of peaceful, mutually beneficial cooperation. I think you share my certainty that such a beneficial turning-point in Soviet-American relations, and government officials who knew how to bring it about, would be applauded not only by Soviet and American peoples but by all to whom peace on our planet is dear.

Therefore, we have not abandoned hope that the Government of the USA irrespective of all difference of world outlook and way of life, will together with us work for the creation of conditions for peaceful, I underline peaceful, competition in the course of which each social system, each country, would demonstrate its possibilities for the satisfaction of the requirements of the people.

The entire foreign political activity of the Soviet Government is subordinate to the service of peace and peaceful co-existence. It is precisely from these positions that we approach the international questions touched upon in your message.

The question of the cessation of nuclear testing is touched upon in your message. As you doubtless know, we have long considered that our Western partners are still far from having traversed their part of the distance to the desired finish—the conclusion of an agreement.

We have now received from you and Prime Minister Macmillan new proposals on this question./3/ Inasmuch as you and the Prime Minister are addressing yourselves to us together and inasmuch as some time is required to study these proposals, I shall not specially dwell here on the question of the cessation of testing and shall write you and the Prime Minister separately./4/ I shall only say that for its part the Soviet

Government has done and will do everything in order in the shortest possible time to approach the final act, which would crown the efforts of many years, to agree on the conclusion of an agreement on the cessation of testing of nuclear weapons.

Here I shall dwell on a question which, although to a certain extent also touches on the cessation of nuclear testing, has itself acquired increasing significance and urgency particularly now in connection with various plans for the creation of nuclear forces of NATO. I have in mind the task which by the will of history has been placed first of all before our countries; to act so that nuclear armaments even before general and complete disarmament should remain walled up in the arsenals of those powers which already possess, them and in order that it would be possible not to fear that sometime the doors of the nuclear club will be broken and we shall hear the triumphant exclamation, shall we say, in the German language, "I am already here!" You of course know well the point of view of the Soviet Government concerning the non-dissemination of nuclear weapons. In brief it consists in this, that if it is not possible immediately to agree on the destruction of such weapons, then at least anticipating this it is necessary not to permit their further dissemination. And seriously if a dam is properly constructed which would not permit a flood of nuclear weapons then the first duty of the builders is to concern themselves that no single crack or outlet canals remain; otherwise all the construction loses its meaning. The proposal of the Soviet Government to conclude an international agreement which on the one hand would contain the requirement of the atomic powers not to transfer any form of nuclear weapons—directly or indirectly including via military alliances to those states which do not possess them—and on the other hand the obligations of other powers not to manufacture or to acquire such weapons serves precisely this purpose./5/ In other words, we are talking here about new states not acquiring or utilizing nuclear weapons in any form.

I note with satisfaction that in your message you confirm that the USA is decisively against the development of additional national nuclear potentials. At the same time you, now as formerly, attempt to convince me that neither the multinational nor multilateral nuclear forces being planned for NATO will increase the danger of the spreading of nuclear weapons and that the Soviet Government can rely on the continuing and decisive opposition of the USA to the dissemination of national nuclear forces. Obviously, some sort of gradual acquiring of, or partial participation in, the control of nuclear armaments in your view is better than an appearance of new national nuclear forces.

But you will agree, Mr. President, that no matter what crack appears, opening the way to atomic weapons, be it only the size of a little finger, it makes no difference; once such a crack exists there will be found fingers which in this fashion will find their way to the control panels of these weapons. I do not speak of the fact that for states tempted by military adventurism and revengism, the degree of acquisition thus received would appear only a temporary step toward the putting forward of further demands which in the final analysis would lead to the unleashing of new nuclear potential which, as you write, the USA seeks to avoid. It seems that this is clear to everyone who looks on all of these things not only from the positions of NATO. The question arises naturally why place yourself before the choice between what is bad and that which is still worse? Would it not be better to cast aside both the bad and the still worse variant and choose the good?

We rapidly believe that the Government of the USA will strive to arrange it so that the multinational and multilateral nuclear forces of NATO, no matter how their creation comes out in practice could never be used without the Government of the USA. But one way or another states which are included in the nuclear pool of NATO, including the FRG, will have a vote there and will participate in the formulation of opinions and, as a consequence, of the final decisions concerning the utilization of nuclear armaments. Indeed, we all witnessed the fact that in NATO the voice of Western Germany is increasingly listened to although everything indicates that at least some members of this bloc not without suspicion look upon the foreign policy of that state remembering the past and knowing from personal experience the habits of the German militarists.

It is also no less clear that if there were concluded a genuine agreement which left no loopholes concerning the non-dissemination of nuclear weapons, then in these conditions neither Western Germany nor anyone else would dare go against the collective will of the participants in that agreement since in that case they would appear in a most unfavorable light before all the world and would be subjected, it may be said, to the moral ostracism of all mankind.

Naturally we will set forward separately in greater detail our views concerning the draft declaration about the non-dissemination of nuclear weapons which the Secretary of State, D. Rusk, recently handed Ambassador A.F. Dobrynin./6/ But it is already possible to say that unfortunately this draft does not bring us any closer to the achievement of agreement. It is impossible not to note that it contains in reality the same positions which formerly deprived us of the possibility of coming to mutual understanding. This particularly relates to the possibility of permitting access to Western Germany of nuclear weapons on which as a practical matter the American draft is based. No one can expect the agreement of the Government of the Soviet Union to the growth of nuclear fangs by the West German Bundeswehr. I believe you will understand that from our point of view the realization of any plans for the creation of collective nuclear forces cannot but shake the ground under the achievement of international agreement concerning the non-dissemination of nuclear weapons in which the USA should be interested no less than the Soviet Union.

Already for a protracted period, in the exchange of opinions between us no matter in what channels they took place, one and the same question has inevitably arisen—concerning the situation around Cuba. To a considerable degree this is understandable if one considers how we passed through a most dangerous crisis in the fall of last year. But it is impossible not to recognize also that tension around Cuba decreases too slowly and at times rises anew not unlike the way the mercury jumps in the thermometers of the present spring.

And of course when one thinks about where the abnormalities are coming from which are making the atmosphere in the region of the Caribbean Sea ever more feverish, one comes to the conclusion that a one-sided approach can least of all help the situation.

If one allows that in the Western Hemisphere uneasiness is evoked by the presence in Cuba of a certain small number of Soviet troops which are helping Cubans to master the weapons delivered by the Soviet Union for the purpose of strengthening the defense capabilities of Cuba, then how much more uneasiness should be evoked in the countries of Europe, Asia and Africa by the hundreds of thousands of American troops in the Eastern Hemisphere? It is sufficient to make such a comparison in order that things can be seen in proper perspective. At our meetings in Vienna we seemed to have agreed to proceed from the fact that the forces of our states were equal. Well, then, if our forces are equal, then there should also be equal possibilities. Why does the United States forget about this?

You know that we have withdrawn from Cuba

a significant part of our military personnel. I can
tell you that we have withdrawn several times
more people than has been stated in the American
press. How this matter will develop in the future
depends on a number of circumstances and in the
first place on the pace at which the atmosphere in
the region of the Caribbean Sea will be normalized, and whether, as could be expected, the reasons which occasioned the necessity for assistance to the Cubans by Soviet military specialists
and instructors will disappear.

I would like to express the thought of how
important it is in evaluating what is happening
around Cuba that one rise above one-sided understandings and base his judgments on the respective estimate of the situation of the interested
parties. From your point of view, as set forth in
your message, the reconnaissance flights of
American aircraft over Cuba are only "peaceful
observation." But if one were to characterize
these flights objectively, without even considering
the point of view, understandable to everyone, of
the country over which they are being carried
out, then they cannot be described other than as
an unrestrained intrusion into the air space of a
sovereign government and as a flagrant violation
of the elementary norms of international law and
the principles of the UN Charter, to which are
affixed the signatures of both the USA and Cuba.
It is natural that no state prizing its sovereignty,
no government solicitous of the interest and dignity of its people, can tolerate such flights.

Perhaps it is desired that we recognize the
right of the USA to violate the Charter of the

United Nations and international norms? But this we cannot do and will not do.

We have honestly carried out the obligations we assumed in the settlement of the crisis in the region of the Caribbean Sea, and withdrew from Cuba even more than we promised to withdraw. There are no grounds for you to doubt the readiness of the Soviet Union to carry out firmly in the future as well the agreement which was reached between us. Why then are reconnaissance flights by American aircraft over Cuba necessary? What are they looking for there when there is not a single thing, seen in the light of the agreement reached, which could cause concern? Trampling on sovereignty in this way can lead to quite serious consequences for us if it is not stopped in time.

And can one pass over in silence or recognize as in accordance with the principles of the UN Charter the continuing efforts to strangle the economy of Cuba? I shall not address myself to this in more detail although of course I could find many words with which to characterize these actions, even from a purely humanitarian point of view.

The Soviet Union gives due credit to the measures which have recently been undertaken by the USA, as well as by England, in connection with the attacks which have taken place ~~~ ves- sels near the Cuban coast. We of underestimate the significance of t and hope that they will be sufficie preclude the possibility of a repe raids against Cuba.

I read with a feeling of satisfaction that passage of your message in which you confirm that you have neither the intention nor the desire to invade Cuba and where you recognize that it is up to Cuban people to determine their fate. That is a good statement. We have always stressed that, like any other people, the Cuban people possess the inalienable right to determine their own fate as they see fit.

A few words about Laos, since you touched on this subject in your message. Certainly the events which have taken place during the past weeks in that country give rise to some concern. Especially alarming is the murder of the Minister of Foreign Affairs K. Pholsena. The life has been cut short of a statesman whose signature was put on the Geneva Agreements on Laos, whose name, together with that of Souvanna Phouma, personified a policy of neutrality for Laos. There are also other facts which show that in that little country great passions continue to boil, leading on occasion to dangerous flare-ups.

There is much to indicate that forces are raising their heads there which also before were resisting the development of the country along the path of peace, independence and neutrality, and information is constantly reaching us indicating that this is taking place with certain outside help. I examined this matter long and carefully in order to see whether this was true and came to the conclusion that the proverb "where there is smoke there is fire" was applicable to the present situation.

It appears to us that the United States can

exert appropriate influence so as to prevent dangerous complications in Laos, which are necessary neither to you nor to us.

As you obviously know, we are at the present time carrying on consultation with the British co-chairman of the Geneva Agreement.

There is no need for me to say that the Soviet Government as formerly is holding firmly to the course of supporting a neutral and independent Laos, which was agreed upon in our meeting in Vienna. We are doing everything that depends on us in order to maintain peace and quiet in that country. If the USA also follows this course firmly, and we think that this should be the case, then it would seem that we can look at the situation in Laos without excessive pessimism.

I received your message dealing with the situation in Laos which you authorized Mr. Harriman to give me./7/ He and I exchanged views on this question, and he obviously will report our conversation in detail to you. Therefore I will limit myself in the present message to what I have said above.

I agree with you that we have before us also other questions and problems aside from those mentioned in your message. In the first instance, I would mention the conclusion of a German peace treaty and normalization of the situation in West Berlin on that basis. The solution of this problem, and given mutual desire that is not now such a difficult matter, would undoubtedly bear the greatest returns both from the standpoint of the interest of consolidating peace and for a serious improvement in Soviet-American relations.

As long as the remnants of the Second World War, which constantly make themselves known continue to exist, then both you and we will be forced to devote ever greater funds to armaments, that is to increasing our ability to destroy each other. And understandably in such a situation it is difficult to count on agreement on disarmament, which requires above all faith and still more faith for its attainment. Therefore, if one realistically evaluates the situation, one cannot but come to the conclusion that the conclusion of a German peace treaty would create better conditions also for the resolution of the question of questions of the modern day—universal and complete disarmament.

I like the proposition you have made concerning a trip to Moscow of your duly authorized personal representative with whom it would be possible to discuss unofficially and frankly problems of interest to both of us. Please be assured that your envoy will receive a good reception in Moscow and complete readiness on the part of the Soviet Government and me personally for a confidential and productive exchange of views.

As concerns the choice of time for your duly authorized personal representative to arrive in Moscow, I am inclined to think, after examining the list of undertakings, in part also of a domestic nature, which demand my participation, that probably the most appropriate period for this meeting would be 10 to 12 June, if of course that is acceptable to you./8/

Thank you for your warm personal greetings to me and to my family. Please accept my cordial greetings. I request you as well to convey my warm greeting to your wife and to all those near you./9/

/1/Source: Department of State, Presidential Correspondence: Lot 77 D 163. Secret; Eyes Only. This letter, which bears the notation "informal translation," was handed to Thompson by Dobrynin on April 29. Four short memoranda of their conversations at that time are in the Kennedy Library, National Security Files, Countries Series, USSR, Dobrynin Talks.
/2/Document 95.
/3/See Document 96.
/4/Document 99.
/5/For text of the Soviet note to the United States, April 8, in which this proposal was made, see *Documents on Disarmament, 1963,* pp. 161-170.
/6/A memorandum of Rusk's conversation on April 12 is in Department of State, Secretary's Memoranda of Conversation: Lot 65 D 330.
/7/See Document 97 and footnote 2 thereto.
/8/See Documents 100 and 101.
/9/Printed from an unsigned copy.

"We wish to make everything quite clear: the Soviet Union would not consent to an agreement which would be detrimental to its security."

99. Letter From Chairman Khrushchev to President Kennedy

Moscow, May 8, 1963./1/

DEAR MR. PRESIDENT: I have carefully studied your message on the question of the cessation of nuclear tests, which was transmitted to me by

Ambassador Kohler on April 24./2/ You stated in this message that you consider·how—from your standpoint—action should be taken for the achievement of the earliest possible understanding, and you offer proposals concerning procedures for further negotiations.

We have considered all this, consulted one another in the government, held consultation once again with specialists, and I want to tell you our considerations in reply to your message. I shall also communicate these considerations to Mr. Macmillan in reply to his message which is identical with yours.

I think that at present it is not necessary to delve deeper into the history of negotiations on the cessation of tests or present in all details our position and our proposals, which have already been stated more than once. You know them well and we have also learned almost by heart the proposals of the Western powers, just as we used to learn "Pater Noster." I merely wish to touch upon some of the main questions and basic differences between our positions.

What is the approach of the Soviet Government to the question of the cessation of nuclear tests? It is very simple: we stand for the cessation of all tests for all time, wherever they may be carried out: in the atmosphere, the cosmos, underground, and under water.

We take such a position first of all because the question regarding the cessation of nuclear weapons tests has an indisputable significance from the moral and humane viewpoint. Its solution would put an end to the contamination of air, water, the bowels and surface of the earth by radio-active substances, harmful to the health of the people now living and for future generations. As it seems to us, this already appears to be a sufficient incentive for coming to an understanding regarding the prohibition of tests.

It appears that the achievement of such an understanding could also exert a definite and positive influence on the international situation. To be sure, the conclusion of an understanding regarding the cessation of tests would not stop the arms race, would not diminish by one charge the stocks of nuclear weapons accumulated by states; it would not even slow down further accumulation of these stocks. The prohibition of tests does not appear to be the key problem for lessening international tension. The roots of this tension lie entirely elsewhere, above all in the fact that the German peace settlement has not yet been reached. And yet the conclusion of an agreement regarding the prohibition of nuclear tests could somewhat clear up the atmosphere in the relations between nuclear powers and would be evaluated everywhere as an expression of their readiness to seek a solution to the questions affecting the interests of both sides. I understood that you also attach significance to this.

We are convinced that it is not difficult to solve the question regarding the cessation of nuclear tests if one manifests a desire to achieve this. Right now, when both sides have completed important series of tests and when your and our scientists are in agreement that for further improvement of nuclear weapons there is no special necessity for new tests, then it seems that it should be even easier than before to come to an agreement on this subject.

On our part we also see no difficulties whatever in the question of control over the carrying out by the states of their obligations under the agreement of prohibition of nuclear tests. We know that national means now available for discovering nuclear explosion, including also underground explosions, are amply sufficient to unmask any state which might try to conduct nuclear weapons tests under cover of secrecy.

If it is necessary to have new confirmation of the fact that even underground nuclear explosions cannot be conducted in such a way that they would not become known, then new proof of this lies in the fact that our seismic stations unerringly caught the vibrations of the earth crust produced by the recent French nuclear tests in the Sahara. I do not doubt that seismologists in the USA also have recorded these vibrations.

But if the Soviet Union is prepared to rely wholly on the national means for verification of the cessation of underground nuclear tests, then there is no reason why the USA could not do the same.

Such, Mr. President, is our approach to the solution of the problem of prohibition of nuclear tests. This is an honest and equitable approach. If an agreement is concluded on this basis, then everybody will gain and no side will lose.

Then why do the Western Powers not accept this approach? Why do they continue to insist on international inspection of the discontinuance of underground nuclear explosions? In the interest of such a cause there is no need of inspection of the cessation of underground tests just as there is no need for international control of the cessation of tests in the atmosphere, in space, and under water with which the Western Powers now agree. But if no inspection is needed for the control of the cessation of underground tests, and yet the Western Powers continue to insist on it, then we are compelled to draw our own conclusions in regard to the reason why such a demand is put forth.

Please, understand me, Mr. President, that under these conditions we cannot regard the demand of the Western Powers for international inspection otherwise than as a policy to charge the Soviet Union for the cessation of the nuclear weapons tests a certain additional price in the form of the admission of NATO's intelligence men to Soviet territory, where, of course, there are many objects of interest to the military intelligence of the states of this bloc. Sometimes, however, the matter is presented in such a way as if equality is ensured by the fact that espionage would be carried out, so to speak, on the basis of reciprocity. But such "reciprocity" would not result in anything good; it could only intensify mistrust in our relations. We do not want to enter on such a path and we have no desire to send our intelligence men to the United States of America.

We wish to make everything quite clear: the Soviet Union would not consent to an agreement which would be detrimental to its security. We are firmly convinced that lasting peace can be founded only on such agreements as would strengthen the security of states and not undermine it.

Well known to the entire world and certainly to you, Mr. President, is our sincere desire to reach as soon as possible an agreement among all states on the matter of disarmament. Such an act would really ensure full security for all nations inhabiting our planet. But heretofore we have not been able to reach such an agreement and, furthermore, we do not see any clear prospects in this direction. Under such conditions the decisive factor is the problem of security of every country, and we, of course, are concerned about the security of our country, and we cannot in this regard permit any concession which military intelligence services may exploit to conduct espionage in our country.

If an agreement for universal and complete disarmament under international control is reached, such control we would not regard as espionage because it would be actually carried out on a reciprocal basis under the stipulation that all states liquidate their armed forces and armaments, and such control would be in the interest of all countries and nations of the world.

You might ask me why, if the Soviet Union considers international inspections for the discontinuance of nuclear tests as a means of espionage, it consented to the conducting of such inspections on Soviet territory four months ago? You know what motivated such a step, because at that time we explained our motives and thoughts on this point. However, since it can be seen from your letter that you interpret them in a somewhat different way, I feel that it would be better if we clarify our position once more.

We consented to inspections not because we came to the conclusion that they were necessary for verification of the states' carrying out their obligations under a treaty for discontinuance of nuclear weapons tests. No, we agreed to this only because we ascribed a definite meaning to your statements, Mr. President, that without a minimum number of on-site inspections you would not be able to succeed in persuading the United States Senate to ratify an agreement for the cessation of tests. And though there was nothing that obligated the Soviet Union to consider the fine points of such purely internal matters as the disposition of forces in the U.S. Senate, we decided to meet you half-way and to agree to a minimum number of inspections on Soviet territory.

I shall not conceal the fact that it was not easy for us to adopt the decision to agree to the number of inspections indicated by us. But we proceed from the premise that they are not relevant to the problem and technically not justified, and so why should we agree to them? For a long time I deliberated as to whether I should take such initiative with our government or not. On the one hand I, as Chairman of the Council of Ministers of the USSR, felt the responsibility for solving questions of disarmament and discontinuance of tests which, as was recognized one year ago, rests with the heads of governments and states participating in negotiations on these questions. On the other hand I, in my position, bear the highest responsibility for guaranteeing the secu-

rity of the Soviet Union and must not forget this
for a moment. And still I have come to the conclusion that it is probably worthwhile in this case
to take a step forward now to meet the Western
powers in order to ensure the swift achievement
of an agreement on stopping tests. In proceeding
in this manner, we, of course, had counted on the
fact that as a result of a peaceful settlement of
the crisis in the Caribbean Sea area on an international basis, as was hoped at that time, the
germs of confidence might begin to sprout. We
had hoped that our new step in the direction of
stopping tests might help these sprouts burst
forth and grow strong.

But this did not mean at all that, as you write,
we had accepted the "principle of verifying on the
spot undetermined phenomena." Not at all! We
have not accepted and do not accept this principle in the sense that there is any necessity for
verification on the spot; there is no need for that.

That is how our agreement arose concerning
inspection. This decision was dictated by purely
political considerations, by the desire to achieve
more quickly the cessation of all nuclear tests,
but in no case did this mean any revision of our
opinion concerning the futility of inspections
from a scientific and technical standpoint.

After we had taken this great step toward
meeting the Western powers, it was directly up to
them and solely up to them as to whether the
subsequent obstacles on the road to agreement
would be removed. We had hoped that the
Western powers, in their turn, would likewise
take an equally important step forward, and the

only remaining step would be to prepare a treaty text for the cessation of tests and sign it.

One can only be sorry that in reality this did not come to pass. Instead of a positive reply to our initiative the Western powers began to haggle concerning the number of inspections and the conditions for conducting them, and this cannot be construed otherwise than meaning that they are really not prepared to conclude an agreement on the cessation of tests on such a basis as would give nobody an advantage and would inflict no damage on anyone. But on any other basis there can be no agreement at all between the powers during our era. When we are requested to make some new concessions in the matter of inspections, this can merely mean that an agreement is becoming more and more remote, that its attainment is becoming less and less likely. Thus the negotiations being conducted lose all sense of direction and cannot get out of the doldrums.

And now I come to that which, apparently, constitutes the very essence of the messages which I received from you and Mr. Macmillan. To summarize briefly what is stated in these messages, their main thought, as I have understood it, reduces itself to the proposal to continue haggling over inspections, but at a higher level. Please pardon me for my straightforwardness, but I could draw no other conclusion, however much I read the messages. Considerations are expressed therein as to how to carry forward the movement as to the figures of annual inspections; reference is made to the possibility of establishing a quota for several years; there is brought up the question of how these inspections should be conducted, etc.

All this merely confirms that the sense and significance of our concession in the matter of inspections have not only not been duly appreciated, but there is a desire to use this concession as some kind of springboard for achieving other objectives and not at all for settling the problem of stopping nuclear tests.

The Soviet Government sincerely desires to reach an agreement for the cessation of nuclear tests, but it cannot and will not approach an understanding on the conditions proposed by the Western powers. Our people would have every right to severely question their government if it entered into negotiations as to how many intelligence agents we would admit annually to our territory and what conditions we would grant to such intelligence agents. But the Western powers in their proposals, which they have advanced in negotiation for the cessation of nuclear weapons tests, insist that in the implementation of any inspection they have the right to check the territory to the extent of 500 square km. Just imagine what an enormous area would be covered by these inspections, if there were seven or eight of them, as the Western powers insist on. And is it possible for you to think that we can seriously regard such a proposal, the unserious character of which is obvious to us.

When we agreed on two or three inspections we thought that these inspections would be very symbolic, and that the question would never arise concerning the inspection of such vast areas—all the more so with the use of various methods of boring, flying about, etc. No, we will not accept that, because there is absolutely no need for that. Thus, if the position of the Western powers is judged by their proposals, then one comes to the conclusion that they really have no serious attitude toward negotiation. And it seems to me that if the Western powers would seriously consider their own proposals and realistically evaluate their partner's position, then they themselves would come to understand that these proposals are unacceptable to us.

If the question is now approached in a businesslike manner, then it must be admitted that the establishment of automatic seismic stations, the so-called "black boxes," is fully sufficient, and to this, as before, we consent. Nothing else is required.

As soon as I had studied your message for the first time, I said to Ambassador F. Kohler/3/ that it was evidently based on the old positions of the Western powers and for that reason cannot provide a basis on which to reach an agreement. This impression of mine has now become even stronger, and I even wonder whether the dispatching of the messages by you and Mr. Macmillan is not connected with some additional internal policy consideration.

In any case we took note of the fact that although the messages of the President of the United States and of the Prime Minister of Great Britain addressed to the Chairman of the Council of Ministers of the USSR were in this case strictly confidential, the content of these messages was

announced by the press of some of the Western
countries several days before they were handed to
the addressee. It is as if someone wanted especially to show who is the initiator of this "constructive" step. We, however, will not participate
in these schemes and will not be drawn into them.

What will the further course of developments
be on the question of stopping nuclear tests? To
tell the truth, I do not know; it depends on the
Western Powers whether there will be an agreement. The explosions of American nuclear
devices in Nevada and of French nuclear devices
in the Sahara cannot but cause us to wonder
whether there are any prospects at present of
reaching an agreement on the banning of tests,
or whether we shall not again have to turn our
attention in another direction, that of taking
measures which would ensure a still more reliable guarantee of the security of the Soviet Union
and other Socialist states. This, obviously, is also
made imperative for us because of the measures
of the Western powers in establishing a joint
nuclear force in NATO.

Is such a development, Mr. President, in harmony with the interests of our two countries? It
seems to me that it is not. But this depends not
so much on the Soviet Union as on the other side,
and on the future actions of the other side.

It gives me no satisfaction to say this. I repeat
that we were anticipating something quite different in the question of stopping nuclear tests—the
conclusion of an agreement. And we are now, as
before, prepared to seek an agreement, provided
that our negotiating partners are also prepared

to do so. It would be even more important to approach a decision on the main problems—disarmament and a peaceful German settlement. But in the disarmament discussions at Geneva there has been, as before, no evidence of any accomplishments except the multiplication of the number of minutes. Such a situation cannot but give rise to anxiety.

In your and Mr. Macmillan's messages you propose sending to Moscow high-ranking representatives who would have full powers to carry on, in your name, discussions about the cessation of nuclear weapons tests. So be it; we are even prepared to try this method of discussion too, and in general we consider it right to use every opportunity in order to effect a rapprochement of the positions of the respective sides. For that reason we shall be happy to receive in Moscow the high-level representatives of the United States and Great Britain. It is important, however, that they be empowered to negotiate on the question of stopping nuclear weapons tests on the same realistic and equitable basis which life itself suggests, i.e., without spying inspections in foreign territories. This is the crux of the whole problem.

We would, of course, also welcome a meeting at the highest level, the possibility of holding which, for the purpose of reaching a definitive understanding on the agreement for banning tests, is mentioned in your message. I should gladly take part in such a meeting, provided that there is hope of its being successful; for that, one thing is now necessary—namely, that the Western powers, too, show a desire to negotiate and come to an agreement.

These are my ideas as regards the thoughts which were set forth by you and Mr. Macmillan in your messages.

With my respects,

N. Khrushchev/4/

/1/Source: Department of State, Presidential Correspondence: Lot 66 D 204. Secret. The source text is a Department of State translation. Another English text is in telegram 2839 from Moscow, May 8. (Ibid., Central Files, DEF 18-4) Another copy is in the Kennedy Library, National Security Files, Countries Series, USSR, Khrushchev Correspondence.
/2/See Document 96.
/3/See telegram 2719 from Moscow, April 24, in vol. VII, pp. 685-686.
/4/Printed from a translation that indicates Khrushchev signed the original Russian-language version. A bracketed note after his signature indicates it was illegible.

"I . . . appreciate the frankness with which you discussed some of the outstanding issues between us, even though I can find little encouragement from the gaps that separate us . . ."

100. Message From President Kennedy to Chairman Khrushchev

Washington, May 13, 1963./1/

DEAR MR. CHAIRMAN: I thank you for your

message of April twenty-ninth/2/ and appreciate the frankness with which you discussed some of the outstanding issues between us, even though I can find little encouragement from the gaps which separate us on these problems. I am especially concerned about Laos, on which I felt we had reached an agreement to which we have on our side given full support.

I have also received your message of May eighth/3/ on the subject of nuclear tests, to which I shall be replying separately.

I am more than ever of the opinion that a visit to Moscow by a personal representative would be useful, and I have asked the Secretary of State, who has long desired to accept Mr. Gromyko's invitation to return his visit to this country, to undertake this task. Unfortunately, for a number of reasons, including the fact that he has some long outstanding commitments, the date of ten to twelve June, which you have suggested, is a very inconvenient time for him. Moreover, he will be accompanying me on my visit to Europe in the latter half of June. He would, however, be prepared to come at any time in July or August that is convenient to you, and I should be grateful if you could suggest a date./4/

/1/Source: Department of State, Presidential Correspondence: Lot 77 D 163. No classification marking. A note on the source text indicates it was handed to Dobrynin by Thompson at 6 p.m. May 13. Another copy is in the Kennedy Library, National Security Files, Countries Series, USSR, Khrushchev Correspondence.
/2/Document 98.
/3/Document 99.
/4/Printed from an unsigned copy.

"We would be glad to see Mr. Rusk here . . ."

101. Letter From Chairman Khrushchev to President Kennedy

Moscow, May 15, 1963./1/

DEAR MR. PRESIDENT: I have received your message of May 13, 1963./2/ I was pleased to learn from it that as your personal representative for a trip to Moscow you have designated Secretary of State Dean Rusk and that he would like to make use in this connection of the invitation once extended to him by Foreign Minister Andrei A. Gromyko.

We will be glad to see Mr. Rusk here and to have a frank exchange of opinion with him on questions of interest for both sides.

You write that you are more than ever of the opinion that a visit to Moscow by your personal representative would be useful.

I want to think so too. Let us hope that the trip by Secretary of State Dean Rusk will turn out to be both useful and fruitful.

As for the date of his arrival, having in mind that in July or in August, as you say, any time is acceptable to you and to the Secretary of State, I suggest that Mr. Dean Rusk arrive in Moscow on July 28, 1963./3/

/1/Source: Department of State, Presidential Correspondence: Lot 77 D 163. Top Secret; Eyes Only. The source text is apparently a Russian translation. Another copy is in the Kennedy Library, National Security Files, Countries Series, USSR, Khrushchev Correspondence.
/2/Document 100.
/3/Printed from an unsigned copy.

"The Soviet people send congratulations and best wishes to the intrepid Cosmonaut Gordon Cooper."

102. Letter From Chairman Khrushchev to President Kennedy

Moscow, May 17, 1963./1/

DEAR MR. PRESIDENT: Accept our cordial congratulations on the successful flight of Cosmonaut G. Cooper on the spaceship "Faith-7" which made a new contribution to the exploration of the expanses of the universe.

The Soviet people send congratulations and best wishes to the intrepid Cosmonaut Gordon Cooper.

N. Khrushchev/2/

/1/Source: Department of State, Presidential Correspondence: Lot 66 D 204. No classification marking. The source text is a Department of State translation of a commercial telegram from Moscow. Another copy is in the Kennedy Library, National Security Files, Countries Series, USSR, Khrushchev Correspondence.
/2/Printed from a copy that bears this typed signature.

"All of Major Cooper's countrymen share a deep sense of satisfaction at his achievement."

103. Telegram From the Department of State to the Embassy in the Soviet Union

Washington, May 19, 1963, 11:15 a.m./1/

2508. The following message dated May 19 for delivery soonest to Khrushchev from the President.

Begin Verbatim Text:

Dear Mr. Chairman:

Thank you for your cordial message of congratulations on the successful completion of astronaut L. Gordon Cooper's orbital flight./2/

All of Major Cooper's countrymen share a deep sense of satisfaction at his achievement.

They know it represents not an American accomplishment alone, but the result of the peaceful application of scientific and technical work by men of all nations.

It is our hope that the flight of the Faith-7 will be a milestone towards the peaceful conquest of space for men of all nations.

Sincerely,

John F. Kennedy.

End Text.

Please inform Department when message delivered. Unless Embassy perceives objections we plan to release exchange of messages 24 hours after delivery.

Rusk

/1/Source: Department of State, Presidential Correspondence: Lot 66 D 204. Limited Official Use; Priority. Drafted by S/S-S Harrison; cleared by Davis, Henry (SOV), Anderson (EUR), Tully (P), and Bromley Smith; and approved by Harrison and Kriebel (S/S). Another copy of this message is in the Kennedy Library, National Security Files, Countries Series, USSR, Khrushchev Correspondence.
/2/Document 102.

". . . the date of July 28, 1963 . . . is satisfactory."

104. Message From President Kennedy to Chairman Khrushchev

Washington, May 29, 1963./1/

DEAR MR. CHAIRMAN: I am happy to inform you that the date of July 28, 1963, which you suggest for the arrival of Secretary Rusk in Moscow, is satisfactory. I have asked Secretary Rusk to get in touch with Minister Gromyko well in advance of this date in order to work out the arrangements, including a public announcement at an appropriate agreed time./2/•

/1/Source: Department of State, Presidential Correspondence: Lot 77 D 163. No classification marking. Another copy
is in the Kennedy Library, National Security Files, Countries
Series, USSR, Khrushchev Correspondence.
/2/Printed from an unsigned copy.

"We hope that the high level discussions we are proposing can take place in Moscow."

105. Telegram From the Department of State to the Embassy in the Soviet Union

Washington, May 30, 1963, 5:56 p.m./1/

2590. Following is final revised text to which we have agreed with the British. Request you compare it with text which Trevelyan receiving separately, and concert with him on immediate delivery to Khrushchev or highest available official. Request you work out with Soviets timing and wording of announcement if they so desire.

Begin Verbatim Text

Dear Mr. Chairman:

1. Since we received your letter of May 8 about the question of the treaty to ban nuclear tests,/2/ Prime Minister Macmillan and I have been carefully considering it and we have now jointly agreed to send you letters in similar terms.

2. Let me say first of all that Prime Minister Macmillan and I are glad that you feel able to accept our suggestion that we should send highly placed representatives to Moscow who would be empowered to carry this question further and would be able to discuss the matter with you. We should be glad to send our representatives to Moscow at a time convenient to you either during the last half of June or, if you would prefer this, in the first half of July. We would hope that our representatives might have the advantage of a personal discussion with you.

3. We realize that our positions are still different, especially on the nature of the problem of inspections, but we agree with you that it is important "to use every opportunity in order to effect a rapprochement of the positions of the respective sides." It is in this spirit that we think a visit of high-level representatives to Moscow would be good, so that both sides can talk fully and freely about ways of bridging the gap between us.

4. If you can accept this proposal, we suggest that the present correspondence should remain confidential but that in view of the world-wide interest an announcement should be made straightaway to the effect that as a result of our correspondence on the subject of a nuclear test ban treaty, it has been agreed that you will receive highly placed representatives of the Prime Minister and me in Moscow during the month of June/July in order to carry forward the discussion of possibilities.

5. There are, however, two points that you

have made in your letter to which we think we should reply in advance of detailed discussions. In the first place, you state that "national means now available for discovering nuclear explosions, including also underground explosions, are amply sufficient to unmask any state which might try to conduct nuclear weapons tests under cover of secrecy." You cite the example of recent French tests in the Sahara, point out that your seismologists detected the vibrations in the earth produced by these tests and state that you have no doubt that our seismologists "also have recorded these vibrations."

6. While we agree that developments in seismological techniques have made it possible now to detect most of the earth tremors produced by subterranean disturbances of significant size, we do not agree that it is possible by these techniques alone to ascertain in many important cases whether these tremors were caused by natural earthquakes or man-made explosions. For such identification on-site inspection is still necessary in many cases. This was, of course, the position agreed by the Geneva Conference of Experts in 1958 in which Soviet scientists participated; and at recent private conferences between scientists of our three countries there has been general agreement that there are underground events which occur in both of our countries whose origin could not be identified with certainty without an on-site inspection.

7. To return to the recent French test in the Sahara, the earth tremors produced by the most recent French test were certainly detected, but

prior to the French test it was generally known that it was going to take place in the fairly near future as well as where it would be. The detection of the earth tremors from the French underground nuclear explosion therefore does not, in our view, prove that all nuclear explosions can be identified by national detection systems alone. This is, of course, the central point in our argument in favor of a reasonable number of on-site inspections for underground tests as part of a treaty to ban all nuclear tests, and we sincerely believe this argument to be well founded on scientific fact.

8. The second point to which we feel we must refer is your suggestion that the purpose of our requirement for a system of on-site inspections is to send intelligence agents on to the Soviet territory so as to carry out espionage. We most sincerely and categorically affirm that we have no such purpose. We had thought that this was made clear by the proposals we have made which in our view would prevent on-site inspections being misused for espionage purposes. If you are still in doubt on this matter, our representatives are prepared to discuss in detail the safeguards which could be arranged in this matter so that we can satisfy each other that we are both prepared to enter into a test ban in good faith. We think that reasonable provisions for on-site inspections will make it possible for us to work out a treaty which will endure and not be liable to break down because of unfounded suspicions which could easily have been dispelled by reasonable provisions for verification. We believe that given good will it

should be possible to reach agreement on a method of inspection and on a number which would satisfy both of us.

Mr. Macmillan and I wish in conclusion to express our pleasure at your belief that the signing of a treaty to end nuclear weapons tests would have value both in itself and because of its positive effect on the international situation. It is in this belief, which we share, that we hope that the high level discussions we are proposing can take place in Moscow.

Sincerely, John F. Kennedy.

End verbatim text.

Rusk

/1/Source: Department of State, Presidential Correspondence: Lot 66 D 204. Top Secret; Operational Immediate; Eyes Only. Drafted and approved by Tyler and cleared by Bundy. Another copy of this message is in the Kennedy Library, National Security Files, Countries Series, USSR, Khrushchev Correspondence.
/2/Document 99.

"Quite recently we have already had experience on this score which cannot be called anything other than painful."

106. Letter From Chairman Khrushchev to President Kennedy

Moscow, June 8, 1963./1/

DEAR MR. PRESIDENT: I have received your message of May 31/2/ on the question of cessation of nuclear tests and, it goes without saying, have studied it with due attention. I received an analogous message from Prime Minister H. Macmillan.

In your letters, you and Mr. H. Macmillan repeat your proposal to send to Moscow high-ranking representatives of the USA and Great Britain, who would be empowered "to discuss ways of overcoming existing differences between us" regarding conditions of agreement on the cessation of nuclear tests. Well, in my previous letter I already expressed my readiness also to try such a method of negotiation. The whole question is where and in what direction to seek for a way of overcoming those differences between our positions, which really exist.

It is our profound conviction that success of any further negotiations on the cessation of tests, wherever these negotiations may be conducted—in Moscow, in Geneva, or in any other place—depends completely, as I wrote to you, on whether both parties are ready to agree on the realistic and equal basis which is prompted by life itself. And that basis is well known. In resolving the question of the cessation of tests, as well as any other international question, it consists of necessity in strictly following the principle of equality of parties and of taking into account the interests of each of them. This means that the attainment of agreement on the cessation of nuclear tests can only be arrived at if neither of the parties attempts to receive any special advantages at the expense of the other party, and, consequently, does not insist on demands which are unacceptable to the other party.

However, we have recently become more and more convinced that those with whom we are negotiating are not inclined to conduct negotiations by proceeding from the principle of equality of parties, and still want to receive from us some kind of bonus for the cessation of nuclear-weapons tests. It is not possible otherwise to understand their stubborn attempt to obtain our consent to the conduct of inspections which would open up the possibility of peeping into the places at which the stranger's eye should not look.

The fact that the Soviet Union will not consent to the conducting of espionage inspections has been mentioned in nearly everyone of our documents on the question of the cessation of tests, and this question, it would seem, should be clear to the utmost degree. For, under present conditions, when the problem of disarmament has not only not been solved, but the nuclear-armaments race is taking on ever greater proportions and, day by day is being spurred on more and more by the leading NATO powers, we are compelled to display particular concern in order not to endanger the security of our country in any way. And permit me to note, Mr. President, that steps recently undertaken on the creation of a NATO nuclear fist in Western Europe, with the participation of the West German revanchists, can in no way stimulate us to relax our vigilance; the opposite is rather the case.

You write that the goal of espionage is not being pursued by the Western powers in the question of inspections of the cessation of nuclear tests. But, unfortunately, most recent facts which have been scrupulously verified and have become public knowledge, have shown with all possible certainty how strong is the interest of the intelligence services of some powers in secrets of our defense and, at the same time, how unscrupulous they are in the choice of methods. One would have to have an exceptional share of naivete to rely on the possibility that appropriate agencies in NATO countries—which, it may be said, day and night devote themselves to the study of, and as they themselves put it, the selection of targets on the territory of the Soviet Union and other peace-loving states for nuclear strikes—would shrink from using for these same purposes the channels which would be opened up if we were to agree to the demands of the Western powers on inspection. If we displayed such naivete, it would not be difficult to image what attitude the Soviet people would take towards such leaders.

Therefore, when you say that representatives of the USA and Great Britain would be prepared to discuss with us in detail guarantees which should remove our doubts concerning inspections, I do not think, to tell the truth, that this would settle the matter. The root of everything is not in guarantees with which inspections might be surrounded, but in why such insistence is displayed by the Western powers on the question of inspections, when actually there is no need for them, when, indeed, there is in fact no need for them at all, if one bears in mind only the interests of control in the fulfillment by states of their obligations under an agreement on the cessation of nuclear tests.

In your message of May 31, you seem to wish again to urge us to start discussion on whether national means of detection of underground nuclear explosions are sufficient or insufficient for controlling the fulfillment of such an agreement. But what is there here to argue about, and what is there to discuss? Facts which confirm complete sufficiency of national means are at hand. And you, too, it seems, have no doubts about, for example, the fact mentioned in my message—namely, that seismic tremors from the French underground nuclear tests in the Sahara were registered by national means of states at a distance of many thousands of kilometers. And nevertheless, for some reason, you do not consider it possible to accept as proof even such indisputable data.

As I recall, Mr. President, in one of your press conferences you stressed that a treaty on the prohibition of nuclear tests must give assurance that, if any country carries out a series of secret underground tests, these tests will be detected. Recently I had occasion to become acquainted with a statement on the question of the cessation of tests, made by a group of well-known American scientists representing scientific centers and universities of the USA known the world over. I think that you read it too. What did these American scientists have to say, what ideas did they come out with, these American scientists who, as they say, know what they're talking about, if one takes into account that it is precisely the USA which has great experience in carrying out of underground nuclear explosions? They declare that, given contemporary means of detection, it is impossible to conceal a series of underground nuclear explosions, even one of small yield. Consequently, those means of detection already in existence satisfy the principal demand which you make for a treaty.

If one considers that national means of detection can be supplemented by automatic seismic stations, how can one fail to admit that all this is more than sufficient for a most reliable control over the cessation of all nuclear tests? Under these conditions no state would undertake secretly to violate an agreement, since such a step would be fraught for it with the risk of being exposed and of receiving such a blow to its prestige on the international scene from which it would be difficult for any state to recover. National means of detection, combined with automatic seismic stations—this, certainly, is a fully reliable guarantee against any attempts to produce secret nuclear explosions in circumvention of an agreement on the cessation of tests. And we are agreeable to the installation of automatic seismic stations; you know this.

In the light of all this, is it necessary for me to repeat once more that, if in December of last year we agreed to the conducting of a certain minimum number of inspections on the cessation of underground tests, we did so only and exclusively out of political considerations, with a view to making easier for you, Mr. President, the ratification of a treaty on the cessation of tests by the Senate of the USA. But as a matter of fact, however, the resolution of the question of the cessation of tests could be handled perfectly well without any inspections. That was true in December 1962, and is all the more true now as well.

Thus, it is completely possible to conclude an agreement on the cessation of nuclear tests on the basis of equality, if only all the participants want this. We are, of course, prepared to discuss this, too, with high-ranking representatives of the USA and Great Britain, whom you and Mr. H. Macmillan propose to send to Moscow. You express the desire that these representatives should have the opportunity to talk with me personally. I agree to this too, if it can be hoped that such meetings would provide useful. With regard to the time of arrival in Moscow of representatives of the USA and Great Britain, it would be most convenient for us, taking into account other, previously planned, arrangements of foreign-policy character, for them to come, if this is suitable for you as well, let us say, on July 15, 1963. The question of an appropriate announcement in this regard may be agreed upon through diplomatic channels.

We should like to count upon the success of the planned exchange of opinions in Moscow on the question of the cessation of nuclear tests. The Soviet Union sincerely wishes to reach agreement as quickly as possible on this question, and is prepared even now to sign an agreement which would prohibit forever the conducting of any and all tests of nuclear weapons. People throughout the world desire the conclusion of such an agreement. Consequently, I cannot be silent about the fact that heavy responsibility would be assumed by those who might continue to impede the achievement of an agreement and, at the same time, in connection with the forthcoming exchange of opinions in Moscow, might sow deceptive illusions among peoples to the effect that the matter was now already approaching a solution of the question of the cessation of tests.

Quite recently we have already had experience on this score which cannot be called anything other than painful. You recall, Mr. President, that after the Soviet Union in December of last year had taken an important step to meet the Western powers in that it agreed to a certain number of inspections, a proposal followed from the Government of the USA to send representatives of the USSR to the United States for talks directed toward the most rapid achievement of an agreement. We immediately responded to that proposal and sent our representatives to the USA. The whole world expected that, under the favorable conditions which had developed as a result of our December step, the talks in the USA would be the final step before the signing of a treaty on the cessation of tests.

But it turned out quite differently. The Western powers did not wish, as it is our custom to say, "to meet us half way," but remained on the old, notoriously unacceptable, positions, and, instead of serious political talks, attempted to draw our representatives into discussions of technical details, which could not fail to remain pointless until political questions of principle had been agreed upon. What is more, your representative declared to our representatives that he would have no occasion at all to cross the ocean if the Soviet Union did not intend to accept the demands of the Western powers. It was this sort of position on the part of those with whom we were negotiating which led at that time to the break-down of the talks, which consequently left nothing but disillusionment behind them.

A repetition of this sort of experience would only harm the cause, and I should like to express the hope that you are aware of this also. Success now depends only upon the question of what baggage representatives of the Western powers bring with them to Moscow.

I am sending a similar message to Prime Minister H. Macmillan.

Sincerely,

N. Khrushchev/3/

/1/Source: Department of State, Presidential Correspondence: Lot 66 D 204. No classification marking. The source text is a Department of State translation. The Russian-language text is ibid. Another copy of this message is in the Kennedy Library, President's Office Files, USSR. An Embassy translation was transmitted in telegram 3104 from Moscow, June 8; see vol. VII, pp. 714-715. According to telegram 3101 from Moscow, June 8, Gromyko handed this letter to Kohler at 4 p.m. that day. (Department of State, Central Files, US-USSR)

/2/See Document 105.
/3/Printed from a translation that indicates Khrushchev signed the original Russian-language copy.

"I congratulate you and the Soviet people on the successful flights of Col. Bykovsky and Lt. Tereshkova . . ."

107. Telegram From the Department of State to the Embassy in the Soviet Union

Washington, June 19, 1963, 11:14 p.m./1/

2818. Deliver following message to Khrushchev from the President.

"Dear Mr. Chairman:

I congratulate you and the Soviet people on the successful flights of Col. Bykovsky and Lt. Tereshkova, and on their record-breaking length. These latest successes stir the imaginations of all people. They are warmly acclaimed in this country, and especially by American space flyers.

John F. Kennedy"

Rusk

TOP SECRET

/1/Source: Department of State, Presidential Correspondence: Lot 66 D 204. Unclassified; Operational Immediate. Drafted by Bundy and approved by Weiner (S/S). Another copy of this message is in the Kennedy Library, National Security Files, Countries Series, USSR, Khrushchev Correspondence.

"... the preservation of peace has become in truth a vital necessity for all mankind."

108. Message From Chairmen Khrushchev and Brezhnev to President Kennedy

Moscow, July 4, 1963./1/

DEAR MR. PRESIDENT, On the occasion of the national holiday of the United States of America—Independence Day—we send to you and the American people our warm congratulations and best wishes for peace and prosperity. In our times—the age of harnessing atomic energy and penetration into the depths of the universe—the preservation of peace has become in truth a vital necessity for all mankind. We are convinced that if the governments of our two countries, together with the governments of other states, displaying a realistic approach, firmly choose the road of elimination of points of international tension and of broadening commercial cooperation, then peoples everywhere will welcome this as a great contribution to the strengthening of universal peace.

N. Khrushchev/2/

L. Brezhnev

/1/Source: Department of State, Presidential Files: Lot 66 D
204. No classification marking. The source text is a
Department of State translation of a commercial telegram
from Moscow. Another copy of this message and the
transliterated Russian text is in the Kennedy Library,
National Security Files, Countries Series, USSR, Khrushchev
Correspondence.
/2/Printed from a copy that bears these typed signatures.

"The American people are grateful for your message of good will . . ."

109. Telegram From the Department of State to the Embassy in the Soviet Union

Washington, July 4, 1963, 6:29 p.m./1/

54. For Ambassador. Please deliver following message to Khrushchev/Brezhnev from the President:

"The American people are grateful for your message of good will on the anniversary of our Independence Day./2/ The American Revolution was based on the desire of our people to build a free nation in a world of peace. Today, that desire for peace is more urgent than ever. The world has long passed that time when armed conflict can be the solution to international problems. That is why I share your desire, expressed in your message of today, that we move forward with understanding towards the solution of those key problems which divide us. I am hopeful that a world peace, just and lasting, can be achieved.

John F. Kennedy"

Flash hour of delivery so that we can set release time here.

Rusk

/1/Source: Department of State, Presidential Correspondence: Lot 66 D 204. Limited Official Use; Operational Immediate. Drafted by General Clifton at the White House and approved by Nobbe (S/S). Another copy of this message is in the Kennedy Library, National Security Files, Countries Series, USSR, Khrushchev Correspondence.
/2/Document 108.

"The Soviet people are proud of the successes of their cosmonauts . . ."

110. Message From Chairman Khrushchev to President Kennedy

Moscow, July 8, 1963./1/

DEAR MR. PRESIDENT: I thank you for the felicitations in connection with the successful protracted flight of Cosmonaut Valeri Bykovski and the first of its kind in the world for a woman—Cosmonaut Valentina Tereshkova./2/

The Soviet people are proud of the successes of their cosmonauts, breaking the trail into unknown expanses of the universe, and consider that cosmic space should be a zone of peace, a field for cooperation among nations. N. Khrushchev/3/

/1/Source: Department of State, Presidential Correspondence: Lot 66 D 204. No classification marking. The source text is a Department of State translation of a telegram from Moscow. The Russian-language text and another copy of this message are in the Kennedy Library, National Security Files, Countries Series, USSR, Khrushchev Correspondence. /2/See Document 107.
/3/Printed from a copy that bears this typed signature.

" . . . there is simply not any interest in using such inspections for espionage of any sort . . . "

111. Telegram From the Department of State to the Embassy in the United Kingdom

Washington, July 12, 1963, 8:11 p.m./1/

306. For Harriman from Bundy.

[Here follow two paragraphs concerning a test ban agreement.]

3. Presidential letter to Khrushchev follows and is for your delivery in any way you see fit. Message open for amendment if you wish to recommend any.

"Dear Mr. Chairman:

I am sending this message by the hand of Averell Harriman, whose visit to Moscow with Lord Hailsham is one that I hope may have important positive consequences for peace.

I am sure you know, but I want to say again, that Mr. Harriman comes with my full personal confidence and is in a position to give you my thinking not only about the problems of disarmament but about other issues as well. I have chosen him also because of his clear record of sympathetic understanding of the Russian people and his service to our common cause in the critical days of World War 2.

As Governor Harriman will explain to you, we continue to believe that it will be best if we can get a comprehensive agreement on the end of all nuclear testing, and we regret the continuing difference between us on the question of the nature and number of the inspections which would be necessary to give confidence in such a comprehensive agreement. I can only repeat again that there simply is not any interest in using such inspections for espionage of any sort, but I know from your recent statements that you have not accepted this explanation. In these circumstances, I believe that we should continue with our efforts to resolve this difference, but in the meantime I share the view which you have put forward in your important statement in Berlin that it is sensible to reach agreement where agreement is now possible, in the area of testing in the atmosphere, under water, and in outer space. Governor Harriman will explain that we continue to be in favor of such a more limited agreement and that we are encouraged by your statement in Berlin to believe that it is now possible.

I will not take your time in this letter to go into greater detail on this and other questions, but will merely repeat my conviction that we are at a moment in which it is important to make progress together. For this reason we attach great importance to Mr. Harriman's visit.

My wife joins me in sending our good wishes to you, to Mrs. Khrushchev, and to all your family.

Sincerely, John F. Kennedy"

Ball

/1/Source: Department of State, Presidential Correspondence: Lot 66 D 204. Secret; Priority; Eyes Only Ban. Drafted by Bundy and approved by Read (S/S). According to telegram 364 (Document 112), this message was delivered to Khrushchev on July 15. Another copy of this message is in the Kennedy Library, National Security Files, Countries Series, USSR, Khrushchev Correspondence. The full text of telegram 306 is printed in vol. VII, pp. 797-798.

"This is a good beginning."

112. Telegram From the Embassy in the Soviet Union to the Department of State

Moscow, July 27, 1963, 1 a.m./1/

364. Following is text Embassy translation of letter addressed to President handed by Khrushchev to Harriman this afternoon (original being carried by Harriman):

"His Excellency John F. Kennedy, President of the United States of America, Washington.

Dear Mr. President:

Thank you for your message transmitted to me by Mr. A. Harriman at the time of my first meeting with him and Lord Hailsham on July 15./2/

I am happy that the visit of Mr. Harriman to Moscow was a success and that our governments together with the Government of Great Britain succeeded in working out an agreed draft treaty on prohibition of nuclear weapons tests in the three environments—the atmosphere, the cosmos and under water./3/

This is a good beginning. I think that you agree with this. Now it seems we can with even greater basis hope that the negotiations which have taken place will have, as you say, serious and positive consequences for the cause of peace.

I agree with you that we are living at a time when it is important to achieve progress together in international affairs. It is particularly important, I would say, that this be really tangible and actual progress creating a new situation—a situation of relaxation of tension, thus opening to us the prospect of solution of other pressing problems and questions.

It should be noted in this connection as a positive result of the negotiations which have taken place that agreement was reached for continuation of discussion of the question regarding the conclusion of a non-aggression pact between the

countries of NATO and the states-participants of
the Warsaw Treaty with the purpose of achieving
agreement./4/

We consider that conclusion of such a pact
would fundamentally improve the international
atmosphere, would facilitate the strengthening of
confidence in relations between states-members
of opposing military groups.

I recall, Mr. President, that you also have
expressed yourself on the usefulness of members
of NATO and Warsaw Pacts taking upon themselves obligations to live in peace with one another and on the readiness of the United States to
consider the question of ways of diminishing tensions in relations between NATO and the Warsaw
Pact.

If the conclusion of a treaty for the cessation
of nuclear tests were followed by the signing of a
pact of non-aggression between the NATO countries and the states of the Warsaw Pact, then this
would be not only an important step toward normalization of the entire world situation, but could
signify the beginning of a turning point in the
history of contemporary international relations,
would open the prospect of transition from the
state of cold war to one of peaceful co-existence,
businesslike cooperation between states.

In the meetings with Mr. Harriman I mentioned other possible steps leading in this direction./5/ I think that by common efforts—and Mr.
President, the matter will not be delayed by us—
we could, as the military say, building upon our
initial success, really make an important contribution to the strengthening of peace throughout

the world.

We would like to continue the discussion of all these questions with Secretary of State D. Rusk if he is authorized to do this by you when he comes to Moscow for the signing of the treaty for the cessation of nuclear weapons tests. It is scarcely necessary to say that Mr. Rusk will be received by us with complete cordiality. In conclusion I can testify that Mr. Harriman showed himself to be worthy of the recommendation which you gave him in your letter. Furthermore, we never doubted this. He is really an old friend of ours. He spent a number of years in the Soviet Union, and in his time did a great deal for the development of Soviet/American relations. We remember this and are always pleased to exchange views with him on questions of interest to our two countries.

Accept, Mr. President, warm greetings and best wishes for you, your wife, your mother whom I met in Vienna, from myself, from my wife Nina Petrovna and from our entire family. Sincerely, N. Khrushchev. 26th July."

Kohler

/1/Source: Department of State, Presidential Correspondence: Lot 66 D 204. Secret; Ban—Eyes Only; Operational Immediate. A slightly different translation is in the Kennedy Library, National Security Files, Countries Series, USSR, Khrushchev Correspondence.

/2/Harriman and Lord Hailsham, British Minister of Science and Lord President of the Council, had been in Moscow since July 14 to negotiate a nuclear test ban treaty. For text of the President's message of July 12, see Document 111; a report on the meeting on July 15 is in vol. VII, pp. 799-801.

/3/For text of the treaty, initialed on July 25 and signed on August 5, see *American Foreign Policy: Current Documents, 1963*, pp. 1032-1034.
/4/At the meeting on July 15 Khrushchev had given Harriman and Hailsham the text of another non-aggression pact between NATO and the Warsaw Pact. The Embassy in Moscow transmitted the text in telegram 152, July 15. (Department of State, Central Files, Def 4 WARSAW PACT)
/5/Khrushchev and Harriman met a second time on July 26 and discussed Germany and Berlin, Laos, Cuba, and the test ban agreement. Reports on these conversations were transmitted in telegram 365 from Moscow, July 27, see vol. XV, pp. 539-544.

"Khrushchev telephoned . . . and asked me to convey his personal distress and his condolences . . ."

113. Telegram From Secretary of State Rusk to the Department of State

Bonn, August 10, 1963, 2 p.m./1/

Secto 55. Personal for the President from the Secretary. No other distribution. Just before my departure Chairman Khrushchev telephoned from Sochi and asked me to convey his personal distress and his condolences to you and Mrs. Kennedy./2/

Rusk

/1/Source: Department of State, Presidential Correspondence: Lot 66 D 204. Confidential; Priority; Eyes Only.
/2/A son born to the Kennedys on August 7 died 2 days after his birth.

"You were very kind to think of us at this difficult time . . ."

114. Letter From President Kennedy to Chairman Khrushchev

Washington, August 16, 1963./1/

DEAR MR. CHAIRMAN: I send you many thanks for your generous message of sympathy./2/ You were very kind to think of us at this difficult time, and your message was a comfort to us. Mrs. Kennedy and I are very grateful to you.

Sincerely,

John Kennedy

/1/Source: Department of State, Presidential Correspondence: Lot 66 D 204. No classification marking.
/2/See Document 113.

"I think both of our Governments feel satisfaction with the signing of the Treaty."

115. Letter From Chairman Khrushchev to President Kennedy

Moscow, August 17, 1963./1/

DEAR MR. PRESIDENT: Availing myself of the return of our Ambassador A. Dobrynin to

548

Washington I would like to express some of my thoughts in connection with the state of things shaping up now after the Treaty on banning nuclear weapon tests has been signed in Moscow.

I think both of our Governments feel satisfaction with the signing of the Treaty. And this is quite understandable since the Treaty is such a matter which brings no losses to either of the sides; on the contrary, from such an agreement equally win both our countries and other countries of the world, all the mankind.

A clear demonstration of the support of this good beginning is in particular also the fact that immediately after the signing of the Treaty by representatives of the USA, the USSR and Britain many other countries not only declared of their readiness to join that Treaty but have already put their signatures under it. Literally from all corners of the globe the Soviet Government is getting now a flood of letters, messages, congratulations. The White House mail is evidently no less busy. This is one more proof that the wide public of the whole world has received not a small satisfaction and welcomes the agreement of the three Governments which not only cleans the atmosphere of the globe of the poisonous fallout but in a certain sense purifies the international political atmosphere as well. All this strengthens the hopes of the peoples for a further relaxation of tension, gives a prospect of solution of other unsettled questions.

So far as I can judge by your statements, Mr. President, as well as by what your Secretary of State Mr. Rusk said here,/2/ you share our con-

viction that it is important now not to stop at
what has been achieved but to make further
steps from the good start taken by us. Of course
the way ahead of us is not an easy one. However
we must follow it stubbornly and persistently—let
this be without hurry but there should be no
slowing down the pace—consistently striving to
solve the ripe international problems which again
would correspond to the interests of not only our
two countries but also of the whole world.

There is hardly need to mention here all these
problems once again. We have more than once
listed them. I mentioned them in my last conversation with Mr. Rusk too. I would only like to
emphasize that these problems are awaiting their
solution. And they should rather be solved without, as it is said, being shelved, they should
rather be solved now when a more calm and consequently more favourable atmosphere has been
created then under other circumstances which
may always arise since serious unsolved problems still remain.

Mr. Rusk has certainly had time to inform you
about his stay in the Soviet Union and about our
talks with him.

We consider the Secretary of State's visit to us
to be useful. In a short period of time Mr. Rusk in
addition to Moscow had a chance to visit
Leningrad—the city of great historic traditions,
and also to visit the Black Sea shore. As I understood him, he was satisfied with his trip. I was
told that the Senators who attended the signing of
the Treaty were also satisfied with the trip. I do
not know to what extent this may facilitate the

process of the ratification of the Treaty by the U.S. Senate but the fact that they visited us and, among other things, had meetings with our deputies to the USSR Supreme Soviet is in our opinion a positive factor. We have always believed that such contracts promote better understanding.

During the talks with the Secretary of State we were able to exchange opinion on a certain number of questions including the questions of bilateral Soviet-American relations. Naturally, an improvement of the relations between our countries would have a beneficial effect and make it easier to look for solutions of the main international problems which divide us now.

Mr. Rusk expressed the wish that after his report to you, Mr. President, an exchange of opinion on all such questions should be continued. We agree with this and, moreover, we consider the continuation of the exchange of opinion to be necessary.

My wife Nina Petrovna, myself and all our family send you, your wife and your family our regards and best wishes.

Accept, Mr. President, our sincere sympathy on the loss that has befallen you—the death of your newly-born son.

Sincerely yours,

N. Khrushchev/3/

/1/Source: Department of State, Presidential Correspondence: Lot 66 D 204. No classification marking. The source
text indicates it is an unofficial translation from Russian.
Another copy is in the Kennedy Library, National Security
Files, Countries Series, USSR, Khrushchev Correspondence.
/2/For documentation on Rusk's visit to the Soviet Union,
see volume V.
/3/Printed from a copy that bears this typed signature.

"This could lead to a real turning point, and the end of the cold war."

116. Memorandum of Conversation

Moscow, September 10, 1963./1/

SUBJECT

United States Actions in Cuba

PARTICIPANTS
Ambassador Anatoliy F. Dobrynin, USSR
Llewellyn E. Thompson, Ambassador-at-Large
Department of State

Ambassador Dobrynin said he had a personal
message for the President, and he considered it
so confidential, that he had not had it typed but
would read from his handwritten notes.

He said that the Soviet Government considered that things had recently taken a turn for the
better in the international situation and in relations between the Soviet Union and the United
States. With the signing of the Test Ban Treaty

and the exchange of views with Secretary Rusk, there had developed a relaxation of tension and the prerequisite for the settlement of other questions had been established. This could lead to a real turning point, and the end of the cold war. The Soviet Union took satisfaction from the willingness of the United States to look for the solution of other international problems. If both countries were determined to accomplish this, it was important that nothing be done contrary to this intention. The Soviets wished to tell the President, frankly, what was of concern to them. There were certain facts which did not fit in with the situation and these were the provocative actions against Cuba, which had increased in recent weeks. Unknown planes had shelled industrial establishments and there had been landings of saboteurs on the Cuban coast. These actions had been intensified after the conclusion of the nuclear Test Ban Treaty. It had been stated that the United States had nothing to do with these actions, but no one could believe this. When the United States took a position against the attacks on Soviet ships in Cuban waters, these attacks had stopped. This action had been understood by the Soviet Union as a measure showing the good intentions of the United States. How then could these recent actions be interpreted? If such attacks continued—and they could only be taken from the United States proper or from countries allied with the United States and with the knowledge and connivance of the United States—this could only lead to a new crisis.

The Soviet Union did not want a new crisis to

emerge. Both sides had expressed their satisfaction over the elimination of the last crisis, which had been resolved after each side had undertaken certain commitments. The President had said that these commitments should be carried out. The Soviets agreed with this. They believed that for the future of our relations, it was important that effective measures be taken to stop the piratic attacks against Cuba. The Soviet Union had undertaken certain commitments in respect to the protection of the independence of Cuba which were aimed exclusively at preventing Cuba from becoming a victim of aggression, and the Soviet Union would certainly fulfill its commitments if aggression were unleashed against Cuba.

The Soviet Union hoped for understanding of the motives that prompted them to convey to the President, personally from N.S. Khrushchev, this assessment of the effect of the activation lately of provocative actions against Cuba.

/1/Source: Department of State, Presidential Correspondence: Lot 77 D 163. Top Secret. Drafted by Thompson. Another copy is in the Kennedy Library, National Security Files, Countries Series, USSR, Dobrynin Talks.

". . . it is not the United States, but the behavior of the Castro regime that is to blame for the difficulties in the Caribbean area."

117. Oral Statement From President Kennedy to Chairman Khrushchev

Washington, undated./1/

The President wishes Mr. Khrushchev to know that he shares his view that the signing of the Test Ban Treaty and the recent exchange of views with the Soviet Government is encouraging, and he hopes it will be possible to proceed to the solution of other problems. The President is hopeful that the Test Ban Treaty will be approved by the United States Senate in the course of next week.

With respect to the Cuban situation, the President also agrees that the emergence of a new crisis would be in the interest neither of the Soviet Union nor of the United States, and can assure him that the United States will faithfully carry out its commitments.

With respect to any air attacks on Cuba, it can be stated categorically that not only was the United States not involved in any way in such attacks, but has been making every effort to prevent them. It is possible, but not likely, that a light private aircraft could take off from one of the large number of private fields in the southeastern portion of the United States. No such illegal flights have been detected by the means available to us. The President has directed, however, that the measures already taken be reviewed to see what further steps could be taken.

In keeping with the March 30, 1963 declaration by the Departments of State and Justice concerning hit and run attacks by Cuban exile groups against targets in Cuba, the law enforcement agencies are taking vigorous measures to

assure that the pertinent laws of the United
States are observed.

Apparently it is assumed that the United
States exercises control over the policies and
actions of the other sovereign, independent states
of this Hemisphere. This assumption betrays a
fundamental misunderstanding of the relationship between the United States and the other
American Republics. The history of inter-
American relations makes abundantly clear that
the American Governments will not tolerate
interference with their foreign or domestic
affairs. The states in this Hemisphere jealously
defend the principle of juridical equality of states
and reject any insinuation that difference of size
and power in any way modifies this fundamental
rule governing their relations.

The United States could, of course, consult
with any government in this Hemisphere from
whose territory we have information indicating
that flights were originating against Cuba, but, in
all candor, we must point out that such consultation would be greatly complicated by the increasing sense of outrage among the governments of
this Hemisphere about Cuba's deliberate stimula-
tions and support of subversive activities
throughout the Hemisphere in direct violation of
international norms. This is not simply a matter
of speeches or words by Castro, as has sometimes
been indicated. Clear evidence of Cuban involve-
ment in this form of aggression is to be found in
the fact that:

a) The Cuban Government is recruiting Latin
Americans, sending them to Cuba for training in

guerrilla tactics and returning them to their countries to engage in terroristic activities. A case in point is the Cuban-trained Peruvians captured on May 14 and 15, 1963, at Puerto Maldonado as they attempted clandestinely to enter Peru from Bolivia.

b) The Cuban Government is furnishing funds to revolutionary groups seeking the overthrow of governments by force and violence. By way of illustration, in May 1963, two leading members of the Ecuadorean Communist Party, Jose Maria Roura and Alejandro Roman were seized as they were returning to Ecuador. They were carrying over $30,000 which they confessed had been given them by Chinese and Cuban sources.

c) The Cuban leaders continue to exhort revolutionaries in Latin American countries to resort to sabotage, terrorism and guerrilla action. Premier Castro returned to this theme in his July twenty-sixth address when he called on activists in Venezuela and other countries to "open the breach" and begin fighting. Major Ernesto Guevera, in an article published in the September issues of Cuba Socialista, strongly advocates guerrilla warfare as the surest road to power in Latin America. Information available to us shows a direct connection between terroristic activities in Venezuela and the Castro regime. In addition to being guilty of such aggression against other American Republics by promoting these and other activities, the Cuban Government recently embarked on a most risky venture of direct violation of the territory and territorial waters of another country in this Hemisphere using units of its armed forces. On August 14, 1963, a Cuban helicopter and two patrol boats furnished by the Soviet Union forcibly removed from Cay Anguila, one of the islands of the Bahamas group, nineteen persons who had sought refuge on the island. This incident led to a vigorous protest by the British Government on August 21, 1963, requesting an apology and return of the persons taken prisoners.

In sum, it is not the United States, but the behavior of the Castro regime that is to blame for the difficulties in the Caribbean area.

/1/Source: Department of State, Presidential Correspondence: Lot 77 D 163. Secret. The source text is attached to a memorandum of conversation by Llewellyn Thompson that indicates that Thompson made the oral statement to Dobrynin on September 13.

"Thus the Nuclear Weapon Test Ban Treaty has come into force."

118. Telegram From the Embassy in the Soviet Union to the Department of State

Moscow, October 10, 1963, 6 p.m./1/

1203. *Verbatim text.* Following is Emb translation letter from Khrushchev to President handed me by Zorin (Acting for Kuznetsov who reportedly "out of town") after deposit ceremony today. Similar letter to Macmillan given British Charge. According Zorin, text letter will be broadcast Moscow radio beginning 0600 Oct 11 Moscow time and published first issue tomorrow's *Pravda:*

Begin Text: Dear Mr. President: Today in the three capitals—Moscow, Washington and London, carrying out the final act in connection with the conclusion of the Treaty Banning Nuclear Weapon Tests in the Atmosphere, in Outer Space and Underwater—the ratification instruments of the original parties to this treaty, the Soviet Union, the United States of America and Great Britain have been deposited.

Thus the Nuclear Weapon Test Ban Treaty has come into force. This undoubtedly is a significant development in international affairs which brings joy to all peoples. Together with the Soviet Union, the United States of America and Great Britain the Nuclear Weapon Test Ban Treaty has been signed by more than one hundred states. It can be said with assurance that this treaty has found warm response and approval among all peoples of good will.

It has been repeatedly noted by representatives of our countries that the Test Ban Treaty is in itself a document of great international significance and the hope has been expressed that the conclusion of this treaty will have a positive influence on the international climate, on relations between states. Actually, the conclusion of the Nuclear Weapon Test Ban Treaty has injected a fresh spirit into the international atmosphere showing that no matter how complicated contemporary problems, no matter how great the differences between social systems of our states, we can find mutually acceptable solutions in the interests of all mankind, in the interests of maintaining peace if we manifest the necessary push (stremleniye) toward this end.

But, it is understood, agreement on banning experimental nuclear explosions with all its importance for peoples, in itself does not solve the principal international problem of our epoch—does not eliminate the danger of war. Now it is necessary—and our governments have spoken out in favor of this—to develop further the success that we have achieved, to seek solutions of other ripe international questions.

These questions are well known, they have been brought forward by life itself, by the whole development of world events. They concern the strengthening of security in Europe, including the liquidation of the remnants of the Second World War, conclusion of a non-aggression pact between countries of NATO and member states of the Warsaw Pact, creation of nuclear free zones in various regions of the world, barring the further spread of the nuclear weapon, banning of launching into orbit objects bearing nuclear weapons, measures for the prevention of surprise attack, and a series of other steps. Their implementation would facilitate a significant strengthening of peace, improvement of international relations, would clear the road to general and complete disarmament, and, consequently, to the delivering of peoples from the threat of war.

Peoples expect that our governments will now manifest still more persistence and consistency in their further activities in the interests of consolidating peace. So far as the Soviet Government is concerned, inalterably following the course of peaceful coexistence of states, it is prepared to exert new efforts, to do everything dependent on it in order that the change for the better in the international situation which has been noted as a result of the conclusion of the Nuclear Weapon Test Ban Treaty should become the beginning of a sharp turn toward broad relaxation of international tension.

Permit me, Mr. President, to express the hope that the Government of the United States of America for its part will make an appropriate contribution to the solution of international problems which is demanded by the interests of weakening international tensions, the interests of insuring universal peace. Respectfully yours, signed N. Khrushchev. *End text.*

Kohler

/1/Source: Department of State, Presidential Correspondence: Lot 66 D 204. Limited Official Use; Priority. The Russian-language text is ibid., Central Files, DEF 18-4. Another copy of this message is in the Kennedy Library, National Security Files, Countries Series, USSR, Khrushchev Correspondence. A slightly different version is printed in *American Foreign Policy: Current Documents, 1963*, pp. 1034-1035.

". . . the gravity of this loss is felt by the whole world, including ourselves, the Soviet people."

119. Letter From Chairman Khrushchev to President Johnson

Moscow, November 24, 1963./1/

DEAR MR. PRESIDENT: I am writing this message to you at a moment that holds a special place in the history of your country. The villainous assassination of Head of the American State John F. Kennedy is a grievous, indeed a very grievous loss for your country. I want to say frankly that the gravity of this loss is felt by the whole world, including ourselves, the Soviet people.

There is no need for me to tell you that the late President John F. Kennedy and I, as the Head of the Government of the socialist Soviet Union, were people of different poles. But I believe that probably you yourself have formed a definite view that it was an awareness of the great responsibility for the destinies of the world that guided the actions of the two Governments—both of the Soviet Union and of the United States—in recent years. These actions were founded on a desire to prevent a disaster and to resolve disputed issues through agreement with due regard for the most important, the most fundamental interests of ensuring peace.

An awareness of this responsibility, which I found John F. Kennedy to possess during our very first conversations in Vienna in 1961, laid down the unseen bridge of mutual understanding which, I venture to say, was not broken to the very last day in the life of President John F. Kennedy. For my own part, I can say quite definitely that the feeling of respect for the late President never left me precisely because, like ourselves, he based his policy on a desire not to permit a military collision of the major powers which carry on their shoulders the burden of the responsibility for the maintenance of peace.

And now, taking the opportunity offered by the visit to the United States of my First Deputy A.I. Mikoyan to attend the funeral of John F. Kennedy, I address these lines to you, as the new President of the United States of America in whom is vested a high responsibility to your people. I do not know how you will react to these words of mine, but let me say outright that in you we saw a comrade-in-arms of the late President, a man who always stood at the President's side and supported his line in foreign policy. This, I believe, gives us grounds to express the hope that the basis, which dictated to the leaders of both countries the need not to permit the outbreak of a new war and to keep the peace, will continue to be the determining factor in the development of relations between our two States.

Needless to say, on our part, and on my own part, as Head of the Government of the Soviet Union, there has been and remains readiness to find, through an exchange of views, mutually acceptable solutions for those problems which still divide us. This applies both to the problems of European security, which have been handed down to the present generation chiefly as a legacy of World War II, and to other international problems.

Judging by experience, exchanges of views and our contacts can assume various forms, including such an avenue as the exchange of personal messages, if this does not run counter to your wishes.

Recently we marked the Thirtieth Anniversary of the establishment of diplomatic relations between the U.S.S.R. and the U.S. This was a historic act in which an outstanding role was played by President Franklin D. Roosevelt. We have always believed that, being a representative of one and the same political party, the late President John F. Kennedy to a certain extent continued in foreign policy Roosevelt's traditions which were based on recognition of the fact that the coinciding interests of the U.S.S.R. and the U.S. prevail over all that divides them.

And it is to you Mr. President, as to a representative of the same trend of the United States policy which brought into the political forefront statesmen, such as Franklin D. Roosevelt and John F. Kennedy, that I want to say that if these great traditions could go on being maintained and strengthened, both Americans and Soviet people could, we are convinced, look optimistically into the future. We are convinced that this development of events would meet the sympathy of every state, and indeed of every individual who espouses and cherishes peace.

I would welcome any desire on your part to express your ideas in connection with the thoughts—though they may, perhaps, be of a somewhat general nature—which I deemed it possible to share with you in this message./2/

Respectfully,

N. Khrushchev/3/

/1/Source: Department of State, Presidential Correspondence: Lot 66 D 204. Confidential. The source text is marked "unofficial translation." President Kennedy was assassinated in Dallas, Texas, on November 22.

/2/On November 24 President Johnson also wrote to Khrushchev. After thanking the Chairman for his letter of condolence, Johnson wrote:

"I should like you to know that I have kept in close touch with the development of relations between the United States and the Soviet Union and that I have been in full accord with the policies of President Kennedy. I shall do my best to continue these policies along the same lines and hope that we can make progress in improving our relations and in resolving the many serious problems that face us.

"May I say that I am fully aware of the heavy responsibility which our two countries bear for the maintenance and consolidation of peace. I hope that we can work together for the achievement of that great goal, despite the many and complex issues which divide us. I can assure you that I shall sincerely devote myself to this purpose."

(Ibid.: Lot 77 D 163)

/3/Printed from a copy that bears this typed signature.

"I read she had tears in her eyes when she left the American embassy in Moscow . . ."

120. Letter From Jacqueline Kennedy to Chairman Khrushchev

Washington, December 1, 1963./1/

DEAR MR. CHAIRMAN PRESIDENT, I would like to thank you for sending Mr. Mikoyan as your representative to my husband's funeral.

He looked so upset when he came through the line, and I was very moved.

I tried to give him a message for you that day—but as it was such a terrible day for me, I do not know if my words came out as I meant them to.

So now, in one of the last nights I will spend in the White House, in one of the last letters I will write on this paper at the White House, I would like to write you my message.

I send it only because I know how much my husband cared about peace, and how the relation between you and him was central to this care in his mind. He used to quote your words in some of his speeches-"In the next war the survivors will envy the dead."

You and he were adversaries, but you were allied in a determination that the world should not be blown up. You respected each other and could deal with each other. I know that President Johnson will make every effort to establish the same relationship with you.

The danger which troubled my husband was that war might be started not so much by the big men as by the little ones.

While big men know the needs for self-control and restraint—little men are sometimes moved more by fear and pride. If only in the future the big men can continue to make the little ones sit down and talk, before they start to fight.

I know that President Johnson will continue the policy in which my husband so deeply believed—a policy of control and restraint—and he will need your help.

I send this letter because I know so deeply of the importance of the relationship which existed between you and my husband, and also because of your kindness, and that of Mrs. Khrushcheva in Vienna.

I read that she had tears in her eyes when she left the American Embassy in Moscow, after signing the book of mourning. Please thank her for that.

Sincerely,

Jacqueline Kennedy

/1/Source: William Manchester, *The Death of a President, November 20-November 25, 1963* (New York, 1963), pp. 653-654. No classification marking. The original letter has not been located. The authenticity of the text printed here has been verified by comparing it to the Russian translation in the Department of History and Records of the Russian Ministry of Foreign Affairs. Mrs. Kennedy wrote the following note on a folder in which she presumably put the letter but which is now empty: "Important: Mrs. Lincoln/This is my letter to Khrushchev to be delivered to him by Ambassador Thompson." (Kennedy Library, President's Office Files, Countries Series, USSR, Khrushchev Correspondence) According to Manchester, the handwritten letter was forwarded to Khrushchev by McGeorge Bundy after clearance at the Department of State by U. Alexis Johnson. Two undated typed drafts of the letter are at the Johnson Library. On one draft Bundy crossed out several words and added several other words in his hand. These revisions were incorporated in the second typed draft. (Bundy Files, Chron) In the final version, one phrase in the second typed draft was reworded and one sentence added.

Bibliography

"Back from the Brink: The Correspondence Between President John F. Kennedy and Chairman Nikita S. Khrushchev on the Cuban Missile Crisis of Autumn, 1962." *Problems of Communism XLI* (Spring 1992): pp. 1–120.

Beschloss, Michael. *The Crisis Years: Kennedy and Khrushchev, 1960–1963.* New York: Harper Collins, 1991.

Claflin, Edward B., ed. *The President Wants to Know: Memos from the President's Office, 1961–1963.* New York: William Morrow, 1991.

Cousins, Norman. *The Improbable Triumvirate: Kennedy, Pope John and Khrushchev.* New York: W.W. Norton, 1972.

Flamini, Roland. *Pope, Premier, President— The Cold War Summit—Why Khrushchev was willing and Kennedy unwilling, to talk peace with John XXIII.* New York: Macmillan, 1980.

Fursenko, Aleksandr and Naftali, Timothy. *"One Hell of a Gamble": Khrushchev, Castro and Kennedy, 1958–1964.* New York: W.W. Norton, Co., 1997.

Gelb, Norman. *The Berlin Wall: Kennedy, Khrushchev & a Showdown in the Heart of Europe.* New York: Times Books, 1987.

McSherry. James E. *Khrushchev and Kennedy in Retrospect.* Palo Alto: Open Door Press, 1971.

Seaburg, Glenn T. *Kennedy, Khrushchev and the Test Ban.* Berkeley: The University of California Press, 1981.

Schlesinger, Arthur M. *Robert Kennedy and His Times.* Boston: Houghton Mifflin, 1978.

Sulzberger, Cyrus L. *The Last of the Giants.* New York: Macmillan, 1970.

Index

About the Editor . . .

Thomas Fensch is the Publisher of New Century Books and the editor of the Top Series series.

He is the author or editor of 25 books of nonfiction; his specialty has been literary biography. Some of his books include:

Steinbeck and Covici:
  The Story of a Friendship
Conversations with John Steinbeck
Conversations with James Thurber
The Man Who Was Walter Mitty:
  The Life and Work of James Thurber
Of Sneetches and Whos and the
  Good Dr. Seuss:
  Essays on the Writings and Life of
  Theodor Geisel
The Man Who Was Dr. Seuss:
  The Life and Work of Theodor Geisel
Oskar Schindler and His List:
  The Man, the Book, the Film,
  the Holocaust and Its Survivors

Thomas Fensch holds a doctorate from Syracuse University and lives near Houston, Texas.

Printed in the United States
3775